THE IDEOLOGIES OF CHILDREN'S RIGHTS

International Studies in Human Rights

VOLUME 23

The Ideologies of Children's Rights

Edited by

MICHAEL FREEMAN
University College, London, U.K.

and

PHILIP VEERMAN
Defence for Children International, Jerusalem, Israel

MARTINUS NIJHOFF PUBLISHERS
DORDRECHT / BOSTON / LONDON

Library of Congress Cataloging-in-Publication Data

The Ideologies on children's rights / edited by Michael Freeman and
  Philip Veerman.
        p.   cm. -- (International studies in human rights ; v. 23)
    Includes bibliographical references (p.   ) and index.
    ISBN 0-7923-1800-5 (hb)
    1. Children's rights.   I. Freeman, Michael D. A.   II. Veerman,
  Philip E.   III. Series.
  HQ789.I34 1992
  305.23--dc20   92-14359

ISBN 0-7923-1800-5

Published by Martinus Nijhoff Publishers,
P.O. Box 163, 3300 AD Dordrecht, The Netherlands

Sold and distributed in the U.S.A. and Canada
by Kluwer Academic Publishers,
101 Philip Drive, Norwell, MA 02061, U.S.A.

In all other countries, sold and distributed
by Kluwer Academic Publishers Group,
P.O. Box 322, 3300 AH Dordrecht, The Netherlands

Printed on acid-free paper

Printed in the Netherlands

Table of Contents

PART II. APPLICATION

List of Contributors

Michael Freeman is Professor of English Law at University College London, U.K.

Susan Wolfson is a philosopher and a lawyer. She teaches at the Education Center of the European Division of the University of Maryland. She lives in London UK.

Adam Lopatka is at present affiliated with the Polish Academy of Sciences in Warsaw. He was the chairman of the UN Working Group drafting the UN Convention on the Rights of the Child.

Cynthia Price Cohen is the United Nations representative of Human Rights Internet and is a research associate at the Ralph Bunche Institute of the United Nations, City University of New York, USA.

Hans-Jachim Heintze is the deputy-director of the Institute for International Studies of the Karl-Marx University in Leipzig and visiting scholar at the Ruhr-University Bochum, Germany.

Eugeen Verhellen is a psychologist and Professor at the State University Ghent in Belgium. He is the director of the Study-and Documentation center on Children's Rights of that University.

David Johnson was at the time of the Study-Group staffmember of the international secretariat of Defence for Children International (DCI). He now works for the United Nations Center for Human Rights in Geneva, Switzerland.

Coby de Graef is a teacher in juvenile law at the University of Amsterdam Faculty of Law, the Netherlands.

Joachim Wolf is research fellow of the Max Planck Institute for Comparative Public Law and International Law, Heidelberg, Germany.

Malfrid Grude Flekkøy, is a psychologist and was the Ombudsman for Children in Norway. She was, at the time of the Study-Group, senior fellow of the UNICEF International Child Development Centre in Florence, Italy. At present she is affiliated with the Nic Waals Institute in Oslo, Norway.

Gwen James is the director of the Voice for the Child in Care in London, UK.

Elaine E. Sutherland is a senior lecturer at the Department of Private Law at the School of Law of the University of Glasgow, Scotland.

Gary B. Melton is the Carl A. Happold Professor of Psychology and Law, University of Nebraska-Lincoln, USA.

Susan P. Limber is a staffmember of the Center on Children, Families, and the Law, University of Nebraska-Lincoln, USA.

Colin A. Wringe is a philosopher. He teaches at the Department of Education of the University of Keele, Keele, UK.

Philip Graham is Professor of Child Psychiatry, Department of Child Psychiatry, Institute of Child Health, London, UK.

Anne McGillivray is Professor of Family Law, University of Manitoba, Winnipeg, Canada.

Leslie Sebba is Professor of Criminology, Faculty of Law, the Hebrew University of Jerusalem, Israel.

Miek de Langen is Professor of Juvenile Law, Faculty of Law, University of Amsterdam, The Netherlands. She is the founder and chairperson of the 'Center of Children's Legal Aid' in Amsterdam, the Netherlands.

Ludwig Salgo is Professor of Family- and Youth Law at the School of Social Work Esslingen and the J. W. Goethe University in Frankfurt, Germany.

Stanley S. Herr is Associate Professor of Law, University of Maryland, Baltimore, Maryland, USA.

Janet Fink is at present working as a legal advisor of the State Assembly of New York. At the time of the Study-Group she was the assistant attorney-in-charge of the Legal Aid Society (Juvenile Rights Division) in New York, NY, USA.

George Kent is Professor in Political Science at the University of Hawaii, Honolulu, Hawaii.

Françoise Krill is a member of the Legal Division of the I.C.R.C., the International Committee of the Red Cross in Geneva, Switzerland.

Philip E. Veerman is co-ordinator of the Israel Section of Defence for Children International (DCI), Jerusalem, Israel.

PART I

Theory

MICHAEL D. A. FREEMAN*

1. Introduction: Rights, Ideology and Children

Children's rights have been argued about for well over a century, and by a variety of different professionals with different perspectives. A century is a short time span in the history of childhood but even within the last century or so we can observe the different values that have attached to children at particular historical moments. Early concerns for children and their rights were voiced by child savers. It was they who were instrumental in establishing separate institutions for children, juvenile courts, distinct penal systems and a system of compulsory education.

These concerns still exist, though many of the institutions so established are now problematized. But discourse about children and their rights has moved on rapidly since the 1960s. The liberationist movement challenged those who claimed the status of children could be advanced exclusively by conferring on children increased protection. The emphasis shifted from protection to autonomy, from nurturance to self-determination, from welfare to justice. In the pithy[1] language of one advocate of the latter (Richard Farson) we began to talk of protecting children's rights as well as, or in substitution for, protecting children. Some early feminist thinking of the 1970s supported this. Shulamith Firestone[2] wished to include the oppression of children in 'any program for feminist revolution' for otherwise, so she argued, 'we will be subject to the same failing of which we have so often accused men: of not having gone deep enough in our analysis, of having missed an important substratum of oppression merely because it did'nt directly concern *us*.'

The courts of a number of countries, though in more measured language, began at roughly the same time to recognise the personality of children. In the United States 'students in school as well as out of school' were held[3] to be '"persons" under the Constitution' and constitutional rights were said[4] not to 'mature and come into being magically only when one attains the state-defined age of majority'. Nor, it was said in the famous *Gault* decision[5] does the 'condition of being a boy' justify 'a kangaroo court'. In England there was talk of access (or visitation) being a child's right[6] in 1973 but this received

* University College, London.

M. Freeman and P. Veerman (eds.), The Ideologies of Children's Rights, 3–6.

statutory affirmation only in 1989.[7] But in England it was the *Gillick*[8] case more than any other official statement which brought the child's rights to autonomy to public attention. This coined what has come to be know as *Gillick*-competence: the yielding of a parental right to the child's right to make his own decisions 'when he reaches a sufficient understanding and intelligence to be capable of making up his own mind on the matter requiring decisions'.

Meanwhile, 1969 saw the United Declaration of the Rights of the Child. There had been a declaration adopted by the fifth Assembly of the League of Nations in 1924. This reflected a concern with the rights of children afflicted by the devastation of the 'Great War' and its aftermath. That declaration emphasised children's material needs. It proclaimed, for example, that children 'must have' means requisite for their normal development, including food for the hungry, nursing for the sick, help for the handicapped, and shelter and succour for the orphan and waif. Nor was this the first such declaration. Janusz Korczak was formulating a declaration long before the Geneva Convention of 1924. And this is strikingly modern:[9] a right to respect, a right to live in the present ('children are not people of tomorrow; they are people today'), a right to be him or herself, a right to make mistakes, a right to be taken seriously, a right to resist educational influence that conflicts with his or her own beliefs are just a few of the rights he advocated.

These ideas did not find their way into the 1959 Declaration of the Rights of the Child. It was based on the premise that 'mankind owes to children the best it has to give'. Implicit was an emphasis on duties to children,[10] and, although the Preamble referred to rights and freedoms, the ten principles set out in it did not embrace children's liberties (or freedoms or autonomy) at all. Indeed the Articles were vague, perhaps deliberately so, as to the rights children should have and, necessarily, as who was to bear the correlative duties. The Declaration was little more than a proclamation of general principles.

The period between the 1959 Declaration and the 1989 Convention was marked by a growing consciousness of the plight of children and of the importance that vesting children with rights might have in coming to grips with some of these problems. It seems difficult to imagine now, but, in 1959, the 'social problem' of child abuse did not exist. The phenomenon was there but neither the whistle had been blown nor the value judgment made.[11] There was a concern with juvenile delinquency (but then adults can be victims of this) but otherwise the issues addressed in Part Two of this volume were rarely spoken of.

1979 was the International Year of the Child. It caught the public imagination more than many other international years. In the United Kingdom it was said[12] to lay down a continuing challenge. Perhaps it had to: twice in 1979 a bill in the UK Parliament to make it unlawful to beat mentally and physically handicapped children failed. That such a spectacle could occur seems inconceivable now but at the time leading organisations in Britain resisted suggestions that there was any link between physical chastisement of a child and child abuse.

The Convention of 1989 and the World Summit of 1990 are thus watersheds in the history of children. They were greeted with euphoria. An African Charter on the Rights and Welfare of The Child followed in 1990. Perhaps the most significant article in the UN Charter is Article 12,[13] requiring states to 'assure to the child who is capable of forming his or her own views the right to express those views freely, on all matters affecting the child, the views of the child being given due consideration in accordance with the age and maturity of the child'. It is surprising (or is it?) that on the content of the Convention children as such were given no opportunity to input their views.

The ideological conflict between those who see children's rights in welfare terms and those who wish to promote a child's self-determination is still present in the Convention. Thus, despite Article 12, Article 3, perhaps the key provision, directs that the 'best interests of the child' is to be a primary consideration.[14] And the Preamble may undermine not just a child's autonomy but his or her welfare as well for it acknowledges that 'due account' should be taken of 'the importance of the traditions and cultural values of each people for the protection and harmonious development of the child'.[15] These 'traditions and cultural values' are not problematized so that the fact that traditional values have undermined the child is ignored. There is recognition also that the child's welfare may well be 'trumped'[16] in certain situations (which are not spelt out) by 'cultural values and traditions'. And, although states are to 'take effective and appropriate measures with a view to abolishing traditional practices prejudicial to the health of children',[17] this is conceptualized as the recognition of a social or cultural right, rather than a civil right, and therefore falls within the realm of progressive obligation.

That conflicts remain is hardly to be wondered at. The Convention is a remarkable achievement. But it is a beginning and not a conclusion to the quests of the last 100 or so years. We have to look now beyond conventions and towards the empowerment of children. Those who participated in the conference, the fruits of which are presented in this book, are amongst the leaders of movements which are pledged to find ways of making the child's voice heard. The Convention, it may be observed, though it gives the child (to take but a couple of examples) the opportunity to participate in proceedings involving his separation from his parents and the right to express views and for these to be accorded due weight, gives him no right to separate representation. The growth of ombudspersons[18] or commissioners[19] has drawn attention to the need, barely recognised in the Convention, for different techniques of children's advocacy.

These themes are explored in the two parts of this book. The first part examines the moral foundations of children's rights, their limits, their relationship to changing images of children and what children themselves think about rights. Although the emphasis is on theory, the relationship to practice is constantly referred to. There are essays also on cultural and ideological conflicts. These themes reassert themselves in the second half of the book where the issues of child abuse, education, child prostitution, drug addiction, health and warfare are addressed specifically from the perspective of the children as a person.

NOTES

1. *Birthrights*, Harmondsworth, Penguin (1978).
2. *The Dialectic of Sex*, New York, William Morrow (1970).
3. *Tinker v Des Moines Independent School District* 393 US 503, 509 (1969).
4. *Planned Parenthood of Central Missouri v Danforth* 428 US 52, 75 (1976).
5. *In Re Gault* 387 US 1, 27–28 (1967).
6. *M v M* (1973) 2 All ER 81.
7. With the Children Act 1989.
8. (1986) A.C. 112, 186. But this has been somewhat undermined by *Re R* (1991) 4 All ER 177.
9. See B. J. Lifton, *The King of Children*, London, Chatto and Windus (1988), pp. 355–356.
10. See also O. O'Neill, 'Children's Rights and Children's Lives', *Ethics* 98, 445 (1988).
11. See W. Waller, 'Social Problems and The Mores' (1936) 1 *American Social Reviews* 922; S. J. Pfohl, 'The Discovery of Child Abuse' (1977) 24 *Social Problems* 310.
12. By J. Stone, *The Continuing Challenge*, IYC Trust (1981).
13. Article VII in the African Charter is similar.
14. The African Charter Article IV says 'the primary consideration'.
15. The Preamble to the African Charter puts it rather differently. It refers to the 'cultural heritage, historical background, and the values of the African civilization' which should 'inspire and characterise their reflection on the concept of the rights and welfare of the child'.
16. In R. Dworkin's well-known expression: see *Taking Rights Seriously*, London, Duckworth (1978).
17. See Article 24 (2).
18. See M. Flekkøy, *A Voice For Children*, London, Jessica Kingsley (1991).
19. See P. Newell and M. Rosenbaum, *Taking Children Seriously*, London, Calouste Gulbenkian Foundation (1991). See also I. Hassall, 'A Children's Rights Commissioner' in Ph. Alston and G. Brennan (eds.), *The UN Children's Convention and Australia*, Canberra, Human Rights and Equal Opportunity Commission (1991), p. 105.

SUSAN A. WOLFSON*

2. Children's Rights: The Theoretical Underpinning of the 'Best Interests of the Child'

Neither the phrase nor the standard 'the best interests of the child' is new. What is quite remarkable about this standard, however, is its persistence taken along side of its complete lack of definite, or seemingly necessary, content. Further, both of these features of this standard also persist. This is despite the fact that on its surface, although not on a deeper level as is argued in this paper, 'the best interests of the child' stands in direct opposition to almost every other standard which liberals profess to rationally hold dear.

There have been innumerable attempts to 'pour content into the "best interests of the child"'.[1] Moreover, the recently adopted United Nations Convention on the Rights of the Child, setting out international and national social and legal standards and guidelines, can rightly be seen as an attempt to articulate and enumerate the practical implications of the standard.[2] Even a cursory glance through the relevant material relating to this standard yields the conclusion that there is such a diversity of opinion as to its meaning and content as to render the standard itself meaningless.

This paper is not yet another attempt to 'pour content' into this heretofore virtually empty vessel, which has remained the uncomfortable theoretical parallel of the Lockean notion of children's primary natures as tabula rasas. It is rather an attempt to make theoretical sense out of what has now become *the* international standard for child regarding practices. In particular, it is an attempt to spell out those relevant features of general rights theory which, when understood, allow us to further understand children's rights. Such understanding of children's rights in turn highlights their compatibility (as well as their singular features due to the unique moral status of children) with this general theory and, more widely, with political liberalism.

* Education Center of the European Division of the University of Maryland.

M. Freeman and P. Veerman (eds.), The Ideologies of Children's Rights, 7–27.
© 1992 *Kluwer Academic Publishers. Printed in the Netherlands.*

1. Objections To Be Countered

There are those who would have us believe that 'rights' in general are a moral fiction based on some outdated metaphysical view of the universe and humanity's place in it. Worse still, some claim that the very existence of moral (and concomitantly legal and institutional) rights is nothing more than a way of maintaining the political status quo – a way to keep the powerful in power. According to these and several other lines of argument, 'moral rights' turn out not to be moral at all; in fact, to perpetuate our ideas and conventions of rights is at the very least morally misguided and at most a grossly immoral thing to do.

There is a point to all of this. It is true that most traditional rights theories (e.g. the theory of natural rights) are based on certain metaphysical views that are no longer so commonly held. They are also sometimes based on views of 'man' which are themselves rationally questionable and possibly sometimes immoral. These views are such in that it can be argued that their entire context is based on ethnocentric and egocentric assumptions about 'man'.[3] Further, it is also true that in many cases rights are attributed, claimed or exercised in ways which are grossly immoral, ways which often serve nefarious purposes of the already powerful. Nevertheless, there are other (and perhaps more morally relevant) ways of grounding rights which have been suggested; and practical applications of theories of rights do not always or necessarily turn out to be flagrantly immoral. That 'moral' reasons of many sorts (not only talk of rights, and then particularly as it is concerned with children) are too often used to cover and 'justify' immoral behaviour is surely no reason to throw all of morality out the window as dangerous.

What we need to know is whether or not rights and the related concepts and conventions, where properly applied, carry any real moral weight. We are especially interested in discovering anything about the nature of rights in general that might shed light on questions of children's rights. The relevant question then is whether or not this constellation of concepts is a significant addition to the moral life. Joel Feinberg suggests a thought experiment which enables us to answer this question.[4] We are told to imagine a world in which there are no rights. No matter how benevolent and possibly even devoted to duty everyone in it is, he says, such a world would be greatly 'morally impoverished' because no one would feel *deserving* of even decent treatment. Rather, inhabitants of this world would feel that they were at the mercy of the whims of everyone else and also feel humble gratitude for the smallest kindness. Imagining this world we can see that people would lack the dignity (and insurance) that come from considering oneself the moral equal of everyone else in the community. As Feinberg puts it, 'The harm to individual self-esteem and character development would be incalculable'.[5]

The thought of such a world with moral rights (or the more generic 'claim rights' as Feinberg refers to them) seems sufficient to convince anyone that the notion of rights and the related concepts are a significant and valuable addition to the moral life. In fact, given (among other losses) the resultant harm to the character development of individuals, one wonders what kind of a moral life would even be possible. Moreover, it seems that this latter point must be particularly relevant to children and our treatment of them. However, beyond being an addition to the moral life, moral rights seem to be a central and perhaps ineliminable part of morality itself.

This becomes even more evident if we consider the function of rights-talk in moral discourse. It is commonly held that rights serve the purpose of establishing either a justified claim[6] or a valid claim[7] which protects one interest or another of the right holder. These interests are not just the desires to seek pleasure and avoid pain that utilitarians commonly discuss, nor are they the passing or superficial whims of overly self-indulgent or egoistic beings, as their initial articulation in social contract theory occasionally suggests. Rather, these interests are comprised of (tentatively and vaguely) the concerns, plans, projects, states of mind and being without which our lives would lose much if not all of their meaning. In other words these interests, however we come to state them precisely and specifically, are what make human life more fully human. As such, the recognition and protection of them that a recognition of rights gives us is of central importance to our morality, the quality of our lives, and often our lives themselves. An ability to protect at least some of these interests is at the very heart of civilization itself.

This is not to inflate the importance of moral rights. Some have objected that it is not rights and their exercising that should govern our behaviours and attitudes, but rather love for our fellows or altruism or some other 'higher' motives and sentiments. This particular objection is also strongly and specifically raised to the notion of the possibility of children's rights. Rights serve to settle conflicts of interests. However, the claim is that in an ideally moral world there would be no such conflicts; everyone would have the same interests or they would at least be able to harmonize their interests. Instead of scrabbling about who has a right to what, things would run smoothly and people would not need to fall back on an adversarial model of which the notion of rights is a part. The exercising of rights is only necessary, it is claimed, when our other moral relations have broken down.

Once again, there is a point to the objection. Rights and their related notions are not the totality of morality (central as they may be) and there are situations in which questions of rights are inappropriate or inapplicable. There are many moral considerations other than rights which are at times more important in a particular case or type of case in deciding what ought to be done or what the appropriate moral attitude should be.

Nevertheless, even if we grant the assumption that people are capable of behaving exclusively from some other 'higher' motives, conflicts of interest will continue to arise, the world being as it is, no matter how 'good' or 'moral' everyone in it strives to be. Moreover, fierce controversy about what constitutes children's interests (not to mention their best interests) will almost certainly continue even if (and probably especially if) the holders of opposing views take their completely independent stands on their own moral high ground. Not only is it a world of inevitable scarcity, as Hart[8] has pointed out, but also one in which people are necessarily vulnerable to each other.

This latter is particularly and obviously so in the case of children. Therefore, even proceeding on the weakest assumption that there is at least the possibility that everyone's interests will not always harmonize is sufficient to establish the necessity for and value of a rights model.[9] Without rights there would be no moral 'bottom line' as it were, to resolve these conflicts, to protect people's truly vital interests, or to ensure that their status as unique individuals with dignity and worth was recognized.[10] Furthermore, even the possibility that we could descend into anything remotely resembling a Hobbesianesque state is sufficient to establish an overriding reason for the retention of rights concepts and practices.[11]

Moreover, the above objection puts the cart before the horse. It is not that having rights causes conflicts of interests, although this may on occasion seem to be the order of things. When this seems to be the case, however, a more plausible general explanation is that prior to the time that rights are attributed or acknowledged people just quietly tolerate any injurious or degrading treatment they are receiving; and again, and very sadly, this is obviously and particularly true as concerns children. Under such circumstances, apart from overt or underhanded retaliation of some sort, what else would the injured parties have the power to do? The point is that not having rights might well make the world a quieter and possibly less openly contentious place to live; and children could conceivably continue indefinitely in their societally (and often legally) prescribed time honoured role of being seen and not heard. It would not, however, make the world a less conflict-free place and certainly not a qualitatively better one.

Having rights, on the other hand, serves to settle either possible conflicts, or disputes after they have arisen; and it does so in a fair, non-arbitrary and consistent way. Further, quite to the contrary to this objection as raised to children's rights, their existence and acknowledgement serves at least equally to harmonize differing interests from the beginning.

Rights are generated by moral principles. When legally or in some way institutionally instantiated, rights, among other things, give the right holder a certain power over some resources[12] and ultimately some control over the behaviour of others which affects (often in crucial ways) the right holder directly. Although it is true that rights are often exercised and stood upon when we would all be better off if they were not, the inconvenience suffered at the hands of a few obnoxiously over-zealous rights claimers is surely better than the alternative. A world without a rights model and conventions would be a world where members of the moral community (or anyone for that matter) had no guarantee of even minimally decent treatment, and no power or basis upon which to redress legitimate grievances. It would, in fact, be a world where everyone was in a situation quite like the real world situation of children.

Beyond the loss to individuals, it seems likely that the life of the larger community would indeed become impossible.

One further general objection must be answered, namely that although rights concepts and conventions may be an addition to a moral scheme and moral life, nevertheless, no coherent or satisfactory theory of rights has been advanced. Such a theory, therefore, may well be unobtainable. In any case the result is that rights theories and talk are confusing, obfuscating, and ultimately untenable. If one accepts such claims, it would follow that we should indeed protect children from catching this adult disease.

Admittedly, when the notion of rights comes onto the scene it is often true that people mean a wide variety of different, and sometimes irreconcilable things. It does not follow, however, that a coherent theory of rights either has not been or can not be advanced. Nor does it mean that there is no common ground or understanding which can be reached. Now that we have established the existence and importance of the retention of rights in general in our moral scheme we need to know more about the nature of the rights to which we shall be referring.

There are, of course, a number of competing and conflicting theories which have been advanced. Nevertheless, there are many relatively non-controversial things which can be said that will help fill in our picture in the relevant areas. Our interest is to discover and articulate whatever can be said surefootedly about the nature of rights in general, and children's rights in particular.

2. A MORALLY LEGITIMATE THEORETICAL FRAMEWORK FOR ANALYSIS

It seems necessary and appropriate to first define more precisely what a right is. Joel Feinberg has defined rights as 'valid claims'; what makes these claims valid is:

> Justification of a peculiar and narrow kind, namely justification within a system of rules.[13]

In the case of moral rights,

> the recognition [of a morally valid claim] is called for . . . by more principles, or the principles of an enlightened conscience.[14]

'A has a moral right to X' then can be taken to mean that 'A has a valid claim to X'. As Feinberg himself points out this definition is somewhat circular (possibly necessarily so) and, therefore, not meant to be a formal definition.[15] It serves our purposes, however, as it expands and clarifies the notion of a right; and as will become apparent, it is used here to refer to the more traditional non-interference rights as well as moral rights to positive assistance.

But not anyone or anything can count as a holder of the valid moral claims; it would be conceptual nonsense, as Feinberg has effectively pointed out, to talk about, for example, the rights of rocks or the rights of a shrimp.[16] Thus when considering who is to count as a right holder, Feinberg comes to a 'tentative conclusion'; this is a principle, 'the interest principle', which states that:

> the sorts of beings that *can* have rights are precisely those that have (or can have) interests.[17]

His reasons for adopting this principle are:

> (1) because a right holder must be capable of being represented and it is impossible to represent a being that has no interests, and (2) because a right holder must be capable of being a beneficiary in his own person, and a being without interests is a being that is incapable of being harmed or benefitted, having no good or 'sake' of its own.[18]

As stated, this interest principle is useful for all the species of claim rights, separating those who can count as right holders from those who can not. Moral rights have this in common with other claim rights, particularly legal rights.

Our assumptions so far then are that to have a moral right is to have a valid claim, its validity arising within a framework where the 'principles of an enlightened conscience' call for its recognition. Further, rights are held by beings that have or can have interests. Since we are thus far on relatively uncontroversial ground, and these conclusions have been successfully established, we shall take them as given. The controversy begins, however, when we attempt to spell out who has or can have interests.

As has been noted by many philosophers, 'interest' is an ambiguous term and concept. A large part of the controversy surrounding questions about moral rights – questions of who has rights, and what they have rights to and why – has to do with which sense or senses of the term 'interests' one takes to be relevant. Although disambiguating the concept will not do all of the work towards settling disputes surrounding rights generally or children's rights in particular, doing so is central and certainly with respect to children's rights.

John Kleinig has given us a clear statement of the different meanings of 'interest':

> (i) One use of 'interest', generally capturable in expressions of the form 'X is interested in Y', refers to an inclination to pay attention to something . . . We speak here of interest being aroused or excited, dampened or suppressed, of it waxing and waning. It is a psychological phenomenon. A person lacking interest in this sense is said to be *uninterested* . . .

> (ii) . . . the interests generally expressible in statements of the form 'X has an interest in Y' . . . Here, my interests are restricted to those projects (my own or others') in which I have some stake. To have a stake in something is to stand to gain or lose from it, because of some investment of energy or goods in it or some project affected by it, or because its outcome affects me advantageously or otherwise. Interests in the second sense are not logically tied to interest in the first sense, though they may not be

completely unrelated at a conceptual level. The correct drafting of my aunt's will may be to my advantage, yet hold no interest for me. I may be *un*interested without being *dis*interested . . .

(iii) We sometimes use expressions of the form 'Y is in X's interests'. Here a person's interests and his desires may well be in conflict. Indeed, a frequent use of such expressions is to draw attention to the fact that what a person desires – even what he has an interest in – is not in his interests . . . Normally, people have an interest in what is in their interests. However, they do not always behave rationally or with sufficient knowledge of the consequences of their actions, and they may acquire wants or stakes in projects which are contrary to their interests. And just occasionally, they may knowingly and reasonably accord certain interests such importance that they will be prepared to jeopardize that which is said to be in their interests.

The interests of which we are now speaking are appropriately referred to as *welfare* interests . . .[19]

It is Professor Kleinig's second two senses of 'interest' which are of direct relevance to rights questions, and his discussion is especially illuminating as applied to children's rights.

Stanley Benn, who has argued that moral agency is a sufficient as well as in most cases necessary condition for a being to have rights, agrees with Feinberg's claim that only one who has interests can have rights. However, the only sense of 'interests' which Benn has taken to be of primary relevance is the sense set out in (ii) above. As he describes them, these are:

the sort of interest that organize or give a consistent direction to otherwise diverse activity . . . rights are related . . . to the kind of interests that give a consistent direction to [one's] activities; they are normative resources that enable [one], by controlling the actions of others, to manipulate [one's] social environment for [one's] own ends . . .[20]

We shall refer to these kinds of interests as 'project interests' since this seems to capture what both Professor Benn, and Professor Kleinig in (ii) above, have in mind.[21]

It seems undeniably true that this sense of 'interests' is in some way related to rights theories and questions. However, the problem with a view such as Professor Benn's is with the claim that this is the only primarily relevant sense of 'interests'. On his analysis, because certain beings have projects that are important to them, they have rights. Rights are grounded in what he refers to as deontological reasons.[22] But his claim regarding the relevant 'interest' makes the criteria for both who is to count as a right holder and what they have rights to much too strict, since it fails to give us an account of any but a very restricted group of core rights cases. On an analysis such as this, it is only full moral agents (or moral persons as Benn calls them) who can qualify as right holders in the full sense, since they are the only beings who can have these sorts of project interests.

He specifies that a moral person is, for one thing a 'natural person'

> someone aware of himself, not just as process or happening (as he may be aware of his digestive processes), but as agent, as having the capacity to make decisions that make a difference to the way the world goes . . .; he is conscious of himself as capable of having projects that constitute certain existing or possible states 'important' of 'unimportant' . . .[23]

Beyond this, besides perceiving her/himself in this manner, a moral person must also recognize that others are natural persons in just the same way; and s/he must further recognize that 'a natural person has a minimal right as a moral person to be considered'.[24]

In short then, a moral person must recognize that both s/he and others have a right that the fact that they are authors of projects and plans be taken into consideration – that is, they have a right to the forbearance of others, so that they might carry out their plans without interference. The category of full fledged right holders on an account such as this is thus limited to full moral agents. Moreover, it seems that he restricts the category of full fledged right holders even further to only moral agents in full possession of their faculties because, on his thinking, it somewhat devalues rights to allow someone other than the right holder to act as a proxy.[25]

As noted above, taking this as the only sense of 'interest' which is of central importance to rights questions is a much too strict criterion, and, therefore, yields an inadequate and unsatisfactory account. Moreover, it is accounts of this nature which have rendered

> The jurisprudence of rights . . . singularly weak in providing the material guarantees of life and dignity flowing from the community to the individual.[26]

This last point seems especially relevant to children's rights considerations.

On an account such as Benn's, the class of cases relegated to borderline status becomes overwhelmingly large. It is also divergent, completely out of line both with common sense and the answers to the questions of who has rights and what they have rights to given by theoretical accounts. What sense can be made of all of the so-called borderline cases, including young children, people in comas, severely mentally and emotionally deficient people etc. – all of the cases that do not involve 'natural persons' as he characterizes them?

For Benn, the telos or purpose of legal rights is:

> to provide natural persons with institutional normative resources to safeguard their capacities for selecting and pursuing their own projects.[27]

Given the conceptual and empirical connections between legal and moral rights, his formulation can be extended. The telos of moral rights then would be ultimately to provide normative social, political, legal resources for natural persons for the same reasons. Even if we allow him that this is indeed *the* telos of rights, which seems highly questionable, it can not include only natural persons as he has described them. To do so would exclude too many cases that our moral (and also institutional/legal) judgments would normally insist that we must include.

If anyone has rights, then surely someone who is temporarily comatose, or temporarily insane does; yet neither of these qualify as natural persons. Moreover, it is certain that a dead person can not qualify as a natural person, while it is far from certain that s/he cannot qualify, in some sense even if an attenuated one, as a right holder. Or even a child who has not quite reached Benn's requisite state of development must have some rights, at least some sort of *right*, for example, not to be treated as the household pet. Beyond that, this young child's rights would seem to be at least as central and constitute as much of a 'core case' as any.

In fact, if we look more closely at these types of cases it becomes evident that not only does taking 'project interests' to be the only or primary relevant sense restrict too greatly the class of right holders, it also too narrowly limits the acceptable content of rights. To take just one case illustratively, consider a teen-age heroin addict who is obviously not now a natural person and possibly can never be. Would it really be acceptable to lock him away in a dungeon indefinitely? Would he not have some right to the best institutional care we could afford, or at the very least a right to be allowed out from his place into the sunshine and fresh air periodically? Moreover, is that right not one which should be legally instantiated and enforced – even though such treatment would have absolutely nothing to do with the youngster's project interests (certainly not directly or in any obvious way), but rather solely with his welfare interests?

Benn attempts to substantiate his claims by making a distinction between two different kinds of moral reasons for actions. He claims that one kind of moral reason for action arises from the fact that something is an object of value, an 'axiotimon' as he calls it, 'something which it is appropriate to value or esteem' on the basis of axiological reasons.[28] Certain objects such as oil paintings, trees, young babies etc. get classified this way; he claims that we have moral reasons to treat such objects in certain ways just because they are axiotima. These kinds of reasons are, however, supposedly distinct from the deontological moral reasons he says we have for according and respecting the rights of persons who are 'properly an object of respect and forbearance'.[29] Since Benn sees respect as a strictly stand-off relationship, equating respect and forbearance, it follows that his legitimate content of rights is unacceptably limited.

According to him it is irrational not to care whether axiotima exist or continue to exist, and whether or not they flourish or decay. For this reason we can and do ascribe needs to these objects, 'conditions necessary for the object to remain that by virtue of which it is are valued'.[30]. He has distinguished moral reasons for administering to the needs of axiotima from the moral reasons we have for attributing and respecting rights. But this distinction will not bear the weight he wishes it to carry.

In the first place, to say that someone has a right to something is not just to say that it would be nice or decent for them to have it. To say that 'A has a right to PHI' is to say that 'A ought to have PHI (or be allowed to PHI)', and also that someone has a corresponding duty, whether of forbearance or a positive duty, to insure that A have PHI. Differences between the moral reasons behind 'A has a right to PHI' and the supposedly distinct moral reasons for action behind acting in a particular way because 'A is an axiotima and A has a need for PHI' are, so far, not apparent. However, to say that 'A has a right to PHI' is to further say that there is a prima facie stronger moral reason for A to have PHI than any of the types of moral reasons mentioned above, taken either singly or combined. In other words, if 'A has a right to PHI', since this is a stronger, more compelling, moral reason, it would override (again, *prima facie*) any of the other type of moral reasons mentioned. This is one of the distinctive features of rights as reasons for actions, distinguishing rights from many other kinds of reasons, including administering to the needs of axiotima.

All of this is not to say, of course, that there are not or can not be over-riding moral reasons for A not to have PHI in a particular instance where A has a right to PHI. But it is to say that if A has a right to PHI, and someone wants to claim that 'A ought not to have PHI', then the burden of proof lies completely with the person who makes this claim. Otherwise, unless it can be shown that there are very strong overriding reasons which mitigate against A having PHI, then A's right to PHI still stands.

This is very unlike the situation with respect to other moral reasons for action where, when one is asserted, it is to be considered on an equal footing and weighed against whatever other reasons are or can also be asserted. We usually consider rights to be such strong moral reasons for action that there is, as Hart puts it,

> a special congruity in the use of force or threat of force to secure what . . . someone's right to have done shall in fact be done.[31]

I suggest that the prima facie overriding strength of rights as moral reasons for actions lies in this congruence.

Further, the congruency exists because we take the treatment that rights insures to be of such fundamental importance[32] that the use of force is justi-fied and appropriate to bring it about, whereas this is not the case with our other moral reasons for action. We institutionalize rights in our social and legal systems in ways which we would not even consider institutionalizing these other moral reasons for action. Other reasons do not seem to be strong enough to justify using coercion to systematically limit the freedom of other people or to make positive demands on them. In other cases we expect or at least hope for people's voluntary compliance. However, if it is not forthcoming we are not prepared to guarantee it with the use of force. This is perhaps because either the harm done is not as great or serious as in rights violation cases, or the prima facie harm done by forcibly restricting people's freedom is more serious or outweighs the other harm done. With respect to rights, however, the situation is different. The possible harm done if rights, including children's rights are violated is just too great to risk the possibility, and so the threat of force is used to ensure that violations do not occur.

Although when Hart speaks of this special congruence he speaks particularly of legal rights, this does seem to be one thing that we can say moral and legal rights have in common. On this latter point Kleinig has said that:

> merely moral rights are not accompanied by the same guarantees, but it can be said of such that where they are unrecognized compulsion would be appropriate.[33]

On our account, a more accurate description of the situation involves a slightly stronger claim. The question which naturally immediately follows Kleinig's proposition is, 'Such compulsion would be appropriate *under what circumstances?*' It is true that moral rights are not necessarily backed up by currently existing specific institutionalized legal guarantees. In this they differ from legal rights. But it is not just that compulsion would be appropriate where moral rights remain unrecognized, but rather as with legal (positive) rights, that compulsion *is* appropriate. If someone wants to claim that it is not appropriate in a particular case, the burden of proof is entirely on her/him to establish her/his claim.

It is not enough to say what Kleinig has concerning this. The danger with doing so lies in this very fact that the natural end of his proposition is, 'appropriate under what circumstances?'. This, of course, strikes at the foundation of all other claims about moral rights and seemingly especially children's rights – and weakens it.

Consider the child again who has not yet reached Benn's requisite stage of development. It seems fairly widely agreed that this child has some kind of a right to some education. It can not be enough that the right is enforced publicly, while at home the child is only provided with the conditions necessary for it to continue as a child – which would be very minimal indeed.

If all of this is correct it now becomes obvious why Benn's distinction will not work. Consider another specific but hypothetical case: suppose the nine year old grocery boy arrives at A's door to make his weekly delivery for which A has already paid. Suppose further that he discovers an abandoned infant on the doorstep, and on calling A to the door finds out that while A is quite happy to take the infant (B) indoors, A has no intention of giving B any food or making any other provision for B's nutritional needs. It does seem incontestable that in this case, while A has a right to PHI (the food), B also has a right to be fed – and most immediately by A. It is inconceivable that A's right to dispose of the contents of the grocery boy's delivery as A sees fit is a prima facie stronger moral reason than whatever the reason behind the demand that B should be fed by A. It is not enough to say that

'B should be fed', 'it would be nice or decent for B to be fed', and 'A has a duty to feed B'. If the infant is not fed, then his rights have been violated and it would be wrong to conclude that the moral damage done arose simply from the fact that the infant is an axiotima, something that it is appropriate to value or esteem. To consider the infant in the latter way seems virtually obscene. We would think it both appropriate and justified to use force or the threat of force to ensure that the infant (or anyone in relevantly similar circumstances) were fed in this case. Moreover, that conclusion seems remarkably unrelated, at least in any direct or obvious way, to the fact that the infant is a holder of future project interests. The moral reasons which motivate the claim that 'B should be fed by A' are at least as strong, and probably more so, as those reasons behind 'A has a right to dispose of his food as he pleases'.

The distinction between axiological and deontological (as those relevant to rights) reasons fails to bear the theoretical weight Benn wants to place on it because such a distinction does not allow us to limit people's freedom of action, or even more especially to make positive demands on them, in cases and for reasons that not only make us think it appropriate to do so, but which our values demand. The abandoned infant does have a claim to A's care and groceries; and this claim has primarily to do with the infant's needs and welfare interests. Moreover, the needs and welfare interests, upon which in the first instance this infant's right is grounded, constitute the same grounding that an adult's right in a similar situation would have. Significantly, the infant's relevant interests here have strikingly little to do with its 'best interests'; B's right to the food is grounded on its interests period. Why in general would protecting people's project interests constitute a prima facie stronger moral reason for action than either protecting their welfare interests or, for that matter, even for administering to the needs of an axiotima? Here we are left at a loss by Benn's theory.

Further, if we go on to ask, why is it to be considered that someone's project interests are so important, important enough for us to institutionalize rights and their surrounding practices as we do, his theory gives us very scant grounds upon which to proceed to answer this.[34] Not only does what he has said not satisfactorily answer this question, but it might well preclude the possibility of a satisfactory answer. In either case, there is a value judgment which takes place in determining rights contents and cases that has not been allowed for in what he has said. If Benn's explanations would admit that anything at all were lost, it seems it would only be a certain kind of power that right holders have, or possibly a cherished part of his self image.

We need only consider Feinberg's Nowheresville once again to see that this is so. In this world, it will be recalled, rights do not exist and consequently people do not see any particular treatment coming to them as their due. In such a world, people would feel gratitude for the smallest kindness, and even if they received the best of treatment they would not see it as owed to them; nor would they see themselves as 'dignified objects' worthy of respect.

A world with claim-rights is one in which all persons, as actual or potential claimants, are dignified objects of respect, both in their own eyes and in the view of others. No amount of love and compassion, or obedience to higher authority, or noblesse oblige, can substitute for those values.[35]

However, as the thought experiment points out, something of great value to us all would be lost in Benn's world, and that arising from a certain attitude – the attitude of respect, in a much broader sense than Benn uses 'respect' as applied to rights. He uses 'respect' here as being virtually equivalent to forbearance; whereas, the sense of 'respect' which accords a certain dignity is reserved as appropriate only to our treatment of axiotima, although he does not refer to this latter as respect.[36]

But this distinction, like the greater one he has made between the two different moral reasons for action, is not applicable in the way he wants. Rather, while respect is often appropriately exhibited to right holders by forbearance, such forbearance is not the equivalent of respect (as he would have it) and is only one form the manifestation of respect can or should take. The appropriate attitude of respect which is applicable to right holders (*all* right holders) is an attitude towards their worth which is an acknowledgement of their worth and dignity and of their status as members of the class of 'persons', members (possibly past, present or future) of the moral community. It is a recognition of their value and importance simply because they are members of the moral community, holders of rights, and in these ways at least the moral equals of everyone else in the moral community. It is simply not enough that others let us (or even help us) get on with our projects; if their actions towards us lack respect in this broader sense, then the quality of our lives would indeed be greatly altered.

An alternative answer to our current central concerns has been suggested by John Kleinig. Kleinig agrees that it is beings who have interests who also have rights, however, for him there is a different sense of 'interests' that is relevant. He argues that welfare interests, which:

in their foundational aspect, are those interests which are indispensable to the pursuit and fulfillment of characteristically human interests, whatever those interests might be,[37]

are necessary prerequisites of project interests. The candidates he has in mind for welfare interests are:

bodily and mental health, normal intellectual development, adequate material security, stable and non-superficial interpersonal relationships, and a fair degree of liberty.[38]

Moreover, he goes one step further claiming that:

It is with welfare interests that rights are primarily concerned. Indeed [he goes so far to suggest that] our politico-moral rights are, in the first instance to the components of our welfare. Other rights that we might claim, though not derivable from judgments of welfare, can be justified only by reference to our welfare rights.[39]

Kleinig has a point. It seems correct, and at least partially for the reasons he says, to protect welfare interests with rights. Empirically speaking, and in the case of children chronologically speaking, a certain level of welfare interest satisfaction is a prerequisite for any concern regarding project interests. For this reason it seems ludicrous, if not entirely pointless, to insist that it is with project interests that rights are mainly or primarily concerned. Further, these rights may even be logically prior to the latter. Whether or not they are logically presupposed by project type rights, it is surely irrational to protect the latter without also protecting the former. Rights lose at least a great deal of their value if, contrary to Benn as well as Kleinig, both kinds of interests are not attended to in a way which gives each equal moral footing.

Even the one telos which Stanley Benn's theory admits of can not be made sense of without considering both. If we take at least one of the telos of ascribing rights to be that rights ensure that the right holder is a dignified object of respect both in her/his own eyes and in the eyes of others as previously suggested, then to protect only or primarily project interests is to undermine the very values which rights are meant to ensure get expressed. A theory such as Benn's makes virtually meaningless any non-interference rights which it does ascribe. Acknowledging rights of non-interference without also including in one's theory at least some rights to positive assistance is very much like saying to a person who is crippled in a wheelchair 'You are free to walk around the room. I shall not interfere; it is your right'. Therefore, Kleinig's point is welcome and historically overdue. It at least provides room for some important 'borderline cases' and leaves leeway for introduction of not yet formally institutionalized rights.

There are problems with Kleinig's view also, however. There is, first, the relatively minor one that just as the term 'human rights' is ambiguous and confusing, so is the term 'characteristically human interests'. It is more explanatory to spell out what these are, as Feinberg does with his 'interests', as those which:

> however the concept [interests] is finally to be analyzed, presupposes at least rudimentary cognitive equipment. Interests are compounded out of *desires* and *aims*, both of which presuppose something like *belief*, or cognitive awareness.[40]

Using 'interests' in this way, beyond being clearer and more specific, goes further towards an explanation which avoids begging the question of who has rights and what the relevant interests are. Further, and rather obviously, children can now be seen as having the relevant interests from the beginning. There is no conceptual reason, for instance, why certain beings such as higher mammals can not have these interests and possibly even rights, and both Benn and Kleinig acknowledge this. There is, however, an obvious conceptual reason why any higher mammal could not have 'characteristically human interests'. Moreover, we can in this way avoid the danger and confusion that would result from automatically conflating all discussions of rights with discussions of human rights.

If we recast Kleinig's analysis with a different terminology, leaving out the question-begging references to characteristically human interests, it is still an open question of who has or can have these welfare interests. However, Kleinig's offered conditions prove too weak to give us an adequate answer. In trying to avoid the mistake which Benn and others have made of making the conditions for being a right holder too strong, Kleinig's considerations become too weak. The sense of ' "interests" . . . [as used to mean those which] must be rational in the sense of conscious projects'[41] is, as he says, too strong, at least on its own, to be the only sense relevant to rights. So he brings in the other sense of 'interests' but to the exclusion of the stronger sense, claiming that welfare interests are the only one relevant to rights. As noted previously, it should be remembered that he remains unsure about this.

To make having welfare interests a sufficient condition for having rights is too weak in that it allows in cases for which it would make no sense to ascribe rights. Since a shrimp can be said to have some welfare interests, for instance, it would follow on such an account that it also had rights.

In other words, to take welfare interests as the only ones to which rights are addressed is again to fail to capture the full telos of rights, and again to fail to protect the values that they are meant to insure. At the very least more needs to be said.

For our purposes it is enough to note that the general rough and ready rule of thumb is obviously connected with just how many of the welfare interests a being can be said to have and also to what 'degree' s/he holds those interests – i.e. how cognitively aware she/he is, now complex and realistic his or her belief system is etc.

Moreover, the connection between this and what exactly any right holder can be said to have a right to is equally obvious. Yet also, cum Kleinig, we must agree that *pace* Benn, having 'a capacity to form conscious plans and projects' is always a sufficient condition for a bearer of interests to be a right holder, although this condition on its own misses the underlying point of rights and related practices; further, from this theoretical gap arises much of the misunderstanding concerning the relationships between the interests which rights protect, the best interests of the child, and children's rights.

Finally, it is clear that what a particular right holder can be legitimately said to have a right to must be significantly affected by whether or not s/he has (or will have or has had) such a capacity. For all of this, however, the heart of the dispute concerning relevant senses of interests remains unresolved. The resolution is necessary not only to determine who legitimately populates our class of right holders, but also to determine what rights they have.

3. THE PARTICULARS OF THE FRAMEWORK FOR
CHILDREN'S RIGHTS ANALYSIS

The most plausible suggestion is that we are referring to both senses of 'interests' when we make the claim that a being must have interests to have rights. 'Interests' is ambiguous. But as we have seen, to distinguish the senses of the term and then assert that it is only one or the other of them that we are talking about without respect to rights leaves us with an inadequate and unacceptable account of who has rights and what the content of those rights is. It is only when we admit that both senses of the term are equally relevant that we can capture the purpose of ascribing moral rights (and ultimately legal rights) at all. It is also only by doing this that we come up with a notion of rights that satisfactorily classifies the cases. In other words, it seems that 'the principles of an enlightened conscience' that we take into account include both senses of the term 'interests'.

The best answer to the questions concerning who are right holders and what the content of their rights are is that moral (and legal) rights are held by those who have interests, which are in some sense intimately and inextricably and inextricably bound up with their personalities. We can take 'interests' to mean roughly 'a capacity to be disposed to form conscious plans and projects'.[42] To Kleinig's formulation we can add that such capacity need not be a present one; it might be a future one (a not too remote potential), or possibly even a past one. Those satisfying this condition are right holders; what they have rights to depends in each instance on which potentials and capabilities they themselves would take to have the crucially relevant (i.e. vital) connections to their personalities at the time the matter is first considered. A right holder has positive rights in so far as non-interference rights would be of no use or value to her or him presently; and this because not to have such positive rights would make the ascription of negative rights at a later time (and possibly even a past one) an unfair or at best a random matter, given that who would qualify by the stronger interest criteria for such rights is largely dependent on how or whether their welfare interests are met. As or when the recognition of these positive rights bring the state of affairs to one where the potentials of the right holders are actual capacities, then the positive rights decrease accordingly and the non-interference rights increase, but always with an eye to their underlying welfare interests.

The overall purpose of ascribing rights is both individual and collective well-being, and without ascribing them consistently with the criterion roughly stated, neither would be possible. In other words, even if we imagine very far-fetched but possible worlds where all might be the same except without this general recognition and acknowledgement, the *quality* of life able to expressed therein would be quite abysmal.

The above criterion answers our central question concerning who is to have rights and what they are entitled to, firstly by taking into account that the capacities required for a right holder develop and are present in each individual at any given time along a continuum as a matter of degree. This is one point at least where society can begin to, theoretically as well as practically, learn from its children. Moreover, it ensures the protection of the potentials as well as the actual capacities, both being considered to be of equal importance.

Very young children, for example, since they satisfy our condition turn out to be right holders, as long as there are no overriding other serious objections. Further, this is consistent with most of our practices and beliefs regarding young children as well as others we normally take to be right holders. Which specific rights they have would be decided according to where they fall along the continuum, rather than by some extraneous, irrelevant or artificially imposed criterion. The right to life in this case, for instance, where the personality of the child involved was to a far greater extent potential rather than capable would entail different treatment than a right to life would entail for a fully formed and developed personality. It would be ludicrous to claim for instance, as an account such as Benn's would require, that a three year old had no right to life as such. Similarly with our case of the comatose individual; as long as the coma was a temporary or possibly temporary condition, the person's right to life would cash out to a positive right to the assistance necessary, within the limits set by the environmental resources available, to remain alive. On the other hand, if the coma was certainly permanently irreversible then the right the person would have might well entail much less, bringing it much closer to a strictly negative right.

Moreover, since not all interests are entitled to be protected by rights, it is just those which should receive protection which it is necessary to protect in order to ensure that the dimension which rights establish in our lives can continue as actualized. This subset of interests which are and should be so protected are those which are vital to our lives as having the extra dimension and quality.

The broad implications that conceiving rights this way has for children in general are that a child could be said to have a right at first that we act in his or her interests, i.e. the welfare interests specified before – providing conditions necessary for 'bodily and mental health, normal intellectual development, adequate material security, stable and non-superficial interpersonal relationships, and a fair degree of liberty'. Moreover, in so far as these interests must be attended to with an eye to protecting the child's later project interests, whatever these turn out to be, then the child has a right that we act *only* in his or her welfare interests, and this only in so far as the capacity to act in his or her own interest has not yet developed.[43] We further have the obligation to provide those conditions and that assistance necessary for these capacities to develop. Beyond that, in so far as the child becomes able to act in her/his own interest we have the obligation to let her/him do so. Acting in a child's best interests, therefore, means that one's child regarding behaviour meets one's responsibilities to the child in these (and *only* these) ways.[44]

Approaching an analysis of rights within this framework gives us a way of analyzing general rights claims which is completely theoretically parallel to analyzing children's rights claims, and, therefore, thoroughly compatible. Beyond that, such a framework allows us (moreover, compels us) to keep in mind at all times during our analysis the morally relevant facts about children. In particular, children are in the first instance especially helpless and vulnerable and particularly to those significant others in their lives (who might have competing rights claims). Secondly, children are both developing as well as potential personalities, and they are also future full personalities – and each of these facts are equally as morally weighty when determining to treat them in this way or that, i.e. in determining what exactly their relevant interests, and their best interests and rights are. Finally, but certainly no less morally significantly, children are not only inconceivable except as firmly rooted within their social setting, but they are also particularly so located (initially) completely as a result of the actions of others, not their own. This latter fact greatly increases our obligatory responsibilities to insure that their best interests really are the determining factor when deciding to treat them in this way or that; and this in turn means in large part that our collective responsibility is to ensure that their rights are protected.

While the model focuses on these facts as ultimately determinative, it also precludes certain other common pitfalls which often confuse children's rights issues. Firstly, it is theoretically impossible to compile a 'list' of all particular rights, not to mention exact content in particular cases. Secondly, it is inadvisable to make a general theoretical framework for rights (or just children's rights) any more specific than is necessary to clearly state it, in that to do so would undermine the very purpose of rights. Taking education as an example, it is clear that the more particular questions concerning rights and curriculum content, child-rearing practices etc. can only be adequately answered in light of further information about the psychological/mental development of the individual child, perhaps even more adequate psychological theory than is currently available, what the nature of the child's socio-economic system is, the state of development of the society etc. However, employing this general theoretical framework allows us to ask these questions in a morally legitimate way and provides us with the specific fundamentals necessary for adequately determining the answers.

NOTES

I would like to thank those at the Institute of Education, University of London who commented on earlier versions of this paper for their insights.

1. J. Goldstein, A. Freud and A. Solnit, *Before the Best Interests of the Child* (1980), New York, Free Press. This book itself constitutes one of the more famous such attempts.
2. The phrase 'the best interests of the child' appears eight times in this document. Not insignificantly, its first appearance is in Article 3 (there are fifty four articles altogether) in the

paragraph stating 'In all actions concerning children . . . the best interests of the child shall be a primary consideration', i.e. for all governments, governmental agencies, communities and even families themselves.

3. See, for example, Hobbes' discussion in his introduction to *Leviathan Parts I and II* (1958), pp. 23–24.

4. Feinberg discusses this point in J. Feinberg *Social Philosophy* (1973) Prentice-Hall Inc., New Jersey, p. 58. As a thought experiment it appears in 'The Nature and Value of Rights', *The Journal of Value Inquiry* 4 (1971)

5. J. Feinberg, *Social Philosophy* (1973), p. 58.

6. A. I. Melden, in *Rights and Persons* (1977), University of California Press, Berkeley & Los Angeles, gives an elaborate and enlightening general justification of rights. He also talks of rights as being justified claims. See, for example, p. 14 of his introduction.

7. See J. Feinberg (1973) op. cit., pp. 65–67, for an interesting elaboration of some of the differences between considering rights as 'justified' claims and considering them as 'valid' claims.

8. H. L. A. Hart, *The Concept of Law* (1961), Clarendon Press, Oxford, p. 176.

9. That this 'weak' possibility exists with respect to children should be fairly uncontentious. Even the most romantic Rousseaun souls need look no further than the nearest teenage 'child' to see that this 'possibility' is almost always not far from the surface, if it is not actually being actualized and played out. For a good discussion of the rights of teen age persons, which seems to be in complete theoretical agreement with this account although what is spelled out in it are some more practical applications, see Richard Lindley, 'Teenagers and Other Children', pp. 72–93, in Geoffrey Scarre (ed.), *Children, Parents and Politics* (1989), Cambridge University Press.

10. This is not to make a claim which is necessarily speciesist, or to say that animals are worthless. It is to say just that personalities have a value, as members of the moral community, which is not open to those who can not be members of that community. It may be that animals have a qualitatively different, although equally as valuable (if this is quantifiable) value, which must be respected, or at least taken into consideration, in appropriate ways. Empirical considerations concerning whether or not it is possible for animals to 'acquire' this value are beyond the scope of this paper, not to mention quite beside the point.

11. For a fuller discussion of the strengths, as well as the weaknesses, of rights models, see R. M. Cover, 'Obligation: A Jewish Jurisprudence of the Social Order', *The Journal of Law and Religion* 5 (1). See also my more complete discussion in 'Modern Liberal Rights Theories and Jewish Law' (forthcoming), *The Journal of Law and Religion*.

12. The notion of rights as 'normative resources' is articulated by S. I. Benn, 'Human Rights – for whom and for what?', in E. Kamenka and A. Erh-Soon Tay (eds.), *Human Rights*, Edward Arnold, London, p. 67. Benn's characterization of what these resources can legitimately protect, however, falls theoretically very short.

13. J. Feinberg, *Social Philosophy* (1973), p. 67.

14. Op. cit.

15. Ibid. p. 64.

16. See J. Feinberg, 'The Rights of Animals and Unborn Generations' in W. T. Blackstone (ed.), *Philosophy and Environmental Crisis* (1974), University of Georgia Press, Athens, Georgia. Being convinced by Feinberg's argument for this proposition, however, does not necessarily commit one to accepting his entire thesis in this article. However, questions about the possible rights of animals, individually or as species, are irrelevant to our concerns.

17. Ibid., p. 51.

18. Ibid.

19. J. Kleinig (1978) 'Crime and the Concept of Harm' (1978), p. 28 and 30, *American Philosophical Quarterly* 15 (1).

20. S. I. Benn, 'Personal Freedom and Environmental Ethics: The Moral Inequality of the Species', in G. Dorsey (ed.) *Equality and Freedom – International & Comparative Jurisprudence*, Oceana Publications, Dobbs Ferry, New York (1977).

21. In fairness to Professor Benn it should be noted that while he makes these claims in this particular article, in 'Human Rights – for whom and for what?' (a slightly later article) he does go some way toward trying to take account of the other sense of 'interests' as it relates to rights, even though the account he takes of it is only a socio-historic one. The contradiction leaves the reader wondering what prescriptive account he would have ultimately endorsed.

22. Again, this is his 1977 account. In the 1978 one, he picks out various human rights as being grounded on axiological reasons.

23. S. I. Benn (1977), op. cit., p. 408.

24. Ibid., p. 409.

25. See, for example, Benn's discussion of the legal rights which have been extended to infants and business corporations in 'Personal Freedom and Environmental Ethics: The Moral Inequality of Species' (1977), supra note 20.

26. R. M. Cover, op. cit., p. 71.

27. S. I. Benn, 'Human Rights – for whom and for what?'(1978), *supra* note 12, p. 67.

28. S. I. Benn (1978), *supra* note 12, p. 68.

29. Ibid., p. 68.

30. Ibid., p. 69.

31. H. L. A. Hart, 'Are There any Natural Rights?', *The Philosophical Review* 64 (2), 178 (1955).

32. This is a point that Kleinig makes in a discussion about a quite similar and closely related issue in (1976) 'Mill, Children, and Rights'(1976), p. 11, *Educational Philosophy and Theory* 8 (1). While we can agree with this point, some of the logic of the remainder of his discussion on rights in general and children's rights in particular is ultimately inadequate as a prescriptive account.

33. J. Kleinig, op. cit., p. 11.

34. It should be remembered that the critique offered here is of a compilation of several of Benn's articles, none of which purports to offer a complete theory of rights.

35. J. Feinberg (1973), *supra* note 4, p. 59.

36. See, for example, Benn's (1977) discussion in 'Personal Freedom and Environmental Ethics: The Moral Inequality of Species' (1977), p. 417, *supra* note 20, where he says: 'But this recognition [of him as a right holder] does not commit me to valuing or esteeming him . . . It is at least plausible, indeed, to suppose the contrary: If, through A's existing and having rights, I am liable to some restraints that he can impose at will on my freedom of action, I have a reason to look forward eagerly to his early extinction, even if I have a duty not to compass it'.

37. J. Kleinig (1978), op. cit., p. 31.

38. Ibid.

39. Ibid., p. 33. To be fair to Kleinig, as well as for our theoretical purposes, it is important to note the following. He says he remains unsure, after claiming that 'The only *actual* interests that need be presupposed are welfare interests . . . ', about the argument that 'unless these welfare interests also function as preconditions for the pursuit of ulterior interests which the being has, or will come to have in the ordinary course of events, then it will not qualify as a possible right-holder'.

40. J. Feinberg (1974), op. cit., p. 52.

41. J. Kleinig (1978), op. cit., p. 33.

42. This comes close to what Kleinig takes to be a more acceptable restatement of Benn's project interests. J. Kleinig (1978), op. cit., p. 33.

43. For a more concrete discussion on how a notion similar to this might work in the world of parents, children and the state see, J. Feinberg 'The Child's Right to an Open Future' (1980), in W. Aiken and H. LaFollette (eds.), *Whose Child: Children's Rights, Parental Authority, and State Power*, Rowman & Littlefield, Totowa, New Jersey. There are significant parts of his general thesis in this article, however, with which this theoretical account fundamentally disagrees.

44. M. D. A. Freeman, in *The Rights and Wrongs of Children*, Frances Pinter Publishers, London (1983), makes much of (and rightfully so) the necessity of recognition of the child's 'personality'. There is, of course, a legal personality of the child which needs to be recognized in order for her/him to be further recognized as having the legal rights that stand on all fours with those of any other right holder. The personality of the child discussed here constitutes the real world, and theoretical, prerequisite for the further recognition of the legal personality.

MICHAEL D. A. FREEMAN*

3. The Limits of Children's Rights

There can be no doubt that children are amongst the most vulnerable and powerless members of our societies to-day. In the past thirty years, but not before, we have been reminded to this each time a dramatic incident of child abuse is brought to public attention. In Britain, if not elsewhere, the sad face or logo of Maria Colwell,[1] a victim at the hands of her step-father, still haunts the consciousness of society. It is perhaps fitting that the vulnerability of children should be associated with parental violence (and, now of course, sexual abuse) because for so long the argument prevailed that parents were the guardians of their children's welfare making the need for and development of children's rights otiose. It would not render children's rights advocacy redundant even were it true (as, of course, it is for most children most of the time) for the love, nurture, care and protection afforded children would still be that which particular parents deemed appropriate. Children are in this sense at their parents' 'mercy' and, as Joel Feinberg put it,[2] 'no amount of love and compassion' is an adequate substitute for the ability to demand what is ours by right.

THE IMPORTANCE OF RIGHTS

Rights are important – few would now deny this. They have been called 'valuable commodities',[3] important moral coinage. In Bandman's[4] words, they 'enable us to stand with dignity, if necessary to demand what is our due without having to grovel, plead or beg'. If we have rights we are entitled to respect and dignity: no amount of benevolence or compassion can be an adequate substitute.

The children's rights movement, in some shape or form, has been with us for a century or more. An article with the title 'The Rights of Children' appeared as early as June 1852.[5] In France Jean Vallès attempted to establish a league for the protection of the rights of children in the aftermath of

* University College London.

M. Freeman and P. Veerman (eds.), The Ideologies of Children's Rights, 29–46.
© 1992 *Kluwer Academic Publishers. Printed in the Netherlands.*

the Paris Commune.[6] This was also the period of the child-saving movement and thus of the development of juvenile justice, as well as of the establishment of compulsory education. But, at this stage, it is the 'investment motive'[7] which is critical to the thinking behind children's rights: society's concern for the child is seen very much in terms of the child's usefulness to society. Children are objects of intervention rather than legal subjects. Talk of children's rights has been couched predominantly in child-saving language, in terms of salvation.[8] Its essential concern has been with protecting children, individual children, rather than with upholding the rights of children in general. And, although the distinction between two approaches to children's rights, between the 'nurturance' and 'self-determination'[9] orientation, has now been widely recognised, it is still the former that largely characterises public debate and social policy.

It is in part because of this that concern for children is still often firmly rooted in the individual child rather than children in general. With advocacy of children's rights it is not a question of protecting a particular child against an abusive or uncaring adult. The children's rights movement has now moved on to a plane where what is in issue is institutional discrimination, not a shortfall in parental or other adult behaviour.

THE IMPORTANCE OF CHILDREN'S RIGHTS

There are still those who argue that, however important rights are, it is not necessary to recognise as such children's rights. Where such arguments are put, they tend to employ one of two myths.

One, to which brief reference has already been made, idealises adult-child relations: it emphasises that adults (and parents in particular) have the best interests of children at heart. Those who argue in this way tend, like Goldstein, Freud and Solnit[10] or indeed the British government which was recently responsible for major children's legislation,[11] to adopt a *laissez-faire* attitude towards the family.[12] Thus, the only right for children which Goldstein *et al.* would appear to accept is the child's right to autonomous parents.[13] A policy of minimum coercive intervention by the state accords, they maintain, with their 'firm belief as citizens in individual freedom and human dignity'.[14] But *whose* freedom and *what* dignity does this uphold? It certainly would not appear to be those of the child. The recent English Children Act of 1989 very much reflects this philosophy.[15] It is somewhat unfortunate that in an age when so much abuse is being uncovered that governments and writers should cling to the 'cereal packet' image of the family.

The second myth can be captured more succinctly. It sees childhood as a golden age, as the best years of our life. Childhood is synonymous with innocence. It is a time when we are spared the rigours of adult life; it is a time of freedom, of joy, of play. The argument runs that, just as we avoid the responsibilities and adversities of adult life in childhood, so there should be no necessity to think in terms of children's rights. Whether or not the premise underlying this is correct or not (and I think that the carefree nature of a child's life can be exaggerated), it represents an ideal state of affairs, and one which ill-reflects the lives of many of to-day's children and adolescents.

There are countries which to-day are systematically exterminating children as if they were vermin (Brazil and Guatemala are two well-documented examples).[16] Poverty, disease, exploitation are rife in every part of the globe: the briefest of glances at the annual *State of the World's Children* publication soon reveals that.[17]

Even in the developed world the lives of children are fraught with deprivation. Thus, the latest data to 'emerge' from Britain reveals that, in a decade in which awareness of children's rights has heightened, child poverty numbers have nearly doubled. In a report just published[18] (written by Jonathan Bradshaw for the National Children's Bureau) the conclusion is drawn that during the 1980s 'children have borne the brunt of the changes that have occurred in the economic conditions, demographic structure and social policies of the United Kingdom'.[19] Three million children in Britain (that is 28 per cent of the total number) live on state benefits which force them to exist at or below (depending upon definition and interpretation) subsistence level. For contrast the percentage in 1979[20] was 17 per cent.

The case posited to attack those who espouse children's rights does not, therefore, command respect. Rights are important because possession of them is part of what is necessary to constitute personality. Those who lack rights are like slaves, means to others' ends, and never their own sovereigns.[21] It is surely significant that when we wish to deny rights to those who have attained chronological adulthood we label them (blacks in South Africa, the mentally retarded) children. To be a child, one does not have to be young. Foucault's aphorism[22] that 'madness is childhood' rings very true. Childhood is, of course, a social construct, a man-made phenomenon: those in authority determine who is a child.[23] That they have not done so with any consistency or, it would seem, coherent thought can not detain us here.

To say that rights are important, and important also for children, is not to gainsay the crucial part which other morally significant values, such as love, friendship and compassion, have and play in life's relationships. John Kleinig[24] is surely correct to argue that 'a morality which has as its motivation merely the giving of what is due . . . is seriously defective'. But, short of a cultural revolution beyond our wildest dreams, rights will remain important.

And, it will remain important to recognise children's rights. As Howard Cohen put it,[25] when he explained the importance of associating the children's rights movement with other rights' movements (women, civil rights etc.), '"rights" is a militant concept to the extent that it is used as part of the ideology in a campaign for social change'. It is generally agreed that denial of rights is a bad thing, so that something should be done about it. 'Rights' enables one to talk in terms of 'entitlements'.

RIGHTS AND DIGNITY

Ronald Dworkin[26] has not given any thought to children's rights but his thesis can be generalised. It is his thesis that if persons have moral rights to something, they are to be accorded these rights even if a utilitarian calculation shows that utility would be maximised by denying it to them. He invokes Rawls's *A Theory of Justice*[27] to illuminate the moral foundations of the rights thesis. Rawls proposes a methodology of reflective equilibrium whereby we try to fashion formulations of moral principles to the coat of moral judgment until we no longer feel inclined to change our judgments to fit the theory or our theory to fit the judgments. The ideal is a perfect fit. The mechanism for this reflective equilibrium is the social contract model: it conceives of persons in the 'original position' behind a 'veil of ignorance' (and thus ignorant of their identity, interests and entitlements) choosing the structure of the society in which they will live. Dworkin believes that these individuals 'have a responsibility to fit the particular judgments on which they act into a coherent program of action'.[28] He sees this as analogous to the way lawyers construct principles from precedent. Thus interpreted, he believes the contractual mechanism can be dropped: it is nothing more than a moral metaphor. Instead, he believes we can, and should focus on the idea that all other principles derive from the principle of equal concern and respect for each person.[29]

For Dworkin, anyone who proposes to 'take rights seriously' must accept the ideas of human dignity and political equality. He argues in favour of a fundamental right to equal concern and respect, and against any general right to liberty. The advantage of his so doing, as acknowledged by Mackie,[30] is that the right to equal concern and respect is a final and not merely 'a prima facie right' in the sense that one person's possession or enjoyment of it does not conflict with another's. Dworkin puts this forward as a 'postulate of political morality',[31] a fundamental political right: governments must treat citizens with equal concern and respect.

RIGHTS – FROM WHERE?

It may be thought that, however persuasive, this argument does not take us far enough. The question still not answered is where rights come from?[32] Why do we 'have' the rights we do? In posing this question, I am asking why we have the 'moral' rights we have (and assuming that we have some), and not posing the same question about legal rights. It is obvious why we have legal rights: on *one* level the answer is that they are set out in laws (the right to consult a lawyer when in police custody[33] or the right, if adopted, to see one's original birth certificate);[34] on *another*, we have them because historical struggles to acquire them have been successful (for example the right to vote or to strike). But it is less clear why we have the moral rights we do. What 'is' there when there 'are' rights? There must be, Narveson argues, 'certain features or properties of those who 'have' them such that we have *good reason to acknowledge* the obligation to refrain from interfering with, or possibly to sometimes help other bearers to do the things they are said to have the right to do, or have those things they are said to have a right to have'.[35]

All then hinges on 'good reason', on moral argument. It is interesting, if surprising, that Robert Nozick,[36] an arch-apostle of rights, should do no more than assert peremptorily that 'individuals have rights'. A common justifying principle is sought in relating rights to interests.[37] Thus, Feinberg writes[38] that 'the sort of beings who can have rights are precisely those who have (or can have) interests.' Though superficially attractive this argument ultimately fails. More than the existence of an interest is required to establish a right. Conversely, so may less for if rights only exist when interests are expressed, we would have to deny rights to the comatose,[39] the mentally handicapped[40] and to babies (as well, of course, to trees,[41] rocks and animals[42] but then those who do this conflate our moral responsibilities to lesser beings and to the environment into rights-type language with unfortunate consequences).

Another argument often put forward is purely formal. It is that all persons ought to be treated alike unless there is good reason for treating them differently.[43] Dworkin accepts this: he sees the right to treatment as an equal as the morally fundamental idea. It is that which requires that each person be accorded the same degree of concern and respect as every other person. The problem with this argument lies in deciding what constitutes a 'good reason' for treating persons differently. Gender and colour are now almost universally accepted as indefensible distinctions, but age, of course, continues to ground (at both ends, be it noted) legitimate discrimination in the opinions of many. The principle looks egalitarian but it can backfire and become an argument used to undermine egalitarianism.

Dworkin himself, attempts to identify the existence of a moral right against the state when for 'some' reason the state would 'do wrong' to treat a person in a certain way, 'even though it would be in the general interest to do so'.[44] But, since what it is 'wrong' for the state to do is what the state has a duty not to do, Dworkin appears to be defining rights in terms of duties. It is 'wrong' for the state to act in a particular way when the individual has a 'right' on which state action of a particular sort would illegitimately trample. The circularity of the argument will be readily apparent.

The Dworkinian thesis then takes us so far – but not, it seems, far enough. Equality by itself cannot explain what Dworkin is trying to explain, namely that rights as such 'trump'[45] countervailing utilitarian considerations. Something more is needed: the concept of autonomy may supply this. A plausible theory of rights may take account not just of equality but of the normative value of autonomy, the idea that persons as such have a set of capacities that enables them to make independent decisions regarding appropriate life choices. The deep structure of the rights thesis is equality and autonomy. Kant expressed this by asserting that persons are equal and autonomous in the kingdom of ends. It is the normative value of equality and autonomy that lies at the root of the Rawlsian contractarian conception. To see people as both equal and autonomous is to repudiate the moral claim of those who would allow utilitarian calculations of the greatest happiness of the greatest number to prevail over the range of significant life choices which the rights thesis facilitates and enhances.

Utilitarianism, by contrast, insists that the pattern of individual life choices be overridden if others are those made better off. To treat persons as utilitarianism requires us to focus almost obsessively on aggregated pleasure as the only ethically significant goal. But this is to ignore the crucial fact that persons experience pleasure, and that pleasure has human and moral significance only in the context of the life that a person chooses to lead. It is the rights thesis that protects the integrity of that person in leading his or her life.

One of Dworkin's insights was to link Rawlsian contractarian theory to the language of rights. One of his failings was not to appreciate that both notions at the root of Kantian moral theory (equality and autonomy) were equally morally significant. When we take both equality and autonomy seriously we are back at the contractarian thinking to be found in Kant and centrally in Rawls's morality. The reason is that equality is best expressed as an original position of equal beings, and that autonomy cannot be expressed better than as the choice of those equal beings under a 'veil of ignorance'.

CHILDREN AND DOUBLE STANDARDS

But what is the relevance of this to children? For, so the argument may be proferred, children are different. They (or at least some of them) have lesser abilities and capacities, are more vulnerable, need nurturance and protection. This, it may be thought, justifies the upholding of the double standard which is deeply embedded in our social practices and well-established in our laws, with one set of rights for adults (providing them with opportunities to exercise their powers) and another for children (providing them with protection and at the same time keeping them under adult control).

A double standard can be considered unjust where the distinction upon which it relies is not relevant: thus, for example, the colour of a person's skin is not a distinguishing mark to justify giving persons of one colour the right to vote and denying this right to persons of another (as institutionalised by the system of *apartheid* in South Africa or, indirectly, through the use of differential literacy tests in the United States before the 1964 Civil Rights Act). Is age then a relevant or a suspect point of distinction? Part of the problem lies in the fact that if we are going to give adults rights and deny them to children we must have a precise place at which to draw the line between the two (or at least that is received wisdom). Most developed countries currently draw the line at 18[46] (though it was common, previously, to set the line at 21 for no other sound reason than that 21 was the age at which medieval England deemed a man strong enough to bear full armour and fight as a knight).

But no one can seriously believe there is a real distinction (in powers, competence etc.) between someone of 18 years and a day and someone of 17 years and 364 days.[47] The drawing of the line is arbitrary. The law abhors uncertainty and has a tendency accordingly to think in dichotomies[48] (guilty/not guilty, though the Scots with a greater penchant for indeterminancy retain a 'not proven' verdict; liable/not liable; male/female – most legal systems are ill at ease with transsexualism).[49] Similarly, the law categorises persons into adults with full capacity and minors with little or none.

But the arguments adduced to deny children and adolescents rights can equally well be produced to deny those of 'mature' years those very same rights. Take, for example, the right to vote. In England, and in most developed countries with sufficient political stability to allow political choice, the right to vote is exercisable at the age of eighteen. However, many 16 years olds, and doubtless many children of a younger age, are politically aware and are capable of making an informed political choice. We do not give them the vote because there is a widely-held belief that children in general are incompetent to exercise the responsibilities and discharge the obligations associated with full citizenship. But, if competence is the test, a by-no-means insignificant proportion of children must be granted full political status and a larger number of adults would have to be disenfranchised. Apart from incompetence, the other argument adduced is the child's lack of experience and understanding. It suggests, or at least implies, that these are gained during the traditional period of childhood. This argument typically adduces the fact (if fact it be) that children lack foresight, that given the capacity to make decisions they will make disastrous ones. But is this not the case with adults too? Look at the governments voted in by adults in Britain, the United States, Israel in recent years! If experience and/or understanding is the criterion, many children would have the vote and many adults would not.

A further argument would justify denying children the franchise in terms of a belief that the decisions of children are not based on rational considerations. Rationality can be judged from a number of perspectives, but it seems common that those who attack children's rights do so from utilitarian considerations. Thus, Scarre[50] (justifying paternalism and not specifically the withholding of democratic rights) argues for intervention in an individual's affairs 'when there is reason to believe his decisions are not based on rational considerations, and that they are likely to result in a diminution of his stock of existing good, or underachievement of his possible stock of good'. To Scarre 'rational actions are those which are directed to maximising the expected utility of the agent'. 'In addition', he says, 'actions backed by rational decisions typically manifest themselves as elements of a systematic approach adopted by the agent for maximizing his good'. Scarre's concept of rationality is unduly confined but leaving that aside, can it really be said that adults' actions are always motivated by rational considerations? Indeed, it would not be difficult to find examples of decisions motivated by rational considerations which did not maximise the agent's utility, nor were expected to do so.

It is relatively easy to demolish the arguments adduced to support the double standard employed in our treatment of adults and children. It is also not difficult to show that children to-day occupy a different status from that of the young in earlier centuries and in different cultures: the line between adulthood and minority was not drawn as clearly by earlier generations.[51] Thus children in past ages participated in what we designate as adult activities (work, sex, leisure) in ways that would shock to-day. What conclusions should we draw from this? If moral argument and history appear to be on the side of the enfranchisers and liberators, are we to admit that we are wrong? Should we abandon the distinction between children and adults, even if this means, as Hafen put it, 'abandoning children to their rights'?[52]

LIBERATING CHILDREN

Few, it would seem, would go quite this far. Even the most extreme proponents of children's liberation would preserve some protective legislation, though wisely they would look at all claims to protect children with scepticism.[53] But the conclusion is nevertheless drawn by some that, if children worked in earlier societies then the sort of restrictions we find on child labour in developed societies should be removed. Thus Martin Hoyles[54] in *Changing Childhood* can write of the 'crucial separation which modern children *suffer* (my emphasis) is the separation from work'. He can write this from the perspective of England (incidentally in 1979, IYC, in a book welcomed by the U.K. Association for the International Year of the Child). In England to-day, if anything, far too many children are *forced* to work,[55] allegedly part-time and often in conditions of exploitation – and they are lucky compared with children in much of the third world.[56] Certainly, when children had the 'right' to work (when 'Victorian values' so beloved of Thatcher and her cronies prevailed) they suffered.[57] Leading liberationalists, like Farson[58] and Holt,[59] would give children the right to work: in Farson's view it is part of the 'a right to economic power'.[60]

But they would give the child the right to do, in general, what any adult may legally do. Thus Holt writes:[61] 'In important matters, nobody can know better than the child himself'. So central is this to his thought that he italicises the sentence to emphasise its significance. But he recognises that young children are egocentric: they are 'animals and sensualists; to them what feels good *is* good. They are self-absorbed and selfish . . . . They are barbarians, primitives'.[62] Farson's manifesto is strikingly similar and so are his arguments. Thus, overriding all 'birthrights', he argues, is the right of self-determination. Children should have the right to decide 'the matters which affect them most directly'.[63] That these arguments are heard less volubly to-day attests to the experiences of the last decade when manifold forms of child exploitation, not least sex abuse, have captured the public imagination.

On the other hand, it must be asked how many of the structures, institutions and practices created, particularly during the twentieth-century and often under the influence of the child-saving or protectionist ideology, to 'protect' children actually achieve this goal.[64] Has this really been achieved, for example, by the juvenile court,[65] whatever its good intentions? Or by the institutions[66] to which children in need of protection are sent? Or by the whole panoply of powers developed to protect children from abuse and neglect? Do systems of mandatory reporting, such as operate in the United States[67] and now elsewhere including parts of Europe,[68] or child 'protection registers' protect children or do they serve rather to ease adult conscience and offer insurance policies to social workers and others involved in the control of the problem?[69] The examples could be multiplied. But the essential failing of these systems as of others is our failure (that is the failure of all of us, and not just professionals) to recognise the moral integrity of children and treat them as persons entitled to equal concern and respect. Thus, for example, few countries only (the Nordic ones and Austria)[70] have now accepted that it is morally wrong to hit children – legislation which is likely to have a greater impact upon the conquest of child abuse than any system of reporting, registers or care legislation.[71]

THE LIMITS OF AUTONOMY

In looking for a children's rights programme we must thus recognise the limits of protection: we must also note the dangers inherent in the liberationist prospectus. Too often writers on children's rights (like lawyers) have dichotomised: there is either salvation or liberation, either nurturance or self-determination – in Farson's pithy phrase[72] the one protects children, the other their rights. To take children's rights seriously requires us to take seriously both protection of children and recognition of their autonomy.

The view I put forward is premised on the need to respect individual autonomy and to treat persons as equals. It is not dependent on actual autonomy but on the capacity for it. For an understanding I turn again to Rawls's theory of justice.[73] It is, as I have indicated,[74] the normative value of equality and autonomy which form the substructure of the Rawlsian conception of the social contract. The principles of justice which Rawls believes we would choose in 'original position' are equal liberty and opportunity, and an arrangement of social and economic inequalities so that they are both to the greatest benefit of the least advantaged and attached to offices and positions open to all under conditions of fair equality and opportunity.[75]

The principles confine paternalism[76] (the philosophy at the root of salvation or protection) without totally eliminating it. Parties to a hypothetical social contract would know that some human beings are less capable than others; they would know about variations in intelligence and strength, and they would know of the very limited capacities of small children and the rather fuller, if incomplete, capacities of adolescents. They would take account of the insights from cognitive psychology, which suggests that children even as young as 12 (and certainly children of 14) are as capable of making decisions about their lives as adults are for them.[77] They would also bear in mind how the actions of those with limited capacities might thwart their autonomy in a future time when their capacities were no longer as limited.

These considerations would lead to an acceptance of interventions in people's lives to protect them against irrational actions. But what is to be regarded as 'irrational' must be strictly confined. Subjective values of the would-be protecter must not intrude. Irrationality must be defined in terms of a neutral theory capable of accommodating pluralistic visions of the 'good'. Further, we should be prepared to dismiss an action as irrational when it is manifestly so, 'severe and systematic', as David Richards puts it,[78] and when taking the action will lead to major, irreversible impairment of interests. We must tolerate mistakes, for, as Dworkin rightly observes,[79] 'someone may have the right to do something that it is wrong for him to do'. We cannot treat persons as equals without also respecting their capacity to take risks and make mistakes. We would not be taking rights seriously if we only respected autonomy when we considered the agent was doing the right thing. But we also do not recognise a child's integrity if we allowed him to take an action (such as using hard drugs or refusing to attend school) which would seriously impair the attainment of full personality and development subsequently. The test of 'irrationality' must also be confined so that it justifies intervention only to the extent necessary to obviate the immediate harm, or to develop the capacities of rational choice by which the individual may have a reasonable chance of avoiding such harms.

The question we should ask ourselves is: what sort of action or conduct would we wish, as children, to be shielded against on the assumption that we would want to mature to a rationally autonomous adulthood and be capable of deciding on our own system of ends as free and rational beings? We would, I believe, choose principles that would enable children to mature to independent adulthood. One definition of irrationality would be such as to preclude action and conduct which would frustrate such a goal. Within the constraints of such a definition we would defend a version of paternalism. This version is not paternalism in its classical sense for within those perimeters there would be little room for children's rights at all. Furthermore, it has to be stressed that this version of paternalism is a two-edged sword in that, since the goal is rational independence, those who exercise constraints must do so in such a way as to enable children to develop their capacities.

All paternalistic restrictions require moral justification. In many cases it is not difficult to adduce sufficient convincing reasoned argument. Thus, it is not difficult to present the case for protecting children against actions which may lead to their death or serious physical injury or mental disability. Nineteenth century legislation making it illegal for children to go down coal mines or be employed as chimney sweeps or undertake arduous work in factories (if paternalistic – for there were undoubtedly other sources also at play) can thus be defended without much trouble. So, I think, can laws designed to protect children from sexual exploitation and harassment. There are clear dangers that the suggestions of Holt, Farson and others that a child's right to self-determination includes the right to a sexual relationship with whomsoever he or she pleases could become a paedophile's charter.[80] On the other hand 'ages of consent', whether pitched at an age like 16 (as in England) or 12 (as new Dutch legislation proposes) are meaningless: the crucial factor is the presence or absence of exploitation, so that age *difference* may be of greater significance than the age of the child. A system of compulsory education (and, concomitantly, restrictions on employment) can also be defended, contrary to the arguments of some liberationists, though, it should be stressed, by 'education' is not necessarily meant education as conventionally defined. This has often been too narrow and now directed towards the development of capacities required for autonomous self-determination.

What should legitimise all these interferences with autonomy is, what has been called,[81] 'future-oriented consent'. The question is: can the restrictions be justified in terms that the child would eventually come to appreciate? Looking back, would the child appreciate and accept the reason for the restriction imposed upon him or her, given what he or she now knows as a rationally autonomous adult?

The dichotomy drawn is thus to some extent a false divide. Dichotomies and other classifications should not divert us away from the fact that true protection of children does protect their rights. It is not a question of whether child-savers or liberationists are right, for they are both correct in pointing out part of what needs recognising, and both wrong in failing to see the claims of the other side. To take children's rights seriously requires us to take seriously nurturance *and* self-determination, demands of us that we adopt policies, practices and laws which both protect children and their rights. Hence the *via media* I propose.[82]

Thus far this paper has looked at the limits to children's rights as these are expressed in the two paradigmatic orientations of protection and self-determination. But the limits to children's rights can be viewed from a quite different perspective as well.

PUTTING RIGHTS INTO PRACTICE: SURMOUNTING LIMITS

First, crucial though it is to see children's rights recognised, we must be careful not to mistake the words for the deeds. The passing of laws is only a beginning: it is a signal that must be taken up by society's institutions. That both national laws (albeit patchily) and international conventions recognise the language of rights and concepts inherent in them like dignity as applied to children is important. The case that children have rights has to a large extent been won: the burden now shifts to monitoring how well governments honour the pledges in their national laws and carry out their international obligations.

Take national laws. What impact has the recognition that juveniles deserve 'due process' had on juvenile court practices.[83] The *Gillick* ruling[84] in England that once a child had sufficient intelligence, maturity and understanding and could weigh up the 'pros and cons' of a decision-making process (in this case about contraception, but the ruling may be generalised), she was in a position to make the decision herself. This ruling has influenced, though not consistently, the most recent children's legislation in England (the Children Act 1989),[85] but the extent to which it has influenced practice is debatable. In England too the courts have established that access (visitation, contact) is a child's right,[86] but contact is still forced upon children in unfavourable circumstances, in ways which suggest the honouring of the right in the breach rather than the observance.[87] We have to guard against mere tokenism. We must be wary for it is easy to take the words for the act and think that because the words have been enacted the condition of children's lives has changed.

The same point can be made of the International Convention. It is an important achievement, particularly given the cultural diversity and widely different legal systems and traditions of the States represented in the General Assembly of the United Nations. But enacting the Convention is one thing: implementing it in the different countries of the world another. There are clearly difficulties. It is doubtful whether poorer countries can by themselves afford the Convention. They have larger populations and smaller incomes and a higher percentage of their populations tend to be children. And, though it tends to be assumed that the developed world should have no difficulty in complying, that cannot be taken for granted.

The United Kingdom for one will not find it easy to convince its critics, both within and without, that it can comply with a number of the most basic of the protections set out in the Convention. For example, Articles 26 (on social security), 27 (on a standard of living adequate for the child's physical, mental, spiritual, moral and social development) and, in some parts of the country, 28 (on the right to education – there are parts of London, for example, within a couple of kilometres of the Bank of England and the Stock Exchange, where primary education is often not available). Indeed, doubt has been cast upon whether the U.K. collects statistics in sufficient detail to demonstrate whether it can meet the rights or not.[88] But, statistics or not, there is little doubt that it does not comply with Article 10 which commits States to deal with applications by a child or his/her parents to enter or leave for the purpose of family reunification 'in a positive, humane and expeditious manner'. The administration of the immigration laws falls far short of this ideal.[89] Indeed, there are hints that Article 10 may prove the stumbling-block to the U.K. ratifying the Convention. But even if this obstacle is overcome, and the U.K. does ratify the Convention, what impact will this have on poverty, social security standards and education? And, if the U.K. cannot comply, what of the poorer nations?

There is a danger, of course, that the Convention may become nothing more than a way of keeping the developed world up to scratch. Much of the world has as much chance of implementing the Convention as sending its citizens to the moon. Unfortunately, most countries would also rather do the latter. Of course, one of the reasons why it is important that we have an international Convention is that the world as a community, having shown a commitment to the rights of children, should now take on international responsibility to ensure that all countries are able to carry out their obligations to children. But international social justice is a pious aspiration and is likely to remain such.

Legislation, national and international, is important as a symbol. This can neither be gainsaid nor underestimated. But the true recognition of children's rights requires implementation in practice. Unimplemented, partially implemented or badly implemented laws (and this applies equally to international legislation) may actually do children more harm than good.

Secondly, the passing of laws can have unfortunate side-effects and unintended consequences. Prohibition in the U.S.A. was not intended to promote the interests of the Mafia. Laws which restrict abortions are not intended, via the crime tariff, to promote the back street abortion. Rights can too easily backfire. Reform movements intended to enhance children's rights and the concomitant development of professional structures to implement such reforms often generate their own sets of problems and these can, not unnaturally, have deleterious effects on children's rights.

The reforms of one era are apt to become the problems of the next. Many examples could be given: the invention of the IQ test,[90] development of the juvenile court,[91] the practice of cautioning juveniles and thus diverting them from formal processes. Looked at in this way, can we be sure that an injection of rights into the juvenile court system (more 'due process') would not at the same time lead to an increase in more informal 'justice without trial',[92] or that more rights for children in the divorce process would not be used as a stick to control their mothers?[93] This is not to advocate caution in furthering children's rights, but care in so doing, and to recommend adequate surveillance of the institutional practices of those to whom the task of operationalising children's rights is entrusted. And it may be doubted whether the structure to be established to oversee children's rights within the Convention is adequate within these terms.

Thirdly, rights without services are meaningless. As Monrad Paulsen wrote,[94] in relation to laws regarding the reporting of child abuse, 'no law can be better than its implementation, and implementation can be no better than resources permit'. In many, indeed most, countries children get far too little of the cake that is handed around. In the U.S.A. the phrase the 'feminization of poverty'[95] has been coined and popularised: families headed by women are said to constitute the 'new poor'. The point can be generalised. There is little point creating an improved legal framework, recognising the existence of children's rights and even heightening rights – consciousness, unless resource allocation is addressed and redressed. Ultimately, the question of rights for children dissolves into questions of distributive justice.[96]

IMPLEMENTING RIGHTS

Where next? The recognition of children's rights, particularly on the international level, is a major advance. But, as just indicated, rights need implementation. The states, the institutions, must adapt their practices to fit in with the new ideology. On the level of national systems, we need to develop institutions like the Norwegian children's ombudsman[97] to make an ongoing assessment of the impact of policies and practices on children. Independent organisations with power and a commitment to promote the interests of children are vital if noble ideals are not to perish on the altar of political expediency. Within institutions themselves such as welfare agencies, the development of monitoring and complaints agencies[98] and advocacy services along the lines of the 'children's rights officer' pioneered in England by Dr Mike Lindsay in Leicestershire is to be commended.[99]

On the international level, it may be doubted whether the Convention pays enough attention to these problems. The implementation of the Convention is to be governed (as is so much national legislation) by the principle of the 'best interests of the child' (Article 3), though this is not further explained and is, of course, a rather indeterminate notion.[100] When the Convention comes into force, a ten-member committee will supervise the implementation of the Convention by States, which are parties to it. This committee will consist of 'experts of high moral standing and recognised competence in the field': they will serve in their personal capacity (Article 43). State Parties are required to submit written reports to the Committee 'on the measures they have adopted which given effect to the rights recognised herein, and on the progress made on the enjoyment of those rights' (Article 44). It is to be assumed, in line with practice elsewhere, that these reports will be discussed by the General Assembly, though, surprisingly, the Convention is silent as to this. The emphasis in the Convention is on assisting State Parties to meet their obligations rather then on penalising non-compliance. Specific provisions (in Article 45) permit reference of requests for technical assistance directly to UNICEF and specialised agencies. These agencies and bodies are, unusually, given a role in the Committee's monitoring process.

These measures create an innovative structure of enforcement but, I fear, an incomplete one. If the concept of an Ombudsman for children can be operationalised in a national context even in a supposedly third world country like Costa Rica, why not in an international one too?[101] If systems for reviewing child complaints can be advocated within domestic orders, why not a system whereby aggrieved children can complain and seek redress when their State, though a party to the Convention, violates rights contained within it?[102] Perhaps these concepts are too ambitious for a nascent development like international children's rights. But these are directions in which we must ultimately look.

CONCLUSION

Children's rights, in a famous aphorism, was once described as a 'slogan in search of a definition'.[103] It has got well beyond that stage now but it has a lot further to go if children's lives are to be measurably improved. It is often said that you can judge a society by its concern and treatment of its less privileged citizens. The same must now be said about the world community.

NOTES

1. J. Howells, *Remember Maria*, Butterworths (1974).
2. 'Duties, Rights and Claims', *American Philosophy Quarterly* 3, 137 (1966).
3. *Per* R. Wasserstrom, 'Rights, Human Rights and Racial Discrimination', *Journal of Philosophy* 61, 628 (1964). See also A. Buchanan, 'What's So Special About Rights?' *Social Philosophy and Policy* 2(1), 61 (1984).
4. 'Do Children Have Any Natural Rights?, *Proceedings of the 29th Annual Meeting of Philosophy of Education Society* (1973), p. 234 at p. 236.
5. By, improbably, one Slogvolk (see *Knickerbocker*, No. 36 (1852), p. 489).
6. On which see T. Zeldin, *France 1848–1945* Oxford University Press (1973).
7. *Per* P. B. Mayer, 'The Exploitation of the American Growing Class', in D. Gottlieb (ed.), *Children's Liberation*, Prentice Hall (1973), p. 51.
8. See A. Platt The Child Savers, Chicago, University of Chicago Press (1977) and also C. R. Margolin, 'Salvation Versus Liberation: the Movement for Children's Rights In a Historical Context', *Social Problems* 22, 441 (1978).
9. See C. M. Rogers and L. S. Wrightsman, 'Attitudes Toward Children's Rights: Nurturance or Self-Determination', *Journal of Social Issues* 34(2), 59 (1978).
10. *Before The Best Interests of The Child*, Free Press, New York (1979).
11. Children Act 1989. Similar ideology is found in the recent New Zealand Children, Young Persons and their Families Act 1989.
12. To some associated with 'privatisation'. See, for example, A. Bainham, 'The Privatisation of the Public Interest in Children', *M.L.R.* 53, 206 (1990) and M. Freeman 'In the Child's Best Interests?' (1992) *C.L.P* 173.
13. Op. cit., note 10, p. 18. See also para. 10.7 on p. 189.
14. Ibid., p. 12.
15. And see A. Bainham, *Children, Parents and The State*, London, Sweet & Maxwell (1988). See also L. Fox Harding, *Perspectives in Child Care Policy*, Harlow, Longman (1991).
16. See A. Vittachi, *Stolen Childhood*, Oxford, Polity Press (1989). According to a recent report a child a day is 'exterminated' in the streets of Rio de Janeiro (*The Times*, November, 30, 1991). Even in New Zealand children have been described as an 'endangered species'. See L. Max, *Children – Endangered Species*, Penguin, Auckland (1990).
17. Published by Oxford University Press on behalf of UNICEF.
18. *Child Poverty and Deprivation in the UK*, National Children's Bureau, London (1990).
19. Ibid. p. 51.
20. The year when the current Conservative Government came to power.
21. See I. Kant in translation by H. Paton, *The Moral Law*, Hutchinson, London (1948) (originally published in 1785).
22. *Madness and Civilisation*, Tavistock, London (1967), p. 252.
23. See A. James and A. Prout, *Constructing and Reconstructing Childhood*, Falmer Press, Basingstoke (1990).
24. 'Mill, Children and Rights', *Educational Philosophy and Theory* 8, 14 (1976).

25. *Equal Rights for Children*, Littlefield, Totowa, New Jersey (1980), p. 45.
26. See, in particular, *Taking Rights Seriously*, Duckworth, London (1978).
27. Published by Harvard University Press, Cambridge, Massachusetts in 1972. Rawls has refined his theory since. For a review of later developments see R. Arneson 'Symposium on Rawlsian Theory of Justice', *Ethics* 99, 695 (1989).
28. Op. cit., note 26, p. 160.
29. This is developed in op. cit. note 26, chs. 7, 9, 11–13. It is noteworthy that in Janusz Korczak's Declaration of Children's Rights the 'right to respect' was placed only after the 'right to love'. On the reverse (more common) see A. Miller, *The Drama of Being a Child*, London, Virago (1988), ch. 3.
30. 'Can There Be a Rights-Based Moral Theory?' in J. Waldron (ed.), *Theories of Rights*, Oxford, Oxford University Press (1964), p. 168.
31. Op. cit. note 26, p. 272.
32. See L. W. Sumner, *The Moral Foundation of Rights*, Oxford, Clarendon Press (1987).
33. In England, see Police and Criminal Evidence Act 1984, s. 58.
34. In England, see Adoption Act 1976, s. 51. But it is not an absolute right (see *R* v *Registrar General ex parte Smith* (1991) 1 FLR 255).
35. 'Contractarian Rights in R. G. Frey (ed.), *Utility and Rights*, Oxford, Blackwell (1984), p. 161 at 164.
36. *Anarchy, State and Utopia*, Blackwell, Oxford (1974).
37. See for example, H. J. McCloskey, 'Rights', *Philosophical Quarterly* 15, 115 (1965).
38. 'The Nature and Value of Rights', *Journal of Value Inquiry* 4, 243 (1970).
39. See H. Rolston, 'The Irreversibly Comatose: Respect for the Sub-Human in Human Life', *Journal of Medicine and Philosphy* 7, 337 (1982).
40. See M. D. A. Freeman, 'Sterilising The Mentally Handicapped' in M. D. A. Freeman (ed.), *Medicine, Ethics and The Law*, Stevens, London (1988).
41. See C. Stone, *Should Trees Have Standing?*, Los Altos, California, William Kaufmann (1974).
42. See T. Regan, *The Case for Animal Rights*, Berkeley, University of California Press (1983). And using Rawls, D Van De Veer 'Of Beasts, Persons and the Original Position', *The Monist* 62, 368 (1979).
43. See P. Westen, *Speaking of Equality*, Princeton University Press, Princeton, New Jersey (1990).
44. Op cit., note 26, p. 139.
45. Ibid., p. 178.
46. Though this does not preclude conferring legal capacities to do specific things (make contracts, get married are examples) at earlier ages and 21 remains the age of majority for homosexual activity.
47. Cf. H. Cohen, op. cit., note 25, p. 49.
48. See V. Aubert, *In Search of The Law*, Oxford, Martin Robertson (1983), p. 93.
49. See I. Kennedy, *Treat Me Right*, Oxford University Press (1988), ch. 9.
50. See 'Children and Paternalism', *Philosophy* 55 (1980), 117.
51. See P. Ariès, *Centuries of Childhood*, J. Cape, London (1962). But cf. L. Pollock, *Forgotten Children*, Cambridge University Press, Cambridge (1983).
52. 'Puberty, Privacy and Protection: the Risks of Children's Rights', *American Bar Association Journal* 63, 1383 (1977).
53. An excellent new history is H. Cunningham, *The Children of The Poor*, Oxford, Blackwell (1991).
54. Writers and Readers Publishing Co-operative, London (1979), p. 5.
55. See C. Pond and A. Searle, *The Hidden Army: Children at Work in the 1990s*, London, Low Pay Unit (1991).
56. The Anti Slavery Society publishes a continuing series on child labour.
57. The expression was first used by R. Boyson in *Down With The Poor* (1971). Mrs. Thatcher first used it in a speech reported in *The Daily Telegraph*, 16 April 1983, bottom of page.

58. *Birthrights*, Penguin, Harmondsworth (1978).
59. *Escape From Childhood*, Penguin, Harmondsworth (1975).
60. Op. cit., note 58, p. 154.
61. Op. cit., note 59, pp. 175–176.
62. Ibid., p. 114.
63. Op. cit., note 58, p. 12.
64. See L. Taylor, R. Lacey and D. Bracken, *In Whose Best Interests?*, London, Cobden Trust and Mind (1979).
65. See, for example, H. Parker *et al., Receiving Juvenile Justice*, Oxford, Blackwell (1982). The juvenile court is to be renamed the 'youth court' in England in 1992.
66. See the account of 'pin-down': A. Levy and B. Kahan, *The Pindown Experience and the Protection of Children*, Stafford, Staffordshire CC (1991).
67. In the US it is reckoned that, despite the law, only a third of all instances of child abuse are reported (K. Burgdorf, *Recognition and Reporting of Child Maltreatment*, Rockville, Md, Westat (1980).
68. See J. Christopherson, 'European Child-Abuse Management Systems' in O. Stevenson (ed.), *Child Abuse*, Brighton, Wheatsheaf (1989), p. 74. Also see further K. Jones in J. Hutton *et al.* (eds.) *Dependency To Enterprise*, London RKP (1991) at p. 34.
69. See A. Solnit 'Child Abuse: The Problem' in J. Eekelaar and S. Katz (eds.), *Family Violence*, Toronto, Butterworths (1978), p. 143.
70. See the discussion in P. Newell, *Children Are People Too*, London, Bedford Square Press (1990).
71. See M. Freeman, *The Rights and Wrongs of Children*, London, Frances Pinter (1983), pp. 111–114.
72. Op. cit., note 58, p. 9.
73. This was set out in *A Theory of Justice*, Cambridge, Mass., Harvard University Press (1971). It has since gone through refinement and reformulation. This article starts from the 1971 statement, though draws in later developments.
74. *Ante*, p. 33.
75. In later Rawlsian writing parties in the hypothetical deliberations of the original position are now identified as giving priority to their Kantian interests in the development and exercise of their moral powers of rational autonomy and fair dealing.
76. See J. Feinberg, 'Legal Paternalism', *Canadian Journal of Philosophy* 1, 105 (1971).
77. See W. Damon, *The Social World of The Child*, San Francisco, Jossey Bass (1977); J. J. Conger, *Adolescence and Youth: Psychological Development in a Changing World*, New York, Harper and Row (1973).
78. The Individual, The Family and The Constitution', *New York University Law Review* 55, 1 at p. 18 (1980). See also his 'Rights and Autonomy', *Ethics* 92, 13 (1981).
79. Op. cit., note 26, pp. 188–189.
80. See T. O'Carroll, *Paedophilia: The Radical Case*, Boston Alyson Publishers (1980). Cf. J. Ennew, *The Sexual Exploitation of Children*, Oxford, Polity Press (1986).
81. By G. Dworkin 'Paternalism' in R. Wasserstrom (ed.), *Morality and the Law*, Belmont, California, Wadsworth (1972), p. 77.
82. And see M. D. A. Freeman, *The Rights and Wrongs of Children*, Frances Pinter, London (1983).
83. In the light of which see G. B. Melton 'Taking *Gault* Seriously: Toward a New Juvenile Court', *Nebraska Law Review* 68, 146 (1989).
84. *Gillick* v *West Norfolk and Wisbech Area Health Authority* (1986) A.C. 112. But see the back-tracking in *Re R* (1991) 4 All E.R. 177.
85. See, for example, section 1, 43, 44.
86. See *M* v *M* (1973) 2 All E.R. 81 and sections 8 and 34 of the Children Act 1989.
87. There are numerous examples of this until very recently.
88. By Jonathan Bradshaw, op. cit., note 18, pp. 3–4, 14–15, 52.
89. See, further, D. McGoldrick, 'The United Nations Convention on the Rights of The Child',

International Journal of Law and the Family 5, 132 (1991); B. Walsh, 'The United Nations Convention on the Rights of the Child: A British View', *International Journal of Law and the Family* 5, 170 (1991).

90. See S. Rose, L. J. Kamin and R. C. Lewontin, *Not In Our Genes*, Harmondsworth, Penguin (1984), ch. 5, where the purposes of Binet in 1905 are described as 'entirely benign' (p. 84).

91. Described as the best plan 'for the conservation of human life and happiness ever conceived by civilized man' (C. W. Hoffman in J. Adams (ed.), *The Child, The Clinic and The Court*, New York, New Republic (1927), p. 266).

92. J. Skolnick, *Justice Without Trial*, Wiley, Chichester (1966).

93. Note the emphasisis on the 'primary caretaker' and its impact on women. See M. Fineman, 'The Politics of Custody and Gender' in C. Smart and S. Sevenhuijsen, *Child Custody and The Politics of Gender*, London, Routledge (1989).

94. 'The Law and Abused Children' in R. Helfer and C. Kempe, *The Battered Child*, University of Chicago Press, Chicago (1974).

95. By Diana Pearce, Welfare Is Not *for* Women: Why The War on Poverty Cannot Conquer The Feminization of Poverty' in L. Gordon (ed.), *Women, The State and Welfare*. University of Wisconsin Press (1990), p. 265.

96. See D. Wikler, 'Paternalism and the Mildly Retarded', *Philosophy and Public Affairs* 8, 377 (1979).

97. See M. G. Flekkoy, *A Voice For Children*, London, Jessica Kingsley (1991).

98. In England, this process has received an impetus from the Children Act 1989 (s. 26(3)) but see M. Lindsay 'Complaints Procedures and Their Limitations' (1991) *J. S.W.F.L.*, 432.

99. See M. Lindsay, 'The Rights of The Child', Panel News (IRCHIN) 9, 10 (1989).

100. And see R. Mnookin, 'Child-Custody Adjudications: Judicial Functions in the Face of Indeterminacy', *Law and Contemporary Problems* 39(3), 226 (1975).

101. See Flekkoy, op. cit., note 97, p. 197–199.

102. As under the European Convention on Human Rights.

103. By H. Rodham, 'Children Under the Law', *Harvard Educational Review* 43, 487 (1973).

ADAM LOPATKA*

4. The Rights of the Child Are Universal: The Perspective of the UN Convention on the Rights of the Child

Human beings have in common certain universal features that are typical of the entire species of *Homo sapiens*. They also have other features that reflect a definite moment in the development of mankind. Separate human beings have individual features which differentiate them from others in respect of physical and mental properties, sensory perception, a complex of both inborn and acquired reactions. Each human being has his or her own autonomy and personality.

The life and development of each human being is conditioned by the development of other human beings with whom he or she has a direct or indirect relationship. This concerns both that person's contemporaries and the past generations to which the present one is heir. Like other living things, human beings live in the natural environment but they also have their own human environment, which they create.

There are certain values that are universally recognized. These include: human dignity, freedom, equality, justice, brotherhood, solidarity, beauty and truth. Today, these constitute a specific heritage of mankind.[1]

Mankind, or a large part of mankind, also suffers common afflictions: disease, famine, poverty, war, danger of destruction of the entire species, made possible by the present state of development of science and technology.

It is on the universal features of our species, on its needs, interests, values and dangers that the universal nature of human rights is based; or, at least those rights' plea to universality. That universality is a reality, and at the same time a specific challenge to overcome the obstacles on the road to its full realization.[2] Some rights and freedoms receive a greater emphasis than others in different societies or cultures.[3] R. Badinter is right to stress, though, that an undue emphasis on those differences might sometimes be both artificial and dangerous. Suffice it to say that the cultural differentiation of mankind and the unequal development of separate societies are common phenomena. It is not only admissible but even desirable to take account of that cultural differentiation, the dissimilarity of national traditions and regional aspira-

---

* Polish Academy of Sciences, Warsaw.

M. Freeman and P. Veerman (eds.), The Ideologies of Children's Rights, 47–52.
© 1992 *Kluwer Academic Publishers. Printed in the Netherlands.*

tions. It is worth stressing that the right to be different from others is now becoming recognised as a universal human right, and that respect for the rights of ethnic, religious and linguistic minorities is acquiring an ever greater importance.[4]

The universality of guarantees of human rights, on both national and international scale, is also becoming part of their overall universality. On the national scale, Such guarantees include the ideology of the rule of law in a State (*rechtsstaat*), the existence of independent courts, a system for the review of the legality of administrative decisions, constitutional courts, the institution of the *Ombudsman*, etc. On the international scale, supervision exercised by different agencies of the United Nations, the International Labour Organization, UNESCO and other organizations is becoming increasingly effective: the notion of sovereignty, furthermore, is ever more infrequently invoked to contest such supervision. The impact of international public opinion is also effective. Public opinion is expressed, *inter alia*, by international non-governmental organizations (NGOs).[5] Moreover, international supervision is regional in nature in some parts of the world, as in Europe, America and Africa.

The rights of the child, as recognized or laid down in the Convention on the Rights of the Child adopted on November 20, 1989 by the UN General Assembly which entered into force on September 2, 1990, are human rights. All that can be said about the universality of human rights in general also applies to those rights. A child enjoys all the human rights laid down or proclaimed in the constitutions of the individual countries, and particularly in international conventions or declarations. But the rights of the child are only those human rights that are granted to the child because 'the child, by reason of his or her physical and mental immaturity, needs special safeguards and care, including appropriate legal protection, before as well as after birth'. This applies to all children. One should also bear in mind though, that in all countries of the world, there are children living under exceptionally difficult conditions and that such children need special consideration. We are concerned here with children who are deprived of their parents or the possibility to grow up in their family environment: refugee children; handicapped children; children of indigenous peoples or those who belong to ethnic, religious or linguistic minorities; children affected by an armed conflict; those subjected to torture or other cruelty, inhuman or degrading treatment, or punishment; children who take narcotic drugs and psychotropic substances, and so on.

The universality of the rights of the child does not mean that those rights should be interpreted and implemented abstracted from their context. Due account must also be taken generally of the importance of the traditions and cultural values of each specific people for the protection and harmonious development of the child.

A grant to the child of certain additional human rights that are specific to him or her, or adjustment of the rights due to all of the child's properties, is by no means exceptional in the system of promotion and protection of human rights. Special additional rights have been granted to women, to disabled and mentally retarded persons, to persons deprived of liberty, to members of ethnic, religious or linguistic minorities. In short, certain additional human rights have been granted to those groups of persons who are weaker than the others for a variety of reasons. Those rights are granted in order to secure for those specific categories of persons an enjoyment of human rights that would be equal to those of the others, and sometimes simply to safeguard their survival.

The physical and mental nature of the child is identical everywhere. Each child has his or her human dignity and the same needs: for protection of his or her personality, for integrity and privacy. The process of growth and adolescence takes a similar course in all children. Their physical and mental needs are also similar. Furthermore, each child has his or her own specific interests. Adults are required by the Convention on the Rights of the Child to ensure fulfillment of these rights in the best interests of the child.

The 'best interests' demand that all children should receive equal treatment without distinction of any kind, such as race, colour, sex, language, religion, political or other opinion, national or social origin, property, birth or other status. The child should not suffer discrimination on account of any of these traits. But discrimination is also banned on account of such traits of the child's parents or legal guardians. The term 'birth' means the fact of the child's being born – in or out of wedlock – and also as a result of artificial insemination. The requirement of equal treatment and a ban on discrimination on account of the above traits should be universal and unconditional.

The situation is similar as far as exploitation of the child is concerned. Exploitation is just as morally repellent and unjust as discrimination. The Convention on the Rights of the Child declares a general ban on exploitation prejudicial to any aspect of the child's welfare. The Convention also specifies the most frequent forms of that exploitation. It demands that the State should protect the child from economic exploitation and from performing any work that is likely to be hazardous to or to interfere with the child's education, or to be harmful to the child's health or physical, mental, spiritual, moral or social development.[6] The State is also obliged to protect the child from all forms of sexual exploitation and sexual abuse.

The child is not the property of his or her parents nor of the State, the Church, or anybody else. Each child is an individual person whose personality and identity should enjoy universal recognition and respect. In all actions concerning children, the best interests of the child should be a primary consideration. The child has the right to preserve his or her identity, including nationality, name and family relations as recognized by law, without unlawful interference. A child who is capable of forming his or her own views has the right to express those views freely in all matters affecting him or her. It is inadmissible to subject the child to arbitrary or unlawful interference with his or her privacy, family, home or correspondence, or to attack his or her honour and reputation. Respect for the child's personality and physical and mental integrity demands that the State should protect the child by every available means from all forms of physical or mental violence, injury or abuse, neglect or negligent treatment or ill-treatment. In protecting the child's personality and integrity, the State is obliged to protect children from the illicit use of narcotic drugs and psychotropic substances and to prevent the use of children in the illicit production of and trafficking in such substances.

Respect for the child's personality and care for his or her proper development demand that no child should be subjected to torture or other cruel, inhuman or degrading treatment or punishment.

The Convention on the Rights of the Child also requires that neither capital punishment nor life imprisonment without the possibility of release should be imposed for offences committed by persons below 18 years of age. Similarly, the State is obliged to take all appropriate measures to prevent the abduction and sale of or trafficking in children for any purpose or in any form whatever.[7] The State is further obliged to combat the illicit transfer and non-return of children abroad.

The Convention recognizes or establishes a long list of personal, social, cultural and political rights enjoyed by all children. Central to that list is without doubt the inherent right of every child to life. The State should ensure to the maximum extent possible the survival and development of the child. The child's right to life and survival is far from universal implementation which, however, by no means affects its universality. The situation is similar with the right of every child to a standard of living adequate for that child's physical, mental, spiritual, moral and social development. What should be a universal right is far from being implemented on a universal scale. Persons obliged to secure its implementation are the child's parents or other persons responsible for that child. The State is obliged, in accordance with the national conditions and within its specific means, to take all appropriate measures to assist parents in implementing this right.

All the other rights contained in the Convention are similarly universal in nature.

The universality of the rights of the child is confirmed and consolidated by the system of review of the realization of the obligations undertaken in the Convention. The Convention provides for the establishment of a Committee on the Rights of the Child. It will be the only body in the world charged with the examination of the progress made by States and/or other parties to the Convention in achieving its implementation. The Committee will have the right to make suggestions and general recommendations basing them on information received. Such suggestions and general recommendations will then be transmitted to the State and/or party concerned and reported to the General Assembly, together with comments, if any, from the States and/or parties concerned.

The universal character of the rights of the child contained in the Convention will not be impaired by adoption in the future of any possible regional systems of promotion and protection of the rights of the child or any possible universal conventions regulating the enjoyment of a specific right of the child.[8]

The rights of the child recognized or established in the Convention are based on universal human values. Part of them are a response to the moral imperative produced by the tragic situation of children in some countries, or of some categories of children. But this strong moral basis by no means impairs the legal nature of the rights of the child. Quite the opposite. It offers greater hopes for a universal and straightforward implementation of those rights. The rights of the child specified in the Convention are not merely an expression of a moral belief. They express first and foremost the legislative will of the States-parties to the Convention. They are internationally established rights, identical to the human rights contained, for instance, in the Covenants on Human Rights and in other conventions in this field.

The fact, that child slavery, sexual abuse and discrimination of specific categories of children are considered to be natural in some countries does not make those phenomena legal in the light of the Convention. Such phenomena are illicit and should be fought against and prevented by all possible means and primarily by making the principles and provisions of the Convention widely known, by appropriate and active means, to adults and children alike.

The recognition of the importance of traditions and cultural values of each people for the protection and harmonious development of the child does not mean that implementation of the lights granted to the child by the Convention should be relinquished if such traditions are inconsistent with the substance of those rights. Similarly, if the values recognised in a given country or the adopted hierarchy of values are inconsistent with the values on which the Convention on the Rights of the Child is based or on the hierarchy of values adopted in it, the aim should be to replace the values that are inconsistent with the Convention with those contained in it. What is good and right should be continued and developed: what is wrong should he changed in accordance with the requirements of universal progress of mankind. The situation is similar as far as values are concerned.

The Convention on the Rights of the Child is a result of cooperation and the unanimous will of the United Nations. It sets moderate rather than unduly ambitious standards of promotion and protection of the rights of the child. Wherever the national standards prove to be lower, the achievement of these standards set by the Covention should be sought. If the national standards are higher than those of the Convention in a specific sphere, they should be maintained and developed further. The Convention should by no means provide an excuse for the lowering of standards. Its provisions are an order for some and an incitement for all, universally, to raise the standards of promotion and protection of the rights of the child in all spheres that concern that child and in all countries of the world.

NOTES

1. See M. Oreja, *Universalité des Droits de l'Homme dans un Monde Pluraliste. Actes du Collogue Organisé par le Conseil de l'Europe en Collaboration avec l'Institut International des Droits de l'Homme.* Strasbourg, 17–19 avril 1989. Edition N. P. Engel (1990), pp. 3–4.
2. See P. Leuprecht, ibid., pp. VIII–IX.
3. See P. H. Imbert, ibid., pp. 167–168.
4. See G. Braibant, *Les Droits de l'Homme: Universalité et Renouveau* 1789–1989. *Travaux Publies sous la Direction de* G. Braibant et G. Marc, Edition l'Harmattan, Paris (1990), p. 412.
5. As rightly pointed out by G. Braibant, ibid., pp. 414–415.
6. The Seminar on the Implementation of the Covention on the Rights of the Child, Syracuse, 24–28 September, 1990, specified over a dozen terms of exploitation of child labour, Forced labour, debt bondage; labour in the unorganized sector, labour in the organized sector, forced marriages, domestic labour, appenticeships, family-supervised labour, and others. The Seminar was organized by the International Association of Penal Law, Defence for Children International, and the International Commission of Jurists.
7. As was stated at the Seminar in Syracuse mentioned in Note 6, supra, it is a global practice, often pursued under the cover of inter-country adoption. Also mentioned were cases of trade in children as donors of organs for transplantation.
8. In all probability, the first such convention will be the Convention on Inter-Country Adoption. Fruitful work on its preparation is being undertaken by the Hague Conference on Private International Law. See Report on *Inter-Country Adoption* drawn up by J. H. A. van Loon. Permanent Bureau of the Conference, The Hague (1990).

CYNTHIA PRICE COHEN*

5. The Relevance of Theories of Natural Law and Legal Positivism

1. INTRODUCTION

One of the main areas of controversy among legal philosophers is the definition of the word *law*. Do laws of nature or rules of morality qualify as law, or is law something else? Must a rule be written down in some form, like the Ten Commandments, in order to be a law? Can one say that a written law alone has no meaning, and therefore is not law, until it has been interpreted by some authoritative body? The debate over the essence of law is one that is centuries old and is still not totally resolved.[1]

In its simplest form the legal theory debate can be divided into two basic points of view. The first view, that there is a 'higher law', can be traced back as far as the Greeks and is exemplified by the play *Antigone*. There are many variations to this 'higher law' concept, however, all of these are usually considered as being subsections of the theory of *natural law*.[2] The second view is that law must be written down in order to qualify as law and that at the very least it must from the sovereign for the guidance of the governed. This theory is known as *legal positivism*.[3]

One of the main sticking points between these two legal theories is the role that morality plays in law. Classical legal positivists, such as Austin and the more contemporary Hart have taken the position that law is only what is written (e.g., legislation) and that morality has no part in it.[4] On the other hand, natural law claims are usually centered around moral concepts. Legal positivism has been the reigning legal theory during most of the twentieth century, yet natural law theory has never been completely laid to rest. It emerges time and again whenever written laws are claimed to be unjust or illegitimate.[5] It is then that natural law theory provides the basis for the new positive law which corrects the claimed injustices.

Development of the international law of human rights has followed this basic pattern of natural law claims for rights, which are then followed by international positive law in the form of treaties. One variation in this pattern has

* Ralph Bunch Institute on the United Nations, City University of New York.

M. Freeman and P. Veerman (eds.), The Ideologies of Children's Rights, 53–70.
© *1992 Kluwer Academic Publishers. Printed in the Netherlands.*

been The United Nations Convention on the Rights of the Child.[6] In this treaty, rights have been granted which were not claimed prior to the treaty-drafting process.

2. Natural Law, Legal Positivism and Human Rights

One of the most consistently accepted theories regarding the basis of human rights treaties is that the roots of these treaties – the positive law of human rights – can be found in earlier concepts of natural law. In tracing the origins of human rights, Henkin states:

> . . . essentially the same political and civil rights and freedoms that the eighteenth century derived from natural right, individual autonomy, and social contract appear in the positive law of diverse national systems and international law.[7]

In other words, just as the natural law claims of The French Declaration of The Rights of Man and Citizen and The American Declaration of Independence were subsequently elaborated in positive national legislation, the various United Nations human rights declarations were embodiments of natural law claims which eventually became the positive law of human rights treaties.

The Universal Declaration of Human Rights[8] is a classic example of this evolutionary transition from an unenforceable declaration, based on natural rights claims, to positive human rights treaty law. The human rights claims of the Universal Declaration are reflected in the texts of the International Covenant on Civil and Political Rights and the International Covenant on Economic, Social and Cultural Rights,[9] with some rights being covered in greater detail in other human rights declarations and treaties.[10]

As stated above, one exception to this two-step – declaration into treaty – process is the United Nations Convention on the Rights of the Child.[11] The final text of the Convention bears only a partial resemblance to its precursor, the 1959 Declaration of the Rights of the Child.[12] Not only does the Convention on the Rights of the Child extensively expand the claims of the children's rights declaration, it includes the protection of rights heretofore never generally recognized as being among the rights legitimately claimed by children.[13] In other words, the Convention on the Rights of the Child is an anomaly among human rights treaties in that an important segment of the positive law of the Convention was not preceded by rights claims based on natural law nor does it faithfully replicate the content of its related declaration. In this case, positive law preceded claims for rights.

2.1. *Universal Declaration of Human Rights and Human Rights Covenants*

2.1.1. *National Law Claims*

Maurice Cranston describes human rights by saying:

> What are nowadays called 'human rights' or the 'rights of man' were once called 'natural rights' and men's understanding of them was limited to their understanding of natural law.[14]

There are varying views as to the exact origins of the idea that man has certain rights simply by virtue of being human. Melden traces the concept of 'human nature' to the Stoic thesis that there was a higher law beyond that of Rome or Athens.[15] Other analysts refer to the writings of Hobbes or Locke to show recognition of the right to self-defense or to life, liberty and property.[16] Although the original source of human rights claims may be somewhat hazy, growing support for rights of the individual eventually led to the drafting of the French and American Declarations. According to Henkin,

> Human rights was an eighteenth century idea, rooted in notions of natural law and natural rights and woven of several strands: original autonomy of the individual, converted in society to popular sovereignty; government by social compact of the people and subject to the continued consent of the governed; government for limited purposes only; the rights reserved for the individual even against the people's representatives in government.[17]

The idea of natural rights was denigrated by Jeremy Bentham who held that natural rights were inferior to positive law. In Bentham's view

> Right is the child of law; from real laws come real rights, but from imaginary laws, from 'laws of nature' come imaginary rights.[18]

Over time, the enactment of 'real laws' guaranteeing real rights in a few specific countries served to heighten world-wide interest in the concept of rights. World War II created a ground swell in the demand for rights, which resulted in a United Nations mandate to translate the theory of human rights into positive treaty law.

The Universal Declaration of Human Rights, the first formal United Nations articulation of rights, reflects the conceptual change from 'natural' to 'human' rights. In the words of Kenneth Minogue:

> Rights are no longer derived from the operations of natural reason, but rather from an idea of what it is to be human. We think that a person who is malnourished, tortured, wrongly imprisoned, illiterate and perhaps lacking in regular paid holidays is not living in a manner appropriate to a human being.[19]

While those rights known as 'civil and political' rights have been recognized since the eighteenth century, 'economic, social and cultural' rights are the outcome of twentieth century demands. In tracing the origins of human rights, the majority of authors have managed to avoid any discussion of the historical roots of this expansion of human rights concepts.[20] Interestingly, the few who do explore the basis of economic, social and cultural rights do not link it to Marxism or socialism. Instead, what is cited is the 1941 address of Franklin Delano Roosevelt in which he pronounced what he called the 'four essential human freedoms':

> . . . freedom of speech and expression . . .
> . . . freedom of every person to worship God in his own way . . .
> . . . freedom from want . . .
> . . . freedom from fear . . .[21]

These concepts were later elaborated in a another speech in 1944 where Roosevelt called for a 'second Bill of Rights' which would guarantee, among other things, the right to work, the right to have a decent home, the right to a good education and the right to medical care.[22]

Even though many of the rights proclaimed in the Universal Declaration of Human Rights were already part of the positive law of a number of nations, from the point of view of international law, since the Universal Declaration is legally unenforceable, it cannot reasonably be considered to be anything other than a formal statement of contemporary natural rights norms. Arguably, Universal Declaration's rights claims did not become part of positive international law until after the two human rights covenants actually went into force.[23]

2.1.2. *Positive Law Response*

Considering the complications encountered in drafting the human rights covenants, drafting of the Universal Declaration of Human Rights was a comparatively easy task. While its drafters encountered some conflicts due to differing political philosophies, much of the time between the first sessions of the Commission on Human Rights in 1947 and adoption of the Universal Declaration on December 10, 1948 was spent on what might be called strategy or policy decisions. Some of the discussions were devoted to deciding whether the Universal Declaration alone was sufficient to support human rights, or whether a legally binding instrument was necessary. This resulted in plans to separate political and civil rights from economic, social and cultural rights, thus creating two separate human rights covenants.[24]

Drafting of the two Covenants began in 1947 and was completed by the Commission on Human Rights in 1954. Controversies over the completed text ranged from major complaints, asserting that certain rights should not be denied, to such minor matters as concern over choices of wording. Deliberations before the Third Committee of the General Assembly lasted from 1954 until 1966, as each article was carefully reviewed and/or revised. During this period an optional protocol allowing for complaints against governments by individuals was also drafted. The two Human Rights Covenants and the

Optional Protocol were adopted by the General Assembly on December 16, 1966. It was approximately ten years before each instrument received sufficient ratifications to enter into force.[25]

The end result of this prolonged treaty drafting process was that, with the exception of the right to property, each of the rights in the Universal Declaration was, quoting Pechota, 'defined and amplified, in treaty language . . .'[26] The right to property was omitted primarily because of disagreements over the types of restrictions which should be applicable to property rights. Again quoting Pechota,

> At a time when property rights had lost much of their previous sanctity, it was inevitable that the Commission would find it difficult to draft a text that would command general acceptance.[27]

On the other hand, the Covenant on Civil and Political Rights does contain some rights which were not included in the Universal Declaration; although it is arguable that none of these rights were totally new, but are logical outgrowths of the Universal Declaration or the United Nations Charter. For example, the Covenants' guarantee of self-determination for peoples can be found in Article 1(2) of the Charter. Other rights added in the Covenant include protection against debt imprisonment and guarantees of humane treatment for detained persons, which could be said to flow from Articles 8, 9, 10 and 11 of the Universal Declaration; prohibition of war propaganda and advocacy of racial or religious hatred, which could be implied by the Declaration's Article 3. Although the protection of the rights of the child is in some way related to the family rights which appear in Articles 16 (3) and 25 of the Universal Declaration, the Covenant's right to birth registration and nationality, also found in the 1959 Declaration of the Rights of the Child, would appear to be a first indication that the child has an independent claim to individual rights under international law.[28]

2.2. Declaration of the Rights of the Child and Convention on the Rights of the Child

2.2.1. Natural Law Claims

Compared to human rights in general, public interest in children's rights is a relatively recent phenomenon, confined to the latter part of the twentieth century. Early sources of children's rights advocacy can be found in the classical stories of mid-19th century rescues undertaken by the Society for the Prevention of Cruelty to Animals to save children from the hands of abusive adults. Also well known are the activities of 'child savers' who established orphanages, schools for handicapped children and created special juvenile justice procedures.[29] Overall, however, the history of childhood is not very attractive. At worst, children were treated as chattel and were abandoned, shipped off to sea or sent into factories. At best children were treated as inferior beings to be given protection by their parents, other adults and the state.[30]

The writings of philosophers, while less factual than that of historians, merely serve to support the thesis that children were not looked upon as individuals. Most philosophical writings about children were intermingled with theories of the family.

Interestingly, unlike Plato, who viewed the family as a nest of individualism and wanted to eliminate it together from the ruling class of his ideal city, Aristotle thought that the nature of the family was a phenomenon of personal and private life. Aristotle saw the young child as being an extension of the family or the parents. Since, according to Aristotle, the just and the unjust always involve more than one person, parents cannot act justly or unjustly towards their young children, because children are part of the parents themselves.[31] Aristotle's idea of the debt grown children owe to their parents is best understood by taking a look at his concepts of the three basic types of friendship, those based on shared pleasure, those based on mutual usefulness and those based on common virtue. Cutting across the distinction between the three types of friendship, Aristotle added the distinction between equal and unequal friendships and he says, 'But there is another kind of friendship that which involves inequality between the parties, e.g., that of father to son and that of general the elder to the younger and that of man to wife and in general that of rulers to subjects.'[32]

Thomas Aquinas also wrote about the relationship of the family. In his opinion the child was an individual human being, separate from the family. He faulted Aristotle for failing to make this distinction.[33] Although he felt that parents had rights over their children, the rights were restrained by the parents' obligation to provide the children with physical, mental and moral and religious education as well as the needs of domestic life. He believed in the positive relationship between parents and children and that parents and children could be friends.[34]

Jean Bodin was probably the first philosopher to consider that the child might need protection within the family.[35] Bodin thought that the family was a nursery for the state, the training ground for citizenship and that children should be trained by their father in order to be good citizens. Although Bodin considered that princes and legislators should revive the ancient laws touching the power of fathers over their children, he also believed that sometimes the purpose of the law was to protect children from their fathers when they demonstrate gross unfitness to raise their children.[36]

Thomas Hobbes' view of the family is somewhat in keeping with his general attitude about relationships between human beings.[37] Hobbes' thesis was that children are in the power of the parents to preserve or destroy them as parents chose fit.[38] According to Hobbes, children tacitly agreed to obey their parents[39] and because they instinctively wanted to remain alive and because they were given to understand that the parents could kill or abandon them if they didn't obey their parents. He saw this consent to obey the parent as being free, even though it may be forced, because 'terror of the alternative only makes it more prudent to consent'.[40] When they are in a state of nature, parents and children are potential adversaries, parents preserve and sustain their children only on the condition that they will not grow up to be their enemies and children promise to obey for the protection they receive from their parents.[41]

John Locke felt that the child's obligation to obey the parent or their decision to obey the parent, resulted not so much from the parent's direct physical power over the child, but the fact that the parent also had the power of controlling whether or not the child would inherit from that parent.[42] That is, Locke felt that inheritance was a key to the interfamilial parent-child relationship.

Rousseau too wrote about the relationships between the child and family. Rousseau agreed with Locke that there were two separate parents, each having a separate role. Rousseau saw the mother as being the real nurse and the real teacher being the father.[43] In his view handing over the education of the child to professional educators involved jeopardizing the integrity and intimacy of the family. He felt that the aim of education was to make self-sufficient adults live at peace with themselves.[44] There was a duty to bring up one's children in a way to achieve this end.[45]

Until the latter part of this century the image of the child as a person, separate from the family, with rights of his or her own was totally missing from the writings of philosophers and/or social scientists. Neither the child saving movement of the nineteenth century nor the child labor movement of the early twentieth century focused on the child as an individual human being. It took almost another half century before child advocates gave any serious consideration to the idea that the child might be entitled to civil and political rights or what might be termed the child's rights of 'individual personality'.[46] During the early 1970s several American authors published books urging children's liberation and full adult privileges for children.[47] The motivation for this radical new approach can probably be attributed to two sources, both related to the particular period of time in which these theories emerged. First, the authors may have been influenced to some extent, by the U.S. Supreme Court decision of *In re Gault*,[48] which reevaluated juvenile justice procedures. Second, at that time concepts of liberation, in general, were being philosophically supported by the popular attack on social institutions brought on by Vietnam War protests.

The main body of children's liberation literature was confined primarily to the years of 1970–1974. The main proponents of children's liberation were John Holt[49] and Richard Farson.[50] While some of their goals, such as the child's right to be free from physical punishment, have slowly begun to gain acceptance, others have not. Among the more controversial rights which both authors advocated for children were the right to work, the right to vote and the right to sexual freedom.[51] Holt went so far as to support the child's right to use drugs.[52] Although the authors made reasonable logical arguments for children's liberation, the pure extremism of their position sometimes created a backlash of public opinion; it also proved to be impractical to implement. In the long run the short-lived popularity of children's liberation theory may have served to heighten public sensitivity to the fact that children are people too. On the other hand, nearly twenty years later children's liberation theory seems to have had only a modest impact on public policy.[53]

The philosopher Laurence Houlgate[54] expressed the split between children's rights advocates in philosophical terms. He saw one group as basing their claims on the *teleological principle of beneficence*. That is, that there is a 'duty to promote the good of others and since children are classed too weak and limited in their emotional and cognitive capacities to be able to protect themselves, we have an especially urgent duty to create special positive and negative claims rights for them.'[55] On the other hand, a second group was described by him as being those child advocates who gave first priority to the *deontological principle of justice*, which is simply equality of treatment.[56] In other words, children should be treated as equals to adults.

As noted by Freeman, who has analyzed the clashing children's rights theories of autonomy vs. notions of paternalism[57] neither of these theories, alone, is satisfactory. Instead, Freeman advocates a theory of what he refers to as *liberal paternalism*. This concept is aimed at maximizing the child's independence and autonomy while justifying parental intervention under certain circumstances. In a quasi-Rawlsian approach, Freeman suggests that parental interventions in a child's life ought to be tested 'in terms of what we might expect persons in the "original position" to approve'.[58]

What can be concluded from this brief theoretical survey is that, at time of the drafting of the Convention on the Rights of the Child, there was no clear consensus as to the extent of children's rights, even in Western countries, and certainly not within the world community. Global interest in children and their rights did not really begin until the 1979 International Year of the Child.

2.2.2. *Positive Law Response*

The international law background of the Convention on the Rights of the Child actually predates the Universal Declaration of Human Rights by nearly a quarter of a century. The first international children's rights declaration was adopted by the League of Nations in 1924,[59] However, it was not until the 1979 International Year of the Child that steps were taken to create a children's rights treaty which would put the 1959 United Nations Declaration of the Rights the Child into legally binding language.[60]

If one continues the analysis of declarations as embodiments of contemporary theories of natural law, comparisons between the 1924 League of Nations Declaration and the 1959 United Nations Declaration show that, while there are slight variations in language between the two declarations, the emphasis of both of them is on the child's protection and not on autonomy. Each declaration calls for assistance in the child's normal development,[61] protection from exploitation,[62] and abandonment,[63] and to receive relief in times of disaster.[64] The 1959 Declaration is more comprehensive and covers standards for play and recreation,[65] parental care,[66] name and nationality,[67] social security,[68] education,[69] and care of the handicapped.[70] On the other hand, the 1924 Declaration includes putting the child in a position to earn a liveli-hood,[71] which is not mentioned in the 1959 Declaration. Both declarations protect the child against discrimination[72] and have provisions which call for preparing the child for peaceful relations with fellow men.[73]

While it is true that there are a number of other international legal instru-ments which define children's rights in one way or another, these too are aimed at protection. The earliest treaties protect children from 'White Slavery'[74] trafficking[75] and various forms of exploitation.[76] Children are also recipients of special care under Geneva Convention IV Relative to the Protection of Civilian Persons in Time of War[77] and are affected directly or indirectly by the standards of many international human rights treaties.[78] Nowhere in this plethora of instruments is there any recognition of what might be called the child's 'individual personality' rights, those rights which protect and support freedom of the individual to act without government interference.[79] Yet, these rights, sometimes called civil and political rights, are an integral part of the Convention on the Rights of the Child.[80]

Of the thirty-eight articles in the Convention on the Rights of the Child which are devoted to substantive rights, at least ten of these have never been recognized for children in any other international instrument.[81] They are all rights of 'individual personality', and include such civil and political rights as the right to leave and return, to privacy, to freedom of expression, assembly, association and religion, among others.[82]

It is difficult to account for this peculiarity in human rights treaty-drafting. Other human rights treaties, including the Convention on the Elimination of All Forms of Racial Discrimination[83] and the Torture Convention,[84] were preceded by the drafting of a declaration, but unlike the Convention on the Rights of the Child, these treaties all follow the pattern set forth in the corresponding declaration, without significant additions. While it is true that in these cases there was a shorter period of time between the drafting of the declaration and the drafting of the treaty, the inclusion of 'individual per-sonality' rights in the Convention cannot be attributed to time alone,[85] especially when these rights were not universally recognized.

This thesis is supported by the fact that the first model of the Convention presented by Poland, the Convention's sponsor, to the Commission on Human Rights as part of the drafting procedure, was nothing more than a replication of the 1959 Declaration plus an implementation mechanism.[86] In fact, after this model was rejected by the Commission, the Polish government submitted a second version of the model convention, which subsequently became the basis for deliberations by the Working Group, which, while written in language more legally enforceable than that of the Declaration still focused almost exclu-sively on protection.[87] The one exception was Article 7 guaranteeing the child's right to freedom of expression.[88] This article in the second Polish model Convention, later adopted by the Working Group, can be seen as the first step toward recognition in positive international law that children have rights of 'individual personality'.

3. Development of the Positive Law of the Child's 'Individual Personality' Rights

Arguably, there are at least ten articles in the Convention on the Rights of the Child which were not preceded by natural law claims for those rights. These are the right to identity, to review of placement, to leave and return, to protection against torture and arbitrary detention, to freedom of expression, to be heard, to association and assembly, to freedom of religion, to privacy and the juvenile justice safeguards.[89] All of these rights can be classified as civil-political rights and are rights of 'individual personality'. While many of these rights are protected by the International Covenant on Civil and Political Rights and, therefore, are not 'new' rights *per se*, it should be remembered that one of the reasons for drafting the Convention on the Rights of the Child was that children's rights were not the same as those of adults and not all of the Covenants' rights were applicable to children.[90]

An examination of the history of Articles 12–16, which includes the right to be heard, to freedom of expression, religion, association and assembly and the right to privacy, provides an interesting insight to how these articles became part of the positive law of children's rights. When studying the articles, it should be remembered that the Convention on the Rights of the Child was a Polish initiative. In other words, it was seen as being an Eastern Bloc idea and, especially since the second Polish model Convention placed such a strong emphasis on economic, social and cultural rights, it was viewed with some skepticism by some Western delegations.[91] The fact is that in the beginning there was little enthusiasm for the treaty either among early participants or observers.[92] It is also important to remember the political climate and the East-West tensions which existed when the drafting began and which diminished as the drafting continued. With this information in mind, it is interesting to note that of the five articles to be examined, one was submitted by Poland. All four of the others were proposed by the United States, arguably, for political reasons.

3.1. *Article 12: The Right to Be Heard*

Article 12, as it appeared in the second Polish model called for States Parties to

> enable the child who is capable of forming his own views the right to express his opinion in matters concerning his own person, and, in particular, marriage, choice of occupation, medical treatment, education and recreation.[93]

In other words, the main focus of this article was on the child's right to express an opinion. The final version of this text as adopted during the first reading at the Working Group's Session in 1981 was quite similar to the original Polish draft, except for a substitution of the words 'freely in all matters' which replaced the list of specific areas. The major players in the redrafting of this text were the United States, Canada, Australia and Denmark.[94]

A second paragraph on the child's right to be heard was added to Article 12 during the second reading reviewing process in the Fall of 1988.[95] While the proposal for this paragraph came from the Finnish delegation, at least sixteen delegations participated in the drafting discussion. Although reservations over parts of the text were expressed by China, Japan and the USSR, the second paragraph was adopted by consensus.[96]

3.2. *Article 13: Freedom of Expression and Information*

This article was not proposed by the United States delegation until the 1988 Session of the Working Group.[97] The right to seek and receive information was originally conceived of as an additional paragraph to the then one paragraph Article 12. A small drafting party made up of Finland, Poland, Senegal and the United States, using Article 19 of the International Covenant on Civil and Political Rights as a reference proposed the text of an entirely new article which was adopted by the Working Group.[98]

During the second reading there was opposition to this article that was spearheaded by the delegate of the German Democratic Republic. In all, nine delegations took part in the debate, which concluded with the articles being adopted without revision.[99]

3.3. *Article 14: Freedom of Thought, Conscience and Religion*

Article 14 was proposed by the United States and the 1983 session of the Working Group. Although there was some support for such an article, it was not adopted at that session.[100] It was introduced again in 1984. At this session two additional texts had been proposed for an article on freedom of religion. One was the Canadian proposal. The other was a joint proposal from Sweden, Denmark, Finland and Norway. There was a lengthy discussion involving eleven delegations, after which a text was finally adopted.[101]

During the second reading Article 14 proved to be a particularly controversial text, mainly due to objections from Islamic delegations who viewed the child's right to freedom of religion as being contrary to the Koran. A drafting party made up of delegates from Bangladesh, China, the Holy See, Morocco, Mexico, the Netherlands and Poland which was joined by observers from the United States, the USSR, Argentina, Algeria, Egypt, Tunisia and two non-governmental organizations deliberated for days without coming to agreement on a text for the Article.[102] In the end, a text made up of four paragraphs, only one of which did not contain square brackets, was placed before the Working Group. Only pressure from the Chairman, coupled by suggestions that the article should be deleted,[103] prodded the Working Group into adopting a very watered-down version of the original proposal.[104] It is unlikely that any delegation was satisfied with the final text.

3.4. *Article 15: Freedom of Association and Assembly*

First proposed by the United States delegation in 1985 as a composite article, including the right to privacy as well,[105] this article languishes through several sessions before finally being adopted in 1988. In 1986 a revised US proposal was supported by Australia and Canada, but was opposed by the USSR and had negative responses from Algeria, China, Iraq and Poland.[106] The 1987 US revision of the article met with support and suggestions from the United Kingdom, Australia, Norway, Argentina, China and Sweden. The USSR stated that it was not in a position to support the draft.[107]

At the suggestion of the Ad Hoc NGO Group on the Drafting of the Convention on the Rights of the Child, in 1988 the United States delegate removed the right of privacy from the text and proposed that there be two separate articles.[108] This version of Article 15 was adopted with minimal discussion. The text was similarly unopposed during the second reading review.[109]

3.5. *Article 16: Right to Privacy*

This article, the spin off of the original US text for Article 15 was put before the Working Group at its 1988 session.[110] It was adopted with little discussion which nevertheless resulted in an important variation in U.S. text. The introductory words to the first reading text, which called on States Parties to 'recognize the right of the child not to be subjected to . . . ' were replaced by the words 'No child shall be subjected to . . . ' While the purpose of this alteration was to bring the text more closely into line with the language of the International Covenant on Civil and Political Rights, what it also did was to make the right of privacy the strongest of all of the rights of the child.[111] Interestingly, an earlier proposal by the US in 1982 called on States Parties to 'ensure that the child and his parents are not subjected to arbitrary or unlawful interference with their privacy, family, home or correspondence.'[112] The 1988 version was alerted to read:

> States Parties to the present Convention recognize the right of the child not to be subjected to arbitrary or unlawful interference with his or her right to privacy, family, home or correspondence nor unlawful attacks on his or her honour or reputation.[113]

In other words, the new version protected the child alone and not the child within the family. The second reading further strengthened the child's right to privacy when it changed the States Parties' obligation from that of mere 'recognition' of the right to language which makes the right total and absolute.[114]

4. CONCLUSION

The history of the drafting of Articles 12–16 does little to clarify the picture of the tensions between theories of natural law and those of legal positivism. In fact, it may even serve to muddy the waters further. While it could be argued that there were existing national practices to support the submission, by Poland, of Article 12 on the right to express opinions, Articles 13–16 appear to have been submitted for no particular reason at all.

True, freedom of religion was originally adopted without undue debate, but there was no groundswell of support for any of these articles. Three of them were adopted during the final sessions of the Working Group, two having languished for years without success. One could theorize that these American initiatives were initially undertaken solely to provocatively illustrate the differences between the East and the West.[115] This seems even more plausible when one considers that the US was pressing for the inclusion of the right of privacy in an international children's rights treaty, when its constitutional law scholars are still debating the matter of whether there is a right to privacy for adult American citizens.[116]

Despite the questionable legislative history of Articles 12–16, the fact is that once they were adopted, they were given subsequent approval by the international community. That these rights did not emerge as a result of the usual declaration to treaty, natural law claim to positive law, pattern is not important. Nor is it important that positive law was created without prior demand and may have been adopted not so much by the Working Group's support as by its lack of objection. What is significant about the Convention on the Rights of the Child is that, once it had been completed by the Working Group, not only was it adopted, without a vote, by the General Assembly, but it has gone into force more quickly than any other previous human rights treaty.[117] No other treaty has had so many countries take part in a signing ceremony and no other treaty has had so many ratifications in such a short period of time.[118] The Convention on the Rights of the Child has been embraced with enthusiasm by the entire world community.

Debates over the continuing existence of natural law theory and whether it continues to be viable in one of its various forms, will not be settled by studying the Convention on the Rights of the Child. Mieczylaw Maneli's theory that natural law was only an element of importance when there were no laws to protect those rights which men were asserting against the government also does not apply to the Covention.[119] Even granting that some countries had positive laws at least partially protecting some of the child's 'individual personality' rights, it cannot be said that these few examples fulfill Maneli's description of positive law obviating natural law. Certainly, prior to the Convention on the Rights of the Child, there was no positive international law which guaranteed the child's rights of 'individual personality'.

While the Convention on the Rights of the Child may had added fuel to the debate over the relevance of theories of natural law and legal positivism, it appears to have conclusively settled the child's protection vs. autonomy question. While not going so far as to guarantee the child's right to vote, the Convention backed by the world community, has come down squarely on the side of the child's right to dignity, respect and to rights of 'individual personality'.

NOTES

1. See, among others, W. Friedmann, *Legal Theory* (5th ed., 1967); D. Lloyd, *The Idea of Law* (1976); G. Christie, *Jurisprudence* (1973); and C. Morris (ed.) *The Great Legal Philosophers* (1959).
2. For a simple overview of theories of natural law see E. Patterson, *Jurisprudence* (1953), Ch. 13. Also see D. Lloyd, *The Idea of Law* (1976), Ch. 4.
3. For a thumbnail sketch of theories of legal positivism see D. Lloyd, *The Idea of Law* (1976), ch. 5. For a somewhat more detailed overview, see M. Maneli, *Juridical Positivism and Human Rights* (1981); Ch. I-VII.
4. See J. Austin, *Lectures on Jurisprudence* 1-25 (5th ed. R. Campbell, 1885). Also see H. L. A. Hart, *Law, Liberty and Morality* (1963).
5. This was especially clear at the Nuremburg Trials, when defendants unsuccessfully tried to hide their culpability behind the false legitimacy of legality. Martin Luther King also appealed to a higher law theory in his discussion of just and unjust laws in *Letter from Birmingham Jail.*
6. See *supra* notes 57–86 and accompanying text. The author is aware of the fact that some legal positivists have raised the question of whether international law itself can be classified as *law*, since it does not fit exactly into the mold of 'command from sovereign to subject'. While that argument may have some legitimacy when applied to treaties between nations – which are contractual in nature – in the author's opinion, to the extent that human rights treaty law codifies the relationship and obligations between sovereign and subject, it fulfills the criteria for positive law.
7. L. Henkin, *The Rights of Man Today* (1978) at 23–24.
8. GA Res. 217, UN Doc. A/810 at 71 (1948).
9. GA Res. 2200A, 21 UN GAOR, Supp. (No. 16) at 49, UN Doc. A/6316 (1966).
10. See among others, The International Convention on the Elimination of All Forms of Racial Discrimination, 660 UNTS (1966); the Convention on the Elimination of All Forms of Discrimination Against Women GA Res. 34/180, 34 UN GAOR Supp. (No. 46) at 193, UN Doc. A/34/46 (1980); and the Convention Against Torture and Other Cruel, Inhuman or Degrading Treatment or Punishment 39 UN GAOR C.3 Annex (Agenda Item 99) at 11, UN Doc. 1/39/708 (1984).
11. UN Doc. A/RES/44/25 (1989).
12. GA RES. 1386 (XIV), 14 UN GAOR Spp. (No. 1b) at 19, UN Doc. A/4354 (1959).
13. *Supra* notes 29-56 and accompanying text.
14. M. Cranston, 'What Are Human Rights'? in W. Lacuer & B. Rubin (eds.) *The Human Rights Reader* (1978) at 17.
15. A. I. Melden, 'Introduction' in A. I. Melden (ed.) *Human Rights* (1970).
16. See K. Minogue, 'The Idea of Human Rights', in W. Loquer and B. Rubin (eds.) *The Human Rights Reader* (1978) at 7–10.
17. L. Henkin, 'Introduction' in L. Henkin (ed.) *The International Bill of Rights* (1981) at 12.
18. As quoted in Cranston, *supra* note 14 at 18.
19. *Supra* note 16 at 14.
20. For a small sample of writings on the origins of human rights see M. McDougal, H.

Lasswell and L. Chen, *Human Rights and World Public Order* (1980) at 63–82; H. Lauterpacht, *International Law and Human Rights* (1968) at Sect. II; and A. Rosenbaum (ed.) *The Philosophy of Human Rights* (1980).

21. See M. Macdonald, 'Natural Rights' in A. I. Melden (ed.) *Human Rights* (1970). Also see, F. Newman & D. Weissbrodt, *International Human Rights* (1990) at 36 and L. Henkin, *The Rights of Man Today* (1978) at 24.

22. F. Newman and D. Weissbrodt, *International Human Rights* (1990) at 362–363.

23. The International Covenant on Economic, Social and Cultural Rights entered into force on January 3, 1976. The International Covenant on Civil and Political Rights entered into force on March 23, 1976.

24. See, V. Pechota, 'Development of the Covenant on Civil and Political Rights' in L. Henkin (ed.) *The International Bill of Rights* (1981) at 41–42.

25. Id. at 64–66. Also see *supra* note 23. The Optional Protocol entered into force on March 23, 1976.

26. Id. at 43.

27. Id. at 44.

28. See International Covenant on Civil and Political Rights, Art. 24. Also see Declaration of the Rights of the Child, principle 3.

29. See among others, A. Platt, *The Child Savers* (1969) and P. Bean and J. Melville, *Lost Children of the Empire* (1989).

30. See among others, P. Aries, *Centuries of Childhood* (1962); L. de Mause (ed.), *The History of Childhood* (1974); and V. Zelizer, *Pricing The Priceless Child* (1985).

31. Aristotle, *Nichomachen Ethics*, 1138b6.

32. Id. at 1162a4.

33. Thomas Aquinas, *Summa Theologiae*, Vol. 37 (Trans. T. Gilby 1975) 2a2ac, question 57, article 4.

34. See *Summa Theologiae*, Vo. 23 (Trans. W. D. Hughes 1969), 1a2ae, question 65, article 3.

35. J. Bodin, *Six Books of the Commonwealth*, trans. M. J. Tooley (1955) Book I at 6.

36. Id.

37. Thomas Hobbes, C.B. MacPherson (ed.) *The Leviathan* (1968). In other words, without government man would be living in a 'state of war of all against all' and life would be 'nasty, solitary, brutish and short'. Hobbes' discussion of the child-parent relationship can be found in the section of the *Leviathan* which is entitled 'Covenants of the Vanquished and the Victor or the Child to the Parent'.

38. Id.

39. Id.

40. Id.

41. Id.

42. John Locke, *Two Treatises of Government* (P. Laslett, ed., 1965) at Second Treatise, Sec. 72.

43. J. J. Rousseau, *Emile* (Trans. B. Foxley 1974) at 16.

44. Id. at 13 and 16.

45. Id. at 34.

46. The author has chosen the words 'individual personality' to describe rights which are personal to the 'individual', in comparison to rights which belong to the group or society in general. This has been done to bring attention to the fact that the Convention on the Rights of the Child recognizes that each child has an 'individual personality' of his or her own and that there are corresponding rights whcih attach to this recognition.

   The term 'individual personality' incorporates two of the many descriptive terms which have been applied to the rights which are generally thought of in international law as civil-political rights. Such rights as freedom of speech, religion, association, assembly and the right to privacy are sometimes called 'individual' rights. They are also referred to as 'personal' rights, 'rights of personality' or 'basic rights'. See, H. Lauterpacht,

International Law and Human Rights (1968) at 280–286. See also M. McDougal, H. Lasswell & L. Chen, *Human Rights and World Public Order* (1980) at 854–856. See also, G. Goodwin-Gill, *The Refugee in International Law* (1985) at 39–40.

47. *Infra* notes 49 and 50 and accompanying text.
48. 387 US 1 (1967). *In re Gault* interjected due process procedures into the previously informal juvenile justice proceedings. During this period, which was characterized by considerable student activism, the Supreme Court handed down a number of other decisions impacting on the rights of children and young people giving them constitutional protection of such rights as free speech and privacy.
49. See J. Holt, *Escape from Childhood* (1974).
50. See, R. Farson, *Birthrights* (1974). For a collection of early writings on children's liberation see P. Adams, L. Berg, N. Berger, A. S. Niel, R. Ollendorff, *Children's Rights* (1971). For a differing view in this same time period see, H. H. Foster, Jr., *A Bill of Rights for Children* (1974).
51. *Supra* note 49 at Chapters 18, 17 and 27 and *supra* note 50 (Farson) at Chapters 10, 11 and 9.
52. *Supra* note 49 at Chapter 25.
53. A more lasting and far-reaching impact was made by another writer of a slightly earlier period, Dr. C. Henry Kempe. Dr. Kempe's report on the 'Battered Child Syndrome' (181 JAMA 17, 1962) continues to have an effect on legislation, public policy and concern for the well-being of the child which has expanded to include inquiries into all types of child abuse including sexual abuse and incest.
54. L. Houlgate, *The Child and the State* (1980).
55. Id. at 15.
56. Id.
57. See M.D.A. Freeman, *The Rights and Wrongs of Children* (1983).
58. Id. at 54–60. Also see John Rawls, *A Theory of Justice* (1972).
59. Known as the 'Declaration of Geneva', this declaration was drafted under the auspices of the Save the Children International Union, led by Eglantyne Jebb.
60. GA Res. 31/169, 31 UN GAOR Supp. (No. 39) at 74; UN Doc. A/31/39 (1976). For background of the drafting of the Convention see C. P. Cohen, 'The Human Rights of Children 12', *Capital U.L. Review* 369 (1983).
61. See 1924 League of Nations Declaration of the Rights of the Child (hereinafter 1924 Dec.) para. 1 and 1959 UN Declaration of the Rights of the Child (hereinafter 1959 Dec.) Principle 2.
62. See 1924 Dec. at para. 4 and 1959 Dec. at Principle 9.
63. See 1924 Dec. at para. 2 and 1959 Dec. at Principle 6.
64. See 1924 Dec. at para. 3 and 1959 Dec. at Principle 8.
65. See 1959 Dec. at Principle 7.
66. See 1959 Dec. at Principle 6.
67. See 1959 Dec. at Principle 3.
68. See 1959 Dec. at Principle 4.
69. See 1959 Dec. at Principle 7.
70. See 1959 Dec. at Principle 5.
71. See 1924 Dec. at para. 4.
72. See 1924 Dec. at Preamble and 1959 Dec. at Principle 1.
73. See 1924 Dec. at para. 5 and 1959 Dec. at Principle 10.
74. See among others, Slavery Convention (signed 1926) 60 LNTS 253, amended by Protocol (1953) UNTS 17. Supplementary Convention on the Abolition of Slavery, the Slave Trade and Institutions and Practices Similar to Slavery (1956) 266 UNTS 3.
75. While many of the 'White Slave' conventions have the word 'traffic' in the title, there is also a League of Nations treaty known as The International Convention for the Suppression of Traffic in Women and Children, which was amended and adopted by the United Nations.

76. The International Labor Organization has adapted numerous treaties relating to exploitation of child labor. The earliest of these was the Minimum Age (Industry) Convention (No. 5) adopted in 1919. The most recent was Convention No. 138 concerning Minimum Age for Admission to Employment, adopted in 1973.
77. 6 UST 3516, TIAS No. 3365, 75 UNTS 135 (1945).
78. For collection of international instruments relating to the rights of the child see *Documentary Supplement to the Comparative Analysis of the Draft Convention on the Rights of the Child and Existing International Legal Instruments Pertaining to the Same Subject Matter* (K. Tomasevski, ed., 1985). The compilation covers only those declarations and treaties adopted prior to 1985.
79. See *supra* note 46.
80. See *infra* notes 87–110 and accompanying text.
81. See Articles 8, 10, 12, 13, 14, 15, 16, 25, 37, 40, among others.
82. Id. Also see *infra* notes 87–110 and accompanying text.
83. See *supra* note 10.
84. Id.
85. There was a period of twenty years between the adoption of the 1959 Declaration and the beginning of the drafting of the Convention, which was not completed for ten years.
86. UN ESCOR Supp. (No. 4), UN Doc. E/CN.4/1292 (1978).
87. UN ESCOR Supp. (No. 16), UN Doc. E/CN.4/1349 (1979).
88. See *infra* notes 91–96 and accompanying text.
89. *Supra* note 79.
90. See C. P. Cohen, 'The Human Rights of Children, 12 *Capital L. Review*, 369 (1983).
91. Government responses to a questionnaire from the Secretary-General of the United Nations about possible support for a children's rights treaty were mixed. Sweden, among others, was very negative toward the idea. Yet, Sweden was the first Western country to ratify. For a statement explaining the changing U.S. attitude toward the Convention see, Statement of Thomas A. Johnson, US Department of State before the United Nations Commission on Human Rights, March 8, 1989. The United States welcomed the expansion of the Convention's text to include civil-political rights.
92. See among others C. P. Cohen, *Status Report*: 'United Nations Convention on the Rights of the Child 8 N.Y.L. Sch. J. Human Rights (1991); C. P. Cohen,' United Nations Convention on the Rights of the Child – Introductory Note' 44 *The Review* 36 (1990) and C. P. Cohen, 'Role of Non-Governmental Organizations in the Drafting of the Convention on the Rights of the Child' 12 *Human Rights Quarterly* 137 (1990).
93. *Supra* note 85. Note the use of the word 'his'. The Polish Model Convention, as well as most of the articles drafted during the first four sessions, always referred to the child in the masculine gender. Midway through the drafting there was a shift to the use of 'his and hers', that is, language was used which was gender neutral or mentioned both genders. During one of the later drafting sessions the child was referred to as 'it'. All of these matters were corrected during the second reading to create a gender-neutral treaty. see UN Doc. E/CN.4/1989/48. Also see 'Technical Review', UN Doc. E/CN.4/1989/WG/CRP (1988)
94. UN ESCOR Supp. (No. 5), UN Doc. E/CN.4/L.1575 (1981) at paras. 73–81.
95. The term 'first reading' is applied to the completed first draft at a treaty text. The 'second reading' is the process by which the original text is corrected and reevaluated by the drafting group to reach the final version.
96. UN Doc. E/CN.4/1989/48 (1989) at paras. 234–267. Consensus is technically 'without a vote'. In reality, consensus signifies not unanimity (i.e., support), but the absence of objections.
97. UN Doc. E/Cn.4/1988/28 (1988) at para. 35.
98. Id. at paras. 36–46.
99. *Supra* note 93 at paras. 258–279.
100. UN Doc. E/CN.4/1983/62 (1983) at paras. 52–57.

101. UN Doc. E/CN.4/1984/71 (1984) at paras. 13–33.
102. See id., especially paras. 280–281.
103. Id. at paras. 282–287.
104. Id. at paras. 288–291.
105. UN Doc. E/CN.4/1985/64 (1985).
106. UN Doc. E/CN.4/1986/39 (1986) at paras. 84–87.
107. UN Doc. E/CN.4/1987/25 (1987) at paras. 111–118.
108. UN Doc. E/CN.4/1988/28 (1988) at paras. 35–54. For an overview of the activities of the Ad Hoc NGO Group on the Drafting of the Convention on the Rights of the Child see, C. P. Cohen, 'Role of Non-Governmental Organizations in the Drafting of the Convention on the Rights of the Child' 12 *Human Rights Quarterly* 137 (1990). Also see C. P. Cohen, 'Juvenile Justice Provisions of the Draft Convention on the Rights of the Child', 7 *N.Y.L.S.J. Human Rights* 1 (1989).
109. *Supra* note 93 at paras. 292–295.
110. UN Doc. E/CN.4/1988/28 at paras. 35–38 and 55–59.
111. For a discussion of the significance of obligatory words see, C. P. Cohen, 'A Linguistic Guide to the Convention on the Rights of the Child' in *Children's Rights in America* (C. P. Cohen and H. A. Davidson, eds., 1990). Also see, C. P. Cohen, 'Elasticity of Obligation and the Drafting of the Convention on the Rights of the Child', 3 *CONN. Journal of International Law* 71 (1987).
112. UN Doc. E/1982/12/Add. 1, Part C at para. 118 (1982).
113. *Supra* note 107 at para. 35.
114. *Supra* note 93 at paras. 296–303.
115. Prior to the adoption by the General Assembly of the Convention Against Torture, that treaty and the Convention on the Rights of the Child were being drafted simultaneously. On ocassion, the East-West political battles of the Torture Convention would spill over into deliberations on the Children's Rights Convention.
116. See J. Bork, *The Right to Privacy*.
117. For example, the Convention Against Torture and Other Forms of Cruel, Inhuman or Degrading Treatment or Punishment was adopted by the General Assembly on December 12, 1984. It was opened for signature February 2, 1985 and went into force on July 26, 1987. The Convention on the Elimination of All Forms of Discrimination Against Women had 53 States participate in the specially arranged signing ceremony. Sixty States signed the Convention on the Rights of the Child. On the anniversary of the signing ceremony of the Convention on the Rights of the Child, 69 States had become Parties. The total had risen to 77 by March of 1991.
118. There were 84 ratifications in about 18 months.
119. *Supra* note 3 (Maneli). Maneli's assertion is that when the right to property, the right to freedom, the right to life, the right to justice did not exist in positive law, there was the necessity of reaching out for some higher law theory with which to support these claims. Now that positive laws exist which protect all these rights, there is no longer the necessity to have a natural law based claim. Natural law was merely an evolutionary phase along the way towards the development of positive law of human rights.

HANS-JOACHIM HEINTZE*

6. The UN Convention and the Network of the International Human Rights Protection by the UN

The history and the current fate of the UN Convention on the Rights of the Child[1] has enjoyed some obvious successes, but there are also deep-rooted problems in the whole system of the protection of human rights by the United Nations. On the one hand, this international organization has a tendency to elaborate an increasing number of instruments of international law for the protection of certain groups of human beings. On the other hand, it seems that the agreement on concrete measures for action within the jurisdiction of the participating parties and on the effective implementation of systems for all these instruments is still a 'hot coal', because it is connected with the very complex problem of the sovereignty of states.

The fact that the UN Convention on the Rights of the Child came into force within only one year after its adoption by the General Assembly and that it has been widely accepted by participating States shows the widespread interest of the community of States in this topic and instrument. On the other hand, one has to accept some negative aspects. It is hard to find among the participating States States which have traditionally felt obliged to observe the idea of an international protection of human rights. The same, unfortunately, is true of States in which gross and mass violations of human rights of children have been (and are still being) practised.

The political will of States to ratify international human rights treaties is a result of a conviction of the usefulness of standards laid down in these documents. Sometimes, one can have little doubt that the codification process within the United Nations is the best possible way: 'The United Nations has recognized that it can be advantageous to particularize the rights of certain groups; e.g., refugees and women'.[2] The result of this process are several norms, which are only valid for certain groups or which repeat existing general standards or, in the worse case, can weaken these general standards.

The UN Convention on the Rights of the Child shows that the opportunity for the progressive development of the international protection of human rights has reached certain limits. These limits result from the diversity of the

---

* Karl Marx University, Leipzig.

M. Freeman and P. Veerman (eds.), The Ideologies of Children's Rights, 71–78.
© 1992 *Kluwer Academic Publishers. Printed in the Netherlands.*

community of States, the different value-systems of these States,[3] their readiness to undertake international obligations and the fact that the subject is becoming increasingly subdivided. Very often a UN instrument represents only a compromise and the lowest common denominator, which means that it only repeats already existing standards.

1. THE GENERAL FRAME OF THE PROTECTION OF CHILDREN'S RIGHTS UNDER INTERNATIONAL LAW

Among international lawyers there is no doubt about the legal basis of human rights protection under international law: 'It was the Charter of the United Nations . . . that elevated human rights to the plane of international law and stipulated legal obligations on the part of the Member States of the United Nations'.[4] As a general document the Charter did not define what is to be understood as a human right and a fundamental freedom under international law and therefore it is no surprise that 'the members of the UN themselves recognized that the charter law was insufficient. Immediately they proceeded to prepare and promulgate the Universal Declaration of Human Rights, making specific the general Charter references to human rights and freedoms for all.'[5] Therefore, the Universal Declaration is the *ius constituendum* of the United Nations Charter to the term 'human rights' and most of the international lawyers support the opinion that its principles are customary international law.[6]

Because of the fact that the Charter obliged the States to 'universal respect and observance of human rights and fundamental freedoms for *all*' children are clearly included within this obligation. This position is confirmed by the Universal Declaration: 'Most of the rights of the Universal Declaration relate to children either directly or indirectly, though some to a greater extent than others. Several of its provisions are particularly or exclusively relevant to children. The Declaration is thus the definitional matrix of internationally proclaimed human rights, in general, and children's rights, in particular.'[7]

It follows from this that an international, binding, general standard of the rights of children can be assumed. This standard has been supplemented by the two International Covenants on Human Rights: the Covenant on Civil and Political Rights of 1966, and the Covenants on Economic, Social and Cultural Rights of 1966. Some Articles involve the position of the child in the family and in cases of divorce (Articles 18 and 24); other rights are connected with education.

Although one can speak of a general framework of children's rights under international law, there has been a need for clarification because of the question as to whether one can extend to children those human rights and freedoms compatible with the circumstances of childhood. The crucial point is always to determine how to provide children with both the care and protection required by childhood and the broadest range of freedom and rights compatible with the physical, intellectual and social conditions of childhood.[8]

2.   THE SPECIAL FRAMEWORK OF THE PROTECTION OF CHILDREN'S RIGHTS UNDER INTERNATIONAL LAW

Mass and gross violations of the basic human rights of children confront and demand international attention. To mention only one example: in 1987/88 the Inter-American Commission on Human Rights was confronted with 'A study about the situation of minor children of disappeared persons who were separated from their parents and who are claimed by members of their legitimate families'.[9] The focus of the study is the situation in which children are direct victims and specific 'targets' of repressive action, even though their kidnapping and theft is meant primarily to punish their parents or grandparents. This is the case when minors and infants are, kidnapped with their parents, or they are born during their mothers' captivity. The phenomenon may sound cruel and heartless, but in Argentina, in particular, hundreds of such cases have been brought to the world's attention.

Such examples show immediately the necessity for the international protection of children's rights. But the 'everyday violation' of the rights of children should also not be forgotten: 'Many children have been exploited, neglected, abandoned, mistreated, abused (sexually or otherwise), beaten, sold into slavery, mutilated, forgotten, ignored, or even killed with impunity, especially in circumstances of hunger, war or other difficulties. Orphaned, illegitimate, disabled and female children have been more often subjected to discrimination, exploitation and even infanticide. They have been the first victims of human rights violations'.[10]

The fact that children have been the first victims of human rights violations had been recognized early on at the international level. The efforts of the League of Nations date back to the year 1921, with the convention prohibiting trafficking in women and children. Another result was the convention on slavery and the slave trade (1926). Parallel to these activities the International Labour Organization adopted numerous instruments against the exploitation of child labour and for the protection of working children. This is not the place to evaluate these documents, but Alston is right to stress in the opening line of a recent article that 'Recognition that there is a Problem is the most Important Step'.[11]

The first comprehensive international instrument was the Geneva Declaration of 1924, also known as the Declaration of the Rights of the Child of 1924. Though it was essentially an aspirational document, by introducing basic principles on the international plane it did prepare the ground for the progressive development of international norms.[12] Indeed, these principles were later to form the structure of the UN Declaration on the Rights of the Child.

The Declaration on the Rights of the Child speaks, for the first time, in terms of rights and entitlement. The idea goes beyond the protection of children, and recognises an entitlement to some rights. However, as a resolution of the General Assembly it was not legally binding.

With the growing specialization of the protection of human rights by the United Nations the international community has recognized the important place of the rights of the child on the international agenda. The General Assembly declared 1979 to be the International Year of the Child. This year provoked an unprecedented response and concern among States, and many follow-up activities.[13]

In 1978 the UN Commission on Human Rights took up the question of a convention on the rights of the child. The convention contains, in legalistic terms, the principles laid down in the Declaration of the Rights of the Child. The Convention on the Rights of the Child contains fifty-four articles; most of them proclaim rights of children which must be respected and ensured by State parties. These provisions span the spectrum from civil and political rights to economic, social and cultural rights. The Convention has taken its place in the growing line of human rights instruments adopted by the UN.

Since most of the standards contained in the Convention on the Rights of the Child repeat almost verbatim standards already applied to children by many prior instruments, the question arises of what greater legal protection the Convention can guarantee to children. Practice in other fields of international law shows that such a repetition is very common. An impressive example is formed by the treaties in which states underline the principle of the prohibition of the use of force in international relations. The duplication of the language from prior instruments should not automatically detract from the promotion of the human rights of children. Because of the fact that most of the pre-existing instruments are subject to ratification, it is possible that more states, or different states, will ratify the convention on the rights of the child. By ratification these governments have signified their determination to ensure that their domestic laws meet the standards set in the Convention.[14]

The most important improvement of the legal status of children is that this document creates the definitive body of international law on children's rights. But what does this mean for the everyday struggle for children's rights within the States? Jupp mentions two aspects: 'The Convention creates a permanent international forum that will force a protracted discussion on the rights of the child. A monitoring system written into the Convention provides for the appointment of a committee of ten experts, to be elected by the ratifying countries . . . the Convention will become a vehicle for mobilization. The Convention will be used for teaching children about their own rights and about the rights of children in other lands . . .'[15]

Jupp does not answer the question whether there is an actual improvement in the situation of children by the General Assembly's adoption of this Convention. Some doubts are permitted, because there are other and more effective instruments for the mobilization of the public. To take the 1975

Final Act of Helsinki of the All-European Conference on Security and Co-operation as an example, one can say that this document did much more to mobilise public opinion to do something to improve the human rights situation in Eastern Europe than the two UN Covenants on Human Rights. Therefore, the chances of the Convention promoting the mobilization of public opinion is not a very convincing reason for passage of such a convention. It seems more important to me to concentrate on an improvement of the legal situation in the spheres of the physical and psychological protection of the child, as well as of the child's education and of the protection of handicapped children.

3. PROGRESSIVE DEVELOPMENT OF EXISTING STANDARDS AND IMPLEMENTATION SYSTEMS BY THE UN CONVENTION ON THE RIGHTS OF THE CHILD

Some aspects of the UN Convention on the Rights of the Child show that, in general, States hesitate to exceed the existing standards.

3.1. *Protection of Minorities*

In regard to the increasing threats to children who belong to minorities, concrete norms for protection would have been desirable. But Article 30 of the Convention on the Rights of the Child reads as follows:

> In those States in which ethnic, religious of linguistic minorities or persons of indigenous origin exist, a child belonging to such a minority or who is indigenous shall not be denied the right, in community with other members of his or her group, to enjoy his or her own culture, to profess and practice his or her own religion, or to use his or her own language.

This is a general repetition of Article 27 of the UN Covenant on Political and Civil Rights.[16] The only addition concerns 'persons of indigenous origin'. Since indigenous children have been mentioned, the specification of these groups should have been further developed. After all, many indigenous people are fighting for their survival, and this specifically concerns their children:

> The process whereby indigenous and tribal peoples have been accompanied by genocide, not only in the nineteenth century during the hayday of colonial expansion, but also in some parts of the world during the present century and in contemporary times. Denunciations about the genocide of ethnic minorities in general and of indigenous and tribal peoples in particular have been brought to the attention of the international community regularly, but the latter has usually been unable or unwilling to do much about it. This has been one of the major failures of the UN system in

recent years, despite the existence of the Convention on the Prevention and Punishment of the Crime of Genocide.[17]

Knowing about these failures suggests a need for greater protection of these rights in the children's Convention.

3.2. *Prohibition of Torture*

The same criticism applies to Article 37:

> No child shall be subjected to torture or other cruel, inhuman or degrading treatment or punishment.

This standard has already been achieved by the UN Covenant on Political and Civil Rights and the Convention against Torture and Other Cruel, Inhuman or Degrading Treatment or Punishment of 1984.

3.3. *International Humanitarian Law*

Article 38, too, which deals with the obligation of States to respect and ensure respect for humanitarian law as it applies to children, does not fulfil the hopes that were placed in it. There is no improvement in comparison with the generally accepted rules of international humanitarian law. The principle has been underlined that no child under 15 may take a direct part in hostilities or be recruited into the armed forces. During the development of the Convention in the UN Working Group the International Committee of the Red Cross pushed, without success, for a progressive development:

> The presence of far too many adolescents on the world's battlefields had led many States to call for the minimum age of combatants to be raised from 15 to 18 years, and the ICRC had repeatedly expressed its support for such a measure while stressing that none of the advances made over the years should be reversed. Unfortunately, one could only conclude that article 38 of the draft convention did not constitute a development of international humanitarian law but instead weakened it. First, Additional Protocol II of 1977 relating to non-armed conflicts offered better protection for the child than Article 38, paragraph 2, because it prohibited both direct and indirect participation of children under 15 years of age. Second, the wording 'all feasible measures' in Article 38, paragraph 4, created a serious risk of weakening international humanitarian law. Many provisions in the Conventions and Protocols designed to protect civilians in general and children in particular laid down absolute obligations and thus provided more effective protection than anything covered by the words 'feasible measures'.[18]

It is disappointing that the Convention on the Rights of the Child does not offer any improvement in connection with these three important problems of international human rights protection.

3.4. *The Implementation System*

Regarding the enforcement of the Convention one can again reiterate the lack of power to enforce directly the standards which it promulgates. Therefore, the Convention contains a similar implementation system as the other UN human rights conventions. Article 43 establishes a committee of independent experts much like those created by the other UN conventions in this field. Under Article 44, State Parties must submit to the committee periodic reports on the status of children's rights. The committee reviews the reports and has the power to request additional information. The important progress in comparison with other UN conventions is that the committee is allowed to cooperate intensively with NGOs[19], as Article 45 demonstrates:

> In order to foster the effective implementation of the Convention and to encourage international co-operation in the field covered by the Convention:
> a. The specialized agencies, UNICEF and other United Nations organs shall be entitled to be represented at the consideration of the implementation . . .
> b. The Committee shall transmit, as it may consider appropriate, to the specialized agencies, UNICEF and other competent bodies, any reports from State Parties that contain a request, or indicate a need, for technical advice or assistance along with the Committees observations and suggestions, if any, on these requests or indications.

This article marks progress in the struggle for effective implementation procedures. On the other hand, it is surprising that the Convention contains no complaint procedures, either for individuals or for states. The UN Covenant on Civil and Political Rights with its Optional Protocol, the Racial Discrimination Convention, and the Convention against Torture also provide for the possibility of both state-to-state complaints and individual petitions.

4. CONCLUSION

In general one can state that the UN Convention on the Rights of the Child is only a small contribution to the progressive development of general human rights protection by international law. Doubtless the Convention is a step forward in comparison with other instruments for the protection of children and manifests the increasing respect for human rights of their group of human beings in the international field.

NOTES

1. See S. Künzel, 'Rechte des Kindes: Konvention jetzt in Kraft', in *Vereinte Nationen* (Kehl) 38 (1990) 5, p. 192ff.
2. H. Schweitzer, 'A Children's Rights Convention – What Is the United Nations Accomplishing?', in R. B. Lillich (ed.), *The Family in International Law: Some Emerging Problems*. Third Sokol Colloquium, Charlottesville (1981), p. 115.
3. See the critical remarks of Barsh of the Four Directions Council: 'In principle, the ongoing process of elaborating interpretive or derivative standards through new declarations and conventions affords recently-independent states an opportunity to raise genuine cross-cultural concern. In actuality, European states have continued to dominate United Nations human rights policy'. R. L. Barsh, 'The Draft Convention on the Rights of the Child: A Case of Eurocentricism in Standard-Setting', in *Nordic Journal of International Law* (Copenhagen), 58 (1989) 1, p. 24.
4. A. Mamalakis Pappas, *Law and the Status of the Child*, New York (1983), p. xxx.
5. L. Henkin, *The International Bill of Rights*, New York (1981), p. 8.
6. Vgl. Humphrey, 'The Universal Declaration of Human Rights: Its History, Impact and Juridical Character', in: B. G. Ramcharan, *Human Rights: Thirty Years After the Universal Declaration*, Dordrecht (1979), p. 27 ff.
7. A. Mamalakis Pappas, op. cit., p. xxxi. A similar position is taken by Wolfrum. See R. Wolfrum, 'Die Konvention über die Rechte des Kindes: Entwicklung, Inhalt und Einbettung in den internationalen Menschenrechtsschutz', in: *Dokumentation 'Die UN-Konvention der Rechte des Kindes'*, München (1990), p. 9.
8. See H. Schweitzer, op. cit., p. 122.
9. The study is a part of the UN Doc. E/CN.4/1989/66.
10. Y. Kubota, 'The Protection of Childrens Rights and the United Nations' *Nordic Journal of International Law* (Copenhagen) 58 (1989) 1, p. 7.
11. See P. Alston, 'Implementing Children's Rights: The Case of Child Labour', *Nordic Journal of International Law* (Copenhagen) 58 (1989) 1, p. 38.
12. See Y. Kubota, op. cit., p. 9.
13. See A.D. Viccica, 'The Promotion and Protection of Children's Rights through Development and Recognition of an International Notion of Juvenile Justice and its Child-Centered Perspective in the United Nations', in *Nordic Journal of International Law* (Copenhagen) 58 (1989) 1, p. 68ff.
14. See D.A. Balton, 'The Convention on the Rights of the Child: Prospects for International Enforcement', in *Human Rights Quarterly* 12 (1990) 1, p. 122.
15. See M. Jupp: 'The UN Convention on the Rights of the Child: An Opportunity for Advocates', in *Human Rights Quarterly* 12 (1990) 1, p. 13.
16. See L.B. Sohn, 'The Rights of Minorities', in L. Henkin, *The International Bill of Rights*, New York (1981), p. 271ff.
17. R. Stavenhagen, *Background Paper, UN Seminar on the Effects of Racism and Racial Discrimination on the Social and Economic Relations Between Indigenous Peoples and States*; UN-Doc. HR/GENEVA/1989/SEM.1/BP.
18. See UN-Doc. E/CN.4/1989/SR.55/Add. 1, P. 4, para. 12.
19. See C.P. Cohen, 'The Role of Nongovernmental Organizations in the Drafting of the Convention on the Rights of the Child', in *Human Rights Quarterly* 12 (1990) 1, p. 137ff.

EUGEEN VERHELLEN*

7. Changes in the Images of the Child

1. INTRODUCTION

When 'respect for family life is at issue (. . .), it is almost always the family life of the parents, rather than of the children which is given dominance'.[1]

This statement, which has recently been published in a report of the Council of Europe, has not passed unnoticed and it leads one to suspect that, in spite of the arrival of the 'age of the child', the attention given to children, and especially respect for them, is rhetorical rather than real. However, the report also leads us to believe that this situation can change. History has revealed to us that, although there have always been children, they have not always been considered in the same way. In other words, different images of the child are possible, which in their turn entail different consequences with regard to relationships. The present, prevalent opinion, that children belong to a 'separate social category', is a relatively recent social construct.

For some decades, however, this image of the child, this position that the child occupies, has been turned into a topic of real discussion for a variety of reasons.[2] In this discussion, some important trends can be noticed. Each of them refers to a different attitude, especially with regard to the children's 'competence'.

Although these trends fit in with more extensive macro-social dynamics, reflected by the rapidly increasing evolution concerning the concept of human rights, they can be recognised in almost all social and legal areas where the child is involved.

This paper focuses especially on possible indications of an increased growth in respect for the fully-fledged legal position of the child. In particular, the reflection in law can refer to a changing image of the child, to a changing relationship with the child. At the centre of this analysis is the demand for the recognition of the child as the bearer of individual human rights (as a legal subject) as well as the demand for the recognition of the child's capacity to implement rights.

* Study and Documentation Centre on Children's Rights, University of Ghent.

M. Freeman and P. Veerman (eds.), The Ideologies of Children's Rights, 79–94.
© 1992 *Kluwer Academic Publishers. Printed in the Netherlands.*

Recent national and international draft rules, jurisdiction and legal doctrine all illustrate the change towards respect for the child as a human being. Thus, the European Convention for the Protection of Human Rights and Fundamental Freedoms is increasingly applied in respect of children.[3]

At the same time, draft rules have been gradually set up at the international level. The UN Convention on the Rights of the Child and the European drafts (of the Convention or additional protocols to the European Convention for the Protection of Human Rights and Fundamental Freedoms) can be mentioned as convincing examples of this evolution.[4] However, there is still more to come. Some aspects in this evolution even point out that the traditional defensive or re-active policy (protective only) is complemented by an accelerated, pro-active policy, so that children are coming to be recognised as partners worthy of respect. This paper not only ends with this conclusion but also with the conviction that this trend could be more forceful than that found so far.

2. THE DISCUSSION ON COMPETENCE

The main feature of the status of children in history is the absence of virtually all civil rights. Children are denied, both philosophically and legally, the right to determine their own lives. Powerlessness is the principal characteristic of their situation: they do not have the right to control their lives freely, as is the case with slaves.[5]

It is therefore not surprising to discover that several 'actors' from a wide range of fields are trying to turn this status of children into an actual topic. This diversity is sometimes referred to as the 'children's rights movement'. Their chief demand is that children should be granted all basic civil rights, as well as the right to assert these rights independently. In other words, what counts is the recognition of the autonomy and the right to self-determination of children and the recognition of their being fully-fledged legal persons.[6] The starting point, rather than the goal, underlying this demand is the equality of persons, regardless of age.[7] However, the idea is not to treat children as adults, but to guarantee children that they can be themselves. It is considered very important that the needs and the qualities of children should be recognised, and not violated to protect the interests of other individuals.

At present, our society has the habit of removing or isolating children from situations which present a genuine danger or in which their needs cannot be fulfilled. It would be preferable, however, to alter the situation or to provide whatever means necessary to be able to fulfil the needs of children, thus assuring that they can remain present and that their rights of freedom and their rights as persons are respected. The children's rights movement is therefore strongly convinced that the liberation of children will have a liberating effect on all members of society. That is the reason why the movement feels it is urgent to try to remove the huge barriers separating the worlds of different age groups.[8]

The children's rights movement also devotes itself to the recognition of the rights of participation for children. Children should have the right to participate in determining their own living conditions and in shaping society. Therefore, they should be given access to the means and the structures which enable them to do so. The right to participate in democratic policy-making processes, the right to self-determination and the right to assert these rights independently are the main pillars of human rights. Therefore, human rights form an essential point of contact with children's rights movement. However, the ideological and scientific discussion on children's rights has been mainly situated at a more pragmatic level. The idea that children should have rights of their own (i.e. the principle of substantive law) has gradually become accepted by a fairly strong public consensus. In the '70s, in particular, there was little discussion of the view that children possess the same personal rights as adults. In contrast, an issue that is still under discussion today is the question of whether or not children are able, and hence entitled, to assert these rights independently. This is the area of procedural law, i.e. the right to assert the provisions of substantive law. The key notion in this discussion is 'competence'.

Indeed, the constantly-recurring, fundamental argument for denying children autonomy and rights is their alleged incompetence in making informed decisions. On this view, children are not only physically, but also intellectually and emotionally labelled immature. Moreover, they lack the experience required to be able to determine what is good for them and what is not. Yet the children's rights movement has made great efforts to try and refute these arguments, by challenging their validity, their relevance and their appropriateness.[9] Taking all this practical experience into account, the children's rights movement truly regrets that children are still not regarded and studied as fully-fledged partners in our society. What children precisely are or what it is that they know or can do, remains 'a black box', and this situation reinforces the presence of the argument of incompetence in the discussion.

Nevertheless, the most striking feature of this discussion on competence, at an underlying level, should be that the recognition of self-determination for children is essential in order to make them more competent, and not vice versa. It is not because they are gradually becoming more competent that their right to self-determination must be gradually recognised. Depending on the position taken in the discussion on competence, several trends can be distinguished.

1. *The reformist trend.* First, there is a trend which basically considers the argument of incompetence to be valid, but which is convinced that our society heavily underestimates the competence of children to make rational and informed decisions. This trend firmly believes that such a competence is acquired at a much younger age than is conventionally accepted, and that this process is a gradual one. These ideas form the basis of their pleas

to bring down the legal age of majority and to grant children their rights gradually.[10]

2. *The radical trend.* The children's liberationists, for their part, challenge the validity of the argument of incompetence on ethical grounds. Their starting point (the highest moral standard) is the equality of all human beings. Any discrimination, including discrimination based on age difference, is in their opinion to be morally condemned. The only possible solution to the problem for them is to grant all human and civil rights to children as well as to adults.[11]

3. *The pragmatic trend.* The pragmatic trend is becoming increasingly important. It wonders what the practical reasons are for not granting children all civil rights and the right to assert them independently. The adherents of this trend feel that there are no such reasons, except for the case where a child's incompetence to assert specific rights can clearly be demonstrated and is not objected to by any group in society.[12] This is the principle of children enjoying all their rights except in certain cases. As to adults, a similar approach has proved to be perfectly possible. The great advantage of this approach over the present-day system would be that the burden of proof in the discussion on competence is removed from the children's shoulders. At present, the position of children is exactly the opposite, and therefore very weak, since the burden of proving that they are entitled to self determination lies completely with them. This is the principle of children enjoying no rights except in certain cases. This explains why so many rights of children are translated into obligations (e.g. the right to learn and go to school becomes compulsory education).

3. Towards a Changing Image of the Child in the Area of Law

I examine here the extent to which the discussions on the social position of children and especially on the changing trends also manifest themselves in present (draft) rules, in jurisdiction and in legal doctrine. I have opted for the law because, enforced by its known inertia, changes within the framework of the law are indeed a reflection of what takes place at a broader and more macro-social level of society.

More specifically, I will first consider whether or not, and how, the law and the rules are present in the attempts to reassess the child as a human being. Another reason is that the law increasingly becomes the most important way of achieving respect.

I try to answer these questions by discussing substantive and procedural law. In view of the assumption that macro-social dynamics are concerned I will not restrict myself to national law but shall also consider European and international law. For the same reason I will not restrict myself to one sector of society (or branch of law) but will cover various areas. At the same time, it should be noticed that no claim to exhaustiveness is made. Some striking examples have been chosen for their heuristic importance. Neither is any image of 'the' reality involved. It is rather 'a' reality which increasingly has to demand attention as well.

3.1.   *Recognition of Basic Rights With Regard to Minors*

3.1.1.   *Children's Rights – Human Rights*
On the 20th November, 1989, the Convention on the Rights of the Child was adopted unanimously by the General Assembly of the United Nations. This important event, given the binding character of the Convention, refers to the growing consensus on recognition of the child as a bearer of rights.

Although this Convention is not concerned with the direct assignment of rights to the child, but rather with the duties of the States Parties with regard to the child, and although so-called protection rights are especially taken into account, some general human rights – and this is new – have been recognised. In this way, important basic rights are recognised, such as the right to freedom of expression, the right to legal aid, the right to information, the right to freedom of association and public meeting, the right to freedom of thought, liberty of conscience and religious liberty.[13] The discussion of the child's rights to self-determination is given forceful acknowledgment through these provisions.

Some recommendations of the Council of Europe can strikingly illustrate this recent turn. In 1979, for example, an initial impetus was given to a European Charter for Children's Rights. The basic principle was described as follows: 'Children must no longer be considered as parents' property, but must be recognised as individuals with their own rights and needs'.[14] Another recommendation invites the various member states 'to regard children no longer as subjects protected by law, but as persons holding legally recognised rights (. . .). Such an approach is consistent with the dignity of the person of the child and with the parents' role'.[15] A reflection on another recommendation starts: 'Considering that children have the same rights as all human beings . . .'.[16]

These numerous examples are a possible indication of an evolution in the interpretation of the children's legal capacity. Although legal capacity is the point of departure in law, also for minors, until recently only the protection rights were primarily taken into consideration. The image of the child as being almost exclusively in need of care was basic to this. At present it seems not only is the child stressed as an object of protection, but also the child as bearer of all basic human rights. Hence, the child is considered, to a greater extent and at an earlier stage, as a fully-fledged participant in society. At a recent UN congress (Eighth United Nations Congress on the Prevention of Crime and Treatment of Offenders – Havana, 27th August – 7th September 1990) the General Assembly adopted a resolution concerning the prevention of juvenile delinquency (Riyadh Guidelines). The starting point is the same: 'Young persons should have an active role and partnership within society and should not be considered as mere objects of socialising or control'. The pro-active point of departure is especially noteworthy: *in order that* young people should play an active role in society.

The recognition of human rights with regard to minors can also be found in the decisions and the jurisdiction of the European Commission and the European Court of Human Rights.[17]

In the decree, relating to Bouamar, of 29th February 1988, the Court condemns the Belgian State for successive placements of a minor in a house of detention (under Article 53 of the Belgian Youth Protection Act) by the juvenile court. Belgium is held to have violated Article 5 of the European Convention on Human Rights which states: 'All persons deprived of their liberty by arrest or detention have the right of a fair trial'.[18] In other words, this was a violation of the right of the arrested or imprisoned human being, including that of the minor, to have the legality of his detention checked by a court of justice within a short space of time.

In 1978 the Court pronounced a judgement concerning corporal punishment at school. A girl complained that she had been subjected to corporal punishment in school, which she considered a humiliating treatment or punishment contrary to Article 3 of the European Convention for the Protection of Human Rights and Fundamental Freedoms. During the investigation of the case by the European Commission, the British government was urged to start working on a law which would prohibit corporal punishment at school. This eventually happened some ten years later in Britain.

The Tyrer decree of 1978 only dealt with the individual consequences for the plaintiff. In 1986, however, the government was asked to adopt the legislation in question. The statement of P. Brenner, assistant secretary of the European Commission on Human Rights, provides a tentative but pointed conclusion: 'Seit bald 40 Jahren haben (also) eingerichteten Institutionen für den praktischen Schutz der Menschenrechte, darunter die Kinderrechte, in Europa gesorgt. Der Europarat beschäftigt sich mit diesen Fragen, damit die Geselschaft allgemein daraus ihre Gesetze weiterentwickeln order der internationalen Verpflichtungen anpassen können'.[19]

3.1.2. *The Child and Criminal Law*

The 'Eighth United Nations Congress on the Prevention of Crime and the Treatment of Offenders' unanimously adopted two new resolutions with regard to the approach of juvenile delinquency and of the juvenile delinquent. Together with the Beijing Rules adopted in 1985 and the UN Convention on the Rights of the Child, both resolutions constitute a 'Compendium of United Nations norms in prevention of delinquency, juvenile justice and the protection of the young'. Here again we find indications of a greater measure of respect for a fully-fledged legal position of children. In this way, Article 15.1 of the Beijing Rules states: 'Throughout the proceedings, the juvenile shall have the right to be represented by a legal adviser or to apply for free legal aid where there is provision for such aid in the country'. This is also found in the statements of the European Court of Human Rights, e.g. in the Bouamar case.

The 'United Nations Rules for the Protection of Juveniles Deprived of their Liberty' is one of the two resolutions which have been adopted by the UN congress mentioned above. The rules included in this resolution want on the one hand to avoid as far as possible the delinquent youth's deprivation of liberty and, on the other hand, to protect the rights of minors deprived of their liberty. Thus Article 12 prescribes: 'The deprivation of liberty should be effected in conditions and circumstances which ensure respect for the human rights of juveniles'. And in Article 13 we learn that 'Juveniles deprived of their liberty shall not for any reason related to their status be denied the civil, political, social or cultural rights . . .'.

3.1.3. *The Child and Civil Law*

3.1.3.1. *Maintenance Obligation.* In family law we also find signs of a full recognition of the child as a bearer of rights. Thus, several justices of the peace in Belgium have considered that the minor, as a result of the parents' maintenance obligation, has a subjective right to maintenance. Until recently, the minor needed a guardian to demand maintenance by legal process. Now, it is stated that, because of the personal character of that right, the minor himself can take action.[20] This implies the recognition of the child as bearer of a subjective right.

3.1.3.2. *Marriage.* Ever since the law on the reduction of the legal age of majority (19th January 1990, Belgian Statute Book, 30th January 1990), young people in Belgium are allowed to marry only from the age of 18. The amended Article 145 of the Civil Code prescribes, however, that the juvenile court can grant exceptions to this requirement for significant reasons. It is, however, also important in this case that the minor himself can start the procedure, if his/her parents do not agree with the marriage.

3.1.4. *The Child and Social Basic Rights*

3.1.4.1. *Social Services to Children.* Social services to children have almost exclusively become a grant and a concern of special youth care. In fact, this obliges children and young people to raise their problems by means of judicial avenues: Juvenile Court, or semi-judicial, Youth Protection Committee – Committee for Special Youth Care. Nevertheless, Article 1 of the Law on Public Welfare Centres (8th July 1976) states that: '*Every* person has the right to social service and that its purpose is to offer everyone the possibility to lead a life which corresponds to the human dignity'. The right to social services belongs to everyone (each person), and hence to the minor as well. Discrimination on grounds of age is excluded. In order to confirm this principle a decree of the Council of State was required.

3.1.4.2. *Health Care.* In the Netherlands, a discussion was quite recently opened as to whether or not euthanasia should be legalised. Special attention was devoted to the situation of minors. The authoritative State Commission which studied this issue, defends the principle that the right to euthanasia cannot be dependent on an age limit. It is not that the child's age should be decisive but rather its insight into the cause of the disease and into the scope of its demand for the ending of life.[21] The State Commission relied for this matter on the advice of the authoritative National Health Council which prohibits medical treatment without the consent of the minor who is below the age of discretion.

Article 10 para. 2 of the Belgian Law on organ transplantation (Law of 13th June 1986, Belgian Statute Book 14th February 1987) determines that a person who is capable of expressing his intention has the right to oppose the removal of organs and tissues after his death. In answer to a parliamentary question the State Secretary of Public Health and Policy on Handicapped Persons specified that a minor from the age of 13 or 14 is capable of expressing his will and hence can express opposition.[22] In England and Québec a kind of 'medical majority' is established: an age which differs from the legal age and which gives the minor the right to express himself about the desirability of a medical treatment. In England this age is 16. The Family Law Reform Act of 1969 states: 'The consent of a minor who has attained the age of sixteen to any surgical, medical or dental treatment which, in the absence of consent, would constitute a trespass to his person, shall be as effective as it would be if he were of full age, and where a minor has by virtue of this section given an effective consent to any treatment it shall not be necessary to obtain any consent to it from his parent or guardian'.[23] In Québec a minor can consent to a medical intervention even from the age of 14. Article 42 of the 'Loi de la Protection de la Santé Publique' (1972) states: 'Un établissement ou un médecin peut fournir les soins ou traitements requis par l'état de santé d'un mineur d'âge de quatorze ans ou plus, avec le consentement de celui-ci, sans qu'il soit nécessaire d'obtenir le consentement du titulaire de l'autorité parentale, l'établissement ou le médecin doit toutefois avertir le titulaire de l'autorité parentale en cas d'hébergement de plus de douze heures ou de traitements prolongés'.[24]

Another example from health care can be found in a statement of the Dutch Central Medical Domestic Tribunal. In this statement the Tribunal confirmed that a 16-year-old patient could be discharged from hospital at her request and with the doctor's consent, even if the parents or those who exercise the parental authority were not informed about the discharge. The Tribunal based its decision on each person's right to physical integrity.[25]

3.1.4.3. *Education.* Article 28 of the UN Convention on the Rights of the Child recognises the children's right to education. Making primary education compulsory is only a means to meeting this right. Article 2 of the first additional protocol to the European Convention for the Protection of Human Rights and Fundamental Freedoms also guarantees the 'droit à l'instruction'. It is the parents' task to assure their children's education and the State, within its reach, has to support the parents. Agostinho dos Reis Monteiro concludes, from a study on this and many other national and international provisions to that effect, that 'l'enfant est devenu le sujet central du droit à l'education, la puissance et l'autorité cédant de plus à la responsabilité parentale. La famille et l'Etat ne sont partant que des sujets auxiliaries, intermédiaires, dépositaires, mandataires des enfants (. . .)'.[26]

In Belgium, by contrast, compulsory education is still the point of departure, and this until the age of 18, ever since the law of the 29th June 1983. However, in the initial government bill which provided for the extension of compulsory education, there was a departure from the right to basic education. This implied a fundamental change with regard to the first Belgian Compulsory Education Law (21st May 1914). Problems with regard to the enforceability of this right, in view of the minor's legal incapacity, made the legislator decide to use compulsory education as the point of departure. Nevertheless, the minor as a fully-fledged legal subject has gradually acquired importance in education in Belgium. This is, among other things, revealed in a recent study by State Councillor Paul Martens.[27] In his introduction, Martens quotes three reasons which, according to him, could explain the fragmentation 'de la résistance qu'on oppose l'école au droit'. The changing image of the child, which we have cited, can partly fill in what Martens indicates as 'l'évolution des mentalités'.

3.2. *The Child's Capacity to Implement His/Her Rights*

3.2.1. *Minority – Parental Authority: Legal Incapacity as Point of Departure*
In Western countries minority is synonymous with legal incapacity. In other words, even if the minor is seen as a bearer of rights, he is not considered to be capable of asserting these rights independently. It is the parental authority which has to implement the child's rights. Hence, parental authority and minority constitute two complementary, legal concepts. However, this construction often prevents the real (re)assessment of the youth's position in society. One can for example refer to the advice of the Belgian Council of State, Department of Legislation, with regard to the law on the extension of compulsory education (1983).[28]

The text reads: 'Every young person has, from the school year which starts in the civil year in which he becomes six, the right to basic education during twelve successive years. Basic education contributes on the one hand to his upbringing to the personal, familial and social life, and on the other hand to an appropriate training to practise a profession. Consequently, the parents or those who have charge of the young person should see to it that the young person . . .'.

The following remarks can be made about this text. The text is rather laborious because it starts the description of compulsory education with the right to basic education with regard to the young person, while, from the civil law rules concerning legal capacity and from the further description of compulsory education, it follows that the right to basic education in question cannot be enforced but by and against the parents or the persons who 'have charge of the young person'. In other words, the person who has to assert the minor's right is at the same time the person against whom this right has to be claimed. To avoid this situation, it seems preferable, for reasons of simplicity and in view of the purpose of the draft, to restrict the description of compulsory education to the determination of the duties which compulsory education includes.

3.2.2. *The Minor's (Conditional) Legal Capacity*

Nevertheless, two recent decrees of the Council of State prove that there are indeed changes with regard to the minor's legal incapacity. I will discuss in detail the first Decree concerning the access to the Public Welfare Centre because it is a fine illustration. In its Decree No. 30.985 of 19th October 1988 the Belgian Council of State states that:

> *Considering* Article 1 of the law of 8th July 1976 which recognises every person's right to social service: In view of Article 1 of the law of 8th July 1976 which states that: '*Every person* has the right to social service. Its purpose is to offer everyone the possibility to live a life which corresponds to the human dignity'.
> *That* Article 57 of the same law charges the Public Welfare Centre with the task to guarantee social service to persons and families.
> *That* Article 71 states in the first paragraph that 'everyone can appeal against a decision concerning individual assistance taken by the Council of the Public Welfare Centre or by one of the organs to which the Council has handed over powers'.
> *Taking into consideration*
> *That* from these provisions follows that the right to social service can be asserted by everyone who is destitute and consequently is not capable of living a life which corresponds to the human dignity.
> *That* this right *also belongs to the minor personally*, who, with or without good reason, has left his parental home and who finds himself destitute.
> *That*, although in principle this right is asserted in the minor's name by his legal representatives, *the minor's legal capacity has to be recognised in order to assert independently his right to social service, when his legal representatives do not do it for him.*[29]

More recently, in another decree of the Belgian Council of State, we find a similar argumentation in the admittance of a complaint from a minor concerning his exclusion from a secondary school. In this decree, there is still more to be found: *the condition, that the legal representatives should first have refused to assert the right in the minor's name, is counteracted.*[30]

3.2.3. *Some Other Recent and Striking Examples*

At the European Court of Human Rights, too, it seems that the reversal of the principle of legal incapacity is no longer so very strange. In this way the Court allowed a complaint of a 14-year-old minor girl who was obliged to return home after she had 'disappeared' with her boyfriend for a couple of days.[31] There is another indication in the UN Convention. Article 12 of this states:

> States Parties shall assure to the child who is capable of forming his or her own views the right to those views freely in all matters affecting the child (. . .) For this purpose, the child shall in particular be provided the opportunity to be heard in any judicial and administrative proceedings affecting the child (. . .).

Familial and even some parental matters, e.g. a divorce, also concern children. However, if we were to look at the different divorce laws and proceedings in European countries we would have to conclude the opposite.[32] A study concerning the Belgian situation reveals that no text of a law obliges a judge to hear a child. And, in spite of the fact that one notices a tendency in jurisdiction to take the child's opinion increasingly into account, the child has no guarantee at all that it is taken into consideration, as Article 12 of the Convention requires.

A similar criticism can be made about English law. The judge freely determines whether or not he wants to hear the child. For that matter, it seems that English judges do not consider the compulsory hearing of minors advisable.[33] In the German Federal Republic, by contrast, 'das Gesetz zur Neuregelung des Rechts der Elterlichen Sorge' (1979) obliges the judge to hear the children concerned from the age of 14.

Recent legislation in the Netherlands (1982) and in France (1987) also deals with this obligation from the ages of 12 and 13 respectively.

But and this is odd – in these countries there is no law which states that the judge also has to take the minor's opinion into account. There is no sanction provided in the law with regard to the disregarding of this opinion. Moreover, the child, once heard, has no possibility of questioning the decision taken.[34]

Some propose that the only solution to this problem is to give the child full status in litigation.[35]

The recent evolution of the obligation to hear the child (and even the demand to make it a party by right) is strengthened in jurisdiction in which the tendency is noticeable to consider the child of legal capacity when its subjective rights are in danger. I again refer to what has been mentioned above, namely that in Belgium more and more Justices of the Peace allow complaints by minors concerning maintenance. A quotation from a judgement of the Justice of the Peace Court in Mons is very illustrative of this: '. . . que l'incapacité du mineur est une mesure de protection et non une sanction à son regard, que la demanderesse ne saurait être d'aucune manière lésée par l'action qu'elle a intentée cette dernière révélant au contraire par ailleurs sa parfaite maturité'.[36]

There is similar argumentation in a decree by the Court of Amsterdam. A request of a minor girl was allowed because her (subjective) right to freedom and security was endangered by her father and the protection of this right is guaranteed for everyone. The girl's legal incapacity was not taken into account as she was considered to have passed the age of discretion, and hence one could conclude that she could personally decide about the opportunity of the proceedings to be followed.[37] The child's incapacity remains, however, the rule, in family law, too. However, to consider the child as indeed having a legal capacity occurs more frequently. Two provisions included in the Belgian law which recently reduced the legal age to 18 can further confirm this. The minor who is 15 and who has no parents, can ask the Justice of the Peace to convene the family council to confer about his emancipation (amended Article 479 of the Civil Code) before the age of 18. Ever since the law on the reduction of the legal age (19th January 1990, Belgian State Book 30th January 1990) young people in Belgium can only marry at 18. The amended Article 145 of the Civil Code prescribes, however, that the Juvenile Court can grant exemption from this age requirement for significant reasons. It is also important, however, that the minor himself can start the procedure, if his parents do not agree with the marriage.

Article 30 para. 2 of the law which from now on regulates the protection of the mentally ill person in Belgium prescribes that '. . . the ill person, *even if he is a minor*, (. . .) (can) lodge an appeal against the judgements pronounced by the justice of the peace with enforcement of this law'.[38] In the parliamentary discussion the question was put forward as to why it was necessary to add the words 'even if a minor'. The answer of the Government confirms the conclusions already mentioned above: the addition is necessary as it is a deviation from common law. It is sensible because it concerns a right which is proper to the person and aimed at his/her special protection.

A final example with regard to the minor's capacity can be found in the jurisdiction of the European Commission of Human Rights. The Commission was called on in a case in which a 12-year-old complained he was illegally detained in a psychiatric hospital, in spite of the mother's consent. The decision of the Commission reads:

> Etant donné qu'il s'agissait d'un enfant de douze ans normallement développé, capable de comprendre sa situation et d'exprimer clairement son opinion (. . .), le consentement de la même n'était pas déterminant.

4. CONCLUSION

This short investigation has demonstrated that within the law there has indeed occurred a change in the image of the child during recent decades. All the more because this analysis was concentrated on two fundamental aspects of the present discussion: the child as fully-fledged bearer of rights (not only children's rights, but also basic rights); and the child being capable of implementing these rights personally. Thus, a more profound respect for children seems to be mainifesting itself.

At the same time, one may wonder whether the observed evolutions in law do not rather follow the macro-social changes, rather than preceeding or bringing them about. The law, in other words, has been reactive. Would it not be more desirable that the law should play a more active role so that these changes to a more humane and respectful relationship with children should take place?[39] There are indications that this is going to happen.

We can also see a gradual transition from a defensive application to a more offensive one with regard to human rights in general, with the law taking a more pro-active role. We are also witnessing a law without borders. The problems with which children come into contact are macro-socially embedded. Why not look for instruments which can intervene at this level? The entrance into force on 2nd September of the UN Convention on the Rights of the Child is one such. And it is already having superfast consequences. Recently, on the 1st February 1990, a Recommendation was adopted by the Parliamentary Assembly of the Council of Europe, which conduces to the development of an additional protocol to the European Convention for the Protection of Human Rights and Fundamental Freedoms concerning the rights of the child, in order to complement the UN Convention. This would be a milestone because, in that case, the rather weak mechanism of monitoring of the UN Convention would be complemented by the stronger, far more compelling monitoring via the European Commission and Court of Human Rights in Strasbourg.[40] At the same time, this recommendation insists that not only political and civil rights but also economic and social ones should be included in the protocol to be prepared.

And there is still more to come. At the 25th session of the Permanent Conference of the local and regional European governments of the Council of Europe, which was held from 6th – 8th March, 1990, a draft resolution was discussed which had already been adopted unanimously by the Commission for Cultural and Social Affairs on 11th January 1990. This draft resolution seeks to encourage the active participation of young persons in their local and regional environment, by developing a charter to that effect.[41] Hence, indications that policy makers are pushing in the direction of a pro-active policy. And they do not lack forceful moral support. The World Summit of political leaders in New York on 29th and 30th September 1990, whose theme was children's rights, is perhaps the peak of the efforts which are made to recognise the child again as a fully-fledged partner in society. The image of the child continues to change – and change rapidly.

NOTES

1. Council of Europe, Parliamentary Assembly, *Report on the Rights of Children*, Doc. 6142, November 6th, 1989, p. 13. A similar oboservation is also included in a quotation from the report which J. P. Rosenczveig published for the benefit of the Conseil d'Etat français on the 7th October 1988: 'dans nos moeurs, l'enfant est d'abord la chose de ses parents et donc de sa famille'; 'dans un pays comme le nôtre, dans cette fin du 20ième siècle, force est de constater que le statut fait à l'enfant souffre limites et contradictions'.
   J. P. Rosenczveig, 'Le Statut Juridique de l'Enfant. Etat et perspectives', In: *Journal du Droit des Jeunes* 9 (1988), pp. 19–22.
2. For a detailed reflection on the historical evolution of the image of the child and the motives through which the present image of the child is put forward as problematical, we would like to refer to : E. Verhellen, 'Naar een Snel Veranderend Kindbeeld?' in, H. Cammaer, E. Verhellen (eds.), *Onmondig en Onvolwassen*, Leuven, Acco (1990).
3. In the period 1984–1989, no fewer than 14 judgements concerning the application of the European Convention for the protection of Human Rights and Fundamental Freedoms with regard to minors were passed at the European Court of Human Rights in Strasbourg. This is remarkable as only five cases with regard to minors were tried in the period 1976 to 1984.
4. UN Convention on the Rights of the Child, adopted New York, November 20, 1989. Conseil de l'Europe, *Projet de Recommandation*, Assemblée parlementaire, Document 6142, 6 novembre 1989, p. iii. P. Boucaud, *Le Conseil de l'Europe et la Protection de l'Enfant, l'Opportunité d'une Convention Européene des Droits de l'Enfant*, Conseil de l'Europe, Strasbourg, 1989.
5. J. McMurtry, 'The Case of Children's Liberation', *Interchange on Educational Policy* 10(3) (1979–1980), pp. 10–28. P. Wald, 'Making Sense out of the Rights of Youth', in: *Welfare* 55(6) (1976), pp. 379–393.
6. Hence, this implies the introduction of the concept 'human rights'. See in this respect e.g.: M. De Langen, J. Sassenburg, 'De Betekenis van Mensenrechten voor Kinderen', *Mensenrechten en Personen- en Familierecht*, Stichting NJCM-Boekerij, Leiden, 1986, pp. 37–62.
7. We point out again that the Universal Declaration of Human Rights under the various criteria, which should not cause discrimination, does not mention the criterion 'age'.
8. E. Boulding, *Children's Rights and the Wheel of Life*, Transaction Books, New Brunswick (1979); E. Boulding, 'Children's Rights', *Society* 15(1) (1977), pp. 39–43; B. Franklin, *Ageïsm and the Political Economy of Childhood*, Studie- en Documentatiecentrum voor Rechten van Kinderen, Cahier (6) R.U. Gent (1989).
9. For an introduction to this (counter-)argument and relevant bibliography, see E. Verhellen, 'Jeugdbescherming en jeugdbeschermingsrecht', op. cit., pp. 362–365.
10. This can be noticed *inter alia* in the motivation to the new 'law on reduction of the legal age' of 19th January 1990 (Belgian Statute Book 30th January 1990), p. 1239–1243.
11. This view is especially found in the Anglo-Saxon School Movement. See *inter alia* P. Adams, *et al.*, *Children's Rights. Towards the Liberation of the Child*, Praeger, New York (1972); H. Cohen, *Equal Rights for Children*, Littlefield, Adams & Co, Towota (1980); R. Farson, *Birth-Rights*, Penguin, Harmondsworth (1974); P. Goodman, *Growing up Absurd*, Random House, New York (1960); D. Gottlieb (ed.), *Children's Liberation*, Englewood Cliffs, Prentice Hall (1973); B. Gross, R. Gross (eds.), *The Children's Rights Movement*, Anchor Press, New York (1977); J. Holt, *Escape from Childhood*, Penguin, Harmondsworth (1975).
12. P. De Loof, 'Naar een Nieuwe Rechtspositie', in: *Verslag Studiedag 'Meer Rechten Voor Jongeren'*, Brussel (1984); L. De Witte, 'Grotere Zelfstandigheid voor Jongeren', *Eindverslag van de Werkgroep Jeugdbescherming*, SEVI, Brussel (1984); C. Ross, 'Of Children and Liberty: An Historian's View', *American Journal of Orthopsychiatry* 52(3)

(1982), pp. 470–480; E. Verhellen, *Jeugdbescherming en Jeugdbeschermingsrecht*, Kluwer, Antwerpen (1988); V. Worsfold, 'A Philosophical Justification for Children's Rights', *Harvard Educational Review* 44(1) (1974), pp. 142–157; J. Rawls, *A Theory of Justice*, Oxford University Press (1972).

13. See *inter alia* the Articles 12, 13, 14, 15, 17, 26.
14. Council of Europe, Parliamentary Assembly, 31st ordinary session: Recommendation 874 (1979) on a European Charter of the Rights of the Child.
15. Recommendation R(84) 4 on Parental Responsibilities.
16. Council of Europe, Parliamentary Assembly, 39th ordinary session. Recommendation 1065 (1987) (on the traffic in children and other forms of child exploitation).
17. United Nations guidelines for the prevention of juvenile delinquency (Riyadh guidelines) adopted by the 8th United Nations Congress on the Prevention of Crime and the Treatment of Offenders (Cuba, Havana, 27th August–7th September 1990).
18. For a very detailed study to that effect we refer to M. Buquicchio-De Boer, 'Les Enfants et la Convention Européenne des Droits de l'Homme', *Journal du Droit des Jeunes* 6 (1990), pp. 3–12.
19. Cour Européenne de Droits de l'Homme, 29 février 1988, Arrêt 22/86/120/169.
20. European Commission of Human Rights, Application nr. 9471/81, Report of the Commission adopted on 18 July 1986. European Convention for the Protection of Human Rights and Fundamental Freedoms, decree Tyrer, dd. 25th April 1977.
21. P. Brenner, 'Kinderrechte International', *Kinderschutz Aktuell* 3 (1988), pp. 22–23.
22. Vred. Sint Gillis, 23.04.1985, T. Vred. (1987), p. 21. Vred. Etterbeek, 29.03.1988, RTDF, 1988, p. 563.
23. *Rapport van de Staatscommissie Euthanasie*, Staatsuitgeverij, Den Haag (1985), pp. 87–98.
24. Quoted in T. Vansweevelt, 'Persoonlijkheidsrechten van Minderjarigen en Grenzen van het Ouderlijk Gezatg: de Toestemming van de Minderjarige in de Medische Behandeling', *Rechtskundig Weekblad* 27 (1987–1988), p. 904.
25. T. Vansweevelt, 'Persoonlijkheidsrechten . . .', op. cit., p. 903, note 41.
26. T. Vansweevelt, 'Persoonlijkheidsrechten . . .', op. cit., p. 903, note 42.
27. T. Vansweevelt, 'Persoonlijkheidsrechten . . .', op. cit., p. 903.
28. A. dos Reis Monteiro, 'Vers un Nouveau Droit à l'éducation'. Communication au Colloque 'Droits de l'Enfant, Droit à l'Enfance en Europe', Organisé par Medel et l'Idef, les 23 et 24 mars 1990 à Strasbourg, p. 11.
29. P. Martens 'Les Droits de l'Homme: à l'école Aussi?' Bruxelles, Centre des Facultés Universitaires Catholiques pour le Recyclage en Droit (1989).
30. Printed Documents, House of Commons, Session 1982–1983, Document n° 645/1, pp. 16–17.
31. Decree n° 30.985 of the Council of State, dd. 19 October 1988, published in Dutch translation, Panopticon 10 (1989), pp. 302–305.
32. Arrêt de Conseil d'Etat, n° 32054 du 22 février 1989, geciteerd, *Jurisprudence de Liège, Mons et Bruxelles* (1989), p. 826. Moreover, the decree specifies that an exclusion from school implies a violation of hte right to education (given Art. 2 of the Additional Protocol to the European Convention for the Protection of Human Rights and Fundamental Freedoms).
33. Cour Européenne des Droits de l'Homme, 11 décembre 1974, Requêtte nr. 6753/74. See also: *Le Journal du Droit des Jeunes* 7 (1989), p. 5. See also M. Buquicchio *La Protection des Droits de l'Enfant*, Conseil de l'Europe, CDDH 87.29 F.
34. J. Gerlo, A. Wylleman, 'Gehoord . . . en daarmee is de kous af' in E. Verhellen, F. Spiesschaert, L. Cattrijsse (eds.), op. cit., pp. 231ff.
35. J. Gerlo, A. Wylleman, op. cit., p. 240.
36. M. De Langen, *Verplicht Kinderen Horen*, N.J.B. (1982), p. 933.
37. C. Maes, 'Eugenetische Benadering van het Zogenaamde Bezoekrecht', *Panopticon* 10(2) (1988), pp. 175ff; A. Wylleman, 'De Procesbekwaamheid van de Minderjarige. Actuele Tendenzen', in E. Verhellen, F. Spiesschaert, L. Cattrijsse (eds.), op. cit., pp. 249ff.
38. Jugement de la Justice de Paix de Mons du 19 avril 1989, *Journal du Droit des Jeunes* 6(1989), pp. 34–35.

39. Judgement of the Court of Justice in Amsterdam, Vacation Court of 13th July 1989, in the case with number 1408/88 KG.
40. Law of 29th June 1990 (Belgian Statute Book 27th July 1990).
41. 'Le droit, par les normes qu'il affichera, peut jouer un rôle indispensable dans le changement du regard que notre société porte sur l'enfant'. J. P. Rosenczveig, 'Le statut juridique de l'enfant. Etat et Perspectives', *Journal du Droit des Jeunes* 9 (1988), p. 17.
42. Conseil de l'Europe, 'Recommandation 1121 (1990) relative aux droits des enfants', Assemblée parlementaire, 1 févriér 1990, p. 3. Due to this, one opted for the additional protocol to the detriment of a separate European Convention (cf. note 3).
43. Conseil de l'Europe, *Rapport sur les Politiques de Jeunesse des Municipalités et des Régions*, Projet de Résolution, Conférence permanente des pouvoirs locaux et régionaux de l'Europe, 25e session, 6–8 mars 1990.

DAVID JOHNSON*

8. Cultural and Regional Pluralism in the Drafting of the UN Convention on the Rights of the Child

INTRODUCTION

In 1988, work on the latest United Nations human rights convention, the draft Convention on the Rights of the Child, was completed. The new international legal instrument is the product of 10 years of negotiation among government delegations, inter-governmental organizations and non-governmental organizations (NGOs) from every part of the world. All provisions had to be adopted by consensus, meaning that at any time a single determined delegation could effectively exercise a veto power over a proposal. In spite of this constraint, the draft convention was not only completed by its target date – 1988, so that it would be adopted by the UN General Assembly in 1989, the 10th anniversary of the International Year of the Child and the 30th anniversary of the UN Declaration on the Rights of the Child but it was reviewed and readopted in its entirety at the Second Reading held November 28th to December 9th, 1988.

The Second Reading was tantamount to a test on the impact of cross-cultural factors in setting international human rights norms. Over the course of 22 meetings, differences arising from cultural, regional, religious, or socio-economic cleavages were salient in the debate over only five issue areas: freedom of religion, inter-country adoption, rights of the unborn, traditional practices harmful to children and the duties of children toward their parents. What follows is a detailed examination of how each of these issues were resolved.

BACKGROUND: MEMBERSHIP IN THE WORKING GROUP

Because the Working Group on the Draft Convention is itself an auxiliary body of the United Nations Commission for Human Rights, its membership parallels the membership of the Commission. Since 1980, the size of the

* United Nations Center for Human Rights in Geneva, Switzerland.

M. Freeman and P. Veerman (eds.), The Ideologies of Children's Rights, 95–114.

Commission has been set at 43 seats which are apportioned to the five regional caucuses as follows:
- 10 seats for the West (Western Europe, US, Canada, Australia and New Zealand)
- 5 seats for the East (the Soviet Union and Socialist Eastern Europe)
- 11 seats for Africa
- 9 seats for Asia
- 8 seats for Latin America

Within the fixed numerical limits of these caucuses, membership may rotate among States so that at any time there is a large number of observers to the Commission. In practice, any State that is interested may participate in the Working Group even if that State is neither a member of nor an observer to the Commission for Human Rights. Delegations with observer status are free to take the floor and make submissions, just as full members of the Commission may, but they cannot vote. However, the Working Group has never in its ten-year history had a recourse to voting, since all decisions are reached by consensus. This means that there is no practical distinction whatsoever between those States delegations that are members of the Working Group and those States delegations that are observers to the proceedings. The Working Group is, after all, 'open-ended' by definition, and seeks the active participation of as many States as possible in the drafting process. The more that the Convention reflects the views and participation of a wide spectrum of States, the more likely it is that the Convention will attract broad support and be ratified by a large number of States. This is, after all, one of the most important measures of success for any international convention.

The number of States that have participated in the Working Group has increased steadily and substantially since 1981, the first year that official attendance records were kept. Table 1 shows the numbers of participating States by caucus since 1981.

Table 1. Number of States Participating in the Draft Convention

Caucus	1981	1982	1983	1984	1985	1986	1987	1988	SR
West	14	13	15	16	18	16	17	17	19
East	5	6	4	6	6	5	5	6	6
Asia	3	4	6	6	7	7	9	10	15
Africa	3	1	3	1	7	4	3	7	9
Latin America	2	4	7	5	9	6	6	7	8
Total	27	28	35	34	47	38	40	47	57

(Source: Annual Reports of the Working Group, 1981–89)

Table 1 overstates the actual participation of States insofar as delegations that participated in only a single day of the proceedings (when, for example, an issue of particular interest to them was considered) are counted. About

16 of the 57 government delegations that attended the Second Reading were present during two days or less of the 11-day proceedings.[1] Furthermore, it is impossible to tell from the attendance list the diplomatic rank of the representative and therefore his or her authority to take positions. The Federal Republic of Germany, for example, was represented for five years by a lower rank civil servant who was sent not so much to represent his government than merely to observe and report back to his government. Only in 1988 did the West German government finally send a representative of sufficient empowerment to speak for his or her government in the debate.[2]

Regardless of the actual level of participation, Table 1 shows that interest in the Convention has increased almost steadily each year and quite naturally peaked during the Second Reading when the Convention was reviewed in its entirety. Among the five regional caucuses, the Western delegations have shown the greatest interest in participating, comprising on an average over 40% of the States represented in the Working Group. The African nations, meanwhile, have shown the least interest in attending the sessions of the Working Group. Most of the African delegations that have participated in the Draft Convention have been from North Africa, an area racially and culturally distinct from the rest of the continent. In fairness to Third World nations – especially those from Sub-Saharan Africa – it should be pointed out that the interest that a State may have in the Convention is tempered by the financial resources available to send a representative. Staffing levels among the permanent missions to the United Nations in Geneva are naturally lower for the smaller and poorer nations of the world. Many countries, the nations of Sub-Saharan Africa foremost among them, simply cannot afford to participate in international fora at a level comparable to that of the Western nations. Interest and financial constraints are thus two key factors determining participation in the creation of new international norms.

BACKGROUND: PURPOSE OF THE SECOND READING

The purpose of the Second Reading was to review the draft convention in its entirety and to make any changes necessary so that it would be not only a consistent and coherent legal document but very importantly that it would not detract from existing norms in international law. The Second Reading also offered a final opportunity to settle contentious issues. By 1988 when it became apparent that the Convention was about to be concluded, many countries that had not extensively participated in the drafting seized the opportunity offered by the Second Reading to propose revisions that corresponded more to their cultural and legal perspectives. A two-week session was held in November–December 1988 to accomplish this. Although the review of the draft convention was, in the end, completed within the allotted time frame, there was not enough time remaining in the regular session for the Working Group to adopt its final report. Three days in mid-February 1989 were later set aside for this final act of the Working Group before its mandate expired.

Issue Area 1: Freedom of Thought, Conscience and Religion

Article 7 bis on freedom of thought, conscience and religion was identified early in the first day of the Second Reading as one of the five issue areas where consensus would be most difficult to achieve. Informal drafting groups of interested delegations were designated for each of these areas with the aim of completing a compromise text which would then be considered by the entire Working Group for adoption. The drafting groups for two of these issue areas were ultimately unable to arrive at a compromise text after more than a week of deliberations. The drafting group for Article 7 bis was one of them.

The drafting group on freedom of thought, conscience and religion consisted of the delegations of Bangladesh, China, Holy See, Italy, Mexico, Netherlands with Morocco as the coordinator. Additionally, a representative of the International Catholic Child Bureau, one of the more than 40 non-governmental organizations (NGOs) having consultative status with the UN Economic and Social Council which were participating in the drafting of the Convention, participated in the work of the drafting group.

The First Reading text of Article 7 bis that served as the basis of discussion for the drafting group was as follows:

1. The States Parties to the present Convention shall respect the right of the child to freedom of thought, conscience and religion.[3]
2. This right shall include in particular the freedom to have or adopt a religion or whatsoever belief of his choice and freedom, either individually or in community with others and in public or private, to manifest his religion or belief, subject only to such limitations as are prescribed by law and are necessary to protect public safety, order, health and morals, and the right to have access to education in the matter of religion or belief.[4]
3. The States Parties shall respect the rights and duties of the parents and, where applicable, legal guardians, to provide direction to the child in the exercise of his right in a manner consistent with the evolving capacities of the child.[5]
4. The States Parties shall equally respect the liberty of the child and his parents and, where applicable, legal guardians, to ensure the religious and moral education of the child in conformity with convictions of their choice.[6]

The article was originally proposed in 1983 by the United States, which has long been a leading advocate in international fora for freedom of religion. The second of the four paragraphs comprising the proposal, taken almost directly from the International Covenant on Civil and Political Rights (ICCPR) Article 18(2) is especially indicative to the importance accorded this individual right in the West:

2. The States Parties to the present Convention shall ensure that no child is subject to coercion which would impair his freedom to have or to adopt a religion or belief of his choice.[7]

This text was, of course, based on a formulation designed to limit the power of the State or any group in society to circumscribe the freedom of an individual. However, the Covenant was not designed in general to address the particular problems of children since Article 2(1), the Covenant's applicability clause, does not forbid discrimination on the basis of age. With regard to the right of freedom of religion, the Covenant did not frame that right in the context of the parents' right to raise the child in the religion or belief system of their choosing. Concern expressed by a number of Western delegations, especially Canada and the Holy See, over the parents' rights led to the inclusion of paragraphs 3 and 4 in the final version of the Article.

Although a number of Moslem delegations were present during the 1984 session of the Working Group[8], none of them blocked the adoption of the final version of the article by opposing consensus. In 1986 however, the representative of Bangladesh submitted the following comment on the article:

Article 7 bis appears to run counter to the major religious systems of the world and in particular to Islam. It appears to infringe upon the sanctioned practice of a child being reared in the religion of his parents. We believe that the Article as presently drafted will give rise to considerable difficulties in application . . .[9]

The following year, the Moroccan delegation added this comment to the record on Article 7 bis:

On the question of religion, the rule adopted in Moroccan legislation is that the child shall follow the religion of his father. In this case the child does not have to choose his religion, as the religion of the State is Islam. Islam guarantees freedom of worship to members of other faiths.[10]

Like the Covenant, the only possible limitation recognized by the article could be a restriction not on the right to *have* a particular religion but on the right to *manifest* it. From the Islamic perspective, Article 7 bis was unacceptable since it did not recognize the Koranic practice of forbidding the child the possibility of changing his or her religion. Consequently, a coalition of 10 Islamic delegations[11] formed by the time of the Second Reading to propose the following change in Article 7 bis:

Paragraphs 1 and 2 should be combined to read as follows: 'The States Parties to the present Convention shall respect the right of the child to freedom of thought, conscience and religion, as well as his right to have access to education in the matter of religion or belief, subject only to such limitations as are prescribed by national laws and legislation and are necessary to protect public safety, order, health and morals.'[12]

On the one hand, the Islamic States felt strongly that the injunction of the Koran proscribing the conversion of a Moslem child to another religion should not be compromised in international law. It was obvious from the outset of the Second Reading that the reformulation of Article 7 bis ranked very high on the agenda of these delegations. On the other hand, there were the concerns primarily of the Western States that freedom of religion should be absolutely protected against State encroachment. If the Islamic proposal were to be adopted, the power of the State would be extended well beyond that of limiting only the manifestation of religion. Freedom of religion is arguably a 'core' universal right, recognized not only in regional conventions such as the European Convention (Article 9) and the American Convention (Article 12), but most importantly in the ICCPR, the operative international standard in this area. Article 8 of the African Charter on Human and Peoples' Rights, the only binding regional human rights instrument having Islamic nations as States Parties, guarantees the 'free practice of religion' but qualifies the right as 'subject to law and order'. The conflict between regional values in the area of freedom of thought, conscience and religion is not so much whether the right exists but rather how far it extends. Debate over this issue narrowly avoided deadlock during the final day of the Second Reading.

The Moroccan delegate, acting as co-ordinator of the drafting group on Article 7 bis, introduced the following text to the Working Group on the final day of the Second Reading:

[1. The States Parties to the present Convention shall respect the right of the child to freedom of thought, conscience and religion].

2. The States shall respect the rights and duties of the parents and, when applicable legal guardians, to provide direction to the child in the exercise of his right in a manner consistent with the evolving capacities of the child.

3. The States Parties shall equally respect the liberty of the parents and when applicable, legal guardians, to ensure the religious and moral education of the child in conformity with their own conviction. [of their choice]

[4. Freedom to manifest one's religion or beliefs may be subject only to such limitations as are prescribed by law and are necessary to protect public safety, order, health or morals or the fundamental rights and freedoms of others.]

5. No restrictions may be placed on the exercise of these rights other than those imposed in conformity with [national] laws and legislation and which are necessary to protect public safety, order, health and morals. [and the fundamental rights and freedoms of others.][13]

The delegate of Morocco explained that consensus could not be reached in the drafting group and that the compromise text was bracketed as a result. This new text potentially represented a significant rollback from the version adopted at the First Reading. Gone was any reference to the freedom to adopt any religion of one's choosing; gone, in fact, was any indication of exactly what comprised freedom of thought, conscience and religion. While paragraph 1 established the freedom in the barest of terms, the subsequent four paragraphs went on to outline the kinds of limitations on the freedom that were permissible. The lowest common denominator of agreement over freedom of thought, conscience and religion had demonstrably fallen in the two decades since the drafting of the ICCPR. Those decades had, of course, witnessed the rise of dogmatic and generally intolerant religious fundamentalism in many parts of the world, particularly in many Islamic States.

The Chairman, noting that paragraph 2 of the compromise text was not bracketed, drew attention to the fact that it was the same as paragraph 3 of the First Reading text and quickly ushered it into adoption. The Finnish delegate took the floor shortly thereafter and declared that it was his delegation's understanding that paragraph 1 of Article 7 which established the child's right to free expression applied to all questions dealt with in Article 7 bis.

The Chairman then remarked that since there was 'only a very small difference' between paragraph 3 of the compromise text and paragraph 4 of the First Reading text, it should be easy to reach consensus. Despite these hopeful remarks, a very long debate followed, however, in which delegates were unable to resolve even the question of whether the First Reading text or the compromise text should be used as the basis of discussion.

One position, taken by the delegate of Libya, was that the right of a child to change religion (extended by the inclusion of the words 'of the child and' following 'liberty' in the First Reading text) stood in contradiction to the abilities of the child. He noted that children had neither political rights nor even the right to manage their own money since it was recognized that these matters required the maturity of an adult. The same was true, he said, for religious freedom. He went on to say that real religious freedom strictly means that there be no religious training at all for children, but that wouldn't be practical either. It was his delegation's position that Article 7 bis should consist only of paragraph 1 and paragraph 5 (without brackets) of the compromise text. If paragraph 3 were to be adopted, it should, he said, be taken from the compromise text and the bracketed words 'of their choice' should be deleted.

The opposing position, set out by Argentina, was that the omission of the reference to the liberty of the child in the matter of religious education detracted from existing international standards as contained in Article 18 of the ICCPR. Since the First Reading text followed the Covenant more closely than the compromise text, it was preferable, he said, to use it rather than working paper 68, the drafting group text, as the basis of discussion for Article 7 bis.

A succession of 30 government delegations took the floor to express their preference for the text to be used as the basis of discussion. On one side were 15 delegations that preferred the First Reading text: Argentina, the Holy See, the Federal Republic of Germany, Italy, Belgium, Netherlands, the United States, Venezuela, Brazil, Australia, Honduras, Spain, India, New Zealand and the German Democratic Republic. Most of the support for this position clearly came from the Western and Latin American caucuses. Opposed to them were fourteen delegations, predominantly Islamic, that preferred the compromise text: Libya, Kuwait, Egypt, Morocco, Japan, Senegal, Bangladesh, Iraq, Algeria, Jordan, China, Tunisia, the Soviet Union and Pakistan. Among these speakers, the delegate of Bangladesh declared his opposition to the 'unmitigated' right of children to change their religion. The Senegalese delegate pointed out that 'we should not de-stabilize the family structure' while the Soviet delegate reminded the Working Group that it was important to have the support of the Islamic countries for the Convention. The Chinese delegation declared that some restrictions on religion were necessary, noting that the incident of the Peoples' Temple of Jonestown showed that the unrestricted freedom of religion can be harmful. China therefore supported the Libyan proposal to adopt paragraphs 1 and 5 of the compromise text.

When the Chairman next spoke, it was to observe that despite the hour and half long discussion, no progress had been made toward the adoption of this article. He added that it would be no problem if the article were not included in the Convention. If the Working Group did want the article, however, he said that they had better discuss the text rather than their principles. He then proposed that paragraph 1, which was taken from the ICCPR be adopted. The Egyptian delegate then asked if it was paragraph 1 of the compromise of First Reading text that was to be considered. When the Chairman replied that it was a moot point since there was no difference between the two, the Egyptian delegate announced his opposition if it were not the compromise text that was under discussion; only that way would he be assured that paragraph 5 would be considered. When the Chairman remarked that further discussion on the article appeared to be futile, the Italian delegate expressed her opinion that a consensus would yet be found.

When the Libyan delegate proposed that paragraph 5 be joined to paragraph 1 to form a single paragraph, the delegate of the United States announced his opposition to the Libyan proposal on the grounds that paragraph 5 represented a major step backward from existing international standards. Explaining that States can place restrictions only on the right to 'manifest' one's religious beliefs, the Libyan formulation would extend the control of the State over the 'exercise' of one's beliefs. Worse yet, if paragraph 5 were to be joined to paragraph 1, the words 'these rights' would refer to 'the right to freedom of thought, conscience and religion' thus subjecting the exercise of all these rights to restriction by the State.

The Libyan proposal was supported by Morocco, while the United States position was supported by France and the delegate of India, who added that if he accepted the Libyan formulation, the many religious minorities in his country – in particular the Moslems – 'would feel very threatened'.

The Chairman then suggested that a formulation of Article 7 bis that would be acceptable to all delegations might consist of paragraph 2 (which was already adopted) along with paragraphs 1 and 4. That way, he explained, 'there would be no problem about changing religion and no threat to the family'. Nine delegations (India, France, Bulgaria, Australia, the Soviet Union, Kuwait,

Senegal, Finland and the United States) took the floor to support the Chairman's proposal and only one delegation (Brazil) opposed it. Most importantly, no objections were voiced by the Libyan, Egyptian or Moroccan delegations which had led the effort to rewrite Article 7 bis. The Chairman then declared that consensus had been reached and paragraphs 1 and 4 were then adopted. Both the Finnish and Swedish delegates (and later the delegates of Italy and the Holy See) then entered their understandings that nothing in the new text would detract from existing international standards.

The new article neither guarantees that there be no coercion in the exercise of thought, conscience and religion as the Western and Latin American delegations had wanted, but nor did it sanction the restriction of this right as the Islamic States had wanted. From the perspective of international law, half an article in this case may not be better than none at all since Article 7 bis, the latest expression of international consensus on the subject of freedom of religion, arguably marks a lowering of previously accepted standards. However, from the point of view of international politics, the fact that the Convention now reflects more of the concerns of the Islamic States removes a potential obstacle for its eventual ratification by these and other Third World nations. The goal of the drafting process was, after all, to codify the highest standard that could reasonably gain broad acceptance among all members of the United Nations. To achieve this goal, there may sometimes be a trade-off between setting high standards and gaining universal acceptance. A document written either with such impossibly high standards that only a handful of nations would ratify it or a universally ratified instrument with standards so low as to be relatively meaningless would mark the failure of the Working Group. A successful Convention, widely ratified yet having 'teeth', balances both of these concerns. Those numerous Islamic delegations who came to the Second Reading with Article 7 bis near the top of their agenda, were proof that human rights conventions are taken seriously by more than just the developed countries.

ISSUE AREA 2: INTER-COUNTRY ADOPTION

In 1982, the Working Group adopted the following text (Article 11) on adoption:

> 1. The States Parties to the present Convention shall undertake measures, where appropriate, to facilitate the process of adoption of the child. Adoption of a child shall be authorized only by competent authorities who determine, in accordance with applicable law and procedures, and on the basis of all pertinent and reliable information, that the adoption is permissible in view of the child's status concerning parents, relatives and guardians and that, if required, the appropriate persons concerned have given their informed consent to the adoption on the basis of such counselling as may be necessary.[14]

2. The States Parties to the present Convention shall take all appropriate measures to secure the best interests of the child who is the subject of intercountry adoption. States Parties shall ensure that placements are made by authorized agencies or appropriate persons under the adequate supervision of competent authorities, providing the same safeguards that are applied in exclusively domestic adoptions. The competent authorities shall make every possible effort to ensure the legal validity of the adoption in the countries involved. States Parties shall endeavor, where appropriate, to promote these objectives by entering into bilateral or multilateral agreements.[15]

The foregoing text was drafted largely by the Western delegations. Of the 27 paragraphs in the 1982 *Report* recording the drafting of the article, only two mention the participation of non-Western delegations (India and Argentina), neither of which was substantive. By the time of the Second Reading, a number of delegations from Latin America, Asia and Africa indicated that in their view Article 11 posed serious problems. The complaints of these delegations were generally either that the controls over intercountry adoption were inadequate or that adoption as an institution could not be recognized under Islamic law. The drafting group of interested delegations that was designated by the chairman to arrive at a compromise text for Article 11 and Article 10, dealing with the related issue of parentless children, contained no less than 13 government delegations, 6 of which were from regional caucuses other than the West.[16] The fact that the drafting group on Articles 10 and 11 was the largest drafting group and was nearly twice as big as the next largest group indicated the importance of the adoption issue.

The first indication that the text had been drafted too narrowly came in 1986 when Bangladesh appended a statement to the Working Group's annual report that Article 11 would create problems in Muslim countries since adoption was not a recognized institution under Muslim law. The statement went on to call for protection against adoption 'for reasons of proselytisation', adding that 'This kind of adoption has in the past created very serious problems and abuses in Bangladesh and other developing countries.'[17]

By the time of the Second Reading, the delegation of Libya had prepared a working paper for general distribution that explained how 'persons who believe in and observe the provisions of the Shari'a [Islamic law] cannot engage in the prohibited practice of adoption'.[18] Another working paper, submitted by a coalition of 10 Islamic States, proposed that both paragraphs of the first reading text be deleted and be replaced by the following single paragraph:

The States Parties to the present Convention shall endeavour, in accordance with their domestic laws and legislation, to provide an alternative family for a child who does not have a natural family.[19]

Obviously, the foregoing text was unacceptable since it contained no guidelines at all for either domestic or intercountry adoption. A solution that took into account the incompatibility of adoption with Islamic law while not diminishing the substance of the provisions had been, in fact, proposed by Libya in its working paper. That solution was simply to qualify the article at the outset as applying only to those countries that recognize the institution of adoption. This was the approach that was finally taken.

A much more difficult issue to deal with was to reconcile the effort of many Western delegations to strengthen international controls over intercountry adoption with the view of a number of Latin American delegations that were philosophically opposed to intercountry adoption in the first place. This latter attitude was evident in the proposal by Mexico to add the following sentence to paragraph 2 of the article:

> It would also be advisable for the adoptive parents to undertake to recognize the original nationality of the adopted child for a period of two years following the adoption and to offer facilities to enable consular officials of the country concerned to make any visits and prepare any reports that may be required.[20]

After more than a week of informal deliberations in which paragraph 2 of Article 11 dealing with intercountry adoption was significantly reformulated, a compromise text was proposed to the Working Group by the delegation of Egypt, acting as drafting group coordinator.[21] The new text reorganized the article into a chapeau and five subpargaraphs. Subparagraph (a), dealing with domestic adoption, was taken almost verbatim from paragraph 1 of the First Reading Text. A notable omission from the new formulation, however, was the passage calling on States Parties 'to facilitate the process of adoption'. In the subsequent four subparagraphs, many elements of the previous paragraph 2 had been incorporated with some new provisions. The compromise text contained two new statements of principles that had been absent in the First Reading text, namely that intercountry adoption should not be considered before other means of alternative care (subparagraph b) and should not result in improper financial gain for those involved in it (subparagraph d). The new text did not retain the passage in previous paragraph 2 calling on State Parties to 'make every possible effort to ensure the legal validity of adoption'. The effect of the compromise text was undeniably to raise new questions concerning intercountry adoptions.

Still, for some Latin American delegations the new text did not go far enough in providing restraints on intercountry adoptions. During the subsequent debate on Article 11, the delegate of Venezuela in particular expressed her reservations that the article as reformulated might 'open the door to exporting children' from one country to another. She declared that at least three of the four subparagraphs on intercountry adoption needed substantial revision. In an effort to allay at least one of her concerns the Egyptian delegate pointed out that sub-paragraph (b) prioritized intercountry adoption as a 'last resort'.

Six delegations subsequently took the floor to support the compromise text (sometimes with minor modifications) while three delegations (Brazil,

Honduras and Mexico) supported the Venezuelan call for a short postponement of the debate on Article 11. Efforts by the Chairman to continue debate despite the opposition of the four Latin American delegations proved to be futile.

When the debate on Article 11 continued later, the Venezuelan delegate argued that the text should reflect the principle that adoption should serve only the best interests of the child (as opposed to the convenience of the adoptive parents) and proposed that the word 'shall' be followed by 'apply only in the best interests of the child'. Attempts to compose a clear and grammatically correct sentence that would incorporate this idea into the chapeau were made by the delegations of Australia and the United Kingdom, as well as the Chairman before the Finnish delegate composed a wording that satisfied all criteria. The chapeau along with subparagraphs (a) and (b) were then adopted without opposition.

Only the delegate of Netherlands spoke in support of keeping the qualifier 'to the maximum extent possible' regarding governments' efforts to ensure that intercountry adoptions are as rigorously regulated as domestic adoptions. Otherwise, he said, impossible standards would be set. The final text of the article was a product of a concerted effort by the delegations of Canada, Australia, Egypt, France and Netherlands to find a clear and concise wording.

The full text of the article on adoption as finally adopted at the Second Reading was:

States Parties which recognize and/or permit the system of adoption shall ensure that the best interests of the child shall be the paramount consideration and they shall:
(a) ensure that the adoption of a child is authorized only by competent authorities who determine, in accordance with applicable law and procedures and on the basis of all pertinent and reliable information, that the adoption is permissable in view of the child's status concerning parents, relatives and legal guardians and that, if required, the persons concerned have given their informed consent to the adoption on the basis of such counselling as may be necessary;
(b) recognize that intercountry adoption may be considered as an alternative means of child's care, if the child cannot be placed in a foster or an adoptive family or cannot in any suitable manner be cared for in the child's country of origin;
(c) ensure that the child concerned by intercountry adoption enjoys safeguards and standards equivalent to those existing in the case of national adoption;
(d) take all appropriate measures to ensure that, in inter-country adoption, the placement does not result in improper financial gain for those involved in it;
(e) promote, where appropriate, the objectives of this article by considering bilateral or multilateral arrangements or agreements, and endeavour,

within this framework, to ensure that the placement of the child in another country is carried out by competent authorities or organs.[22]

This text was the subject of a number of understandings entered into the final report. The delegate of Japan declared that his government may need to enter a reservation on subparagraph (a) since, according to the civil code of Japan, consent of a court is not required in adoptions where juveniles are blood-relations of the adopting families. The Brazilian delegate declared her understanding of subparagraph (b) to mean that intercountry adoption will only be envisaged when all other alternative means of child care are exhausted.[23] The delegate of Venezuela, in a statement of substantial proportions, strongly protested that intercountry adoption has given rise to numerous abuses and should not have been discussed in the same article as domestic adoption. In particular, she criticized the language used in subparagraph (d) on the grounds that 'it was not possible to combat a market which obviously existed in the world and at the same time institutionalize that market by permitting persons dealing with intercountry adoption to make "financial gain"'.[24]

The Venezuelan delegate's view notwithstanding, Article 11 (new Article 21 after the renumbering) was substantially reformulated at the Second Reading to reflect the concerns of the Latin American delegations over the abuses of intercountry adoption. While it was obvious that no other delegation shared the depth of the Venezuelan delegate's misgivings over inter-country adoption, there was sufficient concern among the Latin American caucus that these delegations acted in concert to redirect the debate. As a result of these concerns and the requirements of the Islamic States that do not recognize the institution of adoption, Article 11 (new Article 21 after the renumbering) now reflects a much more broader approach to the subject of adoption than it did at the time it was originally drafted.

ISSUE AREA 3: RIGHTS OF THE UNBORN CHILD

The Declaration on the Rights of the Child, adopted by the United Nations General Assembly in 1959 (Resolution 1386 (XIV)) and considered for years as the most authoritative multilateral instrument on the subject of children's rights, recognized the claim of the unborn child to protection by virtue of the following preambular paragraph:

> Whereas the child, by reason of his physical and mental immaturity, needs special safeguards and care, including appropriate legal protection, before as well as after birth.

Nowhere within the subsequent text were the rights of the unborn either defined or further alluded. When work on the draft Convention began in 1979, the purpose of the new instrument was initially not to supplant but rather to supplement the existing Declaration.[25] To some members of the Working Group, it was important that the new convention reaffirm the claim of the unborn to protection and so a proposal was introduced in 1980 by the Holy See to add the words 'before as well as after birth' to the fifty preambular paragraph, as in the preamble of the 1959 Declaration. The issue proved to be considerably less amenable to consensus in 1980 than it was in 1959.

Those delegations that supported inclusion of the words argued that their national legislation contained provisions protecting the rights of the unborn child from the time of conception. They stated that the purpose of the amendment was not to preclude the possibility of abortion, since many countries had already adopted laws allowing abortion at least in some cases. Delegations that opposed the proposal maintained that the preambular paragraph should be neutral and should not prejudice the definition of the 'child' as contained in Article 1. Furthermore, they said, since national legislation differed greatly on the subject of abortion, the Convention should be neutral if it was to be ratified widely. The American delegate in particular argued that the draft Convention must be carefully worded in such a way that neither proponents nor opponents of abortion would be able to find legal support for their respective positions in the instrument.[26] At the meeting, this was the point of view that prevailed, and the Holy See's proposal was rejected.

Article 1, establishing the upper and lower age limits for defining a child, was likewise the subject of considerable debate. Once again, the discussion was divided between those who argued that childhood should begin "at the moment of conception" as defined in their national legislation and those who argued that any 'attempt to establish a beginning point should be abandoned and that wording should be adopted which was compatible with the wide variety of domestic legislation on this subject'.[27] Again, the latter was the viewpoint that prevailed and the article as adopted did not provide for the inclusion of the unborn in the Convention.

The subject of the rights of the unborn was by no means laid to rest, however. By the first day of the Second Reading, five different proposals had been officially submitted, each of which would in one way or another, include the unborn within the draft Convention. Senegal and Malta both submitted proposals to amend Article 1 to include 'from the moment of conception' in the definition of a child.[28] Three separate proposals were made to amend preambular paragraph 6 (formerly 5) to include 'from the moment of birth'.[29] The delegate of the Federal Republic of Germany, who by virtue of his tenacity and determination on this subject emerged as the leader of the fight for including the unborn in the preamble, vowed that this time 'the minority would not be rolled over'. He asserted his right both to call for a formal vote on the issue and to raise the issue again at any point during the Second Reading. Either threat, if carried out, would have deadlocked the proceedings.

During the course of the heated debate over the proposed preambular change, no less than 27 government delegations took the floor to express their position on the issue. The end result was evenly split: 13 delegations, generally either predominantly Catholic countries or countries where the social/political status of women is among the lowest in the world, favoured recognizing the rights of the unborn[30]; the 13 who were opposed were generally either predominantly Protestant northern countries or developing countries having strict national policies curbing overpopulation.[31] The debate at the Second Reading largely echoed what had been heard in previous years. Proponents of the amendment argued that all national legal systems provide some measure of protection to the unborn and that the draft Convention should not ignore this fact. Opponents of the proposal argued that an unborn child is not literally a person whose rights could already be protected. The main thrust of the convention, they maintained, was to protect children from birth onward. They also pointed out that the Declaration on the Rights of the Child was 30 years old and that there was no need to stick to all of its provisions.

The issue was resolved after an informal drafting group (consisting of the Netherlands, Ireland, Italy, Sweden, the US and Poland with the Federal Republic of Germany as co-ordinator) was designated by the Chairman to reach a compromise solution. By the following morning a solution was reached that was sufficiently satisfactory to all concerned. The provision inserting 'before as well as after birth' was included in the preamble after all. Any legal effect of the reference was tempered, however, by, the following statement that was entered into the *Travaux Préparatoires* as part of the compromise:

> In adopting this preambular paragraph, the Working Group does not intend to prejudice the interpretation of Article 1 or any other provision of the Convention by State Parties.[32]

The issue of the rights of the unborn child can be a very emotional one since it concerns the direct conflict of two fundamental rights – the right to life and the right to make decisions concerning one's body and health. In dealing with the issue, the Working Group was able to reach a much more mutually satisfactory compromise for the principal parties involved in the dispute than has thus far been the case in the domestic politics of many States around the world.

Issue Area 4: Traditional Practices

In 1987, the Working Group decided to consider for adoption a proposal submitted by Radda Barnen (Swedish Save the Children) on behalf of the NGO Ad Hoc of some 40 organizations participating in the drafting of the convention. The proposal read as follows:

> The States Parties to the present Convention shall seek to eradicate traditional practices harmful to the health of children and shall take all

appropriate action including necessary legislative, administrative, social and educational measures to ensure that children are not subjected to such practices.[33]

When the delegate of United Kingdom asked if female circumcision was included as an example of harmful traditional practices, the Senegalese delegate counselled prudence when dealing with issues that entailed differences in cultural values and emphasized the dangers of forcing practices into clandestinity if they were prohibited by States legislation. This advice notwithstanding the delegates of Canada, United Kingdom and the United States all proposed alternative formulations that would refer to female circumcision to indicate that this was the type of practice targeted by the proposed provision.

At that point in the debate, an African NGO (The International Movement for the Fraternal Union Among Races and Peoples) argued that the reference to female circumcision wasn't necessary, since there were other traditional practices harmful to children, such as son preference. The Canadian delegate then proposed that traditional practices be understood to mean all those practices outlined in the 1986 *Report of the Working Group on Traditional Practices affecting the Health of Women and Children*.[34] Japan, Sweden and Venezuela associated themselves with this understanding.

The Senegalese delegate again took the floor to express his objection to any wording that would include the words 'female circumcision'. The final wording adopted for the provision, which was subsequently included under the article on health (Article 24(3) after the Second Reading) was:

> States Parties shall take all effective and appropriate measures with a view to abolishing traditional practices prejudicial to the health of children.[35]

This wording of the provision presented no problem when it was considered for readoption at the Second Reading. The only objectionable element had understandably been the proposed reference to 'female circumcision' which would have had the effect of specifically targeting Africa when, as the study on son preference included in the 1986 Sub-commission report indicated, traditional practices harmful to the health of children were much more pervasive. In light of the discussion at the time this provision was adopted, there can be no doubt in the *Travaux Préparatoires* that the article was intended to include female circumcision. The provision, the only reference in a United Nations human rights treaty to traditional practices, stands as strong evidence of converging international opinion on fundamental human rights standards in areas highly colored by cultural values. Since the Sub-commission report first appeared in 1986, a special non-governmental organization dedicated to eradicate traditional practices that are harmful to women and children has been established in Africa and has grown to include affiliated sections in numerous African countries.

ISSUE AREA 5: DUTIES OF CHILDREN

During the first week of the Second Reading, Senegal introduced a proposal for a new article consisting of the following single sentence: 'The child has a duty to respect his parents and to give them assistance, in case of need.'[36] A similar provision appearing in the African Charter on Human and Peoples' Rights establishes the duty of the individual to 'respect his parents at all times [and] to maintain them in case of need.'[37]

Despite an appeal by the Senegalese delegation to accept 'this cultural value of Africa and Asia', more than two-thirds of the nearly 20 speakers who commented on the proposal in the ensuing debate were against it.[38] Among those opposing the proposal were the delegations of Australia and the United States, both of which declared that the obligation of a child toward his or her parents was unenforceable by the State and was therefore outside the purpose of an international convention. The delegate from the International Labor Organization agreed, adding that requiring a child to render assistance in the case of need was tantamount to a call for child labor. The delegate from Argentina pointed out the practical difficulty of requiring States to report on the implementation of such an article. The delegate of the United Nations Children's Fund (UNICEF) remarked that if this article were to be adopted, it would mark the first time that duties other than those of States would be enumerated in a UN international human rights instrument. He consequently cautioned delegates to 'tread warily before making extraordinary innovations'. Debate on the article ended when Senegal acceded to a suggestion by Canada that the Senegalese delegation join the drafting group on the article on 'Objectives of Education' to press its call for respect for parents there. Some days later, this was accomplished. Article 29(c), as adopted and renumbered at the Second Reading, now includes the Senegalese proposal in the following text:

> State Parties agree that the education of the child shall be directed to . . . the development of respect for the child's parents, his or her own cultural identity, . . . (etc.).

In this way, the legitimate concern of the African delegation was recognized and incorporated into the convention. The concern that was not defensible in international law and subsequently dropped, namely the proposed provision calling for children to support their parents if necessary, was clearly not congruent with either the purposes of the convention or current international norms on the subject of child labor. No one who spoke in favour of the proposal, not even the Senegalese delegation, attempted to defend this part of the provision.

CONCLUSIONS

In spite of Raimundo Panikkar's admonition that there is no universal concept of human rights[39], there have nonetheless been more than a score of international human rights conventions since the Declaration of Human Rights was adopted by the United Nations General Assembly in 1948. The two international covenants, one on Civil and Political Rights, the other on Economic, Social and Cultural Rights, have been ratified by about 90 of the 160 countries comprising the United Nations. Such broad support for international instruments that create obligations in international law for the States that sign them is compelling evidence that, despite their origins in Western political philosophy, human rights represent a cross-cultural consensus on fundamental human values.

The five issues discussed above – freedom of religion, international adoption, rights of the unborn, traditional practices and duties of children – each provided a test case for resolving conflicting cultural and religious perspectives. In each case, a compromise was found without eliminating the issue from the agenda. Compromises may be based on a minimal text (as in the case of freedom of religion), but more often the minority perspective was incorporated in some way into the final text. The result was a document that was arguably richer in values than if a narrower perspective had been more rigorously followed.

These five issue areas were the only cases during the two weeks of negotiations where factors other than strictly legal or political ones appeared to define the debate. Since the draft Convention is a considerably lengthy document – it contains, in addition to its preamble, 54 articles – it is perhaps remarkable that such a level of consensus was in fact reached on so many issues impinging on a culturally sensitive areas like family law. One explanation may be that cleavages in cultural perspectives may be less cross-national in character than rooted in socio-economic factors. This was found to be true in a recent study measuring cross-national differences in the attitudes of parents towards their children. In the study, parents were asked, among other things, why they wanted to have children. The responses showed that economic utility as a goal of child-bearing followed urban/rural cleavages among all countries more than cultural cleavages between countries.[40]

Another explanation may be that, cultural differences notwithstanding, there is after all an irreducible core of common experience and concern in all human lives. This may be especially true if human rights are thought of not in positive terms – i.e. what they might add to enrich the human experience – but rather in negative terms – i.e. that they attempt to curb pain and suffering. This idea was eloquently expressed by the noted human rights jurist Thomas Buergenthal when he said:

Of course there exists in various countries and regions of the world differences, distinctions and preferences in the application and definition of specific human rights and in their conceptual nuances. But when it comes to massive denials of the right to life, of the right not to be tortured, or of the rights to be protected against disappearance and against lengthy detention without trial, those nuances and differences are of no significance. Human tolerance for pain, suffering, hunger and oppression may be greater in one part of the world than in another, but victims of oppression and of human rights violations certainly do not enjoy their suffering any more than anyone else would.[41]

Whatever the underlying reason may be, cross-cultural barriers have not proven to be a significant impediment to achieving consensus over the need for setting international standards to protect the interests and well-being of children globally.

NOTES

1. Most of the States participating on such a limited basis were either Islamic delegations present only to discuss the Article on 'Freedom of Religion, Thought and Conscience', Western delegations present only to discuss the Article on 'Children in Armed Conflict', or Latin American delegations present only to discuss the Article on 'Adoption'.
2. Personal communication to the author by the West German representative at the Second Reading.
3. See 1984 *Report of the Working Group on the Question of a draft Convention on the Rights of the Child* (hereafter cited as *Report*), UN Doc. E/CN.4/1984/71, para. 23.
4. Ibid., para. 28.
5. Ibid., para. 30.
6. Ibid., para. 33.
7. See 1983 *Report*, UN Doc. E/CN.4/1983/62 at paragraph 52.
8. Algeria, Bangladesh, Iran, Morocco and Pakistan.
9. See 1986 *Report*, UN Doc. E/CN.4/1986/39; Annex IV, page 2.
10. See UN Doc. E/CN.4/1987/WG.1/WP. 35; p. 2.
11. Algeria, Egypt, Iraq, Jordan, Kuwait, Libya, Morocco, Oman, Pakistan and Tunisia.
12. See UN Doc. E/CN.4/1989/WG.1/WP.4.
13. UN Doc. E/CN.4/1989/WG.1/WP.68.
14. 1982 *Report*, UN Doc. E/1982/12/Add. 1, C, para. 76.
15. Ibid., para. 87.
16. Participating delegations were Argentina, Australia, Brazil, China, Egypt (co-ordinator), France, Italy, Netherlands, Pakistan, Portugal, Sweden, USSR, and United Kingdom.
17. See 1986 *Report,* UN Doc. E/CN.4/1986/39, Annex IV, page 2.
18. See UN Doc. E/CN.4/1989/WG.1/WP.3, page 2.
19. See UN Doc. E/CN.4/1989/WG.1/WP.4, p. 2.
20. See UN Doc. E/CN.4/1989/WG.1/WP.29.
21. See UN Doc. E/CN.4/WG.1/WP.62.
22. UN Doc. E/CN.4/1989/29, pp. 9–10.
23. See 1989 *Report*, UN Doc. E/CN.4/1989/48, p. 61.
24. See 1989 *Report*, UN Doc. E/CN.4/1989/48, paras. 728–9.
25. DCI/UNICEF Briefing Kit, *The Future United Nations Convention on the Rights of the Child* (1987), Document 2, p. 2.
26. 1980 *Report*, UN Doc. E/CN.4/L1542, paras. 5–19.

27. Ibid., para. 29.
28. UN Docs. E/CN.4/1989/WG.117 (Senegal) and E/CN.4/1989/WG.1/WP.9 (Malta).
29. UN Docs. E/CN.4/WG.1/WP.6 (Federal Republic of Germany), E/CN.4/WG.1/WP.8 (Holy See, Ireland, Malta and the Philippines) and E/CN.4/WG.1/WP.2, page 5 (proposal by UNESCO in the technical review).
30. Argentina, Austria, Colombia, Egypt, Germany (Federal Republic), Holy See, Italy, Jordan, Kuwait, Nepal, Philippines, Senegal, and Venezuela.
31. Australia, Canada, China, Denmark, Germany (Democratic Republic), India, Netherlands, New Zealand, Norway, Poland, Sweden, United States, and the USSR.
32. See 1989 *Report*, UN Doc. E/CN.4/1989/48, para. 43.
33. See 1987 *Report*, UN Doc. E/CN.4/1987/25, paras. 28–39.
34. UN Doc. E/CN.4/1986/42. Mrs. Halima Embarek Warzazi was the Chairman-Rapporteur for the UN Commission on Human Rights report.
35. See 1989 *Report*, UN Doc. E/CN.4/1989/48, para. 433.
36. UN Document E/CN.4/1988/WG.1/WP.17.
37. Article 29 (1).
38. Those supporting the Senegalese proposal were the Federal Republic of Germany, Libya, Ireland, Egypt and Bangladesh.
39. Panikkar, Raimundo 'Is the Notion of Human Rights a Western Concept?' *Diogenes*, No. 120 (1982), p. 82.
40. See Hoffman, Lois Wladis, 'Cross-Cultural Differences in Childrearing Goals', in R. LeVine, P. Miller and M. Maxwell West (eds.), *Parental Behavior in Diverse Societies*, San Francisco: Jossey-Bass Inc. (1988).
41. Buergenthal, Thomas 'International Human Rights: Past and Future, Failures and Accomplishments', in D. Johnson (ed.) *Internationalizing Human Rights*, SUNY-Buffalo; Baldy Center Occasional Papers (1989), p. 4.

COBY DE GRAEF*

9. Rights of Children in a Changing World

INTRODUCTION

In Holland, as in other postwar industrialized countries, a new concept of society began to emerge after a period of reconstruction, immediately following World War II. Reacting to the postwar period with its emphasis on the material welfare of society, the government began to emphasize a trend towards the spiritual and social well-being of the individual. This movement, in the 'sixties and 'seventies, was strongly characterized by the concept of 'equality' – equal chances for all in the areas of power, money, education and culture – and of personal development. Legislation was seen as an instrument for the modification of society. Youth, in particular, was the subject of this movement's attention and its accompanying governmental policy.

In this article the general reports and papers on youth policy will be discussed; the changing attitude towards youth is clearly recognizable from the successive governmental papers on youth policy. Only the papers in which a general view on dealing with youth has been articulated are the subject of research in this article. Specific fields of youth policy, such as education, labour and health care have been left out of consideration. The intention is to describe the general process of growth of 'youth policy', a name for the state's interference with youth, which was used for the first time in the 'sixties.

In this description the gradual extension of state interference during the years following World War II up to the present time forms the central point of attention. It is interesting to note that, in the official papers about youth policy, children are very rarely mentioned. The titles of these documents betray this: they are all named 'paper' or 'report' 'on youth policy'. Is this terminology significant for the way of looking at the 'not-yet-adult'? Are the youngsters getting this attention, because it is thought they ask for it and because their behaviour is worrying the adult? Policy, however – it's in the name – also means tact and prudence: something that the ones who are not yet youngsters also deserve. The title of this article speaks about the rights

* University of Amsterdam Faculty of Law.

M. Freeman and P. Veerman (eds.), The Ideologies of Children's Rights, 115–124.
© 1992 Kluwer Academic Publishers. Printed in the Netherlands.

of children, which means that all not-yet-adults, children and youngsters, are included as the subjects of rights. In the 'eighties one can notice a turning point in youth policy. Compared with the period of the 'sixties and 'seventies, state interference is becoming less pretentious. The lack of effectiveness of legal measures has doubtless contributed to a more realistic view of the role of the state. It turned out that an over-regulation of social life had even introduced a state of disorder. The ability of society to absorb legislation had been overstretched; it is no longer self evident that civilians will follow the rules. To counter this problem, the government has for some years been trying to deregulate, to decrease and simplify the state regulations.

As another negative, substantial effect of the growth of state interference one may mention the consequences for the possibilities for free development. Instead of the potential of the individual's development being enlarged, it was diminished. Governmental involvement in almost all social fields restricted the most important of human qualities, the possibility of self-realisation. This conflicts directly with human dignity and the integrity of body and soul, the very principles on which the classic rights of men are based.

This brings us to the conclusion that the state is not only not able but also not allowed to arrange the life of its citizens in the way it did during the postwar period. To live their lives everyone – adults and children – needs room to develop freely. In particular, children should have this room and the accompanying fundamental rights to realize their potential in a changing society.

CHARACTERISTIC OF THE PERIOD OF RECONSTRUCTION IN POSTWAR HOLLAND

The period immediately following World War II was dominated by the so-called restoration of society. Not only the material, but also the immaterial – that is the spiritual and mental state – in Holland after the war, was extremely disordered and confused. In her Speech from the Throne in 1946 to the members of the Dutch Parliament, the then Queen Wilhelmina presented the purpose of the activities of the government as: 'To establish a strong foundation for the steady restoration of our spiritual and material prosperity'.[1]

The establishment of a special Ministry of Public Affairs and Restoration clearly indicated the seriousness of the Dutch post-war situation from the material point of view. However, the spiritual and moral condition into which the people had drifted as a result of the war was perhaps even worse. The moral disorder after 1945 was acute. As a well-known Dutch professor of penal law, Pompe, has said: 'The people were used to following the example of the (German) occupiers, namely the example of robbery, violence and lying'.[2]

This general attitude of the occupying Germans also had another very important consequence: written law was no longer seen as the leading principle of right. The written laws issued by the German occupation government were so incompatible with the common concept of right that the people found themselves forced to follow their own judgement concerning these laws. This abuse of law by the occupation government, then, resulted in a more positive attitude on behalf of the people towards (unwritten) principles of law. In retrospect we can see this was a new development, because until then Dutch jurists had held a more legalistic view. As Pompe puts it: 'Previously, the principle of the written law dominated'.[3] In other areas, too, the war situation prompted a profound re-evaluation. For example, the Dutch educational system came to be seen as being too 'intellect'-oriented. The Dutch Minister of Education in exile pleaded for a more balanced education, which would particularly emphasise moral values. More specifically, he explained, because 'our people have had so many sorry experiences with so many men for whom only the intellect mattered'.[4]

During the war, the governmental organisation of education was changed radically. Instead of the former Ministry of Education, Arts and Sciences, the Department of Education, Science and the Protection of Culture was established. In addition to its responsibilities for education, this department was given the task of guiding the youth and caring for their 'cultural wellbeing'.[5] The granting of such responsibilities to this department reflected the national-socialist philosophy of education, that the state, and not the parents, played the primary role in youth guidance. Not much appears to be known about the influence of such an extension of the responsibilities of the government, but the statement Queen Wilhelmina made in her speech, that, in supporting the youth movement, the rights of the parents have to be respected, can be seen as a reaction to the Nazi philosophy.

Considering the poor situation during the war, both spiritually and materially, it is remarkable that so little attention was paid to the position of children after the war. Children raised during the war were affected permanently by their own direct war experiences, while those born after the war had to deal with their parents' experiences. During a visit to Holland immediately after the war, Simon Wiesenthal expressed his deep concern about children who had to grow up in the post-war world. With the pressing need for material reconstruction, there was insufficient time to work through the sufferings and to reflect on the traumatic past.

Only recently has a serious start been made on such reflection on the consequences of the war. The editors of a newly-published book, *Traces Everywhere*,[6] state that, in their judgement, research into the effects of the war in literature and other forms of art has hardly started. The educational specialist who contributed to this book deals with the relations between pedagogy and World War II, which he calls 'the great demasque of our western culture'. How is it possible, he asks, to raise children in a world in which humanity has been so severely afflicted and in a culture for which 'the moral base has disappeared?' The post war pedagogy, however, disregarded these basic feelings of despair and was mainly focused on the restoration of Dutch society. For that reason, this specialist criticises the view, represented by Langeveld, the 'father of Dutch post-war pedagogy'. He did not consider Langeveld's pedagogy, in which fundamental aspects of humanity formed the central theme of education, as responding strongly enough to the effects of the war. It ignored the question of the meaning of education 'in a culture in which the madness of World War II was possible'.[7]

However one views Langeveld's pedagogy in retrospect, the fact is that the youth rebelled increasingly against the conditions in which they had to grow up.

Youth Policy in the 'Fifties

Accordingly, government policy concerning youth was also gradually changed. The first reaction, immediately after the war, was a strictly repressive one. The youngers who rebelled against their situation and society in general, were seen as 'problem youth' – problems that had to be solved. An important figure in this field, Professor van der Leeuw, the then Minister of Education, Arts and Sciences, stressed the importance of educational training out of school.[8] He even argued for a compulsory provision of such training, because, he said, 'we can't close our eyes to the fact that precisely those youngsters who needed the voluntary training most, generally did not socialise'. In particular, he worried about the so-called 'mass youth' – the youth who 'for whatsoever reasons, with or without guilt, only know the law of self-interest and of unbridled egoism'. 'Here', he continued, 'only a very powerful effort on behalf of everyone involved in the training of youth, together with the state, can prevent disasters'.[9] To put his ideas into effect, a separate Directorate General was established by this minister, namely the D.G. 'Educational Training Out of School'. As early as 1946, with the fall of the cabinet to which van der Leeuw belonged, this D.G. was abolished; only a division called 'Educational Training Out of School' remained. The ideas of the socialist van der Leeuw did not agree with Catholic and Protestant views on the part that the state should play in education.[10] At this stage, however, it is worth taking note of this short-lived appearance of the ideas of van der Leeuw, as some of them reappear later.

Symptomatic of the general post war view of youth is a 1952 report commissioned by the Minister of Education, Arts and Sciences, with the significant title, *Social degeneration of the mass youth*.[11] The minister ordered a number of scientific institutes to investigate the origin of, and the possibilities of influencing, the mentality of the so-called mass youth. Langeveld, whom we have mentioned above, was the one who drafted the text of this report, and his ideas were easily recognizable in it; for example, the support of the individual's personal life. This was related to his theory of equivalence, which involved the acceptance of the differences between people.

The image of the youth given in this report was quite revealing of the government's attitude at this time. Concerning youth's behaviour and actions, the report says: 'they lean, hang and slouch, etc . . .'; and about their speech and articulation: 'they growl, roar, chatter, scream, yell, whimper and whine'.[12]

The report explicitly states that the degeneration of the youth is not limited to the 'proletarian youth', in contrast to the immediate postwar attitude.[13] It was no longer possible to isolate the problems of the youth to a relatively small group of 'asocials'; nor was it possible to identify the phenomenon of the 'degenerate youth' with that of (pre-)criminality.

'A characteristic of degenerate youth is the loss of a purpose in life', said the report (p. 23); 'they suffer from the loss of socially justified values, which loss is partly to be blamed on the negative tendencies in our society; for instance, during the years of German occupation'.

The measures suggested in the last chapter of the report were sympathetic, and, compared with the empty slogans of the following period of the 'sixties and 'seventies, refreshingly realistic. On the one hand, material measures were suggested, to create and supply better living conditions, particularly housing; on the other hand, pedagogical measures, explicitly focused on the parents. Parents, said the report, had to be better equipped for their task as educators.[14] In this report, too, school training was criticised as being too 'intellect-oriented': the children were only being trained to conduct themselves in society in an economic sense.

The role of the state was a limited one, said the report; the school and parental environment played a primary part in the fight against social degeneration of the youth. As the report said, 'one has to be aware that the juvenile work is only a way to improve the relations in the family'.[15]

YOUTH POLICY IN THE 'SIXTIES AND 'SEVENTIES

The image of youth still presented in the report of 1952 was to crack in the late '50s. The fact that the phenomenon of the 'problem youth' was not limited to the lower social classes only, doubtless contributed to a change in attitude towards the rebellious youngsters. It was time not only for youth to change to fit in with society, but also for society itself to change. This need was expressed in the introduction of a 1955 inquiry into the behaviour of youth in their free time: 'it is necessary to convince the worried adults that they have to widen the margins of the allowable and to consider the conduct of certain groups of youngsters as an acceptable variation of the general pattern'.[16]

The establishment of the Ministry of Culture, Recreation and Social Work (CRS) in 1965 can be considered as the offical recognition of the changed attitude towards the youth problem. It is important to add that the establishment of this ministry resulted from the political need for the governmental parties to reach a balanced redivision of the ministries existing at that time. An important figure in the socialist party, Vondeling, took the initiative for this redivision, which meant that a number of tasks of the Ministry of Education, Arts and Sciences (EAS) was transferred to the Ministry of Social Work, including youth work. This measure resulted in a different approach to juvenile work. The Ministry of EAS was used to a legal approach and to supporting private initiative. The Ministry of Social Work, however, envisioned a far more active role for government, and this view was carried over when the Ministry was broadened into CRS.

These two different views were both evident in the 1976 report of the 'Legal Provision Commission', the so-called Cower Report. This commission was instituted by the Secretary of State of the Ministry of EAS in 1964, but finished its task to 'advise on the possibilities for a legal provision for the subsidy of juvenile training' in 1967, after the establishment of the Ministry of CRS.[17]

The *leitmotiv* in this report clearly differs from the sounds heard before in such reports as that given form by Langeveld in 1952. This fresh way of seeing the young persons, as they are described in this report (the label 'mass youth' no longer appears), signals the rapid evolution in thinking about dealing with youth. The report starts from the position of the youngsters themselves and from that view develops a framework for a good youth policy. 'Society is demanding more and more of the young person', states the report, 'and is less and less able to make clear why it is demanding just this. The purpose of life is not derived from the future. The reason for living is increasingly to be found in the present. Youth do not reach their future by a clear image of where they are going, but by stepping out in the direction of the seeable future'.[18]

For a good youth policy, therefore, room was needed for experiments. The struggle around the subsidy of youth work was clearly visible. The commission was convinced of the importance that youth work should be 100% subsidized.[19] The report expresses a real concern for those young persons who have had to grow up in a rapidly changing society; juvenile work was no longer regarded as a means to grasp the 'elusives' and to place them in the desired social pattern. Sadly, this progress in understanding how to approach youth, presented by this report, was not to be continued. In retrospect, one can say that this Cower Report was a high point of youth policy: modest, realistic, and genuinely concerned.

The next governmental document on youth policy, however, was something very different. This was called *Paper on Youth Policy 1969*,[20] and was essentially the response of the then Minister of CRS to the Cower Report. Its text was loaded with the specific welfare jargon of that period; worse, however, was the remarkably rapid mutation of youth policy. No longer did the 'young person', as he was so sympathetically called in the Cower Report, form the centre of focus, but rather 'society' returned to play the main role in youth policy. This document stated[21] that youth policy should direct its attention to the future society. Outlining the specific aims of the policy, the Minister of CRS wrote: 'Firstly, that juvenile life with its own expressions, its own rules and own needs, should receive optimum chances in society; secondly, that youth should be able to contribute to the design of society, along the paths of their own choice, and can develop themselves to a maturity such as would be required by future society'.[22] The active role of government clearly permeated this document. The role of the parents as educators was virtually neglected, and even the youngsters themselves had to take a back seat. It would appear as if they were merely being used, by being placed in the front line, to achieve what at that time was the desirable 'New Society'.

The same Ministry of CRS pursued this 'New Society' further in a general document about 'welfare policy and welfare legislation', the so-called Bottleneck Paper of 1974.[23] Welfare policy was indissolubly connected with the necessary changes in a society, the paper stated; this included a process of change in which the ideas 'Of equal chances for everybody as far as possible, a justified division of power, knowledge and income, and a sharing of responsibilities as far as possible' formed the document's central thrust.[24] Priority was given to the underprivileged. These ideas were at that time very common, especially among students. It is at least remarkable that the welfare policy, the subject of the Bottleneck Paper, was so closely identified with the concept of equality, which, in contrast to the idea of equivalence, tended to ignore the identity of each individual.

Two explanations can be given for this attitude of the ministry responsible for this welfare policy. Various groups in society expressed their discontent with the *status quo*; this could be explained as a lack of a feeling of welfare. For the 'new' ministry, this was a kind of justification for its existence and the enlargement of its activities. The attitude of the professionals in this department was yet another reason for this self-perceived role in influencing society. Policy-focused sociologists were the main designers of this governmental policy.[25]

A similar policy development was taking place in the Ministry of Justice, which traditionally took care of child protection and juvenile penal law. The ideas presented on the general welfare policy in the Bottleneck Paper of 1974 were worked out for some specific fields of youth welfare. A working group established by the state secretaries of CRS, Justice and Health Care – the Department of Education did not take part in it, strangely enough – published its final report in 1976. This *Youth Welfare Paper* carried the pregnant subtitle: 'On the way to a coherent policy'. This policy needed a 'radical breakdown of those traditional but now irrelevant barriers between Health Care, Social Service, Child Protection, and other sections of care'.[26]

Youth policy and youth aid were presented in this Paper as one and the same thing. Youth aid, which, in the spirit of the 1976 paper, also had to do with the reasons underlying the problems: problems caused by the shortcomings of society. The social worker in youth affairs has to contribute to the fight against these shortcomings by tracing them and by exposing them: 'If necessary this may possibly lead to socio-political action'. Even more strongly than in the previous papers, the dominating thought here is that it is not in the first place youth itself that matters. Rather it is the 'other society' which matters, and thus becomes the focus of attention. This is even worse here, because we may assume that the group of youngsters in need of aid belong to the most needy in society, particularly those who are in contact with child-protection agencies.

From my own experience with an advice centre for youth, I can add that the youngsters who came for assistance just wanted to be helped in solving their problems and didn't care at all about the broader social causes of the problems.

YOUTH POLICY IN THE 'EIGHTIES

The line in welfare thinking and youth policy, started at the end of the 'sixties, lasted until the 'eighties. The Framework paper of 1980 can be seen as the turning point in this process.[27] Although this paper speaks about an optimum development as a focus of youth policy, the state is, compared with the previous period, more reserved in its interference with youth.

An optimum development is rather a lot to ask, and certainly more than the state is able to manage,[28] but again attention is being paid to the specific needs of youth.[29] The concept of equality no longer occurs. Education, however, is still regarded as the responsibility of society; in the first place it is the state which has to create conditions for the education of youth.

This way of thinking about the state as educator is no longer present in the subsequent paper, which appeared four years later. In a relatively short time, the concept of the role of the state in education has changed remarkably. The paper on Youth policy of 1984[30] allocates the primary responsibility for the education of the youth to the natural environment and not to society any longer. According to this new idea, youth policy has: 'To create such conditions that the youngsters can grow up in interaction with the social environment in which they live'. The government plays only a complementary role. From this point of view priority is given to specific groups, such as youngsters who don't succeed in finding work, youngsters who belong to the so-called minorities in Holland, and young drug addicts.[31]

One of the important premises of youth policy in this paper is: 'the growth towards independence as a process of participation and integration in society'. Room for development to gain an identity, which the Framework paper of 1980 still presented as a condition for youth policy, is no longer in discussion. Youth has again to accommodate to society. This is the typical no-nonsense policy of the 'eighties, a reaction, probably, to the concept of the idealized society of the 'sixties and 'seventies. This way of approaching youth in this paper brings us back to the youth policy of the 'fifties. As the leading principles of youth policy, we notice once again the 'problem youth' and the desirable position of the youngster in society.

REFLECTION ON THE POSTWAR YOUTH POLICY

The various views on youth policy that the official government documents make clear how rapidly the notions about the desirable position of youngsters in society were changing. It became evident that these notions were very much dependent on socio-economic conditions and, in relation to this, on the political attitude of the time. Is it permissible to expose youngsters to governmental policy to that degree, to a policy which hardly deserves this name in the true sense of the word? When we go further into this matter, we can draw a distinction between the effectiveness of the governmental measures and the legitimacy of the measures involved. More specifically: is the state able to arrange the lives of its young citizens and secondly, should it do so? In Holland, during recent years in particular, the effectiveness of general governmental policy has been fully debated. In 1984 the Minister of Justice offered Parliament a report which contained suggestions 'about the decrease and simplification of state measures'.[32]

As negative sides of the process of increasing legislation the report mentions a lack of effectiveness of all the separate legal provisions, the social opacity of legal management, and the overloaded government.[33] It was concluded from the recommendations of this report that all legal provisions had to be tested in terms of criteria for a sober and modest legislative policy. There is, however, a general consent about the lack of effectiveness of this specific measure, too. There is no effect in instructing the officials who actually make the laws, and Parliament, too, fails to inspect these instructions. In order to deregulate, a consensus is needed on substantive criteria; only when there is agreement on essential standards, is it possible to assess the need for regulation. This statement leads directly to the question of legitimacy of state interference. Practically no attention has been paid to this question in relation to the subject of youth policy. When state interference reached its peak, terms like 'optimum chances' (Paper on Youth Policy of 1969) and 'optimum development' (Framework Paper on Youth Policy of 1980) appear, without questioning the role of the state. Excessive state interference seems to be generally accepted, but has actually been questioned because of its lack of effectiveness.

However, there is far more to say about a legal system than whether it is effective of not. Legitimacy plays the most important role because this poses questions about the justification of legal measures; it lays the foundation for state interference. Legitimacy is nevertheless not an abstraction. The Universal Declarations, international treaties, and the Dutch Constitution, give leading principles of justice. For that reason, in regarding the desirable treatment of children, the state does not stand with empty hands. In the first place it can cleave to the dominant principle of human rights, namely the right of each individual to determine his or her own life. As the official papers have shown, up till now, governmental youth policy conflicts with this principle; the excessive interference with youth restricts the ability of youth to realize its potential. The dignity of the human being mentioned in the Preamble to the Universal Declaration on Human Rights is thus neglected.

The wish to control citizens, children as well as adults, seems to be a stubborn quality of states. In our fight against this, we profit from the fundamental human rights in international and national legislation. They present a basis for a just society. Although opinions about justice in a specific situation can differ, human rights can be more of a guide than has often been assumed, especially against interference of states, for which they were meant in the first place.

NOTES

1.   Troonrede van 23 juli 1946, Staatsuitgeverij, Den Haag (1964), p. 267.
2.   W. P. J. Pompe, *Bevrijding*, II, Amsterdam (1945), p. 33.
3.   Ibid., p. 33.
4.   G. Bolkestein, 'Overheid en Kunst', in: A. A. van Rhijn (ed.) *Nieuw Nederland – Bijdragen van Buiten Bezet Gebied i.v.m. den Wederopbouw van ons Land*, Amsterdam (1946), p. 305.
5.   F. Vervooren (ed.), *Nederland in den Oorlog*, 3, Utrecht (1942).
6.   D. H. Schram, en C. Geljon (eds.) *Overal Sporen*, Amsterdam (1990).
7.   L. J. A. Vriens, 'Pedagogiek en Tweede Oorlog (Omkijken om een Humane Toekomst te Scheppen', in: *Overal Sporen*, p. 332.
8.   G. van der Leeuw, *Nationale Cultuurtaak*, Den Haag (1947), p. 75.
9.   Ibid., p. 78.
10. See D. Boonstra, *Politiek Vormingswerk en Jeugdbeleid*, Alphen aan de Rijn (1980).
11. *Verwildering van de Massajeugd*, Staatsuitgeverij, Den Haag (1952).
12. Ibid., p. 18.
13. See H. de Liagre Böhl, and G. Meershoek, *De Bevrijding van Amsterdam*, Zwolle (1989), p. 111ff.
14. *Verwildering van de Massajeugd*, p. 33.
15. *Verwildering van de Massajeugd*, p. 71.
16. D. A. Krantz, en E. V. W. Vercruijjssen, *De jeugd in het Geding'*, Amsterdam (1959), p. 7.
17. *Cower rapport*, Staatsuitgeverij, Den Haag (1967).
18. Ibid., p. 162.
19. Ibid., p. 83.
20. *Nota Jeugdbeleid*, Staatsuitgeverij, Den Haag (1969).
21. Ibid., p. 8.
22. Ibid., p. 10.
23. Session of Parliament 1973–1974, nr. 12968.
24. Ibid., p. 8.
25. *Politiek Vormingswerk en Jeugdbeleid* pp. 145–147.
26. *Jeugdwelzijnsbeleid*, Staatsuitgeverij, Den Haag (1976), p. 13.
27. *Raamnota Jeugdbeleid*, Session of Parliament 1979–1980, nr. 16284.
28. The title of a speech of H. van Ewijk 'The Fake Appearance of Youth Policy' is significant in this respect.
29. 'Raamnota Jeugdbeleid', p. 10.
30. *Jeugdbeleid* (1984), Session of Parliament 1983–1984, nr. 18545.
31. Ibid., p. 4.
32. Session of parliament 1983–1984, nr. 17831, nr. 9.
33. Ibid., p. 10.

JOACHIM WOLF*

10. The Concept of the 'Best Interest' in Terms of the UN Convention on the Rights of the Child

1. INTRODUCTION

Since the adoption of the United Nations Declaration on Human Rights in 1948, a considerable number of Human Rights Conventions followed, which conferred rights upon the individual and created state obligations to respect and guarantee those rights. A number of well-known phrases, which are contained in these conventions, like 'everybody has the right', 'no one shall be deprived of', 'the High Contracting Parties shall secure', 'States Parties shall respect and ensure', 'each State Party undertakes to take steps' and so on, no longer give rise to fundamental disputes. As regards their legal content these legal phrases can be categorized into individual human rights and different kinds of state obligations, i.e. strict obligations of result, obligations of conduct, 'due diligence' obligations and promotional or aspirational obligations, which are to be implemented step by step.

Unlike these phases, which are not subject to any fundamental dispute, there is another, which still is very vague and which may even become the subject of considerable dispute, namely the phrase 'in the best interest of the child' which is contained in the Convention on the Rights of the Child. The very subject of my contribution, the standard of 'the best interests of the child', was introduced for the first time in the non-binding Declaration on the Rights of the Child of 1959 (containing only the political programme). Regarding the content and scope of the 'best interest' standard, neither the Declaration nor the subsequent Convention contain any special stipulation.

Principle 2 of this Declaration reads as follows:

> The child shall enjoy special protection, and shall be given opportunities and facilities, by law and by other means, to enable him to develop physically, mentally, morally, spiritually and socially in a healthy and normal manner and in conditions of freedom and dignity. In the enactment of laws for this purpose, the best interests of the child shall be the paramount consideration.

* Max Planck Institute for Comparative Public Law and International Law, Heidelberg.

M. Freeman and P. Veerman (eds.), The Ideologies of Children's Rights, 125–133.
© 1992 *Kluwer Academic Publishers. Printed in the Netherlands.*

In comparison, Article 3 para. 1 of the Convention on the Rights of the Child reads:

> 1. In all actions concerning children, whether undertaken by public or private social welfare institutions, courts of law, administrative authorities or legislative bodies, the best interests of the child shall be a primary consideration.

As I have already pointed out, the concept of the 'best interest' has not been formulated in either of these human rights documents. What, therefore, is meant by 'the best interests of the child'? Is there a legally binding concept for the care and protection of children underlying this Convention? It seems that there might be three possible answers to the question raised. The first possibility is: yes, there is a legally binding concept to be defined in terms of the wording and the structure of the Convention. A second option is: no, a legally binding concept may be envisaged as a political aim but has not yet been elaborated within the framework of the Convention. The third possibility is: only to some extent may one speak of a coherent legal concept, shaped by contextual relations and different categories of individual human rights and different state obligations.

I shall return to this point at the end of my paper and elaborate which of these possibilities ought to be followed. In the mean time we should also take note of direct information, based on the wording of the 'best interest' standard in the 1959 Declaration and the 1989 Convention.

1. The phrase contained in Article 3 of the Convention, namely 'in all actions concerning children . . . the best interests of the child shall be a primary consideration', is addressed to decision makers, *in general*.

2. A legally binding character, presuming there is any, is confined to 'considerations', which typically indicates a discretionary commitment. In contrast to the normal cases of administrative discretion, Article 3 extends a discretionary commitment to legislative bodies.

3. In States with democratically elected legislative bodies upon which primary State authority is conferred, such a discretionary commitment, as conceptualised in Article 3, comes close to a legal limitation of Government. As for the sovereign legal position of state Governments and Parliaments in international law, it would certainly be wrong to speak of strict obligations of result: the discretionary character of the standard is best described as referring to the way States are discharging their responsibilities in the field of child care and protection.

4. As can be inferred from principle 2 of the 1959 Declaration, the 'best interest' standard relates to opportunities and facilities to enable the child to develop physically, mentally, morally, spiritually and socially in a healthy and normal manner. That means that the concept of the 'best interests' covers the all-round development of the child according to its abilities as a human person within a sound human environment.

5. Considering that Article 3 speaks of the 'best interests', 'in all actions

concerning children', the standard refers to the Convention as a whole, including all rights of the child and all related State obligations. This seems to be understood as part of a possible legal concept in the sense I referred to the three possibilities earlier.

A 'best interest' standard having such a character is without precedent in international legal instruments. Regarding governments and legislators there are no rules in terms of public international law as to how to implement limitations made for discretionary decisions. Conventional obligations on the level of Government and Parliament normally coincide with the obligations of the State itself as a party to the respective treaty. It is an interesting question whether or not the 'best interest' standard applies to decision makers, even on a political level. In terms of the 'best interests' standard one could ask whether a special evaluation of the factual position of children shouldn't be required from states, i.e. that they should bear the child's position in mind when making political decisions. One may further ask whether states shouldn't be prohibited from making political decisions which will be to the detriment of the legal and social position of the child.

For example, suppose that free access to drugs is created without any legal restrictions and that this would lead to an increase of drug-addicted juveniles. Here a State Party could be prohibited by the Convention from allowing free access to drugs as a means to combat illegal drug trafficking. Notwithstanding Article 33, which in principle indicates the illegality of the use of narcotic drugs, this prohibition against free access to drugs would follow from the 'best interests' standard itself. Similar legal restrictions of State policies regarding children seem to be possible.

2. PREPARATORY WORK (*TRAVAUX PRÉPARATOIRES*)

The preparatory work of the 1959 Declaration and the later Convention does not provide us with clear definitions of the 'best interest' concept, either. However, according to all signatory States and observers to the Convention, Article 3 para. 1 is meant to be a binding State obligation.

In the view of the observers for Kuwait, Portugal and Australia, Article 3 para. 1 of the Convention reflects existing international standards, for instance as contained in Article 5 of the Convention on the Elimination of All Forms of Discrimination against Women.[1] Article 5 does not speak of the 'best interest' of the child expressly. However, para. 2 of this Article states a very similar rule according to which State Parties shall take all appropriate measures:

(ii) To ensure that family education includes a proper understanding of maternity as a social function and the recognition of the common responsibility of men and women in the upbringing and development of their children is the primordial consideration in all cases.

During the preparatory work of the 1959 Declaration the 'best interest' standard of Principle 2 was not discussed in detail. From the general context of the discussions in the Third Committee, Principle 2 was understood as dealing with the special protection of the child by law and by other means. There seems to be no direct relationship between the rights of the child and decisions of parents and guardians.

Looking at the Convention as it is presently formulated, we are faced with a considerable shift of emphasis from the initial concept of rights of the child as 'special protection' (as laid down in the 1959 Declaration), towards the current idea of a concept of rights of the child as 'individual human rights'.

When a delegate to the preparatory work of the Convention proposed that the Convention should be named 'The Convention on the Protection of the Child' a storm of protest followed. It was obviously rooted in the belief that such a renaming would be a step backwards. Taking a Convention on the Rights of the Child seriously, the crucial question is, whether the 'best interest' standard is presently regarded in view of the old concept of special protection, which is laid down in the Convention as well, *or* the new concept of individual rights. The answer to be given to this question is of decisive importance for the legal standing of the 'best interest' concept. Should the first option prevail, the concept would be confined to an interpretation of a mere attribute of special protection. Should the second option prevail, the Convention would be open to new conceptual interpretation.

3. The Concept of Independent Human Rights of Children

Does the Convention as such guarantee independent human rights for children? If not, we would be faced with state obligations of protection merely referring to independent human rights by implication. To answer the question in the affirmative is a precondition to incorporating those rights in the sphere of discretionary commitments of states and state responsibility under the 'best interest' standard. We are only justified in speaking of a legal concept in the latter instance. The assumption of independent human rights for the child is to be proved, first, in terms of the Convention itself. Secondly, it may be considered under international legal practice.

Article 3 leaves open the issue as to the incorporation of the rights of the child into the 'best interest' concept. Article 3 para. 2 reads as follows:

> State parties undertake to ensure the child such protection and care as is necessary for his or her well-being, taking into account the rights and duties of his or her parents . . .

There is no explicit reference to the rights of the child as such. In terms of para. 3 of the same article 'State Parties shall ensure that the institutions, services and facilities responsible for the care and protection of children shall conform with the standards established by competent authorities, . . .'. Once again, there is no reference to internationally guaranteed rights of the child. In fact, Article 3 deals with all actions which are undertaken by institutions, amongst others, by courts of law, administrative bodies and legislative authorities, and which concern children in regard to their well-being, their protection and care, their safety and health.

It is simple to summarize the contents of this Article as obligating State Parties to provide for, to give protection and participation to children in matters of their well-being. Seen from the point of view of children, the obligation on state parties to 'provide' creates the right to have their basic needs fulfilled (i.e. the right to food, to health care, education, recreation and play); the obligation on state parties to 'protect' them creates the right to be shielded from harmful acts or practices (i.e. commercial or sexual exploitation, physical or mental abuse, engagement in warfare); and the obligation of state parties to 'participate' creates the right to be heard in decisions affecting their own life.

Are we allowed to take this view, namely to interpret Article 3 from the perspective of the child, which is the converse of the state's obligation to provide and to protect the right of the child? Looking at Article 3 within the framework of the Convention the answer to this question *must* be in the affirmative. The first five Articles of the Convention contain basic provisions as to the structure of the Convention. Thereafter, in Articles 6–40, it lists the various rights attributed to the child and the related state obligations. From the perspective of Article 3 only the first part is of relevance.

Article 1 contains the definition of the child in terms of the Convention. Article 2, which is of crucial importance, reads as follows:

> State Parties shall respect and ensure the rights set forth in the present Convention to each child within their jurisdiction without discrimination of any kind . . .

Thus, the rights of the child (Article 2) precede the 'best interest' standard (Article 3). Article 4 contains reference to the duty to implement the rights recognized in the Convention by means of all appropriate legislative, administrative and other measures.

The basic premise of the whole Convention is the application of its provisions with the 'best interests of the child' constantly in mind. There is no way to escape the conclusion that this cannot be done without reference to the rights of the child recognized in the Convention. The basic structure of the Convention is that of a combination of the two elements, i.e. the rights of the child and the 'best interest' standard. The one cannot be separated from the other. The interpretation of the Convention leads to the conclusion that the 'best interest' standard exceeds traditional concepts of protection. It is open to new development and legal explanation.

State Practice

I would like to illustrate this statement with the aid of a number of practical examples which mainly came up for decision in the European Court of Human Rights and the European Commission for Human Rights.

The Convention on the Rights of the Child is said to be the first international legal instrument giving independent human rights to children. In so far as the practice in international courts and commissions is concerned, no direct arguments pro or contra can be expected. Judicial practice in terms of the European Human Rights Convention dealing with the protection of family life (under Article 8) offers some interesting perspectives.

(i) So, for instance, the question has been raised whether the rights to respect for family life within the meaning of Article 8 imply the legal recognition of a bond of relationship between a recognised illegitimate child and its mother's parents.[2] The Commission expressed the opinion that the concept of family life in Article 8 must be understood in the broad sense and that the fact that an illegitimate child remains at law a stranger to its mother's family constitutes a violation of the Convention in relation to the child. In this case the complainant was the mother. The Court, therefore, dealt with the right to family life from the perspective of the complainant and not from that of the child. The implication regarding rights of the child under Article 8 still remains an open question.

(ii) Although the question regarding the rights of the child under the European Convention remains open, the European Commission of Human Rights is willing to grant children separate procedural status. Hence, children can lodge complaints with the Commission without the authority of their legal representatives. For example, the Commission did not hesitate to examine a complaint brought by a 14 year old girl who had run away from home with her boyfriend and who was taken back to her parents by the police against her will.[3] Where, under national law, a parent no longer exercises parental rights, the Commission requires clear evidence of the child's wish to be represented by that parent in proceedings under the Convention. Failing that, the Commission considers the application incompatible *ratione personae*.

(iii) In the case of *Hendriks versus the Netherlands*[4] the applicant, since his former wife's return to the Netherlands in 1973 and the subsequent dissolution of their marriage, did not have access to their son and his efforts to obtain such access from the competent authorities failed. The courts, in their examination of the applicant's request for a visiting arrangement, had to consider not only the position and the interests of the applicant but also those of his son. Their decision to refuse the father's request for a visiting arrangement in order to safeguard the well-being of the child by giving preference to the interests of the child over those of the father interfered with the applicant's right to respect for his family life under Article 8 of the Convention. The Commission considered that the natural link between a parent and a child is of fundamental importance and that, where the actual 'family life' in the sense of 'living together' has come to an end, continued contact between them is desirable and should in principle remain possible. Respect for family life within the meaning of Article 8 thus implies that this contact should not be denied unless there are strong reasons, as set out in para. 2 of that provision, which justify such an interference. In effect, the Commission did not depart from their established practice in terms of which each decision of national authorities, which is based upon detailed consideration of the well-being of the child, can be justified under broad provisions of Article 8 para. 2. As for the 'best interests' of the child, the substance of the decision of the national courts is not tested in terms of international law.

After Hendriks' failure in Strasbourg he took his case for consideration to the Human Rights Committee in Geneva relying on the *Optional Protocol of the United Nations Covenant of Civil and Political Rights*.[5] Again, the issue was the compatibility of the decision of the Dutch authorities with the 'best interests' standard. The Netherlands, as defendant, submitted that:

> In general, it can be assumed that a divorce occasions such tensions that it is essential to the child's interest that only one of the parents can be awarded custody. In cases of this kind, Article 161, paragraph 1, of Book 1 of the Civil Code provides that, after the dissolution of a marriage by divorce, one of the parents shall be appointed guardian. This parent will then have sole custody of the child. The courts decide which parent is to be awarded custody after a divorce. This is done on the basis of the interests of the child.

The position of the complainant, the father, was that in the absence of a clear, legal norm under Dutch law affirming that a parent–child relationship and parental responsibility continue, the Dutch Courts in the exercise of uncontrolled discretion, violated his and his son's rights under the Covenant by denying his applications for visiting rights.

Under Article 23 of the Covenant 'The family is the natural and fundamental group unit of society and is entitled to protection by society and the State'. Under para. 4 of the same article: 'In the case of dissolution, provision shall be made for the necessary protection of any children'. In examining the communication, the Committee considered it important to stress that Article 23 paras. 1 and 4, of the Covenant sets out three rules of equal importance; namely, that the family should be protected, that steps should be taken to ensure equality of rights of spouses upon the dissolution of the marriage, and that provision should be made for the necessary protection of any children. The Committee noted that the Dutch courts recognized the child's right to permanent contact with each of his parents, as well as the right of access of the non-custodial parent, but considered that these rights could not be exercised in this case because of the child's interests.

Two important individual opinions to the report were published. The first opinion, written by Dimitrijevic, El Shafei, Higgins and Zielinski – and couched in cautious overtones – came to the conclusion that it is not for them 'To insist that the courts were wrong, in the assessment of the best interests of the child, in giving priority to the current difficulties and tensions rather than to the long-term importance for the child of contact with both its parents. However, we cannot but point out that this approach does not sustain the family rights to which Mr. Hendriks and his son were entitled under Article 23 of the Covenant'.

The second opinion by Amos Wako did not shy away from expressing a more critical point of view. In Wako's view: 'The Committee's decision finding no violation of Article 23 of the Covenant in this case is predicated on its reluctance to review the evaluation of facts or the exercise of discretion by a local court of a State party'. His first concern is that, though the Committee's practice of not reviewing the decisions of local courts is prudent and appropriate, it is not dictated by the Optional Protocol. The Committee would not be acting as a 'fourth instance' in determining whether a decision of a State party's court was correct according to that State's legislation, but would only examine whether the provisions of the Covenant invoked by the alleged victim have been violated. His second concern was whether the Dutch legislation, as applied to the Hendriks family, is compatible with the Covenant. The Dutch Civil Code does not provide for a statutory right of access to a child by the non-custodial parent, but leaves the question of visiting rights entirely to the discretion of the judge. Thus, the question arises whether the general legislation can be deemed sufficient to guarantee the protection of children, in particular the right of children to have access to both parents.

As justification for his arguments Wako relies on emerging international norms, including the international conventions against the abduction of children by parents, bilateral agreements providing for visiting rights and, most importantly, the then still draft Convention on the Rights of the Child.

4. Conclusion

With the coming into force of the Convention on the Rights of the Child, the 'best interests of the child' has become an international legal concept. For the first time measures and procedural requirements of States which prescribe how they have to exercise their discretion in matters relating to the well-being of children can be tested in terms of an international Convention. I have pointed out that the Convention on the Rights of the Child incorporates human rights of the child as part of the 'best interest' concept. International legal practice shows that up to now existing legal instruments are deficient in regard to the human rights of children. In practice discretionary commitments of states cannot be implemented convincingly without reference to human rights of the child as such.

To come back to the three initial options proposed, I suggest that the third one is correct: one may only speak to some extent of the 'best interest' concept as a coherent legal concept shaped by contextual relations and different categories of individual human rights and State obligations. The restriction, using the phrase 'to some extent', is still necessary because a legal concept as complicated as the 'best interest' standard still needs time for further development. For this reason, I hesitate fully to throw my weight behind the first option. On the one hand, the Convention clearly recognizes the human rights of children as such. On the other, it prescribes State obligations without bringing them in line with a clear cut system of individual rights. The second option fails basically because the 'best interest' standard has already developed beyond a mere political aim.

NOTES

1. E/CN.4/1989/48 p. 22 para. 118.
2. Op. Com., 10 December 1977, *Marckx* case, § 75 Public Court B, Vol. 29. pp. 45–46.
3. Application No. 6753/74 DR 2, p. 118.
4. Op. Com., 8 March 1982, *Hendriks* Case §§ 95–96 p. 21.
5. Communication 201/1985.

MALFRID GRUDE FLEKKØY*

11. Attitudes to Children – Their Consequences for Work for Children

In the Oxford Concise Dictionary attitude is defined as 'settled mode of thinking'. Children are born without attitudes, but learn through experiences of the world around them. Attitudes may be simple or complex, or built up gradually, as learned reaction-patterns. The attitudes of adults are important sources for such learning, sometimes expressed explicitly, but just as often and more effectively demonstrated through actions and reactions, or the lack of actions and reactions. Acquiring attitudes very often occurs through unconscious learning, without much reflection or conscious thought. The attitudes themselves can be unconscious, subconscious or conscious, and the different layers may not always fit together well; they may even be conflicting. New learning can modify attitudes, particularly the conscious and subconscious attitudes, and so unsettle the settled mode of thinking and lead to adjustments of behaviour. This is one reason why information, when accepted, can change the settled mode of thinking we call prejudice.

As individuals and as groups adults have conscious and unconscious attitudes towards children which directly and indirectly influence their work for children. The attitudes expressed may change according to which role the adult is in, particularly if the attitudinal pattern is not consistent, so that different situations bring out different attitudinal layers. One individual may, for example, be a parent, a teacher and a politician, with different views on children in each role. The parent may basically think of children as dependent and needing care and protection. The teacher views the child as a student, expecting independence. The politician sees the child as a member of a population group that requires services that are difficult to provide. Groups may reflect the attitudes of a political party, a religious faith or the current values held by parents of a certain generation. Some attitudes are more prevalent then others in different parts of the world, different cultures, different historical periods and in different individuals. Under certain conditions societies or society leaders may progress, for example, due to a better understanding of children and their needs. Under other circumstances they may regress, turning

* UNICEF International Child Development Center, Florence, Italy.

M. Freeman and P. Veerman (eds.), The Ideologies of Children's Rights, 135–147.
© 1992 Kluwer Academic Publishers. Printed in the Netherlands.

back to attitudes from earlier periods. The different attitude components in a society or between sub-societies may be conflicting, but the composite will determine the views of private as well as public adult responsibility towards children. Adult attitudes towards children will also shape the children themselves, in part determining their development and therefore also what the world will be like in 20–50 years.

Understanding these attitudes and their consequences may help our work with and for children. Being aware that the complexities exist, even if we do not understand them all, in itself may be an advantage. Views on the value and roles of children may play an important part in determining strategies, difficulties, and how far we feel it is reasonable to go in defending and promoting the rights of children.

CHILDREN: POSSESSIONS OF THEIR PARENTS?

A child as a product has similarities to other products of imagination, planning and effort, and distinct differences. The most important difference is the fact that the child is far more personal: a child bears the genes of the parents, is 'their flesh and blood', has roots in generations of the past and creates continuity into the future of the family. The child is the vessel of an emotional involvement rarely seen in relation to other products. Many adults, some on the basis of teachings of their religion, others in spite of intellectual acceptance of the opposite, feel that they have the same right of possession to the child-product as to other products, or that the ownership right to their child is stronger than other rights of possession, even comparing these rights with the legal rights connected with some other products. For instance, artists have copyrights and other legal and moral rights connected with their products. But there are limits to how far the comparison goes where children are concerned. Adults have the right to dispose freely of other property or belongings. Not so with children. Anger and indignation are common reactions when children are sold or bought. Giving away a child is more acceptable, e.g. by adoption, particularly if adoption is considered to be in the best interest of the child. Nonetheless, giving away another human being is complicated, because the other person must be presumed to have a certain right to make decisions on his own behalf, at least if he has the maturity necessary to make the decision on (and take the consequences of) the issue in question. As long as – but only to the extent to which the child is actually unable to decide for himself, parents or other adults may reasonably have the right to make decisions on behalf of the child on issues the child is unable to decide. This does not mean that the child cannot give an opinion, nor that this opinion should not be taken into consideration. But the right to give an opinion is not automatically connected with the right to make a decision. The right to decide generally comes after the right to speak out, although the two rights sometimes go hand in hand. The right to have an opinion does not mean that a child *must* state a clear opinion either, only that the child should be given an opportunity to do so if he/she so wishes. Decisions made on behalf of someone else means that the decision must be based on what one thinks the other person would decide, given the possibility to do so, or at least on one's best judgement of what is in that person's best interest.

If we agree on this principle, we have come a long way from the view that parents have absolute power over their minor offspring and can do whatever they want to or with their children. This development is reflected in Norwegian law, where the term 'parental rights' was deleted in 1982, to be replaced with the term 'parental responsibility'. Norwegian parents still have full responsibility for their children, but no longer the right to make all decisions, regardless of the child's level of maturity. On the contrary, the law also states that parental rights to make decisions on behalf of the child decrease as the child matures, while the child's own right to state his opinions, participate in decision making, and to make his own decisions in personal matters shall increase, his opinions gaining importance with increasing age.

Parental responsibility involves an obligation to satisfy the needs of their children. The right to exercise this responsibility may be lost if the child's basic needs are neglected. In such cases public responsibility (or the extended family responsibility) transcends parental responsibility, and public institutions (or the extended family) may take over. This view has long traditions in Norway, stated in law as early as the year 1630. Public guardians were then appointed in the townships to take care of children whose parents – after due warning – did not see to it that children over the age of 10 years were in school or at work (school was not compulsory until 1739).

Even if the right to possess a child is no longer valid in principle, things sometimes look different in practice. If an adopted child turns out to have been kidnapped or sold for the purpose of adoption, the question of 'ownership' can again surface. Even if that child has been living with adoptive parents for a long time, the question of 'to whom does this child belong?' and the statement 'Blood is thicker than water' indicate that ownership is still an issue, even in cultures where there is a general acceptance that children are 'on loan' and not owned. Even in less dramatic but far more common cases, e.g. in divorce, the children can become part of the bargaining battle between the parents. Fighting about where and with whom the children shall live can be very similar to a battle about which parent shall 'own' the child, and how much – or how little – the other parent shall have access to the child. Such parental conflicts will very often disregard the child's own rights, e.g. the child's right to give an opinion, to make the decision if he is over a certain age (e.g. 16 years old) or the right to have access to and know both his parents.

In similar fashion conflicts based on the idea that parents 'own' their child may occur when public authorities take over responsibility for a child, disregarding 'the best interests of the child' in their concern for the parents. Child welfare then turns into 'parental welfare'. Also, the adults' right to a 'fair trial', with all the possibilities for appeal, may lead to serious neglect of the child's needs, e.g. for a stable home environment. The child's right to a fair trial is rarely at issue. All parties argue 'in the best interest of the child'. What is really in the child's best interest may be difficult to determine, but the views of two opposing parties cannot logically both be right. And even when an ideal solution is found, the child's right may still be infringed upon if implementation proves impossible.

If the prevailing attitude (conscious or unconscious) in a society maintains that children are the possessions of their parents, one consequence may be that adults care only about their own children, disregarding the others. Adults do not intervene when children are in trouble: in 'innocent' trouble like bullying or in really serious trouble, like child abuse. Adults confronted with their lack of concern and action may say that it is really not their responsibility. Or that they don't want to intrude in the private affairs of other families. But why not?

If parents have sole possession of their children, logically they should also have sole responsibility for providing for all the child's needs. Fortunately, this is not the case. Public school systems clearly demonstrate public recognition of the fact that parents cannot supply children with all the knowledge, experience, and skills children need. Changing times, however, lead to changes in the possibilities parents have to provide for the needs of children. In families with only 1–2 children, it is impossible for many parents in our time to provide the necessary social learning and peer-group experience in the pre-school years. Nor can parents on their own provide safe play and activity areas for children and young people. But public responsibility can be avoided if politicians agree that 'Children are naturally the responsibility of the parents' or, – put in another way, 'We do not want our children to be State property'. The implication is that the child is the property of the parents. Leaving all – or too much – responsibility to the parents can be an excuse for not providing public services to meet children's needs that even the best parents are unable to satisfy. In some communities this attitude becomes more dominant when financial resources and the problems of financial distribution between groups become more difficult. It is, for instance, hard to neglect the obvious needs of the elderly – who are vocal, vote, and are elected to decision-making bodies. It is much easier to disregard the needs of children by placing the responsibility squarely, but unfairly, on the shoulders of the parents. This is all the more unfair when many of these parents have a greater number of old people to care for, given the absence of public services for the elderly, than they have children.

CHILDREN: A 'NATURAL PHENOMENON'?

Of course adults have children! Naturally they take care of them and bring them up! – regardless of number. In 'the old days' and in many countries even today, parents simply accepted whatever number of children they were 'blessed' or burdened with, ruled by fate, supernatural power or as an inevitable result of Nature. If children are considered in these ways, a 'happy childhood' and 'good environment' may also be accepted, without reflection, as inevitable. Many 'responsible' adults, remembering their own childhoods, subconsciously believe – or want to believe – that present-day childhood is still like the idyllic memories of their own. They believe, for instance, that parents can still tell their children to run out and play. Memories about their own parents and lack of clear recollections about the daily life of young parents with young children, enable them to hold on to the belief that parents 'naturally' can manage everything by themselves. Many parents share this idea, feeling guilty or ashamed when they realize that they are unable to cope with all needs and demands. They could at least be relieved of that part of their guilt feelings, if they only knew that it is really impossible to solve all problems, manage all situations, alone.

CHILDREN: THE ANSWER TO ADULTS' NEEDS?

Children may have many roles: besides being considered 'a value in their own right', they can be prized as cheap labour, partners, future adults. One role that seems to be gaining importance is the role children can have as need-fulfillers for adults. Adults in industrialized countries, asked why they have children, do not answer 'we need the labour' or 'we need them to take care of us when we are old'. These adults want children because the child fulfills the adults' needs for human contact, for feeling loved and needed, productive and creative. Being a parent also defines a role in society, in relation to the public services and in relation to other parents, that is, parenting leads to belonging. These adult needs, combined with the child's ability to meet them, are – in a normal setting – an advantage, strengthening the adults' enjoyment of the parental role, their love for the child and their wish to care for it. Based on some of these needs, parents have plans, expectations and hopes for their children. Their own frustrations can be the basis for other dreams, perhaps that their children can achieve goals that they themselves could not reach, e.g. in education or in society. In our time, many families have fewer children to fulfill these hopes – one or two as compared to eight or ten who could share the responsibility 100 years ago. Then, if three or four did not live up to parental hopes and expectations, there were still a number who did, thus demonstrating that the parents were not total failures as parents, giving them the satisfaction of at least partial success, of being good parents. Particularly when expectations are unrealistic or spring from the irrational emotional needs of the parents, the responsibility placed on children for fulfilling this adult need can become a heavy burden for growing children, or even the source of pathology.

Children (one or two) may be the only means parents have to avoid feeling lonesome, useless or worthless. Using the child to 'fill' some kind of 'gap' is not unusual, for example when a child must take over the role of 'housewife' for a single father or a working mother, or be the 'friend and protector' of a single mother or father. In such cases adult behaviour, perhaps even 'adult' emotional responses, may be expected from young children. The fear of losing the emotional satisfaction of having a small child may, on the other hand, even in families with two adults, lead to an exaggerated clinging to or infantilizing of a child. The adult may try to keep the child helpless and dependent, protesting openly or in covert ways when the child wants autonomy and independence. When the question of letting other adults (a day-care person, nursery-school or even school teacher) take over some of the parental responsibility, the unconscious conflict may be uncovered, but not always solved.

Present-day parents have fewer siblings and fewer elder relatives than previous generations had. They have had less experience with small children as they grew up. In addition, they also lack direct transmission from parents, relatives, and elder siblings of traditions and experiences regarding parenthood and children. Unrealistic ideas and fantasies about what parenthood actually involves – what having children really is like – are much harder to correct. The security of knowing how to do it and the feeling of succeeding as a parent are harder to achieve. Parents with four or more children often say: 'Now we know how to do it, now we know what parenting is all about'. With only one or two children, how can parents obtain the satisfaction of achievement, pride in their own competence, particularly when there are no support systems to substitute for the extended family? Problems and disappointments can be overwhelming. In the most extreme cases, parents have such abnormal needs themselves, craving care, comfort, support, and love to a degree which their spouses and children cannot possibly satisfy. Such parents have often been neglected, abused, or emotionally deprived as children. If, as very small children, they learned that 'children are to be hated' they have surely repressed the inevitable anxiety, the threat to their very existence and life, inherent in being a hated child. Hating children is not acceptable in most societies. In some cases this hatred of children is therefore counteracted through reaction formation: to prove to themselves and others that they do *not* hate children, they are overtly very loving and caring. This kind of loving attitude is a fragile one, and may crack under stress. But it may also have a different result: in trying to win exaggerated expressions of love from their children, these emotionally starved parents can try to satisfy their own needs through their children, to prove to the adult that the parent is a love-worthy person. Since satisfaction of the adult need is superior, this must lead to deprivation of the emotional needs of the children as well as to inevitable disappointment for the parents. The parents may then neglect or punish the children physically, as an unconscious revenge on their own unsatisfying parents, as well as an expression for their disappointment and frustration with the child. Adults with such tendencies will scarcely be inclined to give children rights superior or even equal to adult rights. But if the vicious circle is not broken, they will produce new generations of parents who may abuse their children.

CHILDREN: THE ADULTS OF THE FUTURE

Children eventually grow up. In many countries this still determines the number of children in a family. The higher the number, the greater the insurance of care for old parents. In other countries this was one motive for having many children – until infant and child mortality rates declined. The use of contraceptive methods increased, followed by stronger demands for improved methods of family planning. With family planning a greater number of children will actually be wanted, although the reasons for wanting children can be mixed, as we have seen. In other parts of the world the opposite message is given: even if an increasing number of couples have children, the number of children in each family is declining, the annual total also going down. So the number of children must increase if there are going to be enough adults to care for the rising number of very old people, 30–50 years hence, enough workers for the labour market, enough consumers and enough tax payers. Only rarely does this view of children lead to programmes to raise the birthrate, to iniatives easing the problems of parents, to make childbearing and child raising more attractive.

For the children themselves there may be reason for concern if children are not considered seriously as potential adults, particularly in adolescence, which can become a period of empty waiting for adult status. Adolescence as a trial-and-error period in transition to adulthood is in itself no new idea. Twenty-five years ago the teenage period was a phase during which young people could try out different roles, test values and behaviour, express various opinions, without having the full responsibility of adults. Thus they could find out – without having to take all the consequences – which values, attitudes, opinions, and behaviour patterns each of them individually and in groups should adopt more permanently, suited to the roles they would have in the adult world. In times when children were considered fully adult at the age of 6–8 years of age (or as late as at 14) such a period of psychological and social 'trial-and-error' was impossible. But on the other extreme and in our society many young people are not economically or socially independent until they are 25 – or even 30 – years old. The adolescent 'moratorium' can last as long as childhood and the goal of becoming a totally responsible and independent adult can be very unclear, because the time-perspective involved is so long and uncertain. Many young people manage to cope, filling the period with education, meaningful training for an adult career, testing bisexual relationships more or less seriously and participating in many ways as adults in society. But some young people internalize a perception of themselves as useless, irresponsible, and worthless and behave accordingly. If the numbers, and not only the sound level, are increasing there is reason for concern. However, a culturally determined trend of this kind is amenable to change. To change it the situation must be recognized and the necessary consequences accepted, for example, by giving children and youth more real responsibility and increased right to participate in decision making. Adults must then be willing to relinquish some of their own power. The extension of the non-adult period has perhaps led to a gradual, but actually unwanted extension of the power of the older generation over the younger generation, so that parents have too much power too long over their offspring. In any case, we know beyond any doubt that children and young people, to be able to participate in a democratic and threatened society, need courage, optimism, and the will to try, which they will not acquire as adults if they are denied learning possibilities when young. They need to learn how they can influence and have an impact on their small society to believe in the possibilities for change in a larger society when they grow up.

Fewer and fewer families can provide such learning opportunities at home. A younger generation with one or two members can never outvote two parents, and the children are always smaller, younger, with less experience than the majority. The children, of course, benefit from this situation, but to learn the rules of democracy, how equals can function together peacefully, children need other children – peer groups – in addition to the family. In the peer group, membership depends on the group as well as on the individual. The group can expel an unwanted member or let a wanted member back in, on conditions or according to implicit or explicit rules formulated by the group. Making rules for group behaviour or for the group's activities teaches children how rules are made, how they can be changed, what makes a leader (which may not be entirely positive), what kinds of behaviour are acceptable to remain in the group. The individual can also leave the group, even 'for ever', perhaps joining other groups instead. Being a long-term or short-term member of a variety of peer groups will also give varied experience.

In the family membership is unconditional. To learn to solve or live with even long-lasting conflicts in long-term relationships to people they belong with, in a group that will not normally exclude the child as a member (nor will the child normally leave this group permanently), the child needs the family. So children should not spend all their time with other children. But nor should they spend all their time under adult control. The sometimes rough but necessary learning amongst children, teaching each other how groups of equals function and how to solve conflicts amongst equals, cannot be achieved if the groups are constantly controlled by adults. Adults may be needed as consultants and as models – in other situations as teachers as well. But children need a spectrum of different social learning situations, spanning a continuum from the peer group (without adults) to the mixed-age group, even with adults as equal members, to adult-led groups and the close-knit stability of the family, and also spanning generations. Even now there is concern about a compartmentalized childhood, split into watertight groups of 'preschool children', 'schoolchildren' and adolescents, with little or no contacts across 'borders' or between generations.

Adult views of children as future adults will naturally influence the goals parents set in bringing up their children and the goals society sets for its efforts for children. What goals the school system has, which values the schools should teach, which potentials in the children should be cultivated and which stemmed depend very much on what present-day adults believe the future adults will need and which qualities they should have. The accelerating changes in society make it more and more difficult to judge future demands. This difficulty increases when we realize that we can hardly expect a new and better world if we try to shape our young people entirely in our own image.

How Long is a Child a Child?

These days, with so many speaking up for the special rights of children, there are also voices protesting the need for special rights for children, as human rights in general also apply to children. Going back in history we find a more varied picture. Children could have the same rights as adults in limited areas. In England, for instance, children in the 13th and 14th century were given the right to possess property, but not the right to dispose of their possessions until they were 12 or 14 years old. Children often obtain rights gradually with increasing age – but at which age may be subject to change. When I was a child, the right to vote, the age of majority, was 21 – now it is 18 in Norway, 16 in Nicaragua. The age level set for marriage has changed from 12–14 years for daughters of the 'best families' (5–8 for royalty, boys as well as girls) 200 years ago to 18 for both sexes now, or to 16 for girls and 18 or more for boys, varying from country to country. This age level does not necessarily have anything to do with puberty or sexual maturity, as the average age of menarche was actually higher two centuries ago. On the other hand, marriage was necessary to support a girl and also a means of combining fortunes, properties or families. Now, marriage is a question of personal commitment, based on personal feelings, at least in many industrialized countries.

One may well ask if it would be beneficial for children to have the same rights as adults have. Sometimes exceptions from adult law can be an advantage. When penalties for begging were introduced, children were excepted – an obvious advantage for those children who had no other means of supporting themselves. The principle of judging children less harshly than adults can be found in Norwegian law going back 700 years. Yet Norway, even today, puts children of 14–15 years (albeit a small number) into adult prisons, judged by trial in adult courts.

In general, most adults feel that children should acquire some adult civil and social rights gradually, according to age and maturational level. But even so, we must ask who or what determines 'appropriate' maturity, as this has also changed through history. From the times of the Roman Empire, through the Middle Ages and the industrial revolution, even going back 'only' 100 years, children of 6–8 years were full-fledged workers on the farms, in shops, factories, and professions. Girls of 8–10 were servants in the households of other families, boys were apprenticed. The ties to home and family loosened early, the children being expected to support themselves at a much earlier age than now. A question which arises, even today, is whether or not children who must support themselves (like street children must) or children who themselves have children – or children who are active soldiers at the age of 12 are still to be considered as children: or are they actually adults? What is 'a child' – and how can we speak of rights for children if the definition of 'a child' is uncertain? Perhaps 'childhood' is defined by circumstances and not by age? Perhaps an individual is 'a child' as long as he (or she) does not have total responsibility, but has other people to protect, help, support, and teach him or her?

Increasing protection of children may in some connection lead to deprivation for some children. Participation in the work of adults can make children feel needed and necessary, increasing self confidence and the feeling of competence, from a very young age. One little girl of two, for instance, was responsible for filling a small basket with chips left over from wood chopping, and carry that basket to the oven. Her contribution was the starting point for all the cooking and heating needed by the family. Her job was obviously important. Such experience may be much harder to obtain today, particularly within the family, when many of the tasks and responsibilities given to children in 'the old days' have simply disappeared or the tasks have been taken over by machines. The other side of the coin was child abuse, the realization of which led to legislation prohibiting child labour – very often proposed and accepted by adults whose own children did not have to contribute to the support of their family. Robert Owen is one example, proposing that all children in England should – like his own – go to school, leading to legislation on compulsory education and a public school system. This, in turn, led to other measures. Parents who could not afford to support their families without the income of the children objected to compulsory education, and free meals – at school – was a necessary supplementary measure. This example also serves to illustrate how public responsibility must complement parental efforts: and also how the need for such supplementary action changes in time. School meals existed in England and in Norway in the childhood of the public school system – in Norway also during and after the Second World War – but not today, when we at least believe that children are adequately fed at home. But even now the question may arise, either as a consequence of longer school hours, out of concern about young people's increasing use of 'junk' foods or from a recognition of a situation where fewer and fewer children learn the social aspects of sharing meals with a group at home.

CHILDREN: A SPECIAL GROUP?

Children are different from adults. Even people who insist that children should have all the same rights as adults must admit that there are demands on adults which children neither can nor should be obliged to handle. Historically, children have been perceived as miniature adults and the aim of education was to make children as adult as possible as quickly as possible, by setting demands they could not possibly live up to or by beating 'evil' (i.e. childish) impulses out of them. More recent research has given us knowledge about children's needs and reasonable expectations as they grow so that this knowledge now determines many of the upbringing and educational practices used. This use of knowledge assumes that the knowledge itself can be trusted. But the fact is that 'truths' about children change. Three decades ago a basic 'truth' was that babies only start to smile as social behavior at the age of 3–4 months. Now they seem able to imitate, recognize faces, distinguish known from unknown people at the age of one week, and enjoy music even before they are born. Other old 'truths' are questioned: are preschool children really so egocentric or children in general so incompetent as the books 10–20 years old tell us?

Even with new answers, often indicating more competence earlier, no-one will insist that children and youth are just like adults, even though in some ways the boundaries between children and adults seem to be breaking down as reflected in the clothes they wear and in the culture they share, where, for instance, television, amongst other effects, has provided much more common knowledge and shared culture for children, youth, and adults of all ages. Children are exposed to information about sex, marital conflicts, aggression, war, disasters – topics from which young children were vigorously shielded two to three generations ago but which are now presented in ways that rarely are tailored to the growing child's level of understanding.

Also, TV might be a factor effecting one of the old 'truths'. According to developmental theory, the ability to distinguish clearly between fact and fiction, fantasy and reality develops at around the age of six or seven. Recent research on children who watch a great deal of television seems to indicate that the boundaries are blurred until the age of eight or nine, probably because the shows they watch are very often not clearly fantasy nor clearly reality. Reality might be too fantastic to believe and quite a lot of fiction is presented as real or in such a way that the children perceive it is real. When for instance a children's programme had adults sailing in on the scene in a big bed, many 6–7 year olds believed that beds can fly, because 'We *saw* it, the bed *did* fly!'

New observations and studies of children may lead to new answers, new ideas and views about children. We must also be prepared to question what we believe and what we are looking for when we observe children. If we tend to look for differences, between children and adults or between children on different age levels or in different cultures, we may overlook or play down similarities. We may also stress what children are unable to do, overlooking what they can do, perhaps because they do things in other ways than older children or adults. Or they may be able to solve part of a problem, but be seen as incompetent as long as they cannot solve the whole. Perhaps we are then getting a wrong picture of the competence of children. In connection with rights for children, this may be important, because so much then depends on the maturity of the child, what they cannot do, what they should not be burdened with or should be protected from – perhaps without investigating the questions properly – or by asking the children themselves how they feel about it.

ATTITUDES SHAPE CHILDREN

Adult attitudes towards children – as individuals and as a group – will influence the children and their development. Adult perception of children and the child's perception of the adult is always to some extent influenced by personal needs and interests. We perceive – to some degree – what we want to see, taking notice of what is important to us at the moment. Less important elements can be disregarded. In any interaction between children and adults there is a continuous feedback system of interpretation of behavior, with the child adjusting behavior according to what the child perceives as important to the adult, the adult adjusting to what is perceived as the child's needs. That is how values, attitudes, and roles of the growing person are learned and developed. This adjustment happens partly on the basis of the child's interpretations (which may be correct or incorrect), partly on the basis of the interpretations of the adult (which may also be wrong) communicated to the child. The child's development of self-confidence, self-respect, identity is determined largely by the signals the child receives about how others – amongst whom loved adults are very important – perceives the child's behaviour, feelings, thoughts, and reactions. Am I good or bad, valuable or worthless, are my attitudes and values in tune with my society, particularly with the people I care for? Do adults communicate that children are valuable as they are – or do the signals indicate that the adults are only waiting for the child to grow up? Do the adults agree, so that the child gets the same message from many adults or are the messages conflicting and confusing? The signals come from many sources – first mostly from the parents. But as the child grows, other adults (teachers and organization leaders) gain importance, as do other children and the signals from mass media, particularly television, including advertising. The communications about values found in the mass media are often contradictory to the values of parents and teachers, but the authorities or persons responsible for what the children are exposed to do not seem willing to take the consequences and introduce the measures which could protect the children. This might serve as one example of a more general discrepancy between professed attitudes and action, the attitudes expressed in principle being that children are important, the actions showing them that this is not true. If, for instance, we maintain that schools are important, but let the children get their education in run-down buildings, with tattered books and outdated information, how can we expect children, in countries that could obviously afford better, to respect school property and feel that they – as pupils – are important? When youth clubs and leisure time facilities, school transportation and health services are the first projects to be obliterated when the local economy is tight, how can children believe that their lives and activities are important? Slogans such as 'Children are our most valuable asset' are not worth much when society does not seriously realize its responsibility for children.

For parents the child as an individual, as a member of the family, as emotionally important, carries most weight. For society the importance of children as future adults perhaps carries more weight. Children and youth as active, participating members of groups, with opinions worth listening to, are not considered important enough, at least not yet.

So what does all this mean in terms of work for the rights of children? In each culture the prevailing attitudes to children must be defined. Attitudes will not be changed by telling parents, professionals, political and religious leaders what their attitudes should be, unless we start where they are themselves. Understanding attitudes and how they can arise will also help understanding how to change them: what kinds of information is needed in each particular case. It also sets the limits – at least for the time being – to how far we can go in the different arenas of children's rights. Finally, we need patience. History has shown that attitudes to children do change, not always for the better. It may be important to be aware of the changes, to be able to encourage progress and not be too disappointed or frustrated by occasional regressions or set backs. The next generations of parents must be brought up to respect the integrity and dignity of all other human beings, including the small ones, as equal although different from themselves. The first step is recognizing in ourselves where our own weak spots are, most easily found, I suspect, if we take a good look at our own attitudes towards our own children as they grow up.

Finally, looking at the value of children in a global perspective, it is obvious that the world needs children – but not only because children represent our future. Children are also the embodiment of global values. Therefore children unite, they do not divide peoples or countries. They also embody certain global duties and they are the indicators of what the world needs. Recognition of the needs and situation of children should bridge the gap between East and West, North and South. And finally, children are also the hope of the future because they give purpose and meaning to life when ideologies crumble, when despair threatens to overwhelm us, when everything else seems to fail.

GWEN JAMES*

12. Theory into Practice:
Lessons from One English Organisation

1. INTRODUCTION

From the viewpoint of a practitioner, an 'ideology' of children's rights is of little use unless it goes hand in hand with ways of ensuring that the children know about their rights and can exercise those rights. In England, the Children Act 1989 is full of recommendations 'that the wishes and feelings of the child' shall be taken into consideration in any decision made about his (its?) life but with no 'teeth' built in to ensure that this happens.[1] The issue is 'power' – the power (fulness?) of the bureaucracy that controls so many aspects of a child's life. It is very often left to those who have the control to give children the information about ways of making complaints or challenging decisions. This is the case with our new Children Act.

An example will illustrate the point: the Children Act gives the following 'rights' to children who are looked after by a local authority. That their wishes and feelings should be taken into consideration, that they should be placed as near to home as possible and that they should not be locked up for longer than is necessary.[2] 'A Voice for the Child in Care', the organisation that I run, was asked for help by a boy who was in a secure unit in London and was placed in a secure private establishment about 200 miles away. He had a drug problem, but had not committed a serious offence. The regime at the establishment where he was sent is behaviour modification and the boy, who is intelligent, felt that he was not getting the right sort of help. Also, he was living with young people who had behaviour problems, some quite bizarre, or who had committed serious offences and he objected to this. The advocate was both a barrister and a social worker but got absolutely nowhere. The psychiatrist, the social worker and the Official Solicitor (he was a ward of court) said that they knew best. The boy ran away and became yet another homeless person on the streets of London.

---

* Voice for the Child in Care, London.

M. Freeman and P. Veerman (eds.), The Ideologies of Children's Rights, 149–154.
© 1992 *Kluwer Academic Publishers. Printed in the Netherlands.*

2. The Voice of the Child In Care

The background to the setting up of the VCC is as follows: In 1970 the Children's Departments in England and Wales became Social Services departments and Child Care Officers became Social Workers. In most departments they began to work with a generic case-load which included the elderly, the disabled, and the mentally ill as well as families and children. This meant that social workers who did not have the necessary training and experience were working with children in care. It has meant over the years that much expertise has been lost.

As an Area Officer, formerly in the Children's Department in Haringey, in North London and then in the Social Services Department, I was one, among many, who was concerned about the effect generic social work was having on the standard of work with children in care. We formed a network 'A Voice for the Child in Care' to try to do something about it.

One of our number, Kay Fitzherbert, was a social worker who, in trying to adopt a child of mixed parentage, had experienced great difficulties with a Social Services Department. She wrote a paper entitled *The Power of Social Workers over Children in Care* which opened our eyes. In the early days we were asked for help in several cases where decisions had been made that the children and those who cared about them found unacceptable. We explored possible avenues to challenge the power of the social services department.

These were:
1. Local Councillors – elected Council members who constitute English local Government
2. Members of Parliament, who represent constituents at a national level and respond to their concerns
3. The Government department responsible for social services – The Department of Health
4. The Local Government Commissioner – The Ombudsman
5. The British Association of Social Workers
6. The Law.

What we found was that the power of the social services department over the child in care was absolute. No matter what happened to the child there was no-one and no-where that the child, or any adult on his or her behalf, could turn for help. Despite the efforts of the VCC and many other people such as Michael Freeman,[3] it remains just as true today.

In 1979, The International Year of the Child the VCC ran a telephone help-line for children in care. We gained more experience trying to help them. Mostly our efforts came up against a brick wall, but we did have some success in using a model of 'conciliation', bringing people together to look at the problem and trying to find a solution that would be acceptable to all parties. The main problem seemed to be that there was no mechanism by which an independent impartial body could look at the problems and disentangle them.

In the early 1980's I turned my attention to complaints procedures on the basis that if effective procedures could be set up it would mean that there were channels for people like the VCC to use to help children in care. For four years I ran a project for complaints procedures for children in care at our National Children's Bureau in London. During this time I was in touch with about 40 local authorities and most of the large voluntary organisations through running workshops and seminars. Several authorities were committed to the idea of setting up an effective procedure and people worked very hard to achieve this, but for one reason or another they were unsuccessful. We did however learn a great deal as we went along.

First of all there is the issue of *power*. As already stated it is virtually impossible in England to challenge what is done to and for children in care; the local authority has total power over them. Unless there is some way of balancing that power there can be no progress. The final stage of an effective complaints procedure must be that there can be an appeal to an outside body which has authority to impose a course of action on those responsible for the child. This is lacking in England. The nearest we have is The Ombudsman, the Local Commissioner, who can only investigate maladministration and whose recommendations are not binding on the local authority.

The children and young people in care are very vulnerable. Even if they know their rights it is hard for them to achieve them. *Advocacy* is an absolute essential if a complaints procedure is to be effective – they are the two sides to the coin. In this context the word 'advocacy' covers the provision of advice, information, support 'helping to speak' and 'speaking for' a child, and a measure of conciliation.

The other main lesson we learnt was that any system established should aim to tackle problems *as early as possible* when they become apparent. A complaints procedure which has as its main emphasis an examination of events which have already taken place can, at its best, only give redress and help to ensure that similar things do not happen again. . . . What children in care need is a process whereby they can get help *before* decisions are finalised, or things get out of hand, in situations which they are finding difficult.

In this context the most successful work so far has been done by Children's Rights officers. In Leicester, (a medium sized county in the Midlands) Mike Lindsay was appointed in 1986 and I acted as consultant to him for three years. Mike was in care himself and had been a residential social worker. That gave him credence with two very important groups. He has set up a Children's Rights *Service* to educate children and staff in what children should have the right to expect if they are in the care of Leicester. He is also available to individual children and young people to take up issues on their behalf. Because this is his full-time job and partly perhaps because his commitment is based on his personal experience, he has been remarkably successful. He has been able to help young people and staff to sort out difficulties before they need to become complaints. Mike is responsible to the social services committee and is accountable to an Assistant Director. He has the strong support of the Director himself. He has so far been able to ride above the people in the department who have tried to undermine him. The authority of his position is well-established within the social services department and the strength of his role is that it is educative as well as adversarial. He is a very good example of how 'person-power' can help to translate the theory of children's rights into practice.[4]

Following on from my work on complaints procedures at The National Childrens' Bureau I acted as consultant for the setting up of a complaints procedure for children in care in the London Borough of Greenwich. This experience showed me that one of the keys to success is the *process* of setting it up. A social worker, newly returned from a course, was seconded for eighteen months to work full-time on setting up the procedure. Because of his commitment and enthusiasm and his untiring energy in going round talking to children and staff at all levels and helping them to 'own' the procedure, we managed to get it off the ground. It is called an 'Advice and Complaints Procedure' and the main emphasis is on giving the children access to independent advisors and advocates so that they can get help, advice and support *before* decisions are made, and things happen. If the problem cannot be solved at that stage, or if it is something which has already happened, the child can make a 'formal' complaint.

The VCC is engaged in providing another successful service which is also designed to safeguard children's rights.

This service provides Independent Representatives (IRs) for young people in secure accommodation. We have in England 35 places where young people can be locked up. There are legal safeguards about why they can be locked up and for how long, and secure accommodation regulations which carry the force of law on how secure units should be run. We provide 'Independent Representatives', who are either attached to the units and visit regularly, or who visit an individual child on behalf of a local authority. The Independent Representatives are able to listen to what the young people want to say in confidence and in private, tell them about their rights and take up any issues on their behalf.

The service is not focussed on problems or complaints, which makes it more acceptable to staff, and many young people just value having someone independent to talk to. They also value being able to ask for information and often to double-check what their social worker has told them. However, if they wish to make a complaint the Independent Representative can act as their supporter and advocate. We work on a regional basis and recruit, train, accredit and support Independent Representatives, who work on a voluntary basis.

In the larger units there are up to three IRs who visit regularly. We also appoint a Link Person to each unit who is responsible for explaining the scheme to the staff and for keeping in touch with them regularly. We hold residential week-ends to publicise the scheme in new areas and to bring those who are working in the scheme together regularly. The advantages of the scheme are that it is cost effective in the use of person-power because it gets independent people right inside to where the most damaged and vulnerable children are – the secure units. They do not have to contact an unknown outsider if they want help or advice – it is readily available to them on a regular basis.

We have made a start by providing the services for young people in secure units but there is no reason why the service should not be adopted for other residential units, particularly our Observation and Assessment units. Any procedure or service is only useful if the people for whom it is designed have faith in it and use it. Many of our experiments have failed because the young people themselves did not trust them, or use them. We have to try to provide what children and young people in care want, rather than what we think they need. We have to take on board the fact that some children in care will only really trust adults who have had the experience of being in care themselves. We have an organisation in England called NAYPIC, the National Association of Young People in Care. When there is an office open and functioning, there is a flood of young people seeking help and support.

The other experiment in England which is very successful is Childline, the telephone help-line for children. This is by no means a new idea but England has been very slow to get this off the ground and it is supported entirely by voluntary funds. This is hampering its extension into providing a comprehensive service.

3. CONCLUSION

Since this paper was written the Children Act 1989 came into force on October 14th 1991. The complaints procedure as finally drafted requires that there should be an Independent Person appointed to take part in the consideration of formal complaints. Although disappointed that there is not a provision for advocacy or representation before a problem reaches this stage, we in the VCC felt that we must grasp the opportunity of providing this service. We have therefore set up a project to run until the end of 1992 in London, Yorkshire, the West Country and Birmingham. Over 35 local authorities and voluntary organisations, including over half of the London Boroughs have registered for the service and we have about 60 Independent Persons. The model works well but there is still a lack of referrals where the child or young person has made the complaint.

The Children Act, while introducing an independent element into a number of situations, does nothing to counterbalance the power of local authorities. Even in the final stage of the complaints procedure the review panel only has the power to recommend. The rights of children will only begin to be safeguarded when there is a powerful external body such as a Childrens' Commissioner or Ombudsperson who has the authority to investigate infringements of childrens' rights and to ensure that justice is done.

NOTES

1.   See M. D. A. Freeman, *Children, Their Families and the Law*, Macmillan (1992).
2.   See, in particular, Sections 22, 23, 25.
3.   See *The Rights and Wrongs of Children*, Frances Pinter (1983).
4.   See his article in *Journal of Social Welfare and Family Law* (1991).

ELAINE E. SUTHERLAND*

13. The Role of Children in the Making of Decisions Which Affect Them

1. INTRODUCTION

Decisions which affect children are taken all the time. A particular decision may be relevant to the life of an individual child or it may be significant for an identifiable group of children. The decision maker may be a carer, a parent, a government official, the legislature or a court.One feature stands out. The decisions will be made by adults. This raises the question of the role of children themselves in the decision-making process.

This question will be examined here in the context of Scots law as providing one example of the approach taken by a legal system operating within a Western democratic framework. The extent to which children have an opportunity to participate in decision making will be considered and assessed in the light of the U.N. Convention on the Rights of the Child.[1] Factors which inhibit children from so participating will then be highlighted and finally, means of enabling greater participation by children will be explored.

2. BACKGROUND

The extent to which Scots law provides children with an opportunity to participate in decision making can be assessed, in part, by reference to legislation and judicial decision. However, this gives an incomplete picture. Decisions taken within the family setting or where children are in institutional care are rarely subject to scrutiny. The extent to which the children involved have been consulted is not known. Thus, for example, when a family moves to live in a different area or when a particular bedtime is determined in a children's home, the decision is taken and implemented. The children involved may have taken an active part in that decision or they may have taken none at all. Furthermore, judicial decisions only illustrate the cases where a dispute has arisen and has been presented to a court. This requires that those

* University of Glasgow, Scotland.

M. Freeman and P. Veerman (eds.), The Ideologies of Children's Rights, 155–166.
© 1992 *Kluwer Academic Publishers. Printed in the Netherlands.*

in dispute are in a position to pursue this course of action – an option available to many adults but few children.

Defining a 'child' is not without its problems. Scots Law,[2] in common with the Convention,[3] defines a child as a person under 18 years of age. However, and particularly in the context of decision making, the age of 16 is of considerable significance in Scotland. At that age a young person may marry,[4] opt out of full-time education,[5] take up full-time employment[6] and leave the family home,[7] all without obtaining the permission of any adult. Court decrees governing custody and access apply only until the young person reaches 16.[8]

A further problem of definition arises over what is truly the 'child's view' in the context of a particular decision. To accept that what a child says is really the child's view is open to the criticism that the child may simply be repeating what he or she has been told by an adult or that the child's view as expressed is the result of indoctrination by an influential adult. It can be argued that adults' decisions are accepted as valid despite the fact that they are not made in vacuum. Nonetheless, children may be more vulnerable to influence and pressure and this possibility must be borne in mind in evaluating what they say. In a recent Scottish case,[9] the court took the view that, while two boys aged 10 and 8, expressed preferences supporting their mother's application to terminate their father's right to access, what they said was not a 'spontaneous and untutored' account of their wishes. Accordingly, while their views were taken into account, access was continued.

In reaching any decision concerning a child, the court is directed to regard the child's welfare as paramount.[10] This is a concept familiar to many legal systems and is the guiding principle set out in the Convention.[11] It is clear, however, that the child's welfare is assessed by the court on the basis of a variety of factors, only one of which will be the child's views. In such circumstances these views may be outweighed by other factors.[12]

3. WEIGHT ATTACHED TO THE CHILD'S VIEWS

In Scotland, the weight attached to the child's views varies depending on the particular type of decision being taken. Four broad categories can be identified.

3.1. *A Right of Consent or Veto*

On occasion, the child is given an absolute right to consent to or veto a decision. Examples of this approach are rare and are confined to adoption of minor children.

At present,[13] and for historical reasons,[14] children are classified as pupils or minors. Pupillarity lasts from birth until a female reaches 12 and a male 14 years of age. Thereafter the child becomes a minor. No adoption order may be made in respect of a minor unless he or she consents, except where the minor is incapable of giving consent.[15] In the latter case the court can dispense with the minor's consent. This contrasts with the weight attached to the views of the birth parents. While adoption usually proceeds on the basis of their having consented, or at least not opposed it, the birth parents' consent can be dispensed with by the court on a number of grounds,[16] including the fact that it is being unreasonably withheld.[17] The child's consent cannot be dispensed with in this way. It is submitted that the acknowledgement of the child's position here has more to do with the significance our legal system attaches to interests in property than recognition of children's rights in its broader sense. Adoption terminates the relationship between the child and his or her birth parents and thereby any right to aliment (maintenance) or of succession arising out of that relationship.[18] Nonetheless, by its very existence, the approach taken in the context of adoption demonstrates that it is possible to provide children with a major role in the decision-making process. Not only is this approach in accordance with the requirement of the Convention[19] that the child should have the right to express his or her views, but it goes further than simply giving 'due weight' to these views.

3.2.   *The Child's Views Are Taken Into Account*

The second, and more common, approach to the child's views is the requirement that these should be taken into account if it is possible to ascertain them. Where, for example, the adoption of a pupil child is being considered, the court is directed to ascertain the child's wishes and give due consideration to them.[20] Again, this accords with the provisions of the Convention.[21]

In the context of the breakdown of the parents' relationship, decisions regarding the custody of and access to the children must be taken. Every year thousands of children are the subject of such *de facto* or *de jure*[22] decisions. Their role here is, therefore, of considerable significance. While the court is directed to regard the child's welfare as paramount and not to make any decision unless it is satisfied that the decision is in the child's interests,[23] there is no requirement that the child be consulted at all. There is a considerable body of opinion supporting the view that, where the opportunity arises, the judge should take the child's views into account.[24] As one judge put it,

> When the child is a minor it would be, in my opinion, quite unrealistic, and indeed wrong, for the Court, in an issue of custody or access, to do other than place very great and usually decisive weight on the wishes of the child provided the Court is satisfied that these wishes as expressed by the child are genuine and in all the circumstances reasonable, and that compliance with them will not involve the child in any risk or positive danger to its welfare.[25]

While this view goes some way towards giving the child a place in the decision-making process, it applies only where the matter is decided in a disputed case before a court. Where the parents have never been married to each other or where they separate in fact, without seeking a judicial separation or a divorce, there is no opportunity for the courts to consider the arrangements made for the children. Indeed, even where there is a divorce the court usually does no more than rubber-stamp the arrangement which the parents have devised. Most divorces are undefended and proceed by way of affidavit evidence. As far as the arrangements for the children are concerned, the judge will usually see only the sworn statements of the pursuer (plaintiff) and one witness, who will frequently be a friend or relative of the pursuer.[26] There is no opportunity to cross examine them, and the judge does not see the child. Affidavits ought to contain considerable information including: the witness's relationship and contact with the child; details of the home conditions in which the child lives and the proposed care arrangements; details of the child's appearance, interests, state of health and educational arrangements; observations on the child's contact with other relatives, and observations on any other person who would be living in the home with the child and that person's relationship with him or her.[27] However, affidavits frequently do not cover all of these matters adequately, if at all.[28] While a detailed report and supplementary affidavits can be ordered, this is rarely done.[29] Thus, frequently the child's views are not sought and there is no way to ascertain the extent to which the child has been consulted in a particular case.

In the small number of cases where the issue of custody or access is disputed, the court will normally hear the views of a child who is old enough to express them. As has been seen, the judge will attempt to ascertain that the view is truly that of the child and not the product of influence or pressure.[30] However, the child's views will not necessarily determine the outcome of the case, and in assessing what is in the child's interest, the court will consider a number of factors. These include: the child's physical,[31] emotional,[32] moral[33] and educational welfare; past conduct of the parents which may affect the child's welfare; and ensuring stability by preservation of the *status quo*.[34] The child's views are, therefore, only one of a number of considerations which will influence the decision.

While in a disputed case the practice of hearing the child's view accords with the requirements of the Convention,[35] it is submitted that the failure to attempt to ascertain these views in the majority of cases where custody and access are uncontested does not. What can and ought to be done to remedy this will be considered presently.[36]

One area where children have the greatest opportunity to participate in decision making is the Children's Hearing System.[37] Briefly, the system deals with children who are both in need of care and protection and children who have committed offences. The latter category is the larger[38] and, in the former, many of the children are too young to express any views. The System is predicated on attempting to find a positive plan for the future aimed at avoiding the problems of the past and is non-punitive in nature.

Cases came into the system by means of referral from various agencies, most frequently the police or a local authority, and individuals[39] to an administrator, the Reporter. He or she must be satisfied both that there is a *prima facie* case supporting the allegations and that the child is in need of compulsory measures of care. At this point approximately 60%[40] of the cases proceed no further. The remaining 40% of cases are referred to a Children's Hearing, comprised of three lay persons.

At the Hearing the allegations are explained to the child and the parents. If they all accept that the allegations are true, the Hearing proceeds. If any one of them does not accept that the grounds on which the case is founded, or if the child is incapable of understanding the grounds, the case must either be dismissed or referred to a court for proof according to the usual rules of evidence and procedure. If proven the case is then referred back to a Hearing.

The task of the Hearing is to facilitate a round-table discussion involving the child, the parents, the panel members and a social worker. In addition, where there may be a conflict of interest between the child and the parents, an independent 'safeguarder' will be appointed to represent the child and that person will be involved in the discussion.[41] The discussion should address all relevant areas including the background to and sources of the problem and what might be done to improve the situation in the future. In particular, the Hearing is directed to try to obtain the views of the child, the parents and any safeguarder on what arrangements would be best for the child.[42] The three Hearing Members then reach their decision on the disposal of the case. The possibilities are: discharging the case; non-residential supervision (usually this results in the child returning to live with his or her parent(s) with social work involvement); or residential supervision.[43] Conditions of a non-punitive nature may be attached to supervision requirements and there is provisions for appeals and reviews.

In the context of the present discussion, it is significant that the Children's Hearing System not only demonstrates that it is possible to involve children as participants in the decision making process, but that participation is an essential element in the System. If this approach can work in one area, there is no reason why it cannot be applied to the whole decision-making process impacting upon children.

Where a decision is made in respect of a child who is in the care of the local authority or a voluntary organisation that body must

> so far as is practicable ascertain the wishes and feelings of the child regarding the decision and give due consideration to them, having regard to his age and understanding.[44]

Thus, at least in theory, the child has the opportunity to participate in decision making if he or she is in care.

The position of children who live with their families is far less clear and, to some extent, depends on the traditional distinction between pupils and minors,[45] as expressed in the brocard, *tutor datur personae, curator rei.*

According to this view,[46] the tutors (guardians) of a pupil child, who will usually be the parents, have control of both the child's person and property and, in acting on behalf of the child, take all decisions. The powers of curators (guardians) of minor children, who again will usually be the parents, is limited to consenting to the minors' decisions in respect of property only. Thus, decisions affecting the minor's person are the province of the minor himself or herself.

It should be noted that the traditional view is not universally accepted and the view has been expressed[47] that the decision-making power is an incident of custody or care and thus, the custodier of any child under 16 has the right to take decisions in respect of the child's person. This is subject to the court's right to intervene where the decision can be shown to be one which is not in the child's best interests.[48]

The current position is clearly unsatisfactory for a number of reasons. First, it appears that pupil children have no general right to participate in decision making unless they are in care. This is in clear breach of the Convention.[49] Secondly, the position of minors is unclear and, as such, is unsatisfactory. A striking example of the problem is consent to medical treatment. On the traditional view, any young person has the right to consent to or veto medical treatment on reaching 12, if female, or 14, if male. However, a Circular[50] sent to all hospitals by the relevant government department takes the view that the child has no such right until he or she reaches 16. It is submitted that this is not a rejection of the 'traditional view', but rather a blind following of the current legislation in England and Wales.[51] The matter has never been argued before a Scottish court and children, parents and the medical profession are left in an uncertain position. Proposals for reforms[52] have recommended that a child under 16 should be able to consent to any surgical, medical or dental procedure or treatment if, in the opinion of a qualified medical practioner attending that person, he or she is capable of understanding the nature and consequences of the treatment proposed.

A third difficulty of the present position is that the court's opportunity to intervene is subject to a case being brought before it. 'Any person with an interest'[53] may apply to the court for an order relating to parental rights (broadly, any matter concerning the welfare or upbringing of a child) and, while, in theory, the child could take this course of action, in practice the likelihood is remote.

The Scottish Law Commission has addressed the question of the child's place in decision making at two separate stages of a general project on Child Law. In its *Report on the Legal Capacity and Responsibility of Minors and Pupils*[54] it recommended that persons under 16 should be able to engage in transaction of a type commonly entered into by a child of the transacting child's age and understanding and made the specific recommendation on consent to medical treatments discussed above. These recommendations have been awaiting legislative action since 1987. The Commission's Discussion Paper on

Parental Responsibilities and Rights, Guardianship and the Administration of Children's Property[55] is currently the subject of extensive public consultation. In it, the Commission asks whether or not consultees would favour a general provision requiring any person with parental rights to ascertain the child's view, at least on 'major decisions', and to give due consideration to these in the light of the child's age and understanding.[56] While it is acknowledged that a reform along these lines is not without its problems such as, for example, the definition of a 'major decision' or 'due consideration' and enforcement of any such requirement, it is to be hoped that it is supported, thus enabling Scotland to meet the standards of the Convention.

3.3. *No Mention Is Made of the Child's Views*

The third category of approaches taken to decision making is that where statute makes provision for participation in the decision-making process, but no mention is made of the child's role. A clear example here is in the field of education. Subject to resources being available, parents and other carers have always had freedom of choice of the school attended by the child in the private sector. Since 1983,[57] this freedom of choice has been extended to the public sector (i.e. state-funded schools). There are extensive provisions on the parents' right to select a particular school and to appeal against refusal to implement their decisions.[58] Nowhere in the legislation is any mention made of the child's right to participate in this decision.

It can be argued that a child who was unhappy with his or her parents' choice could invoke the court's general power to intervene and could have his or her own preference substituted,[59] but this is hardly satisfactory given the lack of access which children have to legal services. Were the Scottish Law Commission's suggestion to be supported then children could be provided with an active role in this context.

3.4. *Policy Decisions and Children's Views*

A fourth category, concerned with general, rather than individual decisions can be identified. This covers decisions on matters of government policy and includes such issues as housing, health care, education and state-funded benefits. While the decisions here are taken by government and, as such, are one step removed from the population, adults at least have the right to participate in democratic elections which produce that government. Children and young persons have no such right. Furthermore, adults can organise themselves into lobbying groups and, while such organisation is not prohibited to children,[60] the opportunity to do so is limited in practice by ignorance and a lack of resources. Some of the suggestions discussed below might help to alleviate this problem.

Inhibitors on Children Participating in the Decision-Making Process and How They Might Be Removed

A fundamental barrier which prevents children from participating in the decision-making process is that while there is a plethora of judicial decisions and legislation dealing with children, the children themselves are rarely perceived as having an active role to play. They are seen as the subjects of protection rather than individuals with the right to have opinions and preferences. It will take a dramatic change in the attitudes of all adults to overcome this problem, but such a change would be possible. The following steps, some of which have been taken on a limited basis in Scotland, could facilitate the change.

When an area of law is being considered with a view to reform the views of children on the issue in general and the specific proposals for reform should be sought. This could be done by circulating information to children through schools, inviting comments and by conducting opinion polls of children. In the process of consultation which proceeded its *Report on the Legal Capacity and Responsibility of Minors and Pupils*, the Scottish Law Commission commissioned a survey of the attitudes of school pupils and school leavers to their proposals[61] and found the responses helpful.

In the course of drafting legislation thought should be given to how children affected by it can be given an opportunity to express their views when the legislation is implemented and decisions based upon it are being made. Two examples here demonstrate that this would not be difficult to achieve. Where parents have decided to seek a divorce each child in the family should be seen by an independent third party whose duty it would be to record the child's views and, perhaps, comment on how genuine these seemed. The judge could examine the statement and, if he or she thought necessary, investigate the matter further. Where parents expressed their preference that a child should attend a particular school, a statement of the child's preference could also be sought. The key element of these suggestions is that the child should automatically be seen as an active participant in the decision-making process.

A second inhibitor on child participation is ignorance. Even when children do have a right to have their views considered, they will frequently be unaware of it. Ignorance of one's rights is not a new phenomenon, nor is it confined to children. Many adults suffer from the same problem but steps taken to alleviate this has met with some success. Consumers, for example, are far more aware of their rights today than they were twenty years ago. Much of this is due to the media in general and television in particular, and this could be utilised in order to inform children of their rights. With children there is the unique additional opportunity to pass on information and engage in discussion through schools. Courses could be devised which would make children aware that they have rights and how they might enforce them. In addition, information booklets aimed at particular age groups could be provided.

Telling children of their rights would not be enough in isolation. Children have little or no access to legal services. It is imperative that they should be able to seek confidential legal advice and, where necessary, pursue that advice through the courts. Experience shows that children are unlikely to consult a solicitor or other legal advice facility and clearly a new method of making advice available must be found. Free telephone advice lines can be of assistance. The Scottish Child Law Centre, established in 1988, provides an information and advice service on this basis, although in 1989 only 2% of the calls came from under-18 year olds themselves.[62] It is likely that the Centre will expand its activities in this respect in the future, funding permitting. Clearly, there is a need for more to be done in this respect. One possibility would be to have lawyers available in schools and community centres for a few lunchtime and evening sessions per week.

A further problem which affects both the opportunity of individual children to have their views represented and the interests of children as a whole to be the focal point of attention on a given issue is the lack of specific representation at government or quasi-government level. A number of government ministers have responsibility for issues which affect children such as social security and health care, but they have many other responsibilities. Children's interests, (as opposed to their views), are promoted by a number of organisations, although in Scotland only the Child Law Centre is solely concerned with the whole area of Child Law. Nonetheless, there is no Minister or Ombudsman for Children. As a result, there is no holistic approach to the promotion of children's rights and interests.

This problem was acknowledged in the Report of the *Review of Child Care Law in Scotland*.[63] While the Review Group acknowledged that it is not directly within the scope of its remit, it felt compelled to recommend that the possibility of a Child Welfare Commission or Ombudsman for Children should be the subject of further examination.[64] It found support for the recommendation on a number of grounds including: achieving an holistic approach to children's needs; providing independent supervision of services available to children; raising public awareness and securing a voice for children's interests; and advising the Secretary of State for Scotland on how best to meet the needs of children. Perhaps most important in the present context is that the Review Group envisaged that any such agency would be available to advise children of their rights and assist them in the enforcement of these rights. Experience in Israel[65] and Norway[66] has demonstrated that an Ombudsman can provide an invaluable service in promoting children's rights in general and in assisting individual children to have an effective voice in matters which concern them. It is to be hoped that the Review Group's recommendation is acted upon as soon as possible.

4. CONCLUSIONS

In the light of the foregoing analysis, it is perhaps stating the obvious to point out that Scots law fails to give children the opportunity to participate in decision-making on a wide number of issues. That fact alone is enough reason to warrant changes and indeed, there is much support for a greater voice for children. In addition, we are failing to meet the universally accepted standards set out in the UN Convention. As a relatively affluent country in world terms, we have least excuse for failing to meet these standards. Thus, the climate is right for reforms which will ensure the active participation of children in decision-making.

Nor is the picture entirely hopeless. We have demonstrated through such examples as the Children's Hearing System and disputed custody cases that it is possible for children to present their views effectively. All that is now required is to apply that thinking in other areas. Of course, there are resource implications but I for one have no doubt that this would not only be money well spent, but money which must be spent.

NOTES

* The author wishes to thank the Anglo-Israel Association and the University of Glasgow. Their support made attendance at the Study-Group and the preparation of this paper possible. All views expressed are, of course, those of the author.

1. Convention on the Rights of the Child, General Assembly Documents, A/RE5/44/25 (5 December 1989).
2. Age of the Majority (Scotland) Act 1969, s. 1(1).
3. Article 1.
4. Marriage (Scotland) Act 1977, s. 1.
5. Education (Scotland) Act 1980, ss. 30 and 31.
6. Children and Young Persons (Scotland) Act 1937, ss. 28–31 (as amended).
7. While the Social Work (Scotland) Act 1968, s. 15 provides that the local authority is under an obligation to take any person under the age of 17 into care where he or she has been abandoned by his or her parents, this obligation only arises where such intervention is necessary for to protect the young person's welfare. In practice, this is not done in respect of young persons over 16.
8. Law Reform (Parent and Child) (Scotland) Act 1986, s. 8 (a).
9. *Marco* v *Marco* 1989 G.W.D. 5–190. See also *Cosh* v *Cosh* 1979 SLT (Notes) 72 where the children's reluctance to visit their father dated only from their mother's remarriage and the Court believed it to be the result of the influence of the mother and step-father. The mother's motion for the termination of access was refused.
10. Law Reform (Parent and Child) (Scotland) Act 1986, s. 3(2).
11. Article 3(1).
12. *Nicol* v *Nicol* 1953 SLT (Notes) 67.
13. Proposals for reform of the law on pupils and minors contained in the Scottish Law Commission's, *Report on the Legal Capacity and Responsibility of Minors and Pupils* (Scot. Law Com. No. 110, 1987), await Government action. In so far as they affect adoption, the proposals would result in 12 being the age at which all children acquire the right to consent to or veto their own adoption irrespective of gender (paras. 3.84–3.86 and Recc. 7.)
14. See, Smith, *A Short Commentary on the Law of Scotland*, W. Green and Son (1962), at pp. 254–257.
15. Adoption (Scotland) Act 1978, s. 12(8).

16. Ibid., s. 16
17. Ibid., s. 16(2)(6)
18. Ibid., s. 12.
19. Article 12.
20. Adoption (Scotland) Act 1978, s. 6.
21. Article 12.
22. In 1988, of a total under-16 population of approximately 1 million, 9,224 children were involved in divorce Registrar General Scotland, *Annual Report* 1988.
23. Parent and Child (Scotland) Act 1986, s. 3(2). Clive, *The Law of Husband and Wife in Scotland*, W. Green and Son (1982) at p. 568.
24. Thomson, *Family Law in Scotland*, Butterworth and Co. and The Law Society of Scotland (1984), at p. 63; Sutherland, 'Parent and Child', *The Laws of Scotland: Stair Memorial Encyclopaedia*, Butterworth and Co., and The Law Society of Scotland (1990), Vol. 10 para. 1287.
25. *Glover* v *Glover* 1969 SLT (Notes) 78, *per* Lord Thomson at p. 78.
26. A study of custody and access decisions in 1984 found that 91% of these affidavits were provided by a relative, friend, neighbour or cohabitee of the pursuer. Seale, *Children in Divorce*, Scottish Office (1984), at p. 19.
27. Guideline issued by Sheriffs Principal, cited in Bennett, *A Short Guide to Divorce in the Sheriff Court*, W. Green and Son (1987), at p. 140.
28. Seale, Note 26, *supra*, at pp. 16–19.
29. Seale, Note 26, *supra*, found that in only 8% of the cases examined was there supplementary evidence in the form of an additional affidavit, a medical report or a letter. Some of these had been requested by the court while others had been presented voluntarily.
30. See p. 156, *supra*.
31. *Geddes* v *Geddes* 1987 GWD 11–349.
32. *O'Hagan* v *O'Hagan* 1989 GWD 8–319; *Morrow* v *Morrow* 1989 GWD 13–533; *Smith* v *Kaid* 1989 GWD 13–534.
33. *McClements* v *McClements* 1958 SC 286; *Early* v *Early* 1989 SLT 114.
34. *Pow* v *Pow* 1931 SLT 485; *Hannah* v *Hannah* 1971 SLT (Notes) 42; *Whitecross* v *Whitecross* 1977 SLT 225; *Mooney* v *Mooney* 1987 GWD 3–80.
35. Article 12(2).
36. See p. 162, *infra*.
37. The system was proposed in the *Report of the Committee on Children and Young Persons* (Cmnd. 2306, 1964) and implemented by the Social Work (Scotland) Act 1968, Part III. It has been in operation since 1971.
38. In 1988, 68% of referrals related to offences, 8% to truancy and 25% to care and protection. *Statistical Bulletin*, No. CH13 1989 (Scottish Education Department, 1989).
39. In 1988, 79% of referrals came from the police, 10% from the Social Work Department, 8% from schools and the remaining 3% from other sources including the public (*Statistical Bulletin*, Note 38, *supra*).
40. *Statistical Bulletin*, Note 38, *supra*.
41. This provision was introduced by the Children Act 1975, s. 66, although it did not come into operation until 1985.
42. The Children's Hearings (Scotland) Rules 1986, SI No. 86/2291, Rule 19(2)(d).
43. In 1988, in 31% of the referrals no further action was taken. This included cases which were abandoned, where the grounds were not established, or where the Hearing discharged the case. Of the 69% of referrals disposed of by means of a supervision requirement, 88% of such supervision was non-residential.
44. Social Work (Scotland) Act 1968, s. 20.
45. See p. 156, *supra*.
46. Smith, op. cit. Note 14, *supra*; Sutherland, 'Parent and Child', *The Laws of Scotland: Stair Memorial Encyclopeadia*, Note 24, *supra*, Vol. 10, paras. 1045–1146.

47.   Thomson, 'Shades of the Prison House' (1986) *Scottish Law Gazette* 60.

48.   Law Reform (Parent and Child) (Scotland) Act 1986, s. 3.

49.   Article 12.

50.   National Health Service Circular 1985 (Gen) 81.

51.   Family Law Reform Act 1969, s. 8(1).

52.   *Report on the Legal Capacity and Responsibility of Minors and Pupils* (Scot. Law Com. No. 110, 1987), paras. 3.61–3.83 and Rec. 6.

53.   Law Reform (Parent and Child) (Scotland) Act 1986, s. 3(1).

54.   Op. cit., note 48, *supra*, at paras. 3.21–3.39 and Rec.3.

55.   Discussion Paper No. 80, 1990.

56.   Ibid., 2.41–2.43.

57.   Education (Scotland) Act 1980, s. 28(1).

58.   Ibid. ss. 28A–28G (added by Education (Scotland) Act 1981). These provisions came into force on 1st Jan. 1983.

59.   Reform (Parent and Child) (Scotland) Act 1986, s. 3(1).

60.   The organisation's own rules may set specific age limits. For example, both the Labour Party (Young Socialists) and the Young Conservatives allow membership to young persons of 15 or over.

61.   Scottish Office Central Research Unit, *The Legal Capacity of Minors and Pupils- Experiences and Attitudes to Change* (May 1987).

62.   In first quarter of 1990, the proportion increased to 2.5%. The remainder of the enquiries came from professionals and adult members of the public seeking information and/or advice (*Scottish Child Law Centre: Annual Report 1989–90*, p. 6).

63.   (HMSO 1990).

64.   Ibid., paras. 23.1–23.6 and Rec. 88.

65.   Horovitz, 'Pilot Project of an Ombudsman for Children and Youth in Jerusalem', in Verhellen and Spiesschaert (eds.), *Ombudswork For Children*, Ghent (1987) at pp. 159–164.

66.   Flekkøy, *Working For The Rights of Children: The Experience of the Norwegian Ombudsman for Children*, UNICEF (1990).

GARY B. MELTON* AND SUSAN P. LIMBER*

14. What Children's Rights Mean to Children: Children's Own Views

WHY STUDY CHILDREN'S OWN VIEWS?

One of the near-certainties of conferences on children's rights (such as the one from which this volume is derived) is that children will not be involved. Starting from that premise, we feel compelled before we describe research on children's views of their rights to explain what may be obvious to readers of this volume: why information about children's perspective on children's rights is of more than academic interest.[1] There are at least four rationales, which we will discuss in turn: (a) providing the foundation for an agenda for child advocacy; (b) informing policymakers about the legal and political structures needed to vindicate children's rights; (c) showing respect for children as persons; (d) enhancing legal and political socialization through participation in decision making.

An Agenda for Advocacy

Inquiry of children themselves often is important in setting an agenda for advocacy. Without systematic surveys of children themselves, professionals who purport to be expert in child psychology and related disciplines rarely are very skilled in identifying those matters that are of most concern to children (at least in the United States[2]). Indeed, the items that children themselves report as serious stressors – assaults on personal integrity (e.g., accusations of lying), school-based threats to self-esteem (e.g., being sent to the principal; receiving a poor report card), conflicts among peers (e.g., trying to make it through the day without getting into a fight), and family strife – for the most part are not ones that are likely even to appear in professionals' discussions of child mental health (see Melton, 1987, for a review; see also Armacost, 1989, and Yamamoto *et al.*, 1987).

Even family strife, the one category on the list that is apt to be given extensive coverage in treatises on child mental health and welfare, is not likely

---

* Center on Children, Families, and the Law, University of Nebraska-Lincoln.

M. Freeman and P. Veerman (eds.), The Ideologies of Children's Rights, 167–187.
© 1992 *Kluwer Academic Publishers. Printed in the Netherlands.*

to be experienced by children as a stressor in precisely the manner that adult professionals often conceptualize it. Children in families of divorce rarely identify the divorce itself when they are asked to list things that they worry about; rather, they identify specific day-to-day events that are especially stressful (e.g., transitions in moving from one parental home to the other; see Wertlieb, 1991) and that may serve as a list of considerations in designing policy on custody dispositions.

In terms of social conditions directly related to public policy, 'youth issues' turn out to be crime (Foundation of Child Development, 1977; Sigel and Hoskin, 1981) and employment (Sigel and Hoskin, 1981). Although these problems are not unique to children and adolescents, the fact that they are of central concern to youth themselves should put them on the agenda for child advocates, with attention to the particular dimensions of the issues as they are experienced by youth (e.g., not having a safe place to play; difficulty in finding a first job; facing age discrimination in conditions of schooling and employment; perhaps most commonly, not being taken seriously by policy makers and program administrators when they act on such issues[3]).

Thus, research on children's experience of their rights may be useful in constructing an agenda for advocacy because it may illuminate that most critical problems for children in fulfillment of their rights. Even more fundamentally, it may help to define the contours of the rights themselves. For example, the first author (Melton, 1983c) and some of his former students (see, e.g., Kagehiro, 1988; Kagehiro and Laufer, 1990; Small, 1990a, 1990b; Small and Wiener, in press) have begun to identify the psychological significance and subjective meaning of privacy (see also Rivlin and Wolfe, 1985; Wolfe, 1978). That line of research may help to establish the critical elements of a concept that has proven slippery for both lawyers and philosophers but that may have extraordinary meaning in government's relation to the individual. It may also illuminate the intrusions on personal boundaries that are most noxious – most violative of personal integrity – to people of different ages and, therefore, that are most important to avoid.

Implementation of Children's Rights

Thus far we have discussed the significance of empirical research as a means of establishing the substantive rights owed children. Information about children's concepts of their rights and the phenomenology of their exercise of rights also may be useful in the design of *structures* and *procedures* for implementation of children's rights in a manner that is most protective of children's dignity.

Even when political and legal authorities have announced their good-faith intention to implement children's rights, a central problem remains in persuading children themselves that they really *do* have rights. Children from disadvantaged backgrounds often are so skeptical that their exercise of rights will go unpunished that their legal rights become virtually meaningless in practice, even in circumstances in which the perception of an absence of rights does not match reality (see, e.g., Lewis, 1983; Melton, 1980; see also Melton, 1983b, discussing Grisso, 1981).[4] Although extraordinary effort may be particularly necessary to convince some lower-class and ethnic-minority children that they actually are empowered to exercise autonomy, the difficulty that *most* minors have in fulfilling their rights means that even adolescents often will require special procedures if newly recognized rights are to be enjoyed. Youth from affluent backgrounds may experience entitlement to that which they need (and have), but they also often may find that their personal concerns are not taken very seriously by the adults important to them (see Coles, 1977).

In what may be primarily a reflection of the socioeconomic background of the juveniles in the United States who actually enter detention, the evidence is quite clear that juvenile respondents, especially those under age 16, rarely invoke the privilege against self-incrimination and that they are less able than adult defendants (who themselves generally are not very competent in absolute terms) to comprehend their rights (Grisso, 1981). In such a context, it perhaps should be unsurprising – although still disturbing – that many (in some states, most) juveniles waive their right to counsel altogether (Feld, 1988, 1989).

Although the problem is more pervasive and more difficult to resolve in lower-class communities, even affluent youth sometimes must be convinced that adults are serious when they recognize children's rights. For example, Belter and Grisso (1984) found that adolescents were as skilled as adults in identifying violations of rights in psychotherapy but that they demonstrated their competence only when they were provided with models, presumably showing that it was all right to challenge adult authority.

Taken together, such findings suggest that due process for minors differs from that for adults (Melton, 1989; Rosenberg, 1980). Even if minors are presumed to have the full panoply of rights owed autonomous persons, special procedures and institutions may be necessary to vindicate those rights, because of (a) children's inexperience in contacting and using professionals; (b) the obstacles that are placed in the way of children's contracting for such representation independently; (c) the disbelief that some children have that their rights will be enforced; and (d) the developmental differences that may exist in the meaning ascribed to various legal procedures and institutions (e.g., the jury; see McKeiver v. Pennsylvania, 1971).

The point about development differences in the phenomenology of the law is implicitly recognized in the United Nations Convention on the Rights of the Child (1989), which requires states-parties to develop procedures in criminal, juvenile, and school-disciplinary proceedings that are 'consistent with the promotion of the child's sense of dignity and worth' (Article 40, para. 1; see also Article 28, para. 2). Note that the standard to be used for assessing the legitimacy of juvenile procedures is subjective, to be judged by their relation to the 'child's *sense* of dignity and worth' (emphasis added).

In short, research on children's concepts of their rights may be critical to development of procedures that will permit children to *feel* that they are being heard, whatever the objective reality of adult authorities' responses to children's complaints.[5] Such research thus is an important step to ensuring not only that children exercise the rights due them but also that the purpose underlying particular rights is fulfilled. Objective autonomy is empty if it is not accompanied by a sense that one's worth as a person is being recognized and respected.

Taking Children Seriously

Indeed, even if there were no instrumental benefit of asking children about their views on their rights, such a step would be an important signal of respect for their personhood. As Minow (1990) argued in her provocative recent treatise on the rights of disadvantaged groups:

> Including children as participants alters their stance in the community, from things or outsiders to members. . .. The assertion of membership accomplishes something important but does not itself disturb or challenge unequal arrangements of political or economic power. . ..
>
> What, then, is the equality signaled by rights discourse? The equality embodied by rights claims is an equality of *attention*. The rights tradition . . . sustains the call that makes those in power at least listen. Rights – as words and as forms – structure attention even for the claimant who is much less powerful than the authorities, and even for individuals and groups treated throughout the community as unequal. Unstated here are assumptions about the presumed standard for comparison: equal to whom? An adult, white, competent male citizen is the likely reference. But by including any who can speak the language of rights and by signaling deserved attention, rights enable a challenge to unstated norms, to exclusion, and the exclusive perspectives. Rights discourse implicates its users in a form of life, a pattern of social and political commitment. (pp. 297–298)

In keeping with the conviction that the least that people in power can do to build a sense of community is to listen to those who are disenfranchised, the UN Convention on the Rights of the Child (1989, Article 12; see also Articles 13 and 14) requires states-parties to ensure that children have the opportunity to express their views about all matters concerning them. Surely the spirit of this provision goes beyond the right to be heard in individual matters (see, e.g., Article 12, para. 2) to the right to voice opinions on matters affecting children as a class. In that regard, periodic systematic surveys of children themselves about matters pertaining to their rights might be an essential element of each nation's implementation of the Convention.

Legal Socialization

The final and, in our view, least important rationale for systematic involvement of children in the definition of their rights is that such involvement
itself may have socializing effects. In other words, even if one does not care
about children's rights for the sake of children themselves, one still might
support the stimulation of thinking about the nature and fulfillment of rights,
because such experiences are likely to result in greater support for democratic values, including responsibility for creating just law and tolerance for
expression of rights by others (Tapp and Levine, 1974). Such participation also
has a myriad of positive psychological effects, notably increased self-esteem,
that are associated with increased perceived control and that are compatible
with the state's interest in the healthy socialization of its citizens (Tremper and
Kelly, 1987). In such a context, support for self-expression by children
may be premised on the social costs involved in the ultimate development of adults who are unable to fulfill the responsibilities of citizens in a
democracy.

Consistent with this view, the UN Convention (1989, Article 40, para. 1)
requires the development of procedures in juvenile justice that not only promote
a child's sense of dignity and worth but that also promote 'the child's respect
for the human rights and fundamental freedoms of others' and take 'into
account. . . the desirability of promoting the child's re-integration and the
child's assuming a constructive role in society'. More generally, the Convention
is oriented toward integration of children into the community as a whole
(Melton, 1991c, 1991d) 'prepared to live an individual life in society, and
brought up in the spirit of the ideals proclaimed in the Charter of the United
Nations, and in particular in the spirit of peace, dignity, tolerance, freedom,
equality, and solidarity' (UN Convention, 1989, Preamble).

Summary

The perspective from which the studies reported in this chapter were designed
was one of *psychological jurisprudence* (see Melton, 1990a, 1990b, in press),
a jurisprudential theory based on the premise that

> the purpose of law is to promote human welfare – a purpose that demands
> taking people seriously. Doing so requires systematic attention to everyday
> experience of citizens, so that legal doctrines and action conform with
> common understanding of important legal constructs and that they protect
> the interests that people regard as most fundamental. . . .. [M]ore impor-
> tant than the specific form of the evidence is the framework that increases
> the congruence between legal action and citizens' expectations. (Melton,
> in press)

In that vein, 'international human rights law already rests on a foundation
that permits a psychological analysis of the range and scope of rights to

which people are entitled, through a determination of the requisites for the subjective experience of human dignity or, conversely, of the conditions that result in belittlement or a loss of self-respect' (Melton, in press). Taking subjective experience as its focus, psychological jurisprudence offers a means of application of psychological mindedness in order to 'begin to develop systematically in directions that ultimately will result in a legal system that is more responsive to human needs and aspirations. Such an approach also is likely to yield a body of knowledge that is substantially more informative about the human condition than most psycholegal research has been thus far' (Melton, in press; see also Melton, 1988, 1989).

Psychological jurisprudence takes a *bottom-up* perspective that institutionalizes concern with 'the significance and subjective meaning of law in everyday life' (Melton, in press; see also Dahl, 1987, and Nader, 1985). Development of law that matches such experience is facilitated by systematic attention to social reality – an approach that is typically facilitated by empirical research:

> If the law is to confirm the importance of the individual, then the meaning of the ideas in the law should match common understanding, the assumptions in the law should not falsify or mystify experience, and the law should protect those interests that are most critical subjectively to maintenance of dignity. (Melton, in press)

Consistent with those aims, the remainder of this chapter is a report of several studies that provide an overview of children's own beliefs and attitudes about their rights. Such research provides a glimpse of the legal interests that are important to children and youth themselves.

CHILDREN'S RIGHTS IN CROSS-CULTURAL CONTEXT

The Populations Studied

Massachusetts. We have conducted a series of studies in which children were interviewed about their concepts of rights and other legal concepts. In the first of these studies (Melton, 1980, 1983a), 90 schoolchildren in the Boston area participated. The participants were first, third, fifth, and seventh graders in an affluent suburb and a working-class suburb (mostly Italian- and Portuguese-American) of Boston, and seventh graders in an inner-city Boston school (majority African-American).

Nebraska. More recently, we interviewed a representative sample of 300 schoolchildren in the American Midwest.[6] Half of the sample lived in an urban area (Lincoln), and the other half were drawn from several rural communities in southeastern Nebraska. Participants included preschool (age 4) through eighth-grade schoolchildren.

Washington State. We also recently completed a study of children in King County, Washington (Seattle). In that study, we interviewed a sample of more than 100 children (aged 4 to 13) going through criminal sexual abuse proceedings (*witnesses*) and an equivalent-size *comparison* sample not known to have been abused and who, of course, were not undergoing a comparable legal process. The comparison sample was matched insofar as possible for age, gender, ethnicity, and family income. However, we were unable to find a sample of sufficiently low socioeconomic status for a true match, so statistical controls also were used for family income.

The participants were interviewed twice. Among the witnesses, the interviews took place (*pre-*) within a week after their initial contacts with the prosecutors, and (*post-*) six months later or when the case concluded, whichever came later. (Because of a strict speedy-trial statute, most criminal sexual abuse cases conclude within six months in Washington State.) Comparison participants were interviewed two times, also with a six-month interlude.

Norway.[7] In the final study that we have conducted thus far, a native Norwegian graduate student in anthropology interviewed a representative sample of 192 school-aged children (grades 1 through 9[8]) from several schools of diverse social class in Trondheim, Norway.

What Has Been Learned

Care obviously must be taken not to overgeneralize our results. Our research thus far has been limited to Western, wealthy countries, although the participants have had a wide range of socioeconomic backgrounds.

As we noted in Note 2, though, available research suggests that principles of socialization are not bound to particular legal and political cultures. Consistent with this view, promotion of human dignity has become well established as a value in international law – a norm that also is reflected in remarkably diverse religious traditions (Melton, in press). Although specific political values appear to be highly susceptible to cultural influence, concern with maintenance of respect for persons and, accordingly, for protection of dignity appears to be central to the human condition.

The question is an empirical one, but we believe that it is likely that a developmental unfolding of such concerns is a human universal. The endpoint of this development may be variable, because of variations in opportunities for practice in self-expression and in the need for concern with simple survival, whether physical (as may be the case in developing nations) or psychological (as may be the case in dictatorships; see Garbarino and Bronfenbrenner, 1976).

What we can say with confidence at this point is that '[a]dvocates need not worry about depriving children of innocence by involving them in political issues. Children, like adults, are political beings by reason of their living in a political society' (Melton, 1987, p. 363). By the end of the primary grades, children are well settled into the political culture in which they are growing up, and they have considerable concern with maintenance of those interests that adults associate with human dignity (e.g., liberty; privacy; preservation of personal integrity, physically and psychologically).

There are a number of key findings that emerge from our own and others' work on legal and political socialization.

Legal socialization theory and research show a developmental progression from views of rights as (I) what one can have or do to (II) what one should be able to have or do (privileges) *to (III) what one must be able to have or do, as a matter of principle* (natural rights).

The average child becomes sufficiently socially aware to have a Level II concept of their rights by about age 8 in Norway and among affluent children in the United States. American children from lower-class backgrounds often do not achieve that level until about two years later. In general, though, by the end of the primary grades, children perceive protection of their rights as a matter of fairness if not one of moral entitlement.

Consistent with the movement away from an egocentric concept of rights based on the concrete limits of what children are permitted to do toward concepts based on moral considerations, children's attitudes towards their rights become more positive as they mature. In the Washington State sample, the correlation between age and attitudes toward children's rights was 0.48; the relationship observed in Norway was similar. With the understanding of the basis of rights in respect for each other, children move developmentally toward increasing understanding of the universality of rights.[9]

Because of the abstract thinking that is required for consideration of entitlement as a matter of principle, the notion that rights are not revocable by authority is not established before early adolescence. Indeed, the majority of adults never adopt such reasoning as their modal approach to analysis of problems in which a right might be asserted (Tapp & Levine, 1974). Thus, as in other moral and legal domains, cognitive development establishes necessary but not sufficient skills for qualitative advances in reasoning about rights.

That a stage-like process is at work can be seen in the patterns of data about legal reasoning. For example, although general legal knowledge shows a steady linear increase across middle childhood, understanding of the equities of the legal system emerge slowly until about seventh grade, at which point there typically is a significant increase in children's understanding of what makes a trial fair. (Even 8-year-olds, though, are usually cognizant of the adversariness of the legal process, and they believe that having a say is a key element of fairness in dispute resolution. Accordingly, an understanding of the rudiments of due process is acquired at a young age, as our interviews about a vignette about fairness in school disciplinary proceedings also indicate.)

Similarly, although the Washington State study showed that general knowledge about the legal process is highly related to children's concepts ($r =$

0.65) and attitudes ($r = 0.48$) about their rights, this relationship can be observed only in limited age ranges. Reflecting consistency of Level II reasoning among children in the intermediate grades, the correlation between general legal knowledge and the level of reasoning about rights exceeds 0.40 only among children in grades K–2 and 6–7, when transitions to higher levels of reasoning typically occur.

Although principled reasoning about rights typically does not occur until adolescence, the conclusion should not be reached that younger children are naive politically and legally. Consistent with their conceptualization of rights as dependent on whether one actually can do or have something without being punished, preschool and primary-grade children are exquisitely aware of who is in charge in the situation in which they commonly find themselves. Accordingly, an awareness of the significance of power occurs early in development. A third grader's comments are illustrative:

> Some people have rights to like take projectors from the library, and Mr. H [the school principal] has the rights about the school, and Mrs. J [the librarian] has rights about the library. And the President has rights about the country, or the king or the queen. (Melton, 1980, p. 37)

Age is the most powerful factor determining concepts of rights.

Among the Nebraska and Washington State samples, age accounted for nearly three-fourths of the variance in knowledge about the legal process and legal concepts ($r = 0.86$). Age also accounts for a substantial proportion of the variance (> 40%) in the Massachusetts sample; > 35% in the Norwegian sample) in reasoning about children's rights. The seemingly weaker relationship between age and concepts of rights than between age and general legal knowledge probably is an artifact of the limited range of levels of reasoning and the consistency of level of reasoning in middle childhood. As already noted, growth in understanding of the nature of rights appears to be a stage-like progression.

Among children themselves, social class is also an important determinant of concepts of and attitudes toward children's rights.

As Coles (1977) showed in his report of interviews of children from wealthy families, affluence offers children the experience of entitlement. It also provides experience with diverse social roles and opportunities for consideration of the requirements for social order and personal satisfaction in an array of situations. Accordingly, as already noted, children's rate of development of an understanding of rights is significantly related to their social class background, although maturation itself is a substantially stronger factor in such development.

In the Washington State sample, general legal knowledge and family income (as reported by the participants' parents) were moderately correlated ($r = 0.22$). A weak relationship was observed between family income and children's concepts of rights ($r = 0.09$), although this difference in the level of correlation, like the one noted in regard to age and concepts of rights, may be a statistical artifact.

The greater ease with which rights are considered and asserted by people of privileged backgrounds is not unique to childhood and adolescence. Although rights-consciousness may be a hallmark of American culture (see Bellah *et al.*, 1985), support for civil liberties [10] is in fact largely limited to elite groups. Summarizing research about such attitudes (e.g., McCloskey and Brill, 1983), we reached conclusions that are also applicable, at least by analogy, to the relationship between social class and libertarianism among youth:

> In general, people who express support for civil liberties tend to be unusually 'worldly'. The modal libertarian is young, lives in a metropolitan area, works in a professional occupation, tends towards 'humanism' in religious beliefs, enjoys complexity, and feels confident of his or her ability to generate interesting ideas.
>
> In short, as a psychological matter, civil liberties are real only to the relatively small segment of our society who experience diversity in social roles and who work in the marketplace of ideas – who in fact are entitled. (Melton and Saks, 1985, p. 267)

Involvement in the legal system does not, by itself, educate children and adolescents about their rights.

Experience *per se* is not socializing; rather, legal socialization requires experiences in which one *does* make choices and *is* heard. Accordingly, experience in the juvenile justice system is unrelated to understanding of *Miranda* rights (Grisso, 1981). Rote recitation of such rights by a police officer does not, by itself, give juveniles any greater confidence that they can assert such rights or any greater comprehension of their significance.

Similarly, we found that child victim/witnesses gained no greater understanding of the legal process than did children of comparable backgrounds who were not involved in the legal process at the time. Moreover, neither the average witness nor the average child in the comparison sample possessed as great an understanding of the legal process as did the average child in a representative sample of school children, probably because the Washington State sample was composed predominantly of children of lower- and lower-middle-class backgrounds. (That skew reflected class bias in the cases that actually enter the legal system.) Also, the comparison sample scored consistently higher than did the witnesses, on average, but the difference did not reach statistical significance.

By the end of the primary grades, children in the general population in the United States have substantial knowledge about the legal process and key legal vocabulary, with the former developing earlier.

In the Nebraska study, the youngest children in the sample (preschoolers and kindergarteners) received very low scores on all scales. They were able to correctly answer less than 15% of the items testing Expressive Vocabulary (legal terms, such as *attorney*), less than 20% of those assessing Knowledge of the Legal Process, and they correctly identified only one-third of the actors in the pictures (Receptive Vocabulary). By the end of the primary grades, however, children exhibited a substantial knowledge of the legal system by receiving over 50% of the total points allowed. The largest gains in knowledge occur between second and fifth grades, after which there is a leveling off in knowledge acquired. Children typically demonstrated an understanding of concepts before they acquired the relevant vocabulary – a finding that suggests that education that builds on children's intuitive understanding of the legal process could facilitate their involvement in the process, if authorities do not expect children to know particular terminology.

There was a high level of consistency in the ages at which particular concepts first appeared – a consistency that was replicated among both witness and comparison participants in the Washington State sample. Similar developmental progressions have been observed in studies involving English-speaking participants (see, e.g., Flin *et al.*, 1989; Saywitz, 1989; Saywitz *et al.*, 1990; Warren-Leubecker *et al.*, 1989).

The easiest legal term for Nebraska schoolchildren to understand was *police*, which was generally understood by even the youngest children in the study. By age 8, most children had gained at least a partial understanding of *arrest, judge, lawyer*, and *prosecutor*. By the age of 9, children had acquired an understanding of the additional concepts *trial, defense lawyer*, and *bail*. Children exhibited an understanding of the terms *oath, testify*, and *jury* by age 11. The most difficult concepts for children to grasp were *defendant* (understood by urban children at age 9, but rural children at age 13) and *attorney* (understood by most 12-year-old urban children but not by rural children of the same age).

For American (but not Norwegian) children, attitudes toward children's rights are differentiable between nurturance and self-determination rights.

The children's rights movement, at least in the United States, has been fractured (although not always overtly) by conflicts between those who would 'save' children and those who would 'liberate' them (see Melton, 1983a; Mnookin, 1978; Rogers and Wrightsman, 1978). Perhaps unsurprisingly, children reflect the same attitudinal schism. Their attitudes toward children's rights divide into factors that appear to involve more specific attitudes towards protection of children and self-determination by children.

Perhaps because such issues are not so starkly presented in social democracies, the factor structure for Norwegian children's attitudes toward their rights is much more complex, with five factors present[11] and no obvious interpretation of the constructs that they represent. For both American and Norwegian children, though, attitudes toward children's rights (i.e., whether they favored children's expression of rights in particular situations) were substantially more situationally linked than their level of reasoning about such issues. Most correlations among items (12 vignettes about situations in which a child might assert a right) are less than 0.20 when the attitude is scored; most inter-item correlations for level of reasoning are greater than 0.20 for Norwegian children and greater than 0.30 for American children.

American children have particular concerns about self-determination and freedom of expression.

When asked what rights children do or should have, American children (from the time that they understand the word) respond in terms of liberty – the ability to make choices, 'do things', or express oneself. Among primary-grade children, this interest is often expressed as a right to play. Older children focus more on freedom of movement, autonomy in decision making, and freedom of expression.

Norwegian children have particular concerns about nurturance rights – special entitlements and protection for children.

In contrast to American children (fewer than 10% of whom mention nurturance rights when asked an open-ended question about the nature of their rights), virtually all Norwegian children who understand the word *right* speak in terms of positive rights (e.g., right to education, freedom from hunger). Indeed, the only other concerns mentioned commonly by Norwegian children were age-specific. About one-fifth of 12- and 13-year-olds mentioned freedom of expression, perhaps reflecting early adolescent concerns with differentiation of oneself. Perhaps reflecting their initial experiences with some independence from home, one-fourth of 7- and 8-year-olds mentioned the ability to make decisions in everyday matters (e.g., the right to decide how to spend one's money).

In answer to the open-ended questions, Norwegian children often listed entitlements and protection from harm. The following examples were typical:

(12-year-old boy) Everyone has the right to free health and health service.

(13-year-old girl) Peace, care, food, clothes, and education.

(10-year-old boy) Right to enough food, a place to live, parents, not to have to work, school, medicines.

(8-year-old girl) Right to have a good life, food, clothes, money.

(11-year-old girl) To have a good and safe home. And the grownups are not allowed to hit us.

Some Norwegian children also answered the open-ended questions in terms of the differences in care available to children in the Third World, as compared with children in developed countries ('those who live in rich countries'), a concern that has never been mentioned by an American child in the hundreds of interviews that we have conducted about children's rights. In a similar concern with equality, Norwegian children sometimes expressed limitations on children's autonomy, because they valued equal treatment above all. A typical reply of this sort was made by a 16-year-old boy, who opposed a hypothetical child's ability to choose courses of study, because that child 'must have the same subjects as the others. There shouldn't be any difference.'

Given their concern with nurturance rights and their experience with a universal health care system, it is unsurprising that Norwegian children (94.8%) virtually always asserted a right of children who are injured to obtain medical care, regardless of their parents' ability to pay. Although the majority of American children answer similarly, older children in the United States sometimes conceptualize the problem as one of *doctors'* right to be paid for their work.

Both American and Norwegian children believe that protection of their privacy is important, but such concerns may be especially salient among Norwegian children.

American research on concepts of privacy (see Melton, 1983c) shows that a concern with privacy is well established even by the primary grades. Its significance may increase developmentally, and the specific nature of concerns (e.g., privacy of space versus privacy of information) also shifts developmentally.

Although American children typically have such concerns, they appear to be even more basic to Norwegian children, where privacy may be a particularly strong value in the culture. More than 90% of Norwegian children advocated a child's ability to maintain privacy of a diary; fewer than three-fourths of the children in our Washington State sample (perhaps a lower proportion than would be found in a representative sample of American children) shared that view.

Responses of children in Norway to the diary vignette were especially adamant and pointed:

(16-year-old girl) No, you have the right to keep what you want inside of you.

(16-year-old girl) No one has the right to know her thoughts.

(9-year-old boy) No [,parents should not be able to see their child's diary]. The parents don't want the children to look at their secrets, either!

(9-year-old boy) No! That is her own!

Such norms of individualism and social-welfare orientation are well established early in the school years.

Three things are striking about the cultural differences that we observed. First, a concern with rights is shared by both American and Norwegian children, and their logic about such matters seems to be shaped much more by developmental than cultural factors. Second, the scope of rights that are salient appears to be highly culturally determined – even though the United States and Norway are both wealthy democracies. Third, those differences that do exist are present even in the primary grades when children first begin to comprehend the word *right*.

A concern with due process and a preference for adversary procedures are established early in the school years and are consistent across cultures.

Regardless of whether a society has an adversary legal process, procedural justice commonly is judged according to the presence (or lack thereof) of the rudiments of adversariness (each party's having an opportunity to have a say, when disputes are being resolved). Due-process rights are important, because they signify authorities' obligation to treat citizens respectfully. Our studies add to the large literature on perceptions of procedural justice (reviewed by Lind and Tyler, 1988) by confirming the significance of such concerns for children and indicating their importance in diverse legal cultures. Notably, on a vignette raising the question whether students accused of breaking school rules must be given a chance to defend themselves, 95.8% of Norwegian participants espoused recognition of a right, more than on any other item.[12]

Being heard is so basic to being taking seriously that its significance to children provides a clear message that personhood is subjectively important to them, as it is for adults. As Minow (1990) has noted, '[t]he right to due process is special, among other rights, in its specific call for communication and attention to the individual's dignity' (p. 295).

Socialization into the political process also appears to be primarily a function of the elementary-school years.

In the conventional wisdom in psychology and education (e.g., Erikson, 1974), political socialization is primarily a task of adolescence. However, just as our studies suggest that most growth in legal knowledge and reasoning occurs during the elementary-school years, research on political socialization indicates the key importance of middle childhood. By eighth grade in the United States, the proportion of the population who have ever engaged in political activity (e.g., campaigning for a candidate) approaches adult levels (Hess and Torney, 1967), and middle childhood has been demonstrated to be the developmental period of greatest change in political interest, attitudes, and identification (Jennings and Niemi, 1974).

Besides providing data about the significance of middle childhood in development in a related domain (the law), our studies in Norway add directly to knowledge about political socialization. In particular, we surveyed our Norwegian sample about their knowledge of the *Barneombudet* (the ombudsman for children; see Flekkøy, 1991, and Melton, 1991b). Even among primary-grade children, two-thirds had heard of the ombudsman. The percentage rose to as high as 95.5% among children in sixth grade (in Norway, mostly 12-year-olds). Among those who had heard about the ombudsman, virtually all had a reasonably good understanding of the ombudsman's work. For example, first graders (7-year-olds) typically described the ombudsman as a helper for children or, less frequently, someone to whom children can tell problems. Such answers were common also among older children, who also often described the ombudsman as assisting maltreated children or protecting children's rights.

More than three-fourths of the children interviewed said that they might call the ombudsman sometime, although almost none had actually done so. Most children indicated that they would call upon the ombudsman if they had serious problems (e.g., problems at home; 'problems' in general) or they were being subjected to maltreatment by adults or harassment (*mobbing*) by other children.

Most participants indicated that children need someone to watch out for them in the government. Their rationales (offered in response to an open-ended question) typically were one of the following: children need an adult with whom to talk; children need a spokesperson; children need someone to protect them; children have a right to protection (an answer that was given most commonly by ninth graders).

Taken together, these data suggest not only that middle childhood is an important period for learning about politics, but also that it is possible to develop a political institution that does represent children of that age and with which they can identify. In that regard, the level of knowledge about the *Barneombudet* is truly remarkable when one considers that the office had been in existence only about eight years at the time that our survey was conducted.

Satisfaction with the legal process and anxiety about participating in it are not incompatible.

'Trauma' related to children's – especially child victims' – involvement in the legal process has been a matter of great concern to policymakers and child advocates in recent years. Without minimizing the seriousness of that concern in some cases (see Goodman *et al.*, 1991), there is reason to believe that advocates' concerns have been too narrow. Adult witnesses experience stress in the legal process, too, but, as already noted, they also are most satisfied when they believe the procedure used to have been a fair one in which each side had an opportunity to put its best case forward. Being cross-examined is hardly fun, but the experience may be perceived as basic to a fair procedure in which the participants all are taken seriously by legal authorities.

Although our studies do not provide a definitive picture of the factors affecting children's perceptions of justice in the legal process, they do lend some support to those who argue that the range of variables of interest goes beyond the stress experienced by witnesses. As already noted, adversary legal procedures closely comport with school-aged children's sense of fairness. In that regard, the Washington State study showed that the more that children knew about the legal process, the more that they perceived it as anxiety-provoking. We also found, though, that the more that they knew about the legal process, the more that they judged it to be fair.

We also found little difference between victim/witnesses' views (even after six months in the system) and those of children without experience as witnesses. Children's responses to our lengthy set of questions about the legal process (including our 'debriefing' interviews about witnesses' interviews by defense attorneys) were remarkable for the lack of intrusion of emotional concerns. Even if the situation was stressful, it was typically viewed as necessary and sensible – in other words, consistent with due-process rights.

Children attribute their knowledge of the legal process to television.

A theme through our discussion thus far has been that, at least by the intermediate grades, children are quite sophisticated about the legal process. Although we are not certain how television affects concepts of rights in particular, we do know that television is playing an important role in legal socialization more broadly.

In Washington State, two-thirds of witnesses and three-fourths of comparison participants attributed their knowledge of the legal process to television. The specificity of children's comments in that regard (e.g, their allusions to various syndicated courtroom shows that are on the air in after-school hours in many American communities) led us to believe that children's attributions were accurate.

We suspect that the influence of television on legal socialization is largely positive. It has the potential to sensitize children to ways that rights can be asserted and the reasons for doing so. We acknowledge, though, that the lack of verisimilitude in many courtroom dramas can lead to misconceptions. The response of a fifth grader in the Washington State sample of victim/witnesses is illustrative. That child defined the work of a jury as follows: 'They listen to the story, and then there's a commercial break. They come back and then tell who did it'.

CONCERNS OF CHILDREN IN TROUBLED SOCIETIES

A closing word of caution about our findings is one that we noted near the beginning: our studies have been conducted in developed, democratic countries with a tradition of respect for human dignity. In many parts of the world (including some communities in the United States; see Garbarino *et al.*, 1991, and US Advisory Board on Child Abuse and Neglect, 1990), preservation even of personal safety still is at risk. Reconcilitation of such experiences with developing concepts of human rights and civil liberties can present substantial cognitive conflict and moral uncertainty:

> In adolescence, the child moves from the relatively restricted milieu of home and classroom into a broader social environment. Even if personal experi-

ence is somewhat restricted, children become progressively more aware through public information sources of societal conditions that may possibly affect their own fate. What do these broadening perspectives do to the chances of an adolescent sustaining a positive mood? Here we must sound a sombre note. Messages frequently received by young people are dolorous: the world is becoming more and more overpopulated; human beings are using their resources too fast; crime is increasing; political institutions are incapable of solving national and international conflicts without violence; and the type of violence that can be unleashed is destructive beyond imagination. In addition, there is a continual disillusionment with, or disparagement of, heroes. Presumably, adequate coping requires hope. It must be difficult indeed for youth to sustain coping efforts directed toward social institutions and public issues in the face of these strongly negative messages about the future. It remains to be seen what coping and defensive maneuvers contemporary youth will increasingly employ as they face the transition to adulthood. (Maccoby, 1983/1988, pp. 231–232)

We believe, though, that a concern with being taken seriously is a healthy phenomenon in the development of children and youth. It signals a sensitivity to the interplay between the political context and human experience and to the moral necessity of respect for persons:

> The use of rights discourse affirms community, but it affirms a particular kind of community: a community dedicated to invigorating words with power to restrain, so that even the powerless can appeal to those words. It is a community that acknowledges and admits the historical uses of power to exclude, deny, and silence – and commits itself to enabling suppressed points of view to be heard, to making covert conflict overt. (Minow, 1990, p. 229)

To return to a point that we made early in this chapter, *power* is a dimension salient to children as well as adults. Recognition of rights provides a way of ensuring that power is used to uplift rather than to oppress. When applied to a class with little power (surely children fit such a description), sensitivity to rights is apt in itself to 'humanize' relationships, especially with authority. It is likely also to have socializing effects, toward a generation that not only demands fulfillment of rights but that also understands the obligations that recognition of rights imposes on the majority (to protect minorities) and the privileged (to protect the powerless).

NOTES

1.   Such information *is* of academic interest. Besides being of obvious significance in the jurisprudence and philosophy of rights and the status of children, research on children's

concepts of and attitudes toward their rights has substantial import for understanding of legal and political socialization – the processes by which societal values are inculcated (see, e.g., Melton, 1988, 1991a; Tapp and Levine, 1974).

2. As far as we are aware, most of the empirical research on children's concepts and exercise of rights has been conducted in the United States. Except where we specifically indicate to the contrary, the reader may assume that the population being studied is American.

    It is likely, though, that the psychological factors discussed in this chapter have significance in most cultures. Yamamoto, *et al.* (1987) found that the stressors that bother children are remarkably similar across cultures. Research involving adults (see Lind and Tyler, 1988, for a review) also has shown substantial cross-cultural consistency in the factors that are perceived to be basic to justice.

    Moreover, anecdotal reports of political concerns of children in war zones and other dangerous and oppressive environments provide consistent evidence of school age children's sensitivity to the political realities of the societies in which they live and their responsiveness to rights education (see, e.g., Cohn and Aber, 1991; Coles, 1986; Garbarino, 1990, 1991; Garbarino and Bronfenbrenner, 1976; Garbarino *et al.*, 1991). Indeed, Garbarino (1990) has concluded that children's psychological adaptation to warfare and other hostilities is often the product of inculcation of an ideology that enables them to construct an explanation for the violence around them.

3. We (Melton, 1991b; see also Flekkøy, 1991) have noted the kinds of questions raised by children themselves to the Norwegian Barneombudet (office of the ombudsman for children) that would not otherwise have occurred to advocates. Some involve day-to-day incidents of not being taken seriously (e.g., grocers giving children candy instead of money for return of bottles; teachers but not children being protected from dangerous or uncomfortable environments by labor laws), and others involve momentous issues of concern to classes of children (e.g., the complaint of a Moroccan child about a marriage contract that she might be forced to fulfill led to the Barneombudet's far broader inquiry into the welfare of asylum-seeking children and families in Norway).

4. Many times, of course, lower-class and ethnic-minority children's hypothesis that their exercise of rights will result in less favorable treatment by authorities may be accurate. In particular, the realities of juvenile courts may be quite discrepant from the law on the books (Melton, 1989; Schwartz, 1989). Also, as will be discussed later, children from disadvantaged backgrounds have few experiences with entitlement. Accordingly, there is little reason for such children to believe the guarantees by a benevolent authority that their rights will be regarded as due entitlements.

5. More clearly applied research evaluating the effects of procedures when they are instituted would also be valuable (see Melton, 1989).

6. Both the Nebraska and the Seattle studies were supported by a grant from the National Center on Child Abuse and Neglect (Grant No. 90-CA-1274). Some of the data have been reported in papers presented at meetings of the American Psychological Association and the American Psychology-Law Society. These studies have been conducted in primary collaboration with Lucy Berliner (Harborview Medical Center, Seattle).

7. The Norwegian study was begun while the first author was a Fulbright professor at the Norwegian Center for Child Research in Trondheim. Support was provided by the Center, the United States Education Foundation in Norway, and the faculty development program of the University of Nebraska. Melton was assisted on the project by Susan Limber, Heidi Steine, and Axel Wolff. Ove Haugeløkken and Per Olav Tiller were helpful consultants in the design and implementation of the project in the Trondheim schools.

8. First grade begins a year later in Norway (age 7) than the United States, so that age/grade comparisons are not equivalent in the two nations.

9. As the correlations reported here indicate, attitudes toward children's rights are a function in part of social-cognitive development. Such attitudes also are dependent on specific polit-

ical and social values, though, so that the relationship between age and attitudes toward children's rights is weaker than the relationship between age and concepts of rights.

10.   We are defining *support for civil liberties* in terms of attitudes about free application of such rights. For example, when asked whether they favor *free speech*, virtually all American adults answer positively. The consensus breaks down when attitudes are solicited about specific situations in which free expression is at issue.

11.   The test for inclusion of factors was eigenvalue > 1.

12.   The proportion of the sample favoring recognition of a right varied from 5.2% (whether children should have the right to choose the courses that they take in school) to three vignettes that elicited support for a right for children from more than 90% of the sample (the other included [a] access to treatment when parents cannot pay for the service and [b] privacy of a child's diary).

REFERENCES

Armacost, R.L. (1989). 'Perceptions of Stressors by High School Students'. *Journal of Adolescent Research* 4, 443–461.

Bellah, R.N., Madsen, R., Sullivan, W.M., Swidler, A. and Tipton, S.M. (1985). *Habits of the Heart: Individualism and Collectivism in American Life.* New York: Harper and Row.

Belter, R.W. and Grisso, T. (1984). 'Children's Recognition of Rights Violations in Counseling'. *Professional Psychology: Research and Practice* 15, 899–910.

Cashmore, J. and Bussey, K. (1990). 'Children's Construction of Court Proceedings'. In J. Spencer, G. Nicholson, R. Flin and R. Bull (eds.), *Children's Evidence in Legal Proceedings.* London: Hawksmere.

Cohn, I. and Aber, J.L. (1991). 'Children's Rights Education and Advocacy: International Perspectives'. *Child, Youth, and Family Services Quarterly* 1, pp. 3–5.

Coles, R. (1977). *Privileged Ones.* Boston: Little, Brown.

Coles, R. (1986). *The Political Life of Children.* Boston: Atlantic Monthly Press.

Dahl, T.S. (1987). *Women's Law: An Introduction to Feminist Jurisprudence* (R.L. Craig, Trans.). Oslo: Norwegian University Press.

Erikson, E.H. (1974). *Dimensions of a New Identity: The 1973 Jefferson Lectures in the Humanities.* New York: Norton.

Feld, B.C. (1988). *In Re Gault* revisited: 'A Cross-state Comparison of the Right to Counsel in Juvenile Court'. *Crime and Delinquency* 34, 393–424.

Feld, B.C. (1989). 'The Right to Counsel in Juvenile Court: An Empirical Study of When Lawyers Appear and the Difference They Make'. *Journal of Criminal Law and Criminology* 79, 1185–1346.

Flekkøy, M.G. (1991). *A Voice for Children: Speaking Out as Their Ombudsman.* London: Jessica Kingsley.

Flin, R., Stevenson, Y. and Davies, G. (1989). 'Children's Knowledge of Court Proceedings'. *British Journal of Psychology* 80, 285–297.

Foundation for Child Development. (1977). *National Survey of Children.* Unpublished manuscript, New York.

Garbarino, J. (1990). 'Youth in Dangerous Environments: Coping with the Consequences'. In K. Hurrelman and F. Losel (eds.), *Health Hazards in Adolescence* (pp. 193–218). Berlin: Walter de Gruyter.

Garbarino, J. (1991). 'The Experience of Children in Kuwait: Occupation, War, and Liberation'. *Child, Youth, and Family Services Quarterly*, pp. 2–3.

Garbarino, J. and Bronfenbrenner, U. (1976). 'The Socialization of Moral Judgment and Behavior in Cross-Cultural Perspective'. In T. Lickona (ed.), *Moral Development and Behavior* (pp. 70–83). New York: Holt, Rinehart and Winston.

Garbarino, J., Kostelny, K. and Dubrow, N. (1991). *No Place to Be a Child: Growing Up in a War Zone.* Lexington, MA: Lexington Books.

Goodman, G.S., Levine, M., Melton, G.B. and Ogden, D.W. (1991). 'Child Witnesses and the Confrontation Clause: The American Psychological Association Brief in *Maryland v. Craig'*. *Law and Human Behavior* 15, 13–29.

Grisso, T. (1981). *Juveniles' Waiver of Rights: Legal and Psychological Competence.* New York: Plenum.

Hess, R.D. and Torney, J.V. (1967). *The Development of Political Attitudes in Children.* Chicago: Aldine.

Jennings, M.K. and Niemi, R.G. (1974). *The Political Character of Adolescence: The Influence of Families and Schools.* Princeton, NJ: Princeton University Press.

Kagehiro, D.K. (1988). 'Perceived Voluntariness of Consent to Warrantless Police Searches'. *Journal of Applied Social Psychology* 18, 38–49.

Kagehiro, D.K. and Laufer, W.S. (1990). 'The Assumption of Risk Doctrine and Third-Party Consent Searches'. *Criminal Law Bulletin* 26, 195–209.

Lewis, C.E. (1983). 'Decision Making Related To Health: When Could/Should Children Act Responsibly?' In G.B. Melton, G.P. Koocher and M.J. Saks (eds.), *Children's Competence to Consent* (pp. 75–91). New York: Plenum.

Lind, E.A. and Tyler, T.R. (1988). *The Social Psychology of Procedural Justice.* New York: Plenum.

Maccoby, E.E. (1988). 'Social-Emotional Development and Response to Stressors'. In N. Garmezy and M. Rutter (eds.), *Stress, Coping and Development in Children* (pp. 217–234). Baltimore: Johns Hopkins University Press (originally published 1983).

McCloskey, H. and Brill, A. (1983). *Dimensions of Tolerance: What Americans Believe About Civil Liberties.* New York: Russell Sage Foundation.

McKeiver v. Pennsylvania, 403 US 528 (1971).

Melton, G.B. (1980). 'Children's Concepts of Their Rights'. *Journal of Clinical Child Psychology* 9, 186–190.

Melton, G.B. (1983a). *Child Advocacy: Psychological Issues and Interventions.* New York: Plenum.

Melton, G.B. (1983b). 'Making Room for Psychology in Miranda Doctrine: Juveniles' Waiver of Rights'. *Law and Human Behavior* 7, 67–85.

Melton, G.B. (1983c). 'Minors and Privacy: Are Legal and Psychological Concepts Compatible?' *Nebraska Law Review* 62, 455–493.

Melton, G.B. (1987). 'Children, Politics, and Morality: The Ethics of Child Advocacy'. *Journal of Clinical Child Psychology* 16, 357–367.

Melton, G.B. (1988). 'The Significance of Law in the Everyday Lives of Children and Families'. *Georgia Law Review* 22, 851–895.

Melton, G.B. (1989). 'Taking *Gault* Seriously: Toward a New Juvenile Court'. *Nebraska Law Review* 68, 146–181.

Melton, G.B. (1990a). 'Law, Science, and Humanity: The Normative Foundation of Social Science in Law'. *Law and Human Behavior* 14, 315–332.

Melton, G.B. (1990b). 'Realism in Psychology and Humanism in Law: Psychological Studies at Nebraska'. *Nebraska Law Review* 69, 251–275.

Melton, G.B. (1991a). 'Children as Legal Actors'. In D.K. Kagehiro and W.S. Laufer (eds), *Handbook of Psychology and Law* (pp. 275–291). New York: Springer-Verlag.

Melton, G.B. (1991b). 'Lessons from Norway: The Ombudsman as a Voice for Children'. *Case Western Reserve Journal of International Law* 23, 197–254.

Melton, G.B. (1991c). 'Preserving the Dignity of Children around the World: The UN Convention on the Rights on the Child'. *Child Abuse and Neglect* 15, 343–350.

Melton, G.B. (1991d). 'Socialization into the Global Community: Respect for the Dignity of Children'. *American Psychologist* 46, 66–71.

Melton, G.B. (in press). 'The Law is a Good Thing (Psychology is, Too): Human Rights in Psychological Jurisprudence'. *Law and Human Behavior.*

Melton, G.B. and Limber, S. (1989). 'Psychologists' Involvement in Cases of Child Maltreatment: Limits of Role and Expertise'. *American Psychologist* 44, 1225–1233.

Melton, G.B. and Saks, M.J. (1985). 'The Law as an Instrument of Socialization and Social Structure'. In G.B. Melton (ed.), *Nebraska Symposium on Motivation: Vol. 33. The Law as a Behavioral Instrument* (pp. 235–277). Lincoln: University of Nebraska Press.

Minow, M. (1990). *Making all the Difference: Inclusion, Exclusion, and American Law*. Ithaca, NY: Cornell University Press.

Mnookin, R.H. (1978). 'Children's Rights: Beyond Kiddie Libbers and Child Savers'. *Journal of Clinical Child Psychology* 7, 163–167.

Nader, L. (1985). 'A User Theory of Legal Change as Applied to Gender'. In G.B. Melton (ed.), *Nebraska Symposium on Motivation: Vol. 33. The Law as a Behavioral Instrument* (pp. 1–33). Lincoln: University of Nebraska Press.

Rivlin, L.G. and Wolfe, M. (1985). *Institutional Settings in Children's Lives*. New York: Wiley.

Rogers, C.M. and Wrightsman, L.S. (1978). 'Attitudes Toward Children's Rights: Nurturance or Self-Determination'. *Journal of Social Issues* 34(2), 59–68.

Rosenberg, I.M. (1980). 'The Constitutional Rights of Children Charged with Crime: Proposal for a Return to the Not So Distant Past'. *UCLA Law Review* 27, 656–721.

Saywitz, K.J. (1989). 'Children's Conceptions of the Legal System: "Court is a place to play basketball". In S.J. Ceci, D.F. Ross and M.P. Toglia (eds.), *Perspectives on Children's Testimony* (pp. 131–157). New York: Springer-Verlag.

Saywitz, K.J. Jaenicke, C. and Camparo, L. (1990). 'Children's Knowledge of Legal Terminology'. *Law and Human Behavior* 14, 523–536.

Schwartz, I.M. (1989). *(In)justice for Juveniles: Rethinking the Best Interests of the Child*. Lexington, MA: Lexington Books.

Small, M.A. (1990a). *The Need for a Psychology of Jurisprudence*. Paper presented at the meeting of the American Psychological Association, Boston.

Small, M.A. (1990b). *The Role of Perceptions of Privacy Invasions in a Psychology of Jurisprudence*. Unpublished doctoral dissertation, University of Nebraska-Lincoln.

Small, M.A. and Wiener, R.L. (in press). 'Rethinking Privacy Torts: A View Towards a Psycholegal Perspective'. In D.K. Kagehiro and W. Laufer (eds), *Handbook of Psychology and Law*. New York: Springer-Verlag.

Tapp, J.L. and Levine, F.J. (1974). 'Legal Socialization: Strategies for an Ethical Legality'. *Stanford Law Review* 27, 1–72.

Tremper, C.R. and Kelly, M.P. (1987). 'The Mental Health Rationales For Policies Fostering Minors' Autonomy'. *International Journal of Law and Psychiatry* 10, 111–127.

United Nations Convention on the Rights of the Child. UN Doc. A/Res/44/25 (1989).

US Advisory Board on Child Abuse and Neglect. (1990). *Child Abuse and Neglect: Critical First Steps in Response to a National Emergency*. Washington, DC: U.S. Government Printing Office.

Warren-Leubecker, A., Tate, C.S., Hinton, I.D. and Ozbek, I.N. (1989). 'What Do Children Know About the Legal System and When Do They Know It? First Steps Down a Less Traveled Path in Child Witness Research'. In S.J. Ceci, D.F. Ross and M.P. Toglia (eds.), *Perspectives on Children's Testimony* (pp. 158–183). New York: Springer-Verlag.

Wertlieb, D.N. (1991). 'Children and Divorce: Stress and Coping in Developmental Perspective'. In J. Eckenrode (ed.), *The Social Context of Coping* (pp. 31–54). New York: Plenum.

Wolfe, M. (1978). 'Childhood and Privacy'. In I. Altman and J.F. Wohlwill (eds), *Human Behavior and Environment: Advances in Theory and Research* (Vol.3, pp. 175–222). New York: Plenum.

Yamamoto, K., Soliman, A., Parsons, J. and Davies, O.L., Jr. (1987). 'Voices in Unison: Stressful Events in the Lives of Children in Six Countries'. *Journal of Child Psychology and Psychiatry* 28, 855–864.

PART II

Application

COLIN WRINGE*

15. The Ideology of Liberal Individualism, Welfare Rights and the Right to Education

Welfare Rights and Liberal Individualism

In a world in which many thousands of children are at this moment dying amid cruel abuse and degrading deprivation it may seem difficult to justify a paper that presents no horrific new data to emphasise the degree to which childhood is abused, no comparative studies to show how the law affecting children is better or worse in one country than another and no achievements of the writer's own to relate, of hardships endured or effective organisations set up to detect and counter the abuse of childhood. The impression of irrelevance may be heightened by the fact that we now actually have a Convention on the Rights of the Child so that, in the minds of many, the time for justification and analysis may seem to be past and our minds properly turned to the practical task of implementation.

Against this I would make two points. First, with the honourable exceptions of France and the Soviet Union, the powerful nations of the world upon whom the implementation of many of the stated rights of the child largely depend, as yet remain unpersuaded of the rightness of endorsing the Convention. Second, even where and when it is endorsed, the extent and rapidity of its implementation will depend not only on the effectiveness of monitoring procedures, but on the degree to which the rights claimed are seen to be congruent with prevailing social and political ideologies.

It is my purpose to examine the notion of a welfare right within the context of liberal individualism, and to argue that the right to education is properly seen as such a right. My reason for undertaking this particular task is not that I regard liberal individualism as the only valid ideology but rather because it is, at this moment, an exceedingly influential ideology, especially in many of the aforesaid countries that have not signed the convention and whose commitment may be essential to its widespread implementation. It is a feature of this ideology that it finds the very notion of a welfare right difficult to

* University of Keele.

M. Freeman and P. Veerman (eds.), The Ideologies of Children's Rights, 191–202.
© 1992 Kluwer Academic Publishers. Printed in the Netherlands.

accommodate and many of its adherents are inclined to deny that welfare rights are properly rights at all.

Welfare rights are, of course, possessed not only by children, but by all human beings, children and adults alike and the effects of failing to implement even the right to education may be more keenly felt later, during adult life, than during childhood itself. This, however, is no more than a further illustration of the commonplace that if the rights of children are not respected, it is not only childhood but the whole life that may be damaged or lost. Many of the rights claimed for children in the United Nations Convention are, in fact, welfare rights and such rights are of particular significance for children who, by their very nature, may be unable to fend for themselves and are therefore dependent on others. Accordingly, I believe it can be shown to be appropriate to consider whether, properly understood, the grounds commonly given in support of liberal individualism may not in fact also entail welfare rights of the kind so often scornfully rejected by those who embrace that ideology most strongly.

All discussion of rights is necessarily contentious and contention is readily compounded by misunderstanding. It will therefore be helpful to define some of my key terms.

By *liberal individualism* I mean the doctrine that the prior condition of humankind is moral freedom, subject only to such agreements as we choose to make for ourselves and those which free and equal individuals must be presumed to assent to in order to live together peaceably in the social state. In the Anglo-Saxon tradition this ideology has been associated with such names as Locke, Paine, Mill and more recently, the thinkers of the so-called 'New Right'. Its tenets have been embodied in collections of variously called Rights of Man, Rights of the Citizen or, more pejoratively, Bourgeois Rights. They also constitute the first twenty or so articles of the 1948 United Nations *Universal Declaration of Human Rights*.

Initially this ideology enabled a rising middle class to combat older, feudal, generally theistic ideologies. These, for all their restrictive character, at least had the merit of providing some protection for the poor, the sick and above all children as being of special concern to God and having a limited claim on his bounty. Subsequently, as we know, the function of the bourgeois Rights of Man has been less to promote social progress than to serve as a bulwark against such things as humane labour laws, welfare legislation and social justice generally.

By a *welfare right* I mean a right to have certain necessities provided by the community at large if one is unable to provide them for oneself. Traditionally, these have included protection from starvation, the provision of minimum medical care and shelter from the elements. In the third and final section of this paper I shall argue that they should also include the right to education. Hopefully, it will scarcely be necessary to add that in arguing for welfare rights, I am arguing not for general duties of charity, the timing and direction of whose performance can be left to the provider, but a duty of perfect obligation, to which the recipient or potential recipient has a right *hic et nunc*. Failure to receive which is properly a signal not for supplication, but indignation and as in the case of other rights, ultimately legitimates the use of force, either by the rightholders themselves, or by others on their behalf.

As regards the *right to education*, I shall argue that this is not simply the right to an induction into the knowledge, beliefs and folkways of one's own limited social group or sub-culture but something akin to schooling, an introduction to mainstream world culture.

A common tactic when discussing rights, including those of children, is to begin by dividing rights claims into certain categories according to what is being claimed or what kind of justification may be sought or given for claiming it. Some such list as the following may be suggested. Firstly, legal rights and then, within the general category of moral rights, rights of freedom (both positive freedom to act and negative freedom from interference or molestation) special rights created by transactions or role relationships and, last of all, welfare rights. On the face of it, this looks like a very sensible procedure. If justification is our aim, it seems to make sense to begin by sorting out the different kinds of things that need to be justified.

The problem with this kind of procedure is that, from the outset, it fundamentally biases the discussion against anyone attempting to present a moral justification for welfare rights, precisely by defining them *as* welfare rights which cannot be justified as freedoms or the creation of specific transactions or relationships voluntarily entered into by the person against whom the right is held.

If a certain right to receive gratuitous help from others is claimed, the argument tends to proceed as follows: 'We are, of course, not here concerned with legal rights. Legal rights to welfare or whatever in a given state can always in principle be determined by reference to texts or tested in the courts or perhaps in less advanced societies, by reference to observed or remembered custom and practices. Nor are we concerned with statements of rights contained in international documents like the 1948 *Universal Declaration of Human Rights* or 1990 *Convention on the Rights of the Child*. The latter do not so much create rights as recognise rights which are already supposed to exist. The act of endorsement is simply a device for strengthening the hands of supporters of the right and bringing implementation a step nearer.'

As regards the various categories of moral rights, the person who wants people to receive such basic goods as food, medical care or education which they are unable to provide for themselves finds little support in the justification given either for positive or negative rights of freedom. If, for example, the right to education is at issue, the hypothetical opponent is able to reply: 'If by a right to education you mean that children ought not to be prevented from educating themselves by religious bigots or authoritarian regimes, then fine, I am with you. If you are saying that people should not have the schools they have built destroyed by invaders, then I am with you again. But you are asking for people's schooling (food, medical care, housing or whatever) to be paid for out of someone else's pocket. Now that's something rather different. We do care about these things of course, we care desperately, but right now there are other priorities.'

And so there will always be in a free society of rational individuals or a free society of nations until the provision for need brings some tangible advantage to the provider. This may be some crude material advantage like economic return, political influence or social approval, or some more subtle benefit such as the easing of a tender conscience. This last, however, may all too easily be dismissed as weakness of mind or countered by the harsh Malthusian argument that by 'giving' people things we may actually be doing them more harm than good.

Consideration of these standard liberal responses serves to emphasise just why it is important to establish that welfare rights are rights indeed and are not simply expressions of extreme need or appeals to the humane instincts of others. For, if someone has a right against us, the fact that *we* have other priorities is irrelevant, as is the consideration that if we accord them their right we may, by some tenuous concatenation of causes, in some complex roundabout way, actually be doing them harm. We are not, that is, entitled to deny someone their rights because we think that by doing so we may be doing them a good turn.

Along with rights of freedom, liberal individualism also recognises special rights created by various transactions and role relationships. These, however, are as unhelpful to the welfare rights advocate as rights of freedom. In claiming rights to food, medical care, shelter and education we are rarely concerned with the predicament of those who have *paid* for these goods and services and been denied them. The poor, the sick and the ignorant have usually been given no overt promises and, especially in the case of children, may not have been in a position to 'earn' any rights. Nor are individuals in the affluent world usually prepared to admit that any action on another's part has contributed to the plight of the destitute in such a way as to merit compensation.

As a result of this kind of analysis within the framework of an ideology which accords serious recognition only to rights of freedom and special rights, the proponent of welfare rights sees himself progressively pushed out on to shaky ground. If he does not wish to embrace some theistic ideology according to which a powerful creator awards some part of his bounty to the needy and commands his subjects to see that they get it, he must rely on equally metaphysical humanistic notions such as common human dignity, the universal brotherhood of man, the universal bond of sympathy, or whatever. These are, in themselves, difficult to explicate and even more difficult to link with the obligations of others.

It is tempting at this point to say, 'Well, in that case the ideology must be abandoned in favour of another that is more humane. These are our principles, but if you do not like them, we have others.' The way forward then becomes, not argument but struggle. If political violence plays such an important part in our world it is partly because many humane, practically minded people in many places have come to this conclusion. The alternative is to re-examine our ideology and its justifications to see whether we have not been led astray. For that in extreme circumstances a helpless individual has no right to receive aid from those easily able to provide it or that we cannot compel others to provide it without doing wrong is a conclusion so perverse as to suggest either some gross incoherence in the ideology itself, or some palpable error of reasoning.

JUSTIFYING WELFARE RIGHTS

One hesitates to resuscitate old debates about the right of property with its Fourrièrist overtones, hyperbolic slogans and quaint evocations of Humanity's primeval innocence in communal enjoyment of Nature's bounties. Welfare rights, however, essentially concern the distribution of this world's goods and we cannot avoid examining an account of things that seeks to justify a situation in which a large part of the human race is supposed to have no right of access to any part of those goods.

Versions of the Enlightenment myth from which our ideology derives tell how individuals agree to a common *modus vivendi*, calculated to ensure securities of person and property. A will not slaughter B while B is asleep, or plunder his fields and cattle, provided B will similarly refrain. Both will keep their contracts absolutely. The accent here is not, as is often supposed, on freedom but upon a series of agreed abstentions from which all are supposed to benefit.

This story is of course to be seen, not as a chronological narrative of events actually supposed to have happened in the past, but as representing, in fable form, the logic of a contemporary state of affairs that everyone could be expected to agree to. What is immediately striking is that this allegorical interpretation – and any other interpretation is too fanciful to entertain – ought to justify not only the rights traditionally recognised by liberal individualism but also the right to receive support and assistance in times of extreme need. For it is scarcely to be believed that anyone would freely give up his right to take what he needed for his own survival in return for an arrangement that might leave him to starve or die from easily cured diseases while assenting to property laws forbidding him to take what he needed to prevent this happening.

In Rawlsian terms (Rawls, 1973, pp. 11–21), individuals behind a veil of ignorance about their future circumstances and prudently choosing the social structure least detrimental to the worst off, would hardly choose one in which they stood a statistically very good chance of starving to death in the presence of plenty.

Common to many proponents of the liberal ideology is the claim that the individual cannot rationally consent to give up his right to shift for himself if society and its laws do not protect his life from attack (see for example, Hobbes, 1651, II, 21, pp. 268–9). It is equally difficult to see how he can rationally give up his right to do the same when he is left unprotected from starvation or curable disease.

In both cases he no longer benefits from society but is outside and at war with it, and as such is entitled to avail himself of force or fraud and all the other 'helps and stratagems of war' in order to save his life. Society can no longer demand that he obey the law and respect the persons and property of others, particularly of those whom he must come to see as his oppressors. The point of this argument is not to justify terrorism, civil disorder or theft but to show that an attempt to explain how we can stand upon both our right of freedom and securities of person is incomplete and inconclusive unless we also acknowledge a right not to anything approaching equality in the distribution of goods, but at least to protection against extreme destitution.

So transparently evident would this seem that some explanation is required as to how such an apparently benign and reasonable account of things produces an ideology so effective in the hands of those seeking to maintain the very opposite conclusion, that to take some of the surplus of the world's haves to provide minimal assistance for its have-nots is a kind of unjustified imposition. The myth begins, as it must, with an initial state of equality. We are, as Locke (1690, II, 2, iv. p. 298) puts it, 'promiscuously born' with no evident sign of superiority or subordination, one to the other. No-one, despite the differences between us, is born subject to an obligation to obey anyone else or subordinate his or her interests to theirs. The hierarchies and conventions existing in the world are as yet of no concern to the individual who has not yet consented to them. He is therefore morally free to disregard them if he pleases, and if he dares.

Progressively, however, this liberty must be traded off against the securities and immunities mentioned earlier. This, as we saw, ought to result in the human being finding himself in a situation of approximately equal freedom and equal affluence with others. Differences of inclination and capacity may lead some to accept less strenuous and less affluent lifestyles, or a degree of wise direction from others. But none may be assumed – for none may be supposed to find it advantageous – to trade the initial freedom to shift for oneself for absolute obedience or life-threatening destitution.

Many proponents of the ideology, however, have tried to show how both extreme inequality and destitution unto death are possible in a just world because they would result from an agreement between free and equal individuals.

This is achieved by means of two devices, both of which rest on major fallacies. The first of these is an ambiguity in the notion of a contract. The second is to treat the initial contract between free and equal individuals, not as an allegory in the manner indicated earlier but as an actual event taking place at a particular time in the past and followed by a series of other contracts of a radically different kind. The absolutely binding promise of A and B not to slay each other while they sleep or whatever is a legitimate metaphor for the insight that all must obey the rules if civilised life is to be possible. Such a use of the notion does not legitimate gross inequalities, assuming as justification of the ideology requires, that all are more or less equally prudent and astute and also equally free to choose what their interest demands. Different, however, is the situation when, for example, it is argued (Hobbes, 1651, II, 20, pp. 251–7) that conquered peoples who accept foreign government rather than be put to the sword are bound by their implied promise to obey, or that later generations receive property from the earlier on whatever terms the latter may determine (Locke, 1960, II, 8, 116, p. 364).

These are but paradigm cases of what may be termed 'unequal contracts', that is contracts between individuals whose bargaining power is grossly unequal due to fortuitous historical circumstances. They are in no sense agreements between free and equal consenting parties but are morally analogous to that of a drowning millionaire who promises to make over all his wealth to a passer-by if only he will reach out his hand and pull him to safety.

Both historically and in many versions of the Enlightenment myth, such contracts have played an important part in justifying actual inequality; they quickly enable the strong, the unscrupulous and the fortunate, or their descendants, to gain a predominance of wealth and power, particularly once the means of production are in their hands. For to have the power of barring someone's access to the means of production is to have the power of life and death over them, leaving them with the option of agreeing to accept productive labour on whatever disadvantageous conditions are offered, or starving. A series of such unequal contracts may result in destitution, including the mass destitution of whole populations, and one justification of welfare rights would be as restitution for this systematically unjust process. Contracts of this kind have little to do with the kind of metaphorical agreement by which liberal individualism is justified. For if the justification is to be seen as valid the agreement must be thought of as taking place outside time and space between free and equal individuals, each new member of the human race contracting on the same basis as everybody else.

Thus, in Rawls' account, all human beings, past, present and future choose their preferred form of society without being aware of their own particular place in it.

To regard as legitimate the social inequalities and destitution of the many deriving from the unequal contracts we have been discussing is to treat the social contract as if, contrary to all plausibility, it were a kind of once and for all carve-up at a particular time in the past leaving most members of later generations to bargain their way in to a share of the world and what it has to offer on grossly disadvantageous terms, or even be unable to do so at all, and therefore permanently dispossessed. In such extreme, if all too frequently occurring cases, the rights that would most readily relieve destitution would not be rights to be 'given' something at all but a return of the right of freedom that the destitute are fraudulently supposed to have given up, in this case freedom of access to the means of producing either one's own sustenance or goods that might be exchanged for it. The literalist view of the social contract between free and equal individuals as something that took place once and for all in the past causes us to see the destitute as passive supplicants, legitimately dispossessed by their own consent, rather than as individuals progressively excluded from a share of what the world has to offer by a series of exchanges made under duress.

Unlike the mythical contract establishing a just world and taking place outside time and space, the unequal contracts that have led to the present distribution of goods really are historical events taking place in real time. Their outcomes are determined not by reason and justice but by individuals' relative bargaining power determined by such fortuitous circumstances as time, place, local convention, social affiliation, and so on.

Nozick (1974) in his version of the liberal myth, moves spectacularly from one form of contract to the other in explaining how objects taken from a state of nature may be voluntarily given, sold or bequeathed to others in such a way as to leave some individuals bereft of the means of survival unless the 'haves' in their generosity choose otherwise. Nozick, however, acknowledges (pp. 178–82) that he has difficulty in accounting for what he terms 'Locke's proviso' that when something is appropriated from the State of Nature, enough and as good must be left for others. This is Locke's recognition that there can be no legitimate once and for all acquisition of the world's goods, but that future generations stand on the same basis of equality as present and past. If we appropriate more than is our due so that others are left with nothing, they are entitled to be compensated. In addition, therefore, to whatever welfare rights they may have, the destitute would also seem entitled to benefit from a right well recognised by the ideology of liberal individualism, namely a right of restitution for harm done.

There is one further inconsistency in the literalist interpretation of the liberal social contract we have referred to. This is the fact that if newcomers enter the world without possessions, by the same token they also do so without obligations, including the obligation to keep their hands off the possessions of others. They are as yet under no moral obligation to meekly wait around to be given or bequeathed goods by others or seek to obtain what they need in return for labour on whatever terms the present possessor may determine. When it comes to the all-important trade-off of freedom for security, one of the most powerful cards in their hands is the freedom to shift for themselves and, individually or in combination with others who find themselves in like circumstances, to seize not only what they need to survive, but whatever takes their fancy.

In return for the very considerable abstention represented by obedience to our law – I say ours, for it is not yet theirs – they may at least expect to receive an assurance that they will be given the minimum necessities of life, if our property arrangements do not allow them access to the means of producing them for themselves. The objection that the new-born infant is weak, helpless and in no position to make demands would be a final and ludicrous example of the literalist or chronological fallacy which confuses an allegorical agreement between all human beings on equal terms (which is necessarily implied by the justification of a liberal society) with conditions in the real world in which the bargaining power of individuals is determined by arbitrary circumstances.

In this section, I have tried to argue for welfare rights within the terms of liberal individualism using justifications analogous to those commonly used within that ideology to justify securities of person and property. In passing I have also tried to show how the needs of those whose plight provokes the call for welfare rights may also partly be met without recourse to welfare rights at all, by a less partial application of the liberal rights of freedom and special rights. In doing this I have attempted to avoid reliance on such metaphysical notions as 'our common humanity', 'the brotherhood of man', 'essential human dignity', the 'prerogatives of reason' and so on, of which others may be able to give some convincing account.

THE RIGHT TO EDUCATION AS A WELFARE RIGHT

In arguing for this right I propose, as before, to remain within the framework of liberal individualism and, in particular, to avoid such arguments as that recently identified by Nelson (1990) to the effect that, given human beings' supposed capacity to reason, there must be a human right to develop that capacity. As Nelson points out (in an argument that otherwise seems totally flawed) human beings have a great many capacities that certainly do not justify claims to rights. I am therefore limited in my attempts to justify a welfare right to education to the claim that, like elementary medical care, food and shelter, education forms part of the very minimum the individual must demand in return for respecting the rights of others, or that others may properly use some form of coercion in obtaining for him.

One strategy for arguing this point has been to evoke the plight of someone well fed, sheltered and cared for medically, but not even minimally educated: e.g., not given the opportunity to acquire language, with no knowledge of even the proximate environment, no knowledge of goals other than the satisfaction of immediate needs and appetites and so on. Clearly such an individual would be an object of pity, but within our ideology, pity is a spur to charity rather than a ground of rights.

It could also be said that the life of such an individual would not be a recognisably human life but more like that of a well loved pet animal. Unfortunately, this argument, like some of those I have dismissed earlier, appears to depend on some not easily defined assumptions about what it is to be human, or on the value judgement that a truly human life, however construed, would be not only preferable, but so preferable that the individual would be prepared to return to a state of war with society rather than forego it. Psychologically speaking, of course, many individuals might be prepared to do so, but the question is whether they may be presumed to come to such a choice upon rational consideration of their interests. Might not the rational choice be to settle for (literally) mindless but less painful security instead?

This objection, is to rather miss the point of welfare rights. Their justification lies not in the pain and suffering of those who are deprived, however helpful these may be in appealing to the charity of others. If pain and suffering were the main consideration, people's welfare rights would be met if death from starvation, curable illness or exposure could be rendered painless. The deprivation from which welfare rights must protect us is the loss of life itself, and the opportunities offered by life which, with the ideology of liberal individualism, no-one can be presumed voluntarily to forego.

There is little point in debating the unanswerable question of whether this vegetative existence hypothesised as a kind of limiting case, with its opportunities restricted to those of sensation, can be considered a 'life' or not. The least that can be said is that the answer cannot be unequivocally positive. Fortunately, there are further reasons for saying that the individual could not be presumed to accept such an existence in exchange for the benefits of society membership.

The first of these is that he would not hereby become a member of society at all. In no sense could it be said that in return for food, shelter and medical care, such an individual might be presumed to agree to respect the rights of others by obeying society's laws. Obedience to a law, as opposed to mere conformity with it, such as might be secured by some such process as conditioning, presupposes quite a substantial level of cognitive development and understanding. To this extent the hypothetical situation is incoherent.

Secondly, to accept cognitive deprivation is to accept total dependence on others to an even greater extent than the person who, in early versions of the liberal myth, promises total obedience to the sovereign. Even Hobbes (1651, I, 14, p. 192) recognises that such a promise may become void under certain circumstances such as when life is threatened. But the person who accepts total cognitive deprivation denies himself the possibility of rebellion, even if he were able to understand that his life was threatened, or what this entailed.

The situation envisaged above is, of course, a highly artificial one in which adults do not actually prevent children from engaging in human intercourse, thereby acquiring some minimal induction into the cognitive structures of their group, but nevertheless contrive to leave them without opportunities for so doing. At the same time they benevolently provide them with food, shelter and medical care. Obviously no such situation could realistically arise in the real world. To totally prevent the cognitive development that results from human intercourse requires a great deal of interference with the individual's freedom, which would infringe not merely the child's welfare rights, but other rights more readily familiar to liberal individualism. In any real situation, such individuals would be subject to exploitation and abuse of the cruellest kinds. We also know that in the real world such powerless individuals would not have their more obviously identifiable welfare rights provided for either, and would, indeed, be unlikely to survive once the support and guidance of other adults was withdrawn. In practice this would mean, in a liberal society, once they were no longer useful to others.

Our purpose in considering such a bizarre situation was to rule out the extreme position that total cultural deprivation (provided other basic needs were met) would be morally compatible with the obligations of society membership. The individual's minimal rights in any society, including a liberal society, must therefore include not only protection against certain obvious and fairly easily avoidable causes of physical death, but also a modicum of education, at least in the form of an induction into the ways and understandings of the society whose norms he or she is expected to obey. Failing this, individuals remain morally outside society even when living physically within its territory. Vis-à-vis that society they are in a state of unbridled competition for resources and living space, i.e. within their limited capacities, morally in the state of war familiar from the previous section.

In the real world, concern with the right to education does not normally relate to the kind of extreme limiting case considered above. In even the most isolated or deprived milieux, individuals' normal intercourse with parents and fellows enables them to acquire language and sufficient of the group's ways and understandings to find their allotted place in its way of life. This might suggest that the level of education to which the individual had a right depended on the nature of the society in which he found himself and would, in non-advanced societies, simply take care of itself as part of the normal process of growing up. This complacent view sometimes receives support from the contention that, far from being a right, anything more, such as western style schooling, constitutes a positive abuse, an instrument of cultural imperialism, destroying a community's existing culture and giving nothing of value in return.

Such claims seem to represent a hopelessly naive view of the way the world is. If there were a chance that communities separated from the mainstream of world civilisation were likely to continue in their idyllic way, to be inhabited by the modern equivalent of Rousseau's noble savage with nothing to gain and everything to lose by contact with our civilisation, then maybe we ought to restrain the enthusiasm of Western educators. Even then, however, it would be patronising in the extreme (and a denial of their rights of freedom) to set up reservation fences to exclude such people from what *they* saw as the benefits of urban life and schooling for their children.

In fact, however, this picture of noble independence was never realistic and is certainly not so now. Communities which remain detached from mainstream economic and political developments are increasingly doomed by the activities of organisations that have little commitment either to their education or to any other of their other rights. If their members are not already being incorporated into modern economic activity on highly disadvantageous terms because of their lack of schooling, their future is no doubt already being discussed and decided in places to which, because of their lack of knowledge and education, they have no access.

Only a very small number of human groups now seems destined to remain for long totally outside mainstream world society or isolated from its effects, and all may eventually be required to conform to its laws and practices. To those whose cultural induction does not enable them to understand these laws and practices, they must appear as oppressive as the white man's laws must have appeared to the North American Indian. Indeed they will actually be oppressive in terms of that interpretation of liberal individualism according to which political obligation entails informed participation.

At this point it will be felt that our argument is moving some way from the very basic welfare rights which we sought to justify earlier. If, on account of this, it is doubted that education and especially schooling, is itself a welfare right, then at least it may be justified as a kind of secondary right, the necessary means to goods to which the welfare right is more immediately evident. In a world in which illiterate labour may be paid at starvation level and increasingly may not be economically negotiable at all, schooling, even if not itself a welfare right, may be the only avenue by which large numbers of people may obtain such things as minimal subsistence.

Equally clearly, as adumbrated a few moments ago, education, and this means quite a sophisticated level of education, may be the sine qua non of exercising or even understanding certain political rights which no liberal individualist can deny. In this respect the level of education received by the vast majority of the world's population may well fall below the level to which they are entitled in a world community by whose norms their destinies are increasingly governed.

REFERENCES

Hobbes, T. (1651). *Leviathan*, C. B. Macpherson (ed.), Harmondsworth, Penguin (1968).
Locke, J. (1690). *Two Treatises of Government*, P. Laslett (ed.), Cambridge, Cambridge University Press (1960).
Nelson, J. O. (1990). 'Against Human Rights', *Philosophy* 65, no. 253, pp. 341–348.
Nozick, R. (1974). *Anarchy, State and Utopia*, Oxford, Oxford University Press.
Rawls, J. (1973). *A Theory of Justice*, London, Oxford University Press.

PHILIP GRAHAM*

16. The Child's Right to Health

INTRODUCTION – DEFINITIONAL ISSUES

I do not intend to define health, but let me instead consider some issues that are relevant to a consideration of what 'health' means. First, health can be defined positively in terms of a state of mind or body that allow an individual to achieve his or her full potential, or negatively in terms of an absence of disease or disability. World Health Organization documents have helpfully considered negative definitions in terms of handicap (a disadvantage, resulting from an impairment or disability that prevents the fulfilment of an expected role in the social environment in which the individual lives); impairment (involving loss or abnormality of psychological, physiological or anatomical structure or function), and disability (involving restriction or lack of ability to perform an activity in a manner usually considered normal).

A second issue relating to definition, whether positive or negative, is the need to include mental as well as physical states. People cannot achieve their potential without motivation, the ability to concentrate and to cope with frustration. These psychological assets are undermined by the presence of behaviour and emotional disturbances. Further, psychological disability can be as impairing as physical disability. The child who is physically well may be as or more disabled by his inability to make friends, aggressive behaviour or depression, as if he was mentally well but in a wheelchair, crippled, for example, by muscular dystrophy. The right to health must include the right to mental health.

A third definitional issue is one that is relevant to many of the topics raised at this meeting. Health, like education and freedom, must be considered in the light of historical context and the social setting in which the child and family are living. A healthy child in Shakespeare's time was not as healthy as a well child of the 20th century. The environmental disadvantages of the late 16th century, the relative lack of hygiene, safe water and low level of nutrition, meant that the healthy child of that age could not

* Department of Child Psychiatry, Institute of Child Health, London.

M. Freeman and P. Veerman (eds.), The Ideologies of Children's Rights, 203–211.
© 1992 *Kluwer Academic Publishers. Printed in the Netherlands.*

expect to grow as tall or live as long as the child of today. Yet the Elizabethans were surely not wrong to think of many of their children as healthy, just as we today are not wrong to think of our healthy children as healthy, even though we may expect the next few decades to bring advances in genetic engineering and an understanding of the immune system which will further transform the growth and life expectancy of our child population. To this historical relativism must be added economic relativism in defining health, but here we must be more cautious. It is not reasonable to expect poor countries to achieve as satisfactory a level of health in their child population as rich countries. Poor countries are not only poor in income, but they are also likely to be poor in educational resources, and in knowledge to combat malnutrition and infection. But it is easy to develop health expectations that are too low, purely on the basis of an economic appraisal. Sri Lanka, for example, had a GNP per capita in 1987 of 400 US dollars, but achieved an under 5 mortality of 43 per 1,000. Nicaragua, Honduras and Saudi Arabia all had under 5 mortality rates at least three times as high as this, with GNPs at least double that of Sri Lanka. The distribution of income and the organisation of services are important contributors to health as well as the wealth of the country. Nor does national wealth guarantee good health. The USA, the second richest country in the world in GNP per capita terms in 1987 was 21st in the under 5 mortality league in 1988. In these days when knowledge about the promotion of health and the limitation of disability is so easily disseminated, those countries that wish to put child health at the top of their list of priorities should, at least in theory, have no difficulties in achieving as satisfactory an outcome as countries with a similar level of financial resources.

The final definitional issue on which I must touch is the distinction between the subjective experience of health and its objective existence. People who have serious disease can feel perfectly well. When children with chronic disease such as cystic fibrosis are asked if they have any health problems, they will often deny them because they accept their physical state as a fact of normal life. A child with a respiratory disease will often think of ill health as something extra to that which he ordinarily suffers and, of course, there are clear adaptive advantages to taking this point of view. Therefore, in measuring health – a subject to which I will briefly return later, it is important to consider not only to presence or absence of objective criteria of health, but also the subjective experience of those involved. This is not just a detail – children brought up in slum conditions may feel fine, but have far too low expectations for their own health. The right to health implies not just a right to feel healthy, but to be healthy.

THE CONDITIONS NECESSARY FOR PHYSICAL HEALTH

If children have a right to health, as measured in objective terms, they must also have a right to the conditions for health, mental as well as physical.

Most of these are uncontroversial, and their achievement implies only a commitment to divert human and financial resources. These include universal breast-feeding, at least for the first four to six months, early universal immunisation, clean water, regular weighing in the first three years, with referral if there is no weight gain over a two to three month period, and the availability of oral rehydration for diarrhoeal diseases. Of course, developing a commitment, even in relation to these apparently straightforward aims, may not be easy. The path to universal breast-feeding may, for example, be obstructed by milk marketing companies whose investment may be contributing to the wealth of a country in other ways.

Some conditions for health do however carry the potential for conflict with the basic beliefs held by members of different societies or religious groups, and it is important that these should not be glossed over, but that they are faced, though hopefully not in a confrontational manner, both by religious leaders and by health planners and politicians.

The dilemma is not restricted to, but is particularly marked, in the question of birth spacing. On the one hand it is clear that not just infant survival, but also the quality of life and health are improved if families are restricted to two or three children spaced two or more years apart. Weaning in these circumstances does not need to be abrupt or to lead to nutritional inadequacy. On the other hand, there is the injunction, not merely in the Bible, but in all religious writings to 'go forth and multiply' - an emphasis on the blessing of fertility and a deep concern for the sanctity of life expressing itself not just in a revulsion against abortion, but in a positive encouragement to parents to have large numbers of children.

The positive attitude to fertility has material as well as spiritual roots. Nations have need of large numbers of children to serve in armies and fight for territory. Parents have need of children to work in the fields or factories, and then to look after them in their old age. This materialist argument is now countered in many countries without too much difficulty. Adequate birth spacing ensures the survival of more, not fewer children, and these children are likely to be sturdier and healthier. Having few children will allow the mother, in particular, to retain her strength and work for many more productive and fulfilling years.

The spiritual argument for fertility is much less easier to counter, and, almost by definition, arguments based on deep feelings and the interpretation of ancient scripts are not open to argument. Change in these circumstances is most likely to come about not by winning arguments but by alterations in society that change attitudes and reduce ignorance. The secularisation of health services away from the religious charitable foundations that have done so much remarkable work in the past, would ensure that family planning advice is available from health workers who wish to inform prospective parents about the ways they can limit their families without persuading them to embark on one course or another. It is increasingly obvious that one can be as good a Catholic, Muslim or Jew with few or even no children, as one can with many. As religious leaders themselves have fewer and fewer children, so their congregations will follow. The way forward therefore surely lies in diverting state or secular resources into the provision of good health services, including maternal and child health services. The way forward surely does not lie in a dismissive or denigrating attitude by health planners towards spiritual values. It can well be pointed out that the woman with two children has far greater opportunities to extend the spiritual aspects of her life than one with seven or eight children. Further, it may well be questioned whether the achievement of a higher material standard of living for a few would be worth the sacrifice of spiritual values. As Disraeli, a nineteenth century British prime minister, Christian, but of Jewish origins, wrote in one of his novels about 'progress' – 'Progress to what and from where? . . .the European talks of progress because by an ingenious application of some scientific acquirements he has established a society which has mistaken comfort for civilisation'. Mistaking comfort for civilisation must surely be seen as the great mistake not just of the nineteenth but also of the twentieth century.

RESOURCES TO PROTECT CHILD HEALTH

The procreation of children for whose nourishment and protection sufficient resources are not available, and whose existence threatens the health of children already born, must surely be seen as a primary form of child abuse. The second most severe form of child abuse must be allowing children to die unnecessarily. Each year there are, in the world, about 14 million child deaths. These occur almost entirely in third world countries. Of these 14 million child deaths, about two-thirds are due to diarrhoea, respiratory infections, measles and neonatal tetanus. The great majority of these deaths could be prevented by cheap, readily available, well established methods that can be applied without side effects – namely immunisation and oral re-hydration. Virtually the only obstruction to the application of these relatively cheap methods is the inertia of governments to provide the relatively inexpensive training of health workers, the relatively cheap establishment of a structure for the delivery of a service, and the extremely cheap vaccines etc. that would be necessary to achieve a massive reduction in preventable child deaths. It has been calculated that the additional costs of a programme to prevent the great majority of child deaths and child malnutrition over the next ten years would reach approximately 2.5 billion dollars per year by the late 1990s. As UNICEF has pointed out, this is a lot of money. It is as much as US companies spend each year on cigarette advertising. It is as much as the Soviet Union spends on vodka each month. It is as much as the developing world is paying each week just to service its debts. It is perhaps not quite as much money as might appear to be the case.

The cost of not providing the resources required to combat child deaths is of course immense. Let me mention first, because it is so easy to forget it, the cost in human suffering. There is no reason to believe that the death of a child in a third world country is to any degree less distressing to parents and the rest of the family than it is in developed countries. But, in addition, in hard financial terms, there is the cost of bringing into the world, for however short a time, a being that consumes but is economically unproductive, and the cost of the time of the parent, especially the mother, in child upbringing. There is also the cost of the children who suffer these diseases but do not die, remaining instead handicapped and, at least partly dependent throughout their lives.

CHILD MENTAL HEALTH IN DEVELOPED COUNTRIES

If the abuse of the right of the child to health is mainly seen in third world countries in relation to preventable deaths and handicap, in what ways does such abuse mainly occur in the developed world? Here the death of children is a relatively rare event, and, when it occurs, it is very often due to genetically inherited disease or cancer which we do not have the knowledge or means to prevent or treat successfully. This is not to say that preventable deaths do not occur in economically developed countries – they do and probably account (if one includes those due to avoidable injuries and others indirectly related to social disadvantage), to as many as a third of such deaths, but the total numbers are relatively small. The under 5 mortality rate in the 20 countries performing best on this criterion is 12 per 1,000 or less, whereas in the 20 countries performing least well on this criterion it is 190 or more. In fact, if one wishes to look to the main abuse of children's rights in relation to health in developed countries, one has to look at their mental health.

As many as 5-10% of children living in developed countries suffer significant behaviour and emotional problems, such that they are impaired in their functioning to a notable degree. (I should add that the number of disturbed children is not fewer in third world countries, it is merely that in these countries other health issues seem more important.) To what degree are these emotional and behaviour problems a reflection of an abuse of the child's right to health? I would argue that they must be seen in this way if they arise from circumstances that we know how to prevent, or that they arise because children's needs are, in law or in commonly held attitudes, overlooked to a degree that causes unnecessary suffering. Now not all child psychiatric disorder or mental ill health falls into this category. Children may suffer from serious mental conditions such as autism which, at this time, we do not have the knowledge to prevent or treat successfully. Some children also suffer from minor disturbances which do not seem understandable in the light of their circumstances. But, more commonly, disturbed children are victims of preventable circumstances which are only too readily understood. Parental marital disharmony is a major cause of disturbance. Lack of adequate substitute child care facilities where both parents choose or need to go out to work is another. The ignoring of a child's wishes and welfare when divorce arrangements are made is another. The causes of disturbance by no means always lie in the home, though that is a popular fallacy. Bullying in school by other children is a potent source of unhappiness, and it has been well demonstrated in a project in Norway that bullying in school is not an inevitable phenomenon, but can be prevented.

Now the needs of children for satisfactory mental health are not difficult to enumerate. They include a continuous, loving relationship with at least one and preferably two adults, the provision of adequate substitute care when, especially because of employment arrangements, one of the parents cannot look after the child, positively orientated discipline, appropriate stimulation and sensitivity to the child's emotional needs both at home and at school.

CHILD ABUSE

The presence of an emotional or behavioural disturbance in a child is a significant but not a certain indicator that a child's right to mental health is being contravened. A much more certain indicator is the identification of child abuse.

There are four major ways in which child abuse occurs, and in three of these the child's physical as well as mental health is impaired. In the fourth (child sexual abuse), while physical effects may occur, they are by no means invariable. *Physical abuse* is common in both the developing and developed world. In the UK about 1 per 10,000 children is killed by his or her parents, and about 1 per 1,000 under the age of three years is severely physically traumatised to the extent of bone fractures, retinal haemorrhages or other serious physical damage. Minor physical abuse is much more difficult to define, and is much more common. Parents who abuse their children are usually young, socially isolated, materially deprived and have explosive personalities, but there are many parents who do not fit this stereotype. Very few have any mental illness. *Child sexual abuse* is also common and also probably occurs in all societies, although it is better concealed in some than in others. The phenomenon, although previously documented, has only been a matter of serious public and professional concern for about the last fifteen years in the US and for about the last 10 years in the UK. About 10% of adult women give an account of having been abused in childhood. About 1-2% have suffered penetrative abuse and the remainder lesser, though nevertheless still extremely unpleasant forms of abuse such as being forced to masturbate the perpetrator or having their own genitalia fondled. Many girls are abused well before the age of puberty. Often indeed in the first seven or eight years of life and occasionally even in infancy. Boys are also frequently abused, but only about 25% as often as girls. About 9 in 10 perpetrators are male, and about half of these have been abused earlier in their lives. Much serious abuse, perhaps about a half to two-thirds, occurs in the family, and in some families, teenage boys are simultaneously being abused by their fathers or step-fathers, and are themselves abusing their younger brothers.

Emotional abuse involves child abuse and often scapegoating, derision and denigration. Emotionally abused children often fail to thrive physically simply because they are not given enough to eat. Emotional abuse is very difficult to define and there are no good figures on its prevalence – it is certainly common. Finally, there is a form of abuse known as *Munchausen's syndrome by proxy*. In these cases the mother makes her child ill by feeding the child sleeping tablets or other medicines, or artificially producing physical symptoms in her child, for example by scratching the skin or putting dye into the child's urine to make it look bloody. This condition is unusual, but by no means rare.

In considering the means to achieve better child protection, it is perhaps first necessary to acknowledge that, in most countries, excellent, sensible child protection legislation already exists. It is improbable that abuse of children will be reduced by altering laws. Secondly, there is very little or no correlation between the occurrence of abuse and the level of professional resources, whether these be medical, psychiatric or social work. Of course, social workers and doctors play an invaluable part in identifying abuse and managing its consequences, but there is little evidence that resource increases on any realistic scale will result in a reduction of abuse. Instead, if children's rights to health by prevention of abuse are to be sustained, one must look to social and educational policy, and to curriculum development.

Social policies likely to exert a significant preventive effect include: i) the provision of adequate financial support for women who wish to stay at home to look after their young children; ii) the provision for parents of young children who do wish to go to work of substitute care facilities that meet the emotional and physical needs of young children and are flexible in their arrangements to take account of the fact that working hours vary, and that young children frequently suffer minor infections; iii) a commitment to provide early suitable long-term fostering or adoptive care when parents are clearly seen, from the child's infancy, not to be able to provide adequate care; and iv) educational policies to ensure that the curriculum includes sufficient attractive material to prepare youngsters for parenthood as well as the skills to prevent themselves being abused, both within the family and outside it. The Child to Child programme developed in my own institution is an example of an imaginative educational initiative now being taken up worldwide, in which children are taught to look after their own younger brothers and sisters in a way that will stand them in good stead as parents later in their lives.

MISCELLANEOUS ISSUES

In considering children's rights in relation to health, the issues I have discussed so far, – the massive preventable mortality and morbidity in third world countries, the mental health of children in developed countries, and child protection from abuse throughout the world, seem to me self-evidently those that should be given greatest priority. There are however a number of issues, in relation to health and children's rights, which preoccupy doctors, lawyers and some parents in developed countries, and perhaps require some consideration even though they are of lesser significance when the total picture of child health is examined.

The first is the right of the child to life when he has been born handicapped. The child may be born with a condition that is incompatible with later independence, and who could only survive if exceptional life-saving measures are taken. Should such life-saving measures be instituted? How should one judge the quality of later life? Is a child with trisomy-21 (Down Syndrome or mongolism), who will be capable of language, forming relationships, but not getting a job or able to marry or parent, be considered on a par with a much more seriously impaired baby? How life-saving should one be – feed normally, provide antibiotics for an infection, carry out a complicated surgical operation?

A second issue relates to the parents' right to compensation or extra financial resources if the child is handicapped either by bad luck or negligence. In most developed countries, vast sums may be paid to children who suffer as a result of proven medical negligence, but equally handicapped children suffering as a result of nature's mistakes, such as genetic defects, receive derisory amounts from the state. The issue of no-fault compensation is a live one in many countries and, because the quality of a handicapped child's life and health is related to the financial resources available to him and his parents, this is a relevant issue to consider.

A third issue concerns the development of new treatments and the child's rights in relation to systematic and unsystematic investigation. Over the last 50 years there have been major improvements achievement in the treatment of many previously invariably fatal childhood illnesses. Leukaemia that used to be 100% fatal is now curable in 60-70% of cases. Many previously inoperable congenital heart conditions can now be successfully treated surgically. These advances have not been achieved without cost. In the development of successful treatments, many children have suffered unnecessary pain and other unpleasant symptoms in unsuccessful attempts to prolong their lives. Further, systematic enquiries often require random allocation of children to different forms of treatment in a manner that inevitably means some will not get the best treatment available. Many of these issues are now well considered by ethical committees that have been set up in most developed countries, but the problems they consider are often not easy to resolve. Working as I do in an institution that is buzzing with doctors and non-medical scientists, determined to achieve better results, you will not be surprised that I am concerned to protect the rights of those who wish to advance knowledge. But there is no doubt that, while the process is going on, a good deal of thought needs to be put into protecting the rights of the child, not just to health, but if death is inevitable, to the most comfortable terminal stages that can be devised.

CONCLUSION

In conclusion, may I say that the worldwide abuse of children's right to health seems to me to represent the greatest current infringement. Such abuse is not amenable to single or simple solutions, but a commitment on the part of all governments in line with the UN Convention on the Rights of the Child, backed by the appropriate allocation of resources to ensure the implementation of these rights in relation to health, would make a vast difference to the present, appalling situation.

ANNE MCGILLIVRAY*

17. Reconstructing Child Abuse:
Western Definition and Non-Western Experience

1. INTRODUCTION

Like art, law does not just reproduce the visible: it makes visible.[1] Law inter-
prets human interactions, giving them shared and public meaning. The resulting
construct is the public or conventional definition of the behaviour. Law has
the power to expose private abuses, habitual injustices, atrocities justified as
rights. Interactions ignored by law remain in the realm of the private and
unconstructed. Law confirms desired norms by exposing undesirable conduct.
By implicitly or explicitly declaring certain types of interactions to be outside
its realm, law legitimizes them.

Although parentally-induced injury to children has been observed and sometimes censured for centuries, 'child abuse' is only about thirty years old.
Despite its youth, it has received massive state, professional, lay and media
attention. Although the West[2] has had over a century of experience with bureaucratic child welfare decision-making and an even longer history of equitable
and criminal involvement in selected cases, the conduct continues, new abuses
and new harms are identified and the public remains unclear as to what exactly
is the conduct impugned and, by corollary, what parents should and should
not do to children.

Poverty and racism harm far more children than parental abuse and are
implicated in abuse, but they are harder to deal with and easier to ignore. Child
abuse as socially constructed serves a distractive political function: it is both
shaped by, and used as scapegoat for, other social problems. Child abuse as
empirical fact exposes fundamental paradoxes in the sociolegal construction
of childhood. Childrearing practices rest on deep, competing and often unquestioned norms. Child abuse questions those norms. If the questions are cast
in terms of legal rights, then the inconsistency in law and legal policy demonstrates the lack of a coherent theory of children's rights: laws affecting children
are a bundle of opposing ideologies rarely centred on the needs of the child.
Child abuse exposes fundamental contradictions in the construction of privacy

---

* Faculty of Law, The University of Manitoba.

M. Freeman and P. Veerman (eds.), The Ideologies of Children's Rights, 213–236.

and in configurations of children's rights. All this has in turn influenced the construction of child abuse.

Child abuse is the hard case for children's rights. That hard cases make bad law is a legal truism. Hard cases are the anomalies which challenge existing doctrine. Their resolution requires bending or overturning traditional solutions which work well enough in the ordinary case. By demonstrating the anomalies in the sociolegal construct of childhood, hard cases can make good law where social justice for children is at stake. Child abuse constitutes the horns of the dilemma of what children are as human and legal beings. Moral panics about injured children spur the rights debate.

The child abuse provisions of the 1989 UN *Convention on the Rights of the Child* reflect current Western constructs of abuse developed within the larger constructs or ideologies of the public-private distinction and children's legal rights, ideologies unique to the liberal democracy. The Convention is a clear invitation to search for common ground; paradoxically, its provisions must be translated into the cultural idiom in order to appeal to what is universal in human experience. Without a universally tenable theory of childbeing and childrearing, these provisions will lack cultural meaning. As a first step in this interpretive process, they should be divested of the ethnocentric baggage of their generative culture.

2. PUBLIC PARENTS, PRIVATE CHILDREN

> What is good for the individual can be destructive to the family; what preserves the family can be harsh on both the individual and the tribe to which the family belongs; what promotes the tribe can weaken the family and destroy the individual; and so on upward through the permutations of levels of organization.
>
> E.O. Wilson, 1975.[3]

Cross-cultural, biosocial and historical study demonstrate the power of ideology and environment to modify childrearing practices and the resistance of parent-child relations to radical change.[4] Mere ideas have little effect on highly intimate behaviour, except perhaps to justify what people are already doing. Ideas backed by cultural, religious or legal sanctions have greater impact. Ideas which form the inarticulate core of social and legal systems have effects which are both subtle and profound. One idea historically unique to the West and embedded in the sociolegal system has deeply influenced state-parent relations, the social construction of child abuse and the purpose and threshold of state intervention. This is the public-private distinction.

Central to Western legal philosophy is the idea that there are distinct spheres of activity properly regulated by the state; all else falls into the realm of the private and unregulated. For John Stuart Mill, 'the only part of the conduct of any one, for which he is amenable to society, is that which concerns others'. This 'appropriate region of human liberty' includes thought and conscience, opinion and expression, 'liberty of tastes and pursuits; of framing the plan of our life to suit our own character'.[5] Other things have been placed in the private realm, traditionally the sphere of women and children: the family, intimate relations, parent-child relations, family goals and values, the home. Privacy may also denote a legally-recognized right to freedom from state intrusion and to a wide sphere of personal, including family, autonomy. Certainly it entails a host of legal guarantees involving civil liberties and due process of law. The paradigm of the private is the home. The paradigm of the public is the market, the traditionally male realm in which law, policy and history are made. This poses special problems for those who are not prime players in the public realm. Law plays a powerful role in demarcing public and private areas, in effect keeping the state out of some places, letting it enter others. In so doing, it defines both.

Childhood and the autonomous patriarchal nuclear family are sociolegal constructs of relatively recent origin designed to serve interests apart from children's needs.[6] They are traditionally protected by the three faces of privacy: legal, physical and ideological. Physical privacy first became a reality and a social value with architectural innovations of the 1700s.[7] Where physical privacy is lacking, an ideological wall of privacy is constructed: if child abuse is viewed as a private matter, it is ignored by neighbours as well as the state, suggesting that the threat of publicity may be a strong deterrent to borderline abusers.

Liberalism sharply distinguished private from public and placed individual over collective interests. In doing so, it detached family concerns from direct state control and formally placed children under the control of their parents. It is in the public interest to ensure that children pose no threat to society.[8] The liberal state sought to accomplish this by backing parental power, intervening only when they were deemed to have failed to control or properly maintain children. While the line between public and private has changed over time with redefinition of acceptable degrees of corporal punishment and redesignation of the standard of care, the concept remains central to protective intervention. Essentially, the story goes, the state will regulate parental conduct only in 'serious' cases; intervention is then swift and necessarily intrusive. Where children are concerned, the line is either complete and impenetrable; or nonexistent.

Is it true to say that by not regulating certain conduct, law has no influence on that conduct? By marking the outer limits of privacy, law gives shape to the private. By declaring it private, law confirms the activities and relationships occurring within. In making parent-child relations part of the private, existing power structures and controls are tacitly approved and for the most part left unexamined by legal institutions. It is only in hard cases of severe failure and disclosed injury that the private becomes public. This, too, confirms the validity of controls in place in those families not exposed to public scrutiny.

A seemingly swift and decisive state response in selected cases does little to challenge 'normal' practices but provides the appearance of a caring society.

Law responds to public values and shapes the way values are perceived. It achieves this through dispute resolution and through the symbols it creates in the process. Values abhorring parental injury of children and upholding compassion and nurturance rest with the community, but law invests them with greater or lesser significance. When law designates an act as abusive, the act achieves a certain level of public importance; the import is even greater if the same act is designated criminal. When law designates an act private, assessment of its significance is left to private conscience or to informal social controls; it is divested of public significance. By constituting the ground of the act as private, the relationships of control have been legally ratified. In choosing not to intervene, law has intervened anyway.[9]

The establishment of a separate body of law and specialized agencies to deal with abuse and neglect both justifies and ensures differential treatment of children. The system penetrates only open-textured families: open because of obvious malfunction, usually poverty, or complete dysfunction in the case of abandoned or severely neglected children; sometimes opened by the victims themselves. Criminal laws excusing corporal punishment reinforce the low status of children and are used by parents to justify abusive practices. Family privacy is strengthened by 'non-interventionist' decisions upholding the right of parents to dictate educational, disciplinary, religious and residential choice. This legitimizes the power of parents to interpret the child's reality. In a dysfunctional relationship, this interpretive power displaces the child's view, making disclosure unlikely and detection difficult. The value given to the archetype of the family as a private cohesive unit joined by ties of blood, affection and economic interdependence contributes to the ideology of family loyalty. Children fear breaching the family compact by disclosing problems to outsiders and recant where family cohesiveness is threatened.

The intervention debates is tied to issues of family privacy and rules protecting personal privacy or liberty. As historian Linda Gordon points out, the question is 'Whose privacy? Whose liberties?'[10] Until the present century, rights of the individual against the state belonged to male heads of households; subordinates were not protected as a matter of right from oppression within the family.[11] The greater the value accorded by law to privacy, the higher the threshold of direct discretionary state intervention.

The ideology of the public/private distinction is being dismantled. Some critics point out that the distinction is metaphorical rather than legally determinate; others suggest the metaphor is used to mystify the extent of both state regulatory involvement and power differentials in the family. Nikolas Rose argues that the real relations created between people and state do not fit this construct.[12] The pluralistic nature of the state – the many loci of social control, the variety of expert discourses – indicates that it is the outcome rather than the origin of a multitude of processes and agencies. In order to maintain itself, it must create a 'subjectivity of citizenship'. The liberal state over the last two centuries has accomplished this through the 'familialization' of society. Basing his argument in part on the works of Foucault and Donzelot, Rose argues that the family was co-opted to serve state socialization goals not through force but through tutelage: parents seek out the advice of a variety of experts and participate in the education and care of themselves and their families. As Rose notes, 'If the family came to serve social objectives, it was not in spite of the wishes of women and men, but because it came to work as a private, voluntary and responsible agency for the rearing and moralizing of children'.[13] Tutelage constitutes a relationship which can be said to be neither public nor private.

Groups opposing reforms base much of their argument on the value of family privacy and autonomy: freedom from state intervention is the only way to strengthen the family and a strong family is the cure to social ills. Groups supporting a hands-off view of the family equate loss of privacy with gain in victim rights and view power as a zero-sum game. But the sources of power are many and child abuse harms families as well as victims. The public/private dichotomy in supporting parental autonomy isolated children as a group from public visibility, prevented the forging of a direct relationship between child and state and stifled the development of a coherent intervention policy.[14] Although it was possible to talk of rights for men and women within this construct, it made children's rights an oxymoron.

3. IDEOLOGIES OF CHILDREN'S RIGHTS

> It follows, according to the actual progression of human beings, that the next influx or irradiation which our enlighteners are pouring on us, will illuminate the world with the grave descants on the rights of youth, the rights of children, the rights of babies.
>
> Hannah More, 1799.[15]

> The question 'What is a child?' is one answered by adults.
>
> Michael Freeman, 1983.[16]

Children have been portrayed as innocent and as corrupt; as blank slates to be written on and as savages to be tamed and broken. Childhood is a condition which varies according to social convenience and social conscience. To ask 'What is a child?' is to ask what rights, if any, children have. Ideologies of children's rights are tied to ideologies of the family and the role of the state. In order to disentangle children's rights from the vested interests of adults, we would ideally put ourselves in the place of the child as the child, now grown, might wish to have been treated.[17] Although public interest in children spans centuries, concern with children's rights per se dates back only a few decades, reaching public visibility with the 1979 International Year of the Child.[18] Their legal rights are constructed in terms of traditional parental rights and state interests in social control.

Although the Roman patriarchy was abolished by edict, its incidents are reflected in common and statutory law: the private autonomous household ruled by the father, the actual or virtual ownership of children, the blood tie, filial piety, the power and limits of corporal punishment, the expectation of maintenance and the diminished relationship between child and state. Parents are guardians of their children as of right, a right which includes custodial authority based on property in the child. The property nature of the interest continues to influence the treatment and valuation of children.[19] The blood-tie was until recently given primary importance in custody decisions. Although displaced by a showing of unfitness or a strongly bonded relationship with another adult, it emerges in cases involving interracial custody determination and adoption policy[20] and is popularly used as an argument for commanding obedience and respect from children. Corporal punishment, if reasonable and disciplinary, remains a parental power.[21]

3.1. *The Liberalization of Rights*

Feminist and youth movements of the 1960s and 1970s, critical of both public and private violence and of the public/private distinction manifested in professionalism and patriarchy, created an atmosphere of self-help and citizen action in which family violence could be addressed. This time around, the adult victim was active in defining and treating the problem. The new liberalism or welfarism of the 1960s made it possible directly to address the issue of children's rights.[22] The liberalization of rights, spreading downward and outward from the aristocracy to landholders, men, women and − if we deconstruct the public-private distinction − to children suggests children are to be treated on a juridically equal footing with others: special consideration of children's rights ought not be necessary. But few are prepared to concede that children should be treated exactly like adults. This would pose too great a threat to adult rights and to the social order.

Juridical equality requires accommodation of inequality: the equal or identical treatment of unequal persons results in inequality. Are children the same as adults, with some minor differences, or different from adults, requiring special protection and preparation for adult status? Are parents and children individuals with separate interests or is the child-parent relationship an identification of interests? These opposing themes of autonomy and dependance/nurture are central to the rights debate. Children's rights arguments consequently tend to be framed in a developmental and relational context, a context which seems both desirable and inevitable.

Unfortunately, this too easily obscures other, competing interests. One is that of the abusive parent in maintaining control over the child and avoiding stigmatization or punishment. Another is that of the state in maintaining the appearance of family autonomy and the paradigm of privacy: too much meddling weakens the family, meaning parental autonomy and commitment, to the detriment of children; alternatives are unattractive or expensive; it is politically unwise to dispute too strongly the public mythology of the loving and united family; it is politically unacceptable to institute universal support systems which would bypass reliance on parental resource provision and control.[23]

A broad and bewildering array of formulations and codes of children's rights has emerged in the past twenty years. The conservative laissez-faire model of Goldstein, Solnit and Freud supports the family-as-haven ideology of earlier decades; the liberal distributive justice model of Dingwall and Eekelaar sets children's rights into a trust context; Minow's feminist/corrective justice model struggles to bridge the gap between relational interests and children's autonomy interests; the formalist 'rule of law' model would suggest children's rights are, first and foremost, human rights, with child-centred concerns taken into the balance at every stage.

3.2. *The Right to a Family*

The most commonly recognized and least contestable of rights has been called the right to a family, meaning right to a parent.[24] This is associated with rights to nurture and maintenance; to cultural continuity; and to an almost absolute security of placement and parenting. Among the strongest proponents of this view of rights are psychologists Goldstein, Solnit and Freud, who argue that once the child is in the care of the 'psychological parent', the state should not intervene.[25] The parental role is supreme and the state role essentially one of distant support. The major harm to the child, in this view, is the breaking of psychological bonds through state intervention.

Although biological in its emphasis on bonding, this view presents serious problems for child protection and the differentiation of child-parent interests. Phrases like 'blood tie' and 'parental rights' are avoided and the analysis appears to be undertaken from the child's viewpoint, but the ideal of an unbroken integrity of relationship and the presumption of shared interests give paramountcy to parental interests of privacy and control. Consideration of the child's right to protection should the parent prove harmful, or of the needs and interests of children for which the parent should be expected to provide, is minimal. As the private autonomous child-parent relationship has proven in countless cases to be harmful to the children involved, as Robert Dingwall and John Eekelaar point out, it cannot be said to be an unqualified right of children.[26]

3.3. *The Equitable Trust*

The equality principle described Dingwall and Eekelaar is based on 19th century liberalism and John Stuart Mill's contention that it is 'unjust to penalize children for the irresponsibility, poor judgement or economic failure of their parents'.[27] Families are preferred childrearing environments from the child's viewpoint but social inequality leads to disadvantage; therefore there is a collective duty to limit inequality by redistributing wealth directly or indirectly through service provision. As children lack access to such resources, parents must act as their agents and trustees. Giving up resources to equalize children's opportunities creates a collective right to monitor the degree to which the child benefits; if it is insufficient, the parent is held to account.

This distributive justice model recognizes relational and autonomy rights or interests and casts these into a legalistic mold: as parents are trustees of their children's interests, breach results in loss of parental autonomy or privacy commensurate with the breach. This formulation presumes a shared knowledge of children's rights and interests without specifying what these are. The conclusion that the process should continue to be overseen by localized low-level magistrates' courts, as a local 'people's court' is most familiar with local norms, is problematic. What happens if local norms are unusually punitive or neglectful? Why should there not be universal standard governing treatment of children, as there is for adults? When is the parent's trust discharged?

If full autonomy for children is practically or politically unacceptable, the idea of variable competence has met with wide approval and appears to govern the line-drawing defining children's participation in society.[28] The problem here is that, although the results may benefit children, children are not the focus of the majority of laws and rules which affect them.[29] Definitions of 'child' and 'capacity' implied in these rules are contradictory and irreconcilable. As Martha Minow suggests, this represents competing interests rather than competing definitions of childhood.[30]

3.4. *Relational Rights*

Martha Minow outlines three types of children's rights which recognize the importance to children of relations with adults: the right to state protection, invocable by the child to penetrate family privacy and establish a direct relationship between child and state; the right to be protected from the state by reinforcing parental authority; the right to invoke state support for autonomous decisions. These double layers of parental and state control point in contrasting directions. Her rights paradigm is the failure of juvenile justice[31] which she suggests results from adopting into law only some of the features of 'the right to care, connection, and indeed custody'. She recommends introducing the idea of duty into juvenile justice: the court and its social welfare extension is to become an educator, teaching juveniles their duties to parents, state and community. But her resolution is problematic.

This relational rights argument does not account for situations of absolute opposition of parent-child interests. Differences in development and capacity central to resolution of the autonomy/dependence rights debate, central to the control of juvenile crime and child abuse, are not considered.[32] Autonomy is always relative;[33] what is meant by autonomy for children is the measured right to self-determination, the increasing freedom to make one's own mistakes.

The central issue in the rights debate is to what extent we leave children of what age to experience the unadulterated social consequences of those mistakes.[34]

Imposing duties on children as a requirement of rights contradicts the meaning of rights.[35] What duties are to be imposed on infants? What should responsibility mean to an injured child? If 'relational rights' are of a different order than other rights, this is not made clear.[36] The rights debate, with its rigorous insistence on individualism and autonomy, on line-drawing and side-taking, on broad claims narrowed only by clear showing of righteous boundaries, is an awkward vehicle for the exploration of children's terrain, but this resolution suffers from the problems she identifies in other approaches and fails to clearly take the side of the child.[37] Relational rights can be adjudicated by the ordinary courts, the designated experts on rights and, with careful advocacy, something more child-centred, more closely in tune with the interests of the child, may emerge.[38]

3.5. *The Rule of Law*

An alternative view of rights is the formalist view. In this model, law makes no distinction between persons: age is as irrelevant or relevant as gender, class, race or handicap. Formalism suggests that the question of children's rights is better phrased as one of equality: derogation from the notional equality of human beings, whether characterized as child abuse, crime or parental right, is susceptible to social correction. The same law applies to everyone, irrespective of age or status.

The rule of law has historically not been a reality for minorities, women and children: equal treatment of the unequal perpetuates inequality. But all legally relevant personalized attributes can be weighed in the balance, in terms of equalizing access, reforming systemic and judicial bias and making the changes necessary to ensure procedural fairness. Victim inequality has important implications for remedies. The greater the susceptibility of the victim, the greater the wrongdoing by the offender and the heavier the penalty or damages for correction of the harm; the more trusting the relationship, the greater the breach of trust. The challenge in making this model work lies in redefining what characteristics of children are legally relevant and in equalizing system access through child-specific procedural refinements to ensure substantive justice.[39] The larger issue, then, is whether the laws satisfy the broader requirements of justice.

Child abuse challenges children's rights ideologies and exposes inherent contradictions. One solution is to separate out child abuse response issues from the more generalized issues of nurture, care and socialization and subject them to special treatment, as was done in the Convention on the Rights of the Child. This does not solve the logical conundrum posed by situating children's rights in the context of traditional parental rights. Other solutions have not been particularly satisfactory. Children's rights movements are conducted by adults. Adults are the source of protection and injury, adults have interests separate from those of children and adults define children's rights. They are free to do so without meaningful challenge from children. Child abuse presents one such challenge.

4. Rights and Forums

> The child shall enjoy special protection, and shall be given opportunities and facilities, by law and by other means, to enable him to develop physically, mentally, morally, spiritually and socially in a healthy and normal manner and in conditions of freedom and dignity. In the enactment of laws for this purpose, the best interests of the child shall be paramount.
>
> UN *Declaration of the Rights of the Child*[40]

> 15(1). Every individual is equal before and under the law and has the right to the equal protection and equal benefit of the law without discrimination and, in particular, without discrimination based on race, national or ethnic origin, colour, religion, sex, age or mental or physical disability.
>
> *Canadian Charter of Rights and Freedoms*[41]

All else being equal, children are better off in a family environment and best off with their biological parents: empirical evidence supports cultural beliefs in the special nature of family bonds. But the empirical reality is obscured by ownership constructs, which not only reflect a focus on parents rather than children but also justify a wide range of damaging and abusive conduct. The characterization of the family relationship as a right of the child in such cases in misleading and perilous. If children's rights are constructed within a state-as-alternative-parent framework, the problem of adult-centred definition and standards is acute. In this framework, the onus is on the state to intervene where a parent is deemed to have failed. But this process is tautological: in setting intervention standards, the state sets parenting standards.

If children's rights are constructed in terms of actual or notional equality with adult rights, a solution which avoids this tautology, the question of how far these rights should extend in law is more easily settled. Whether or not children should be given the vote, permitted to operate motor vehicles, allowed to choose their own residence or engage in sexual activity are questions related to maturity and capacity. Access to justice is not. Legal solutions to the problem of child abuse reveal much of the construct of both child abuse and children's rights. The form or forum chosen for children's remedies against parents demonstrates a particular configuration of children's rights.

4.1. *Tutelage and Rescue*

On the first level are the private, informal and extra-judicial forums based on kin or community support systems. Here traditional indigenous systems are exposed to new knowledge and ideas by 'experts' who serve a tutelary function but have no sanctioning power. This level is free of individual rights consciousness but does recognize a community right or interest in child welfare. On the second level are the publicly-funded bureaucracies which operate primarily through tutelage and resource provision and secondarily through the temporary removal of the child from dangerous family circumstances. These serve no judicial function other than to make case-specific findings for treatment or funding purposes. They can apply to the courts for wardship and other remedies and they may encourage or discourage criminal prosecution. They are the primary gatekeepers to the judicial process in child abuse cases.

The third and fourth levels involve the public court system, but the differences are significant. On the third level are the separate specialized family courts, halfway houses intended to resolve the dilemma inherent in the configuration of children's rights. Children are rarely parties in these cases; the agency, representing the state, is the applicant and parents or caretakers are respondents.[42] These courts are private in the sense that the cases are rarely the subject of media attention and can apply only a limited range of remedies. Although exposure to family courts is stigmatizing as indicative of family dysfunction, and the results potentially damaging in that the state can sever parent-child relations, their purpose is not to denounce and punish abusers but to protect children. They are concerned with continuing conduct and prevention of harm rather than with the abuser's intent and they deal only with cases of intrafamilial abuse. The standard of proof is the relatively low balance of probabilities. The focus is the preservation of the family insofar as this is in the best interests of the child.

4.2. *The Ordinary Courts*

On the fourth level are the ordinary courts of civil and criminal jurisdiction. Children's access to these courts indicates a shift towards judicial equality and full legal rights. The civil process is now receiving some attention as a child abuse remedy, mainly by adult victims of childhood abuse. Compared to the criminal process, civil cases can take years rather than months to resolve and prosecution is private and expensive. The civil process is somewhat less stigmatizing and it is the stigma which is thought to influence behavioural norms. However, the civil process has the advantages of monetary compensation, a didacticism more subtle and intricate than that of the criminal law and a lower standard of proof. The payment of damages may be more punitive for some defendants than a criminal conviction. It is open to the courts to award punitive damages where the conduct is judged to be a deep derogation from community standards. For these reasons, the private lawsuit may well become an important child abuse remedy.

Probably the most visible change in North American child abuse management is the submission of cases, usually involving sexual abuse, to the criminal courts. The purpose is to establish standards by identifying child abuse with crime and to invite the public denunciation which confirms appropriate norms. Because of its didactic powers and the stigma which attaches to conviction and punishment, the criminal law is believed to have deterrent effect. Although children have not been legally barred from criminal courts, their participation posed evidentiary and therapeutic problems. Beliefs about the truthfulness of children shaped rules for the reception of children's evidence. Concerns about the trauma caused to the child by testifying, facing the abuser in the courtroom, splitting up the family and criminalizing a parent shaped agency decisions about the involvement of police in child abuse cases. These concerns reflect, and influenced, the construction of child abuse as private and civil rather than public and criminal. They have been addressed in recent legislation and court decisions.[43] In effect, it is the accommodations made for children's testimony, rather than the bare potential for access, which indicates recognition of equal rights for children.

Western nations continue to experiment with almost every conceivable combination, judicial and extra-judicial, public and private. It is presently thought that submitting disputes to public and impartial tribunals is an important step in reconstructing ideology. To submit something as private, as personal as child abuse to a public court, whatever the adjustments made to protect the identity of the child, is in itself a strong statement about harm and public interest. The more public and stigmatizing the court, the stronger is the message. Adjudication applies the general principle to the particular case, giving form to the ideal and particularizing the general. Disposition bears a strong message to the public as well as to the parties involved. Judicial discourse with the parties to the case and from case to case is a highly visible expression of ideology. At the least, law has the potential to make suffering visible. Optimally, law will remedy the injustice in the specific case. Ideally, law will strengthen perception of the right and the good, supporting cultural values, ideological change and behavioural reform.

5. Reconstructing Child Abuse

> In all societies the helpless infant. . . must be changed into a responsible adult obeying the rules of his society. Child training everywhere seems to be in considerable part concerned with problems which arise from universal characteristics of the human infant and from universal characteristics of adult culture which are incompatible with the continuation of infantile behaviour.
>
> Whiting and Child, 1953.[44]

Parenting reflects cultural values. It is designed not just to ensure infant survival but to instill culturally-valued characteristics: obedience, filial piety, modesty, courage, violence, compassion. Cross-cultural study reveals wide childrearing variation tied to cultural values and unity in goal: to raise children to be successful adults, within the parameters set on one hand by children and on the other by the rules of the society. Parental success is measured by survival of children to reproductive maturity and successful socialization. What is considered harmful to children varies: practices injuring or endangering children are supported where the presumed benefit in the child's social standing outweighs the dangers; or where the dangers are not perceived. Finding out how children are treated involves evaluation. Little involving children is value-neutral. To avoid the extremes of cultural relativism and ethnocentricity, assessment must include both points of view.

5.1. *Non-Western Constructs*

Cross-cultural assessment of child abuse arises on three levels, according to classifications established by anthropologist Jill Korbin.[45] On the first are practices accepted by one culture but considered abusive by another. Child abuse definitions here are confounded by conflicting values.[46] At the second level are cultural criteria for identifying child abuse, defined as idiosyncratic behaviour outside the range of culturally-accepted practices; and the levels of social control developed by that culture.[47] At the third are environmental conditions which injure children and are not preventable by their parents. These are not of themselves child abuse in any but the most visionary sense but they may precipitate second-level child abuse.[48]

Causal theories of child abuse are usefully measured against the cross-cultural experience. Fostering and stepparenting relationships and child-specific characteristics[49] are implicated in infanticide, abandonment, neglect and abuse in both Western and non-Western cultures. Situations posing heightened risk of abuse, such as social isolation,[50] may be more clearly revealed in cross-cultural comparisons. Formal social controls vary from none to a variety of programs: welfare bureaucracies, health and daycare systems, exclusive use of criminal sanctions, advertising and any combination of these.

How societies publicly define child abuse varies widely. The discovery of child abuse is its chief international characteristic. What is labelled child abuse depends on the discoverer. Rapid social change through industrialization and the ensuing loss of traditional ways is cited by third world countries as responsible for increasing idiosyncratic abuse. Nutritional deficit, decline of cultural practices and family disruption is abuse to some modernizing cultures; others focus on eradicating cultural practices viewed by Western observers as abusive, such as clitoridectomy and suturing, footbinding, scarification and mutilation; and for general improvements in childcare. Etiology differs and is usually univariate: residual feudal male domination of women and children, the cult of filial piety, historical preference for male children, modernization, parental pathology.[51] The cultural value of children and alternate caretaker capability are important factors in the cross-cultural control picture. Study of cross-cultural response is confounded by denial, lack of organized concern and lack of study by outside researchers.[52] There is no way to know if child abuse occurs at similar rates everywhere. What seems certain is that it is universal. While constructs of child abuse current in the West may prove illusory, cross-cultural experience closely corresponds to stages in the Western history of child abuse construction.[53]

5.2. *Western Reconstruction*

Child abuse, however defined, has for centuries cycled between discovery and invisibility, panic and indifference. It has been moralized, bureaucratized, scientized, medicalized, legalized, politicized and criminalized. Different forms of abuse have been discovered, denounced and forgotten. Definitions of abuse – the nature and intentionality of the conduct, the degree of harm, the requisite child-adult relationship – vary to the point that the term 'child abuse' has no inherent medical or legal meaning. Its ambit for child protection purposes is contained by statute and defined by policy. It otherwise carries the meaning ascribed by its user.

Exposure to the elements, exposure to immorality, physical and emotional neglect, corporal punishment, physical and emotional abuse, incest, sexual assault, sexual exploitation, fetal damage, transracial or transcultural adoption, ritual or satanic abuse: all have been labelled child abuse. Explanations range from social deviance to individual pathology; circumstantial variants such as divorce or alcoholism; systemic factors such as economic stress or racism; to ecological or multivariate models; and all the way back again. Remedies have ranged from the individual to the systemic: lecturing and tutoring, apprehension or institutionalization of the child, criminal actions against parents, public education, poverty relief, daycare and improvement of social and educational facilities, visionary calls for massive social reform or revolution. The politics of abuse have ranged from moral entrepreneurship, through bureaucratic expansionism and expansion of expert prestige, to the promotion to tribal, feminist, conservative, fundamentalist and medical interests.

5.2.1. *The Moral Construct: Cruelty to Children*
Although what we now view as child abuse has always been publicly visible,[54] so strong was the ideology of the private and so little done in any concerted fashion that even its public face was rendered invisible. Its private face, intrafamilial abuse, was denied by the 18th century Enlightenment portrayal of the affectively-bonded family and the 19th century idealization of the middle-class patriarchal family. Child abuse as we know it did not exist: it had not been socially constructed. The new wealth of the 19th century middle classes, a rising social and feminist conscience and a general belief in the betterment

of humanity engendered private action on behalf of visibly afflicted children. These moral crusades for child welfare resulted in the formal involvement of the state in child welfare. The prototype of child abuse, cruelty to children, emerged in the 1870s.[55]

Post-1870 child abuse management was the meeting-place of feminists and male moral crusaders who constructed abuse as a moral problem located in the 'bestiality' of lower-class males and in perceived inadequacies of immigrant mothers. The construct included the contemporary range of harms (neglect, incest and a form of emotional or psychological abuse in 'immoral influence') but excluded any concept of the child as having separate interests: children remained the property and subordinates of their parents. Responses included private charitable involvement, moral crusades, the export of abandoned children overseas as cheap labour and the development of male-run agencies staffed by volunteer women. The equation of child abuse with immorality or deviance rather than with parental rights clearly identified it as a social rather than private problem and led to protective legislation permitting the removal of children and requiring the prosecution of parents. The requirement was soon dropped and the focus turned back to the family unit. Child abuse was again privatized, but this time the agencies were in there too.

5.2.2. *The Scientific Construct: Hygiene and Psychopathy*
In the first decade of this century, professional social workers began to staff the agencies and to bring a scientific view to their family work. The agencies were now the designated experts in child abuse management. Child abuse was reconstructed as neglect; moral hygiene was reconstructed as physical and mental hygiene; abusive men were no longer brutes, criminals or deviants but were to be pitied, as poverty or unemployment excused their bad behaviour. Co-incident with the fall of feminism, abuse became a buried sub-category of neglect and the sex offender became a stranger rather than a parent or stepfather or uncle, and the property of psychiatry rather than the law.[56] Intrafamilial sexual abuse, by far the largest category of sexual abuse cases, was reconstructed as sexual delinquency: girls who had been abused were 'sex offenders' under juvenile delinquency legislation. Psychiatry was introduced into the agency roster of remedies in the 1940s and 50s; the goal of therapy, as with all agency remedies since the 1910s, was to keep the family together regardless of the cost to women and children. Public awareness of child abuse was once again effectively nil. Child abuse did not exist.

5.2.3. *The Medical Construct: The Battered Child Syndrome*
The silence was broken in 1962 with the publication of 'The Battered Child Syndrome',[57] a designation chosen by the authors as less incriminating, more coolly medical, than 'child abuse'. The 'syndrome' consisted of patterned repeated physical injury to children, 'probably' inflicted by parents. The moral

panic surrounding the battered child inaugurated the present era in child abuse construction. The primary actors were members of the medical profession: pediatric radiologists whose research orientation freed them from patient confidentiality concerns published their findings and thereby achieved professional prestige; pediatricians who controlled discovery, definition, treatment and legislative processes and spearheaded citizen action groups. The medical univariate construct of child abuse, premised on a parental psychopathy model, dominated child abuse theory for close to a decade. The family was again identified as the source of the problem and the locus of treatment and, as the relationship of offender and victim fit the social work family orientation, child welfare legislation was rewritten to strengthen agency mandates.

5.2.4. *The Ecological Construct: Child Abuse*
The new activism of sociologists involved in child abuse intervention and treatment resulted in a proliferation of research as well as law reform. The environmental orientation of sociology led to the displacement of the univariate medical model with a multivariate ecological model. Child abuse was reconstructed as a complex of predisposing factors requiring a complex of responses, including further legislative change to permit a broad range of counselling, protective and support services and an enormous increase in funding. Despite a much-reduced birthrate, agencies doubled or more in size. Theorists and reformers were obsessed with definitional issues. Bureaucratization and legalization, and the participation of social workers in definition, theory and law reform, gave the agencies prestige and sole responsibility for prevention. It soon became apparent that agencies could not prevent child abuse. Missed cases and misjudgments resulting in a series of child murders were seized upon by the media. Backlash to perceived overintervention in the family, which challenged strongly-held values of autonomy and privacy, coalesced into vocal lobby groups. Workers and the public questioned agency decisionmaking, family orientation and mission. Increasing dissatisfaction with the agency model and its family focus sparked searches for new explanations and new controls. It was into this environment that the feminist rediscovery of sexual abuse fell.

5.2.5. *The Political Construct: Sexual Abuse*
Sexual abuse as constructed in the late 1970s and 80s is a highly gendered issue: the aggressor is male, the victim usually female and the context home and family-centred relationships. The root cause is patriarchy and its control of the private. Child abuse, always a locus of political expediency, became overtly politicized. With thousands of children disclosing sexual abuse year after year as a result of programs designed to encourage victim complaint and a public who now believes them; and a proliferation of studies indicating high levels of sexual victimization, this construct has received strong em-

pirical support. Despite the fact that the victims of a single homosexual pedophile may number in the hundreds, meaning that male victims numerically may equal female victims, the construct remains little challenged. Incest – sexual intercourse within a proscribed range of blood relationships – has been popularly reconstructed as any sexual contact with a child in any relationship of trust. Sexual abuse is constructed as classless and pervasive. For now, child abuse is sexual abuse and sexual abuse is crime.

Several results flow from this construct. First, protection policy is shifting from a social welfare focus on the family to the direct and immediate interests of the child victim. This focus both reflects and magnifies public awareness of children's rights. Second, there is a clear preference on the part of agencies, and a growing preference on the part of the public, for a criminal justice resolution. Third, child abuse in the popular consciousness now means sexual contact with a child.[58] Neglect, emotional or psychological abuse and physical abuse have sunk in public visibility.[59] Racism, poverty and other environmental factors play only a minor role in the popular understanding of causation, releasing governments from responsibility for the larger and more expensive prevention issues.

5.2.6. *Trans-cultural Reconstruction*

'Child abuse' is a post-1960 theoretical construct for the child-centred focus of state resources and social conscience, a political umbrella term for whatever conduct is to be denounced. After much trial and error, legislative standards broad enough to cover any conduct offensive to compassionate norms have been devised; overbreadth is dealt with as a procedural concern and statutes now offer some protection to fundamental justice rights of parents. But intervention thresholds remain problematic. The challenge of cross-cultural study has yielded a definition of child abuse which embraces both emic and etic perspectives and roots control in cultural beliefs. Child abuse, as defined by Korbin and Finkelhor, is not just any harm which befalls children: it is harm resulting from human action which is 'proscribed, proximate and preventable'.[60] Stretching definition to embrace difference lends not only cultural legitimacy but practicality: Korbin and Finkelhor's definition is elastic without overbreadth and could effectively base protective intervention in multicultural Western nations. But the requirement of proscription may pose a problem.

'Child abuse' embraces both actual behaviour and the culturally constructed determination of culpability. It is not restricted to any particular type of society.[61] Although endemic to the human species, it is wasteful of human resources and offensive to human values. As Korbin and Finkelhor point out, child abuse is 'a powerful concept that can be the basis for strong international action' to improve the status of all children. The Convention on the Rights of the Child may be the focus of such action.

6. CONCLUSION

> 19.1. States Parties shall take all appropriate
> legislative, administrative, social and educational
> measures to protect the child from all forms of
> physical or mental violence, injury or abuse, neglect
> or negligent treatment, maltreatment or exploitation,
> including sexual abuse, while in the care of
> parent(s), legal guardian(s) or any other person who
> has the care of the child.
> UN *Convention on the Rights of the Child*, 1989.

> Childcare workers and teachers/ they didn't do their
> part 'Cause I grew up in Auschwitz/ with a bitch
> that had no heart.
> *4 1/2 Reasons for Retroactive Abortion*, 1989.[62]

The suffering of children is intolerable: for the child and for the child become adult; for the compassionate and for those who count the social cost of generations of dropouts, runaways, the impaired, the dysfunctional. An adequate theory of children's rights will embrace the hard case of child abuse. It will be based on factual information about how children are treated and provide a framework for consideration of how children ought to be treated. It will deal with the fact of children's changing dependence. It will cut through the ideologies of privacy and parental rights. It will distinguish the preservation of adult supremacy from the child's need for intimacy, protection and nurture.

The suffering of children at the hands of the family is the hard case for law. The primacy of the family as the locus of childrearing and the foundational social unit is recognized in all societies. Respect may be expressed in protection of paternal or parental authority through doctrines of privacy which discourage scrutiny of parenting practices, confound development of coherent state-child relations and children's rights theory, render child abuse invisible and remove it from the ambit of 'grown-up' or principled law. When child abuse is played out against configurations of children's rights, contradictions are apparent, raising questions of both the suitability of a rights-based framework and the real nature of children's rights.

Child abuse is a recent construct which has grown out of what may be a uniquely Western experience. Definition and response have been shaped by Western institutions and sensibilities and influenced by rapidly changing notions of children's rights. Although the construct may be inapplicable to other types of societies, there is increasing evidence that the range of behaviours variously defined as child abuse occurs in every society, modern, modernizing or untouched. They may not be locally recognized as such; where they are, controls vary widely. From a Western point of view, developing nations reflect our own child abuse history. This history of rediscovery accompanied by the rapid evolution and devolution of theory, model and policy is more than just a lesson in the making of a social problem. It demonstrates the difficulty of seeing what we do not want to see. The Western lesson is instructive for countries which do not acknowledge the existence of child abuse or attribute it to politically expedient causes, just as Western nations have done for much of their history.

The goal of raising healthy children to fully functional adulthood, whatever the sociospecific mode of childrearing, is universal. Setting broad international standards, such as those contained in the UN *Convention on the Rights of the Child*, is for this reason appropriate. The Convention is highly reflective of the Western construct of child abuse. It is expected that states whose culture and ethos is decidedly non-Western will not only adopt this particular view of injury to children but will also take effective action. To resolve the problem of variable social construction and find universality, we need to explore the folklore surrounding the treatment of children: the inarticulate beliefs, culturally-defined responses, social conventions and pretensions, formalistic manifestations of state concern. In so doing, we move from the conventional to the challenging and from acquiesence to revolution.

NOTES

1. Cf. Mahatma Ghandi on justice and Paul Klee on art.
2. Here defined as liberal democracies, primary referents being Canada, the US and Great Britain, whose child abuse/ children's rights histories are closely parallel.
3. E.O. Wilson, *Sociobiology: the New Synthesis*. Cambridge, Mass. (1975) at 4.
4. On history, see L. Stone, *The Family, Sex and Marriage in England 1500–1800* (1979); for a different view see L.A. Pollock, *Forgotten Children: Parent-Child Relations from 1500 to 1900* (1973); for cross-cultural perspectives, see J.E. Korbin (ed.), *Child Abuse & Neglect: Cross-Cultural Perspectives* (1981); for biosocial perspectives on child-parent interaction, see B. Wenegrat, *Sociobiology and Mental Disorder: A New View* (1984).
5. 'On Liberty'.
6. They belong to the individualist ethos originating after the fall of feudal communitarianism, continued by the Reformation, strengthened and articulated by liberal philosophy and inherent in concepts fundamental to modern law. These values, insofar as they impact on the family, are termed by Stone 'affective individualism', involving among other things 'a strong sense of individual autonomy and the right to freedom in the pursuit of happiness' and 'a growing desire for physical privacy'. Stone, note 3 at 22.
7. Stone, note 3 at 245. The inventions of the dumbwaiter and the hallway took the servants out of dining rooms and bedrooms. Further innovations (separate bedrooms for parents and children, soundproofing, central heating) have in the last hundred years extended physical privacy to the majority of Western peoples. Migration from villages to cities during industrialization brought another kind of privacy in the separation of families from kin and community, with wide implications for family violence rates and the passage of control from informal social systems to state regulation. According to anthropologist Richard Lee, 'Privacy is a key element [in family violence]. It is a stunningly novel factor in human history'. Interview, University of Toronto (1988).
8. E.g. C.L. Brace (1872): '[T]he class of a large city most dangerous to its property, its morals and its political life, are the ignorant, destitute, untrained and abandoned youth: the outcast street children grown up to be voters, to be the implements of demagogues, the "feeders" of the criminals, and the sources of domestic outbreaks and violations of the law'. *The*

Dangerous Classes of New York and Twenty Years' Work Among Them. New York, Winkoop and Hollenbeck (1872). Protection of society from the idle, unskilled and rebellious has justified protective intervention for centuries: social order, not children, was the issue.

9. For other analyses of the constituent power of law in this context, see F. Olsen, 'The Myth of State Intervention in the Family' (1985) *Journal of Law Reform* 18, 835; 'The Family and the Market: A Study of Ideology and Legal Reform' (1983), *Harvard Law Review*, 1497; and Martha Minow, 'Beyond State Intervention in the Family: For Baby Jane Doe' (1985) *U. Michigan J.L.* 18, ref. 933.

10. L. Gordon, *Heroes of Their Own Lives: The Politics and History of Family Violence, Boston 1880–1960* (1988).

11. The courts of equity assumed a paternalistic jurisdiction over the child in the name of the state as guardian of all persons under legal disability. This 'parens patriae' power, now accruing to all superior courts with the 19th century fusion of equity and law, permits the court to displace the parent who has injured the morals or interests of the child. The child's welfare will be provided for by the state, not as a matter of right but as a matter of equity. Common law and equitable rules have now been displaced or augmented by a bundle of statutes regulating parental conduct and defining the state role in such areas as divorce, custody, adoption, education and protection. Children have always been presumed to have the same rights as adults in tort, contract and criminal law but special rules and policies governed or restricted their actual participation; some have recently been abrogated.

12. N. Rose, 'Beyond the Public/Private Division: Law, Power and the Family' (1987), *J. Law and Society* 14, 61.

13. This was accomplished 'through the activation of individual guilt, personal anxiety and private disappointment'. Id. at 73.

14. Despite the expansion of legal protections and the value of the ideology to the liberal state, there were no noteworthy philosophical discussions of privacy until the late 1960s, the decade of massive agency expansion. While privacy permits the flourishing of positive ideas and relationships, it also 'creates the context in which both deceit and hypocrisy may flourish. It provides the cover under which most human wrongdoing takes place, and then it protects the guilty from taking responsibility for their transgressions once committed. The right to privacy often stands in the way of vigourous public debate on matters of moral significance'. F. Schoeman, 'Privacy: Philosophical Dimensions of the Literature', in *Philosophical Dimensions of Privacy: An Anthology* (1984) at 1.

15. H. More, *Strictures on the Modern System of Female Education* (1799), vol. 1, pp. 172–173.

16. M.D.A. Freeman, *The Rights and Wrongs of Children* (1983). Ch. 1.

17. J. Eekelaar, 'The Emergence of Children's Rights' (1986) *Oxford Journal of Legal Studies* 6, 161 at 169.

18. For discussion of the evolution of the concept of children's rights and a partial listing of works dealing with children's rights, see Freeman, note 16.

19. Runaways are routinely returned to parental custody and children are expected by law to obey their parents and respect their wishes; indeed, an identification of parent-child interest is presumed. According to biosocial and economic theory, parental valuation of individual children depends in part on their investment of emotional and physical resources or 'property' in that child.

20. A. McGillivray, 'Transracial Adoption and the Status Indian Child' (1986) *Canadian Journal of Family Law* 5, 437–467.

21. 'Patria potestas' and the juridically independent patriarchal family was abolished by Justinian in 560 AD in an edict which stands as one of the earliest examples of state intervention on behalf of children. Justinian left with parents only the power of punishment to correct the faults of minors should good example fail; if the offence were beyond the limits of domestic correction, the child was to be judged in the public courts. Killing a child was punishable by provisions formerly reserved for patricide, the most serious murder under Roman law. Parents were required to maintain children but no sanctions were imposed. The disciplinary rule became part of the common law and is included in Canada's Criminal

Code to excuse assaults on children by parents and those standing in the place of a parent. The requirement of maintenance remained, as Blackstone noted, a moral duty and voluntary obligation sustained on begetting a child; he speculated that the grief brought parents by 'uninstructed' children might have been thought sufficient punishment. Although Blackstone called maintenance a 'perfect right' of the child, it is not a true legal right because it has no remedy: no legal duty was imposed.

22. The accretion of rights to women and their participation in the public sphere is altering the balance of power between men and women. There is some evidence in custody determination that a similar shift is occurring between parents and children. Fran Olsen characterizes this as the liberalization of the family, a shift from hierarchy to equality, from patriarchy to 'egalitarian family of juridical equals'; and from group to individual, from corporate unit to 'voluntary association of individuals'. Fran Olsen, 'The Politics of Family Law' (1984) *Law and Inequality* 2, 1 at 8. Whether this is an accurate description of power relations in intact families or merely the inevitable result of the application of the best interests of the child test when families break up is problematic.

23. This theme is not new, the 19th c. reformer Lord Shaftesbury who worked to safeguard children from exploitation by factory owners, opposed compulsory education as an infringement of parental rights to raise their children as they saw fit. The Charity Organization Society opposed free school meals on grounds that it was in the public interest to allow 'the sins of the parents to be visited on the children, than to impair the principle of the solidarity of the family and run the risk of permanently demoralising large numbers of the population'.

24. Although it is now being argued in connection with reproductive rights and new technologies; from an adult perspective, it is constructed as a privacy issue.

25. Goldstein, Solnit and Freud, *Beyond the Best Interests of the Child* (1980). The state's role essentially is to uphold parental autonomy.

26. R. Dingwall and J. Eekelaar, 'Rethinking Child Protection' in M.D.A. Freeman (ed.), *The State, the Law and the Family* (1984): 'There can be no escape from the fact that the recognition of children's interests necessarily entails the abridgement of family autonomy. The trade-off between them is a political decision'.

27. In Dingwall and Eekelaar's formulation, '[A]ll children should have an equal opportunity to maximize the resources available for them during their childhood (including their own inherent abilities) so as to minimize the extent to which they enter adult life affected by avoidable prejudices incurred during their childhood'.

28. Such as education, driving, medical care, drinking, armed services, public affairs, the labour force, the social welfare system, sexual activity, marriage and access to justice.

29. Laws restricting the sexual activities of girls, for example, were originally based on the father's right of property in his daughter's chastity. Policies restricting the access of children to criminal justice were based on the idealization of family integrity and fictions of children's fantasizing.

30. M. Minow, 'Rights for the Next Generation: A Feminist Approach to Children's Rights' (1986) *Harvard Women's Law Journal* 9, 1.

31. Juvenile courts prior to the 1980s were based on a welfare model: legal rights were denied and paternalistic dependency relations between child and state were established; many children received long detentions in hostile situations as a result. Reforms giving children legal rights to restrain state action they have merely shortened the gap between adult and juvenile offender. The result has been more custodial sentences, fewer discharges and generally more punitive response. See e.g. R.R. Corrado and A. Markwart, 'The Prices of Rights and Responsibilities: An Examination of the Impact of *The Young Offenders Act* in British Columbia' (1988) *Canadian Journal of Family Law* 7, 93.

32. Capacity is also relevant to children's participation in decisions affecting residence, education and medical care. In Canada, children 12 and under are deemed incapable of criminal intent; children over 17 are tried as adults; those in between are subject to reduced penalties and separate proceedings.

33. That both children and adults 'need environments where they can learn what is just, learn what it means to have their needs met, and learn what it means to have and fulfill obligations' is indisputable but misses the point. Minow, note 30.

34. Giving children this kind of freedom is terrifying both to parents who risk losing control, whether exercised in their child's interest or their own, and to a public historically fearful of unsocialized children. But autonomy is also a requirement of passage to adulthood. It is seized where it is not given. Arbitrary legal lines pose no impediments to children ready for adulthood.

35. A legal right imposes duties, not on the rightholder, but on someone else. 'A law creates a right if it is based on and expresses the view that someone has an interest which is sufficient ground for holding another to be subject to a duty'. Joseph Raz, 'Legal Rights' (1984) *Oxford Journal of Legal Studies* 4, 1 at 13.

36. Minow's 'mender of social fabric' concept depends on state bureaucracy and the ability of the courts to commandeer resources on a case-by-case basis. Whether this is an appropriate forum for addressing children's problems overall – adolescent suicide, neonatal death, poverty-related neglect, racism, sexual abuse, physical abuse, adolescent crime – is itself problematic. There is something mildly offensive in the idea of state welfare workers lecturing disaffected adolescents on their social responsibilities. (But, if not the state, then whom?)

37. In a later analysis of recent US court decisions on aspects of children's rights, Minow concludes that, despite the ambiguity of the remedies in these cases, rights discourse after all 'is right for children': taking children's cases to the courts, particularly where carefully selected by children's advocates, opens up the broader dialogue required to improve conditions for children. 'Are "Rights" Right for Children?' (1987) *A.B.A. Foundation Research J.*, 203.

38. 'Litigators could press courts themselves to identify the shortcomings in the knowledge base and conflicts in values; to talk about the needs of children, not just legal doctrine; to expose the competing claims about cost and allocation of burdens on various adults, and to orchestrate a conversation among new participants about how, temporarily, to resolve these problems'. Id. at 222.

39. This model is distinguished from liberationist rights propositions (granting children all incidents of adulthood) on grounds that difference is relevant.

40. Proclaimed by General Assembly resolution 1386 (XIV) of 20 November 1959.

41. *Constitution Act, 1982* RSC 1985, Schedule B, Part 1.

42. In Britain, children are *de jure* respondents. In Canada and Britain, a court of superior jurisdiction (based on its inherent parens patriae powers) can appoint a lawyer amicus curiae to represent the child's interests; for the lower courts, the child will be represented only where authorized by statute.

43. See e.g. A. McGillivray, 'Federal Initiatives in the Criminalization of Child Abuse' [working title] (1990), *Annual Review of Manitoba Law* [upcoming]; *The Criminalization of Child Abuse*. LL.M. Thesis. University of Toronto (1988).

44. Cited in Korbin, note 4 at 2.

45. Korbin, id. at 3.

46. Parents who prevented a child from participating in painful initiation rites would be considered abusive by the community for denying the child adult status. Conflicting values can inspire mutual assessment of practices to discover positive childcare standards: the Western practice of isolating infants from the mother, for example, is considered abusive in most of the world's cultures. Inflicting pain through culturally-sanctioned practices like scarification, while objectively harmful, is less damaging than behaviours termed abusive in the West: when the behaviour is prevalent, unquestioned and viewed as socially valuable and the child is secure in parental goodwill, the act lacks the rejection and breach of trust which underline abuse.

47. Practices such as radical clitoridectomy and vaginal infibulation carry grave risks and no amount of good will or gain in social status prevents suffering, disease and death. Richard

Lee notes, 'In the Sudan, the government tried to abolish vaginal infibulation but women oppose it: severely "circumcised" women had achieved high social status which gave them certain power and they wanted to pass this on to their daughters . . . patriarchy of the worst kind has taken a loop through women's consciousness and has been taken on by women, although now men want to abolish the practices'. Note 7. Clitoridectomy was widely practiced in Europe and used in the US from about 1890 to the late 1930s to prevent masturbation, control sexuality and save husbands from their wives' 'demanding explosive sexuality'. It declined when masturbation was unlinked from insanity and women rejected routine circumcision of new born girls. See A.T. Slack, 'Female Circumcision: A Critical Appraisal' (1988) *Human Rights Quarterly* 10, 437. Slack discusses the point at which a culture's right to self-determination is outweighed by the need to protect individual human rights; until opposition is seen as stemming from within the culture itself, the practice will not cease.

48. Poverty, malnutrition and poor health care characterized life in Western nations until recently and still affect millions of children. Where parents cannot mitigate these problems but continue to provide protection and care, they cannot be considered abusive. But such conditions may precipitate ideosyncratic abuse.

49. Such as female, nonvalued traits, born under conditions of stress, age capabilities and development, illegitimacy, physical deformity or handicap, retardation and high birth order.

50. Social isolation has been implicated both as a precipitant of abuse and as a factor in failure to protect children. Strong kin and community networks are crucial in maintaining child-care standards and preventing ideosyncratic departure. Available temporary caretakers from the mother's kin group is a form of social control common to many cultures and lost to mothers in more mobile industrialized societies.

51. This was a dominant theme of early Western studies. It is the variable least amenable to cross-cultural comparison because it accounts only for a minority of cases and is tautological and retrospective. Alcoholism is responsible for deterioration in childcare in many cultures but Korbin [note 4] classifies this as environmental rather than pathological.

52. C.L. McGehee, 'Responses to Child Abuse in World Perspective' (1983) *Victimology* 10, 140.

53. The West has experienced all of this: denial, discovery and ascribing abuse to politically-expedient causes; and association of child abuse with industrialization, social fragmentation and poverty; the imposition of 'unnatural' mores founded in religious or social rules restricting marriage, infanticide, abortion and birth control or located in patriarchal practices which submit children's interests to those of parents and define female sexuality and reproduction as male property; and from practices thought to be 'good' for children.

54. The bodies of abandoned infants were found in London parks in the 19th century at the rate of up to five a day; neglected or abandoned children lived on the streets; children worked the streets, brothels, mines and factories; residential schools well into this century 'graduated' thousands of children tutored in physical and sexual abuses.

55. The focus in the early 19th century on abandoned or poorly-socialized children reflected not only fear of children but also an appreciation of their economic value. On this 'child-saving' panic, careers were founded and bureaucracies built. A second moral panic later in the century, under the banner of 'Cruelty to Children', was created following the New York *Mary Ellen* case in which an abused child houseworker could be judicially protected only under animal protection laws. Child protection societies based on the animal protection model sprang up in the US, Canada and Britain. As the poor yield privacy and autonomy on the basis of need and were (and are) the families most often seen by charities or agencies, it was with the poor that problems of family violence and child maltreatment were located. Physical and sexual abuse of children and child neglect occurred 'only' in poor, ethnic-minority families.

56. Psychiatrists became the experts on sexual offences in 1930s. They were instrumental in the formulation of legal policy and the treatment of child molesters. The offender was

medically redefined first as a 'sexual psychopath' and later as a 'mentally disordered sex offender'.

57. C.H. Kempe *et al.*, 'The Battered Child Syndrome' (1962) *Journal of the American Medical Association* 181, 17.

58. Although child abuse, family violence and the inadequacy of child welfare systems receive steady media coverage, including 'background' coverage of causation theories, 'child abuse' is primarily sexual, deviant and criminal.

59. It is difficult to project the next stage in reconstructing child abuse. Moral panic periodically forms around ritual or satanic cult abuse and media attention to the subject reflects much the same response as sexual abuse allegations did a decade ago: curiosity, disbelief, speculation. Disclosure of abuses perpetrated by religious residential school and orphanages is drawing attention to institutional abuses including emotional abuse, and to racism. Emotional abuse and the abolition of the corporal punishment excuse (most Canadian schools appear to have quietly hidden away their straps) remain high on many agenda.

60. This definition is modified by six 'dimensions': 'social sanction vs. social censure', distinguishing cigarette burns from ritual scarification; 'international consensus' supplemented by scientific knowledge, which may properly censure certain acts despite cultural approval; 'societal vs. individual causation', a reminder that acts of governments, institutions and religions can directly as well as indirectly harm children; 'children as joint victims [with adults] vs. children as sole victims'; and the culturally-determined 'personhood of the child', important in differentiating infanticide or abortion from abuse. D. Finkelhor and J. Korbin, 'Child Abuse as an International Issue' (1988) *Child Abuse & Neglect* 12, 3.

61. The romanticization of the primitive can obscure or distort the harm of parenting practices. See e.g. D. Freeman, *Margaret Mead and Samoa: the Making and Unmaking of an Anthropological Myth* (1983).

62. 4 1/2 Reasons for Retroactive Abortion, 'Growing Up in Auschwitz'. Toronto. Unpublished lyrics (copyright 1989). The lyrics, to be taken literally and written by the child, now 21, are:

Dad's cheque's not here/ No food just fear
And it wasn't my fault/ It was child assault

Growing up in Auschwitz/ Beat until you're black and blue
Growing up in Auschwitz/ Forced and told what to do
Growing up in Auschwitz/ Lies a fucking bitch would say
Growing up in Auschwitz/ Forgive you, there's no fucking way

Sick psychotic parents/ Can fuck right up a child
In an oven that's turned on/ It's really fucking wild
Child care workers and teachers/ They didn't do their part
' 　 Cause I grew up in Austchwitz/ With a bitch that had no heart

LESLIE SEBBA*

18. Juvenile Justice Policy: Mapping the Criteria

BACKGROUND

Juvenile courts were established in most western countries early in the twentieth century. While the adoption of a welfarist orientation (sometimes explicitly based upon the doctrine of *parens patriae* (Kittrie 1971)) was the *raison d'etre* of these courts, some jurisdictions, notably in the United States and Scandinavia (Dahl 1976), applied this philosophy with such enthusiasm that the procedures ceased to bear any resemblance to those generally prevailing in a court of law – and in particular to those prevailing in a criminal court.

This approach was challenged in the leading US Supreme Court case *Re Gault*,[1] which declared that the juvenile court was in substance a criminal court and that in consequence juvenile defendants were guaranteed constitutional rights similar to those enjoyed by adults. Moreover the changing perspective of the child as a bearer of rights (cf. Verhellen's contribution to this Volume), rather than as an object of welfare, has tended to support such a development. Finally, recent criticisms of the rehabilitation ideal which lay at the foundation of modern penology, and the concomitant movement towards a 'just desert' model for adult offenders, have rubbed off onto the juvenile justice system also.

These pressures have not, however, led to the unequivocal adoption of a legalistic or 'justice' model in the juvenile court. They have led rather to a number of compromises and 'trade-offs', tensions and uncertainties in the various components of the system.[2] Moreover the choice is not necessarily a dichotomous one, between a 'welfare' or a 'justice' model; there may rather be a *continuum* extending from extreme welfarism to extreme legalism.[3] Thus, in an analysis of the Israel juvenile justice system (Sebba 1981) the author of this paper noted *five* alternative models discernible in this system. These alternatives are summarized in Table 1.

* Institute of Criminology, Faculty of Law, Hebrew University of Jerusalem.

M. Freeman and P. Veerman (eds.), The Ideologies of Children's Rights, 237–254.
© 1992 *Kluwer Academic Publishers. Printed in the Netherlands.*

Table 1. Juvenile justice orientations

I	Adult Model
II	Modified Adult Model
	Juvenile Court – modified procedures – conviction – sentence – modified sanctions
III	Juvenile Delinquency Model
	Juvenile court – modified procedures – 'act committed' – treatment
IV	Diversion Model
V	Care and Protection Model
	Juvenile court – welfare procedure – 'neediness'

Israel's Juvenile Justice System

The most extreme form of legalism applicable to juveniles is to treat them as adults.[4] This takes place in the United States in the form of the so-called 'waiver' procedure whereby juveniles are referred for trial to the adult courts. This option is not presently available in Israel. However until relatively recently boys aged 16–18 were tried by the adult court, and some pressure has been exerted from time to time on the part of the police to assimilate this age group with adults, at least in respect of the maximum period for remand in custody following arrest. Moreover, most of the juvenile court provisions are not applicable to persons aged 16–18 tried in the military court.[5] In the administered territories, too, military courts try both adults and minors, although certain special provisions apply to the latter.[6]

A modified form of legalism is reflected in the second model. Minors charged with offences perceived as being serious will be tried in the juvenile court with its special procedures (e.g., participation of parent and enhanced role of probation officer), but may then be convicted and sentenced to the forms of punishment available in respect of adult offenders – with slight modifications: e.g., a secure home is available as an alternative to imprisonment.

The third model refers to the same system of trial in the juvenile court, but in lieu of conviction and sentence (and to avoid the stigma arising therefrom) the court 'finds that the act has been committed', following which a wide choice of treatments become available. This option is likely to be chosen if the delinquent act is not perceived as very serious and the perpetrator not regarded as a 'hard-core' offender.

The fourth option carries this logic one stage further. The desire to avoid stigma and formality results in the file being closed for 'lack of public interest' in a large proportion of the cases, and the suspect being sent home. In many other jurisdictions such cases would be 'diverted' to a community programme.

The final alternative, like the second and third, involves the juvenile court; but in this case the court is exercising not its delinquency, but its 'care and supervision' jurisdiction. The child is regarded as 'needy' – one criterion for which (according to the relevant statutory provision) is the commission of an offence for which he/she has not been charged.[7] However there are no charges or findings of guilt, but rather findings of 'neediness' and protective dispositions; no involvement of police or probation officers, but of welfare officers. Unlike all the previously mentioned alternatives, which are only available to minors over the age of criminal responsibility (currently 12), this procedure has no minimum age limit.

THE PROBLEM

In the light of the institutionalization of these alternative normative modes of reacting to acts of delinquency or deviance committed by minors, it might be assumed that there was a clear policy on the part of the bodies responsible for creating and defining these alternatives, as to their respective purposes, and as to the optimal functioning of the system as a whole. However, it appears that these bodies, rather than enlightening the public (or the consumers) as to the *raison d'etre* behind these alternatives and clarifying the manner in which they should be utilised, seem to have added to the general confusion in this matter.

For example: The Israeli legislature, as noted, provided three main alternatives for dealing with delinquent youth – termed here the Modified Adult Model (minor deserving conviction and punishment), the Juvenile Delinquency Model (minor perceived as offender but not deserving punishment), and the Care and Protection Model (minor perceived as 'needy'). This suggests that minors will be processed under the one or the other model according to their or society's needs. Yet an analysis of the relevant statutory provisions indicates that juveniles processed under *any* of the models may today be committed to a secure home.[8] Can these widely differing philosophies really be accommodated in adjacent beds in the same institution?[9] Or has there been a failure to think through the significance of the different models and their application?

The Israeli courts appear to be equally confused. In a recent case (see *A. & B. v. State of Israel*[10]) involving a serious offence – the defendants violently robbed a blind old man about to draw his pension – the District Court (which sat as a juvenile court) declared that in the light of the gravity of the circumstances the defendants should be convicted and should be sentenced to imprisonment (i.e., Model 2, not Model 3). The court nevertheless decided to take into consideration the youthfulness of the defendants and ordered that the terms of imprisonment be served in a secure home. However, while the law provides that the court may sentence to a secure home *in lieu of* imprisonment, it is not empowered to order *a prison term to be served in a secure home*.

The District Court decision was consequently overturned by the Supreme Court. This court also took the view that the defendants should be convicted and sentenced; but it, too, endeavoured to combine this with a welfarist approach to the actual dispositions. In the case of one defendant, the prison sentence was suspended so that he could perform his military service – which in the Israeli cultural context has a rehabilitative connotation. With regard to the other defendant, the court noted that he was currently living in a non-secure (or open) home and that it would be a pity to move him. However the court had not power to order residence in such a home following conviction (although it could have done so had it adopted Model 3). It therefore ordered the defendant to be sent to a secure home, but stipulated that the implementation of this order be suspended to give time to the Superintendent of Homes to consider the exercise of his power to transfer the youth from a secure to an open home. This power may be exercised under the law 'where the circumstances justify such transfer' and 'on condition that the minor has been held in a secure home for a reasonable period'.[11] Yet it was clearly the court's intention that the defendant in question should spend no time whatsoever in a secure home, but rather should remain in the open home in which he was already residing – thereby evading the legislative restrictions laid down in Model 2.

It is apparent that in the above example both the District Court and the Supreme Court manifested a high degree of ambivalence regarding the selection of the appropriate model; and in spite of the flexibility of the statutory provisions referred to above, both courts found it necessary to strain the meaning of these provisions in order to achieve the particular combination which reflected their ambivalence, viz., a punitive verdict characteristic of Model 2, combined with a treatment disposition characteristic of Model 3.

It would be reasonable to expect that internationally agreed standards purporting to apply to juvenile justice policy would resolve the uncertainties and ambiguities prevailing in national systems, either by expressing a clear-cut preference for a particular model, or by presenting alternative models – but with clear indications as to the circumstances in which each model should be applied. A perusal of the recently adopted standards in this area, however, only adds to the confusion.

Rule 5 of the Standard Minimum Rules for the Administration of Juvenile Justice (the 'Beijing Rules'), adopted by the General Assembly of the United Nations in 1985, states as follows:

> The juvenile justice system shall emphasize the well-being of the juvenile and shall ensure that any reaction to juvenile offenders shall always be in proportion to the circumstances of both the offenders and the offence.

There are three operative components to this standard. Dispositions of the juvenile court must (1) emphasize the well-being of the offender; (2) be proportional to the circumstances to the offender; and (3) be proportional to the circumstances of the offence. The first two components reflect concern for the individual offender and are clearly welfarist in orientation (even though the idea of 'proportionality to the circumstances of the offender' is somewhat obtuse – and the accompanying commentary does not altogether dispel this obtuseness[12]). The third component, on the other hand, indicates a clear preference for the justice model, under which the disposition would be 'proportion(al) to the circumstances of the offence', which presumably means severity, and seems *ipso facto* to override considerations related to the offender.

Similar contradictions appear in Article 40(4) of the UN Convention on the Rights of the Child (adopted by the General Assembly in 1989),[13] which, unlike the standards, is legally binding on the signatory parties. Thus international standards clearly fail to express any clear preference regarding the optimal orientation of the juvenile justice system – at least insofar as dispositions are concerned.[14]

The view is sometimes expressed that there is no need to adopt a specific orientation towards the juvenile justice system, in that the optimal orientation is in fact a compromise between the two main models, adopting some such slogan as 'justice with a human face', or 'welfare tempered with justice'. On a charitable view, this may have been the intention of the framers of the international documents referred to above.

This approach, however, fails to provide solutions to specific quandaries which arise from time to time. Two such quandaries – one specific, the other more general – may be cited from recent Israeli experience. The present law provides that a youth who has been committed to a home (i.e., an open home) for a determinate period may be brought back to court and have this period extended for up to one year 'if it appears to the court that this is required for the minor's benefit' and 'in order to complete his/her treatment or to train him/her for a profession'.[15] Legislation has been drafted which would apply this principle to secure homes too. These provisions reflect a strongly welfarist ideology, placing unequivocal priority on treatment considerations rather than principles of due process and proportionality. On the other hand, were the latter principles to prevail, no such provisions would appear in the statute book. It is hard to see how the conflicting ideologies could be reconciled in this matter, or indeed how any compromise could be adopted.

The more general quandary relates to the minimum age of criminal responsibility. After heated debate, this was raised a few years ago from nine to thirteen (and subsequently reduced again to twelve). While many issues were involved in this debate (see Hassin 1981, Sebba 1981), the basic question concerned the appropriateness of Models 2 and 3 as a response to delinquent acts committed by this age group, as opposed to Model 5. In other words, should a purely welfarist model be adopted, or some form of modified justice model?

It appears that the recurring need to resolve such issues requires that continuing attention be given to the welfare-justice debate. The remainder of this paper will be directed at developing a framework whereby this debate may be effectively advanced.

THE RELEVANT VARIABLES AND THEIR CLASSIFICATION

One of the obstacles to constructive discourse in the context of the justice-welfare debate – and hence also to policy formulation with regard to juvenile justice – is that the parties to this debate may be concerned with different issues. One party may be concerned with the issue of stigmatization of the child and be advocating the model which seems likely to minimize such stigmatization, while another may be focussing on constitutional issues. It is rare for writers in this field to consider more than a very small number of issues, although these may be analyzed in great depth. Moreover, there appears to have been little attempt in the literature hitherto to identify all those factors which may have some bearing upon the debate.[16] The remainder of this paper constitutes an attempt to develop a comprehensive list of such factors – i.e., to specify all those variables [17] which seem to be relevant to the justice-welfare debate (in the context of minors). These variables could serve as criteria for evaluating prevailing juvenile justice systems,[18] and for determining the optimal juvenile justice system for a particular country or jurisdiction. (The need to differentiate by country will become evident in the course of the analysis.)

The variables identified as being relevant to juvenile justice policy are listed in Table 2. As evident from this Table, thirteen such variables have been identified. These have been classified according to the domain to which they belong. Thus variables are characterized as being (1) Philosophical, (2) Criminological/Penological, (3) Psychological, or (4) Normative/Institutional.

Table 2. Juvenile justice variables

I   *Philosophical*
    a.   Ideologies of Rights
    b.   Ideologies of Children's Rights
    c.   Image of Child in National and International Documents
II   *Criminological/Penological*
    d.   Delinquency Reduction
    e.   Image of Child in Delinquency Theory
    f.   "Net-Widening"
    g.   Adult Penal Philosophy
III   *Psychological*
    h.   Perceived Social Stigma
    i.   Perceived Justice
    j.   Psychological Development
IV   *Normative/Institutional*
    k.   National Constitution
    l.   International Documents
    m.   Appropriateness of Relevant Agencies

Philosophical Variables

The first philosophical variable relates to *rights ideologies*. This involves the application of rights analyses which are current in the literature of jurisprudence and social and moral philosophy to the field of juvenile justice. Thus, for example, considerable attention in modern times has been devoted to Rawls' theory of justice. Consideration should therefore also be given to the implications for juvenile justice of Rawls' principle that: 'Each person has a right to the most extensive total system of equal basic liberties compatible with a similar system of liberty for all' (Rawls 1971, p. 302).

To posit that the rights of minors in the justice system should be examined from the perspective of general principles of rights is not necessarily to argue that juveniles are to be equated with adults, but rather that the same philosophical framework should be adopted *ab initio* – precisely in order to determine whether and to what extent the principles applying to juvenile justice should indeed differ from those applying to adults. This approach is rare. (See, however, Freeman 1983, and Adler 1985.) Most discussions of children's rights in general, and of juvenile justice in particular, focus exclusively upon child-related issues, rather than first considering general principles applicable to the matter at hand.

The second philosophical variable, *ideologies of children's rights*, may be considered as the complement to the above approach. Unlike the previous variable, which was concerned with rights applying to minors which were derived from general rights, the present category relates to rights' analyses emerging from the literature dealing specifically with the status of children – although not necessarily with juvenile *justice*. Here again, it is surprising how much of the literature concerned with juvenile justice is narrowly inward-looking, taking a stand within the 'justice versus welfare' debate, while ignoring the relevance of the wider debates relating to the status of minors, such as those emerging from such latter-day 'classics' of this genre such as Aries (1962), with his account of the 'invention' of childhood, Farson (1978), with his 'liberationist' approach, or Goldstein, Freud, and Solnit (1979), with their family autonomy approach.

Thus, for example, while the juvenile justice debate, as noted, is usually (in essence) dichotomous, focussing on justice and welfare, the wider debate generally posits at least three main approaches – state paternalism, family rights, and children's rights (or liberation).[19] Clearly, the traditional justice-welfare dichotomy does not reflect the more complex analysis which almost inevitably follows from the adoption of a wider perspective.

The third and final variable which has been categorised here as 'philosophical' relates to the *image of the child in national and international documents*. This variable is analytically similar to the preceding one, in that it, too, endeavours to link juvenile justice to prevailing concepts of children's rights. It differs mainly in its source of inspiration: rather than looking to the general literature (philosophical, psychological, juridical) on the status of children, reference is made here to official national and international documents – and in particular to normative standards – dealing with the same subject matter. The intention here is not to refer to standards dealing specifically with juvenile justice; these are dealt with below under the 'normative/institutional' heading. The focus here is rather on the norms and standards relating to the status of juveniles in other areas, e.g. schooling, adoption, etc., which must be examined in order to determine the image of the child (or minor) which emerges from these norms – insofar as any coherent and consistent image does in fact emerge.

The purpose of the second and third variables presented here is essentially the same. Logic (as well as practical considerations) dictates that there should be some consistency as to the legal standing of children in the different areas for which norms are being established. It would seem illogical if minors were to have equal status with adults in the area of criminal justice, but would be totally subservient to their parents (or to the state) in some other area, e.g., with regard to their education. Hence in determining the policy which is to be adopted in the context of juvenile justice, regard should be had to prevailing concepts relating to children's rights in other spheres, as they emerge both from the general literature in this area and from standards laid down in official national and international documents.

Penological/Criminological Variables

The first variable to be dealt with under this heading is *delinquency reduction*. If any utilitarian function is to be attributed to the juvenile justice system, this will almost certainly involve delinquency reduction as at least one of its objectives – whether the emphasis be placed on reducing the delinquency of the minor in question, or on deterring others. All (the main) utilitarian objectives – deterring, rehabilitating or incapacitating the offender, or deterring others – are subsumed here. In modern times rehabilitation has of course been the dominant objective of juvenile justice, at least until recently. Penological research, however, has cast serious doubt upon the ability of the penal system (including its welfare component) to achieve this objective.[20] Indeed, doubts have been cast regarding the feasibility of the other utilitarian objectives too.[21] These doubts have, of course, been central to the justice-welfare debate. Nevertheless, only a diehard anti-utilitarian (surely a rare bird among policy-makers?) would hold this variable to be irrelevant.

The next variable – the *image of the child in delinquency theory* – is also related to delinquency prevention but has a more theoretical orientation. Underlying any theory of delinquency there is (at least implicitly) a particular perception of the delinquent child: he/she may be viewed as suffering from a pathological condition, as having been deprived of appropriate parental affection or controls, as having been exposed to negative learning processes or to negative labelling, as having been deprived of appropriate educational or economic opportunities or as being a product of a delinquent sub-culture. The particular perspective adopted has (or should have) implications for the type of correctional policy which will be deemed appropriate (see, e.g., Cressey 1964), which in turn should affect the nature and orientation of the juvenile justice process.

It may be noted, however, that while the interrelationship between delinquency theory and penal policy may seem self-evident, it seems often to be ignored. Thus, most of the modern literature dealing with the aetiology of delinquency tends to be sociological in orientation, and stresses structural and cultural factors; judicial processes and correctional responses, on the other hand, are oriented rather towards individual and pathological factors. (A similar dichomotonization seems to be have taken place in the drafting of the Beijing Rules. The background discussion laid emphasis on social and economic opportunities and cultural factors, while the formulation of the rules themselves appear to emphasize personal circumstances).[22]

A related variable which has to be considered is the issue of *'net-widening'*. The growing literature on the sociology of prisons (e.g., Clemmer 1940, and Sykes 1958) tending to support the perception of prisons as 'schools of crime', coupled with the problem of prison overcrowding, have resulted in a constant search by both academics and policy-makers for 'alternatives to prison'. It has been argued, however, that these 'alternatives' are in practice used primarily for offenders who would otherwise have been released or have received a nominal sanction, and that their availability tends to increase the numbers of minors (or adults) 'caught in the net' of the state social control system (Cohen 1979). This controversy may have implications for delinquency reduction, but it also raises ideological issues related to the dimensions of state intervention and the liberty of the individual.[23]

The last variable under this heading is of a rather different type. It is suggested here that at least one of the starting points in a discussion of juvenile justice should be *adult penal philosophy* (or adult justice). All things being equal, prevailing justice principles should apply to minors also. Insofar as all things – or persons – are not equal (in the instant case – adults and minors), any ensuing departures from adult penal philosophy should correspond in some meaningful way to those differences between adults and minors which have been shown to be relevant to the matter in hand. Thus, for example, if rehabilitation has been rejected in the adult system because of lack of efficacy, it would not be justifiable to adopt this objective for juveniles unless there were grounds to believe that juvenile rehabilitation programmes were more efficacious than adult programmes.

This variable may be regarded as a corollary of variable A, which posits that general (or adult) rights should be the point of departure in analyzing juvenile rights.

Psychological Variables

There are at least three psychological variables which appear to be relevant to juvenile justice policy. These variables are concerned with perceptional and developmental issues related to minors.

The first psychological variable relates to *perceived social stigma*. The avoidance of stigma has played a central role in modern juvenile justice theory, and has led to reforms such as the adoption of diversion programmes. (A more legalistic outcome has been the adoption of rules for the expungement of juvenile court records.) This orientation derives from labelling theory, which posits that to label a juvenile a delinquent has implications regarding the way he will be treated both by criminal justice personnel and by his social environment (family, school, peer group, etc.); this in turn will determine his self-image, and his own subsequent behaviour (Hagan 1987: 202–3). Hence the desirability of avoiding formal criminal processes and official labels.

This, however, is an argument the validity of which must be examined empirically.[24] Moreover the degree of stigmatisation of official delinquency proceedings must be compared with *the degree of stigmatization of the alternative procedures* adopted – in particular where other formal welfare procedures are employed, such as those which designate the minor as being 'in need of care and protection'.

It may of course emerge that a particular procedure may be more stigmatizing in the eyes of the minor's peer group (where, for example, a welfare label may be stigmatizing but a criminal record 'macho'), but less stigmatizing in the view of some relevant agency such as school or employer. There might even be different perceptions among the different agencies. It might then become necessary to sub-divide this variable in accordance with such findings, and to determine the relative importance of each agency in the creation of the minor's self-image.

On the other hand, the degree of perceived stigma might be considered a relevant variable in its own right, i.e., irrespective of its effect on the minor's self-image and subsequent conduct (which could then be subsumed under the 'delinquency reduction' variable). In particular, it might be considered desirable that the public (as well as the parties concerned) should perceive the nature of the official reaction as appropriate to the type of act committed. To adopt this approach is in effect to regard the nature and degree of stigma as related to the concept of justice.

This leads to the second psychological variable, *perceived justice*. It is obviously undesirable that a minor should be subjected to processes which are viewed as unjust, even if positive results ensue therefrom. This will apply both to the procedures themselves and to their outcomes. It is desirable that both the ultimate disposition of the case and the mechanism by which it was arrived at should be perceived to be fair. It might be assumed that this consideration would inevitably operate in favour of 'justice' or legal models, based on desert and equality. Yet research indicates at least some support among offenders for rehabilitationist orientations. There is a need for a close examination of the available literature (cf. Martin *et al.* 1981; Parker *et al.* 1981) and for further research on this topic.

Here, too, it will be necessary to sub-divide the variable and to distinguish between the justice needs of the delinquent (or suspected delinquent) minor him/herself, and those of two other relevant categories: (a) the victims, and (b) the general public (cf. Sebba 1989). While it is sometimes assumed that the public is supportive of a welfarist approach towards minors, and that victims are generally vengeful, these stereotypes have undoubtedly to be questioned. Since, however, the justice perceptions of these categories are likely to conflict either with each other or with those of the minors involved, it will almost certainly be necessary to determine priorities in this respect.[25] Further, in assessing the public's expectations from the justice system, it may also be necessary to differentiate between their expectations in relation to the delinquent and their expectations in relation to the victim. As noted above, one may also have to distinguish in this connection between process and outcome expectations.

The last of the psychological variables relates to the *psychological development* of children. Studies of cognitive and moral development in the traditions of Piaget and Kohlberg would seem to be relevant to various aspects of the justice-welfare debate, including the issues of criminal responsibility, responsiveness to formal procedures and the appropriateness of punitive sanctions as compared with treatments. While there is a growing literature applying psychological concepts, including developmental concepts, to the legal system, research of this nature applied specifically to juvenile justice is sparse (cf. Peterson 1988).

Normative/Institutional Variables

It is evident that in determining juvenile justice policy certain normative and institutional constraints must be taken into account, and these constitute the last category in the present analysis.

One such variable is the *constitution* of the country in question. In most legal systems (Britain and Israel are notable exceptions), the validity of legal norms and institutions are determined by their compliance with formally prescribed constitutional principles. The best-known example of the relevance of this variable (in the present context) is of course the *Gault* case,[26] in which juvenile justice practices then prevailing in the United States were held to be unconstitutional, since the principles of due process were not adhered to.

Increasingly, however, national policy must take account not only of the fundamental principles laid down in the laws of the particular country, but also the standards laid down in *international documents*, and this constitutes the second variable dealt with in the present category.

The scope and importance of such standards are constantly growing, not least in the area of juvenile justice. As noted above, the so-called 'Beijing Rules' laid down minimum standards for the administration of juvenile justice (United Nations 1986). Specific 'Rules for the Protection of Juveniles Deprived of Liberty' have recently been approved by the UN General Assembly (United Nations 1990: 49). Reference has already been made to the Convention on the Rights of the Child – discussed in greater detail elsewhere in this Volume. Juvenile justice is only one of many topics dealt with in the Convention. On the other hand, unlike the other documents referred to here, the Convention is *binding* on the states which have ratified it. (As noted above, however, its terminology – at least in the area under consideration here – tends to be somewhat vague.) Finally, in addition to these documents which are intended to be of universal application, supra-national *regional* standards are also being developed, notably by the Council of Europe.[27]

The last variable in our list to be considered here has been designated *'appropriateness of relevant agencies'*. This is primarily a practical consideration which takes into account the identity and role of any agencies which would be involved in the implementation of any particular policy. Thus, a move towards legalism will tend to enhance the role of lawyers in the system (whether as prosecutors, defence counsel or judges), and the orientation and skills of these personnel become a relevant factor in determining the policy.

Another example may be found in the context of the Israeli debate on the age of criminal responsibility. One result of raising the age from nine to thirteen was that delinquent children in this age category were excluded from the jurisdiction of the probation officer (as well as of the police), but could be treated by welfare officers as 'children in need'. One of the objections raised (but not heeded) was that welfare officers, unlike probation officers, were non-specialized social workers employed by the local authority lacking the skills needed to deal with the population in question. On the other hand, the objective originally posited by the proponent of the reform in question was to leave the schools to deal with the problem. However, the powers that be considered the skills and resources of the educational personnel to be inadequate for this purpose, and responsibility was effectively placed with the welfare officers.

The relevance of this variable may, however, be considered somewhat problematical. It might be argued that institutional arrangements should follow policy decisions rather than determine them, and that to consider the functioning – or even the views – of existing agencies in the formulation of policy will result in the domination of bureaucratic considerations. (Thus, for example, some observers feel that the survival of parole *supervision* in some US jurisdictions in which parole *release* has been abolished is the product of this type of approach.) On the other hand, policy must presumably operate within the limits of certain cultural and professional traditions, and a policy adopted without any consideration of these traditions might prove to be ineffective.

It may be observed that this last variable may have a strong political component. It might, indeed, have been appropriate to have added 'political constraints' to the list of variables to be considered in the formulation of juvenile justice policy. However, since many of the preceding variables, whether ideological or pragmatic, may also have political overtones, it was decided not to attribute independent status to this variable.

SOME OUTSTANDING PROBLEMS

Even if there were agreement as to the above list of variables, both in terms of the exhaustiveness of this list and in terms of the relevance of all its components, its practical application to individual juvenile justice systems would still be fraught with many difficulties. Areas in which problems may be anticipated include the following:
1. operationalization of the variables;
2. consistency of policy implications;
3. homogeneity of the components of the system; and
4. homogeneity of national cultures.
Each of these issues will be discussed briefly.

1. *Operationalization of the Variables.* The current essay purported only to *identify* the variables which juvenile justice policy should take into account, without specifying the precise policy implications of taking any particular variable into consideration. Would taking into account the possibility of stigmatization of the minor, or having regard to prevailing children's rights ideologies, lead to an emphasis on welfarism or on legalism? To assess the implications of almost any one of these variables would constitute a major research task; in many cases existing data may be inadequate for this purpose. Such research, however, is a necessary prerequisite for the development of operational criteria.

2. *Consistency of Policy Implications.* Under the scheme described above, the examination of each variable will lead to a preference either for a more legalistic or for a more welfaristic orientation in the juvenile justice system. For example, if it should emerge that children aged fourteen have a moral development akin to that of an adult, this would be an argument for favouring the application of a legalistic or 'justice' approach (rather than a welfarist approach) to this age group. What, however, if the examination of some of the variables were to indicate a legalist solution, while the examination of others were to indicate a welfarist solution – an outcome which surely has a high probability given the number of variables incorporated in the model?

There is clearly no simple solution to this dilemma. This, indeed, may be one of the reasons why the welfarism-legalism controversy remains unresolved; it may be that the parties to the controversy do not differ greatly in their views on *individual* issues but rather emphasize *different* issues.

A simple numerical count of the variables favouring welfarism versus those favouring legalism would clearly provide too simplistic and mechanistic a solution. The usual approach when views are expressed on the juvenile justice system is probably to make implicit value-judgments as to the variables which the particular analyst regards as deserving priority. One method of rendering these judgments both more explicit and more scientific would be to devise some sort of weighting system, whereby each variable would be allocated a weight in accordance with its perceived importance. Further, if welfarism-legalism can be regarded as a continuum which could be quantified,[28] the analysis of each variable would produce a score on this continuum, which would reflect the extent to which support was indicated for legalism or welfarism. A mean score could then be calculated for all variables, taking into account the respective weights which had been assigned to each.[29]

3. *Homogenity of the Components of the System.* The juvenile justice system can be dichomotized into its procedural and its substantive aspects, and can be further sub-divided into various stages: pre-trial procedures, pre-trial dispositions, trial procedures, trial dispositions, treatment and punishment regimes, release procedures, after-care. Should the multi-faceted analysis posited here be applied to each of these stages separately, or to the system as a whole?[30]

In principle it seems that at least some of the above differentiations should be made during the course of the analysis, since different conclusions might be drawn with regard to the optimal amount of welfarism or legalism desirable according to the stage of the juvenile justice system to which the analysis was being applied. For example, an examination of the moral development issue may lead to the conclusion that a minor of a particular age can respond positively to a sophisticated legal procedure, but not to a punishment regime. A related issue currently being researched concerns American 'waiver' procedures, whereby minors may be tried as adults; should this necessarily imply a punitive *disposition* by the adult court?

It is sometimes suggested that there may be a 'trade-off' in these matters, whereby a harsher policy is applied at one stage of the system, a milder one at another stage. This term of course implies that the apparently inconsistent policy derives from political considerations – some kind of deal or bargain – rather than from a careful examination of the merits of the relevant issues as suggested in this paper.

4. *Homogeneity – or Diversity – of Different National Cultures.* The orientation of this paper has been towards the development of national policies on juvenile justice; the prevailing international standards were viewed in this context as one of the relevant (independent) variables to be taken into account. The model would have to be modified if this variable were to become the *dependent* variable, i.e., if the objective were to develop an international or universal policy, as has been attempted in some of the documents referred to above.

In some respects a model focussing on universal policies would be simpler than the one presented here, in that purely local considerations, such as constitutional limitations (variable K), would be omitted. Nor would it be necessary to reconcile juvenile justice principles with other ideologies in related fields (variable G) prevailing in local systems, or to take into account local practicalities (variable M). On the other hand, the empirical issues – such as the effect of particular policies on delinquency reduction and the psychological variables – might prove impossible to resolve, in view of the likelihood of extreme diversity among different cultures. (Indeed, even within multi-cultural societies these issues are likely to prove problematical.) It is perhaps this possibility – or even probability – that different conclusions will be reached in different cultures which accounts for the high level of ambiguity expressed in the formulations appearing in the international documents on the welfare-justice issue cited above.

CONCLUDING COMMENT

In the light of the above an agenda for juvenile justice research may now be tentatively proffered. The first step would be to review the analytical framework presented in this paper, and modify it if deemed necessary. Research could than be conducted on specific juvenile justice systems from this perspective, i.e., incorporating philosophical, criminological/penological, psychological and normative/institutional variables. Such research should provide indication as to the optimal direction these systems should take.

Hopefully, some of the dilemmas raised in the latter part of the paper would also then be clarified: it would become evident to what extent there were problems involved in researching the variables in order to adduce their policy implications, how far there was a pattern of inconsistency among the variables in relation to their policy implications, and to what extent there was a lack of homogeneity among the different parts of individual juvenile justice systems, and a diversity among different cultures. This, in turn, would indicate the feasibility of developing comprehensive national policies on juvenile justice which were both empirically valid and conceptually sound – and the potential for the formulation of meaningful international norms in this area.

NOTES

1. In *Re Gault*, 387 US 1, 18 L Ed. 2d 527 (1967).
2. For a review of recent trends in the United States, see Feld (1988).
3. In this paper the terms (a) 'justice' versus 'welfare' or (b) 'legalism' versus 'welfarism' are used interchangeably to refer to the dichotomy on which the discussion is focussed. In neither case is the terminology entirely satisfactory: as to (a), supporters of a welfare approach do not regard this approach as exclusive of justice; as to (b) welfarism today

generally operates within the framework of statutory provisions and is thus not lacking in 'legalism'.

4.   Melton (1989), however, believes (based on the psychological evidence) that a juvenile court should provide *more* procedural protections than an adult court.

5.   See *Youth (Trial, Punishment and Modes of Treatment) Law* (1971), sec. 45A.

6.   See, e.g., *Order Regarding the Trial of Young Offenders (West Bank Area)*, no. 132 (1967).

7.   *Youth (Care and Supervision) Law* (1960), sec. 2.

8.   The possibility of having a 'needy' child committed to a secure home was introduced in 1977 as part of the legislative package whereby the minimum age of criminal responsibility was raised from nine to thirteen. It was apparently intended to ensure that the welfare provisions (Model 3), which would now be the sole option available to deal with delinquents in this age group, would have enough 'teeth' to handle tough cases. The package may thus be seen to be an illustration of the concept of 'trade-off' referred to elsewhere in the paper.

9.   I am grateful to Dr. Menachem Horowitz for the graphic aspects of this illustration.

10.   Criminal Appeal 403/88, *Piskei Din* 42(3), p. 570.

11.   *Youth (Trial, Punishment and Modes of Treatment) Law* (1971), sec. 31(a).

12.   See: United Nations (1986: 5).

13.   According to this article: 'A variety of dispositions, such as care, guidance and supervision orders; counselling; probation; foster care; education and vocational training programmes and other alternatives to institutional care shall be available to ensure that children are dealt with in a manner appropriate to their well-being and *proportionate both to their circumstances and the offence*'. (Emphasis added.)

14.   *Procedural* standards formulated in recent documents seem to be orientated fairly consistently towards a more legalistic approach, emphasizing, e.g., the minor's right to be heard and to be represented by a lawyer.

15.   *Youth (Trial, Punishment and Modes of Treatment) Law* (1971), sec. 33.

16.   Cf. the present writer's preliminary attempt to identify the factors relevant to the issue of whether delinquent minors aged between nine and thirteen should be dealt with under delinquency or care proceedings: see Sebba (1981).

17.   The factors deemed relevant to the determination of juvenile justice policy will be referred to in this paper as 'variables' since their content may vary over time, by culture – and even over different areas of the juvenile justice system. (See the concluding section to this paper.)

18.   To render these variables operational, however, would first require in depth research beyond the scope of the present paper, which is merely concerned with *identifying*, the variables. (See the concluding sections to this paper.)

19.   In both areas, there are, of course, variations among different writers. Thus, in the context of juvenile justice, Pratt (1989) has suggested a third approach, which in his view is replacing the justice and welfare models, namely, 'corporatism'; while another threefold classification was discussed in the course of the background discussion on the Beijing Rules (United Nations, 1984). With regard to children's rights in general, Landever (1979) proposes a fourth approach (i.e., in addition to state, family and children's rights), namely, 'due process advocates'; but this seems merely to indicate a technique for reform rather representing a substantive approach. Mention may also be made here to Freeman's modified or composite approach which he calls 'liberal paternalism'. (See Freeman, 1983.)

20.   See, e.g., Martinson (1974).

21.   See, e.g., Blumstein *et al.* (1978).

22.   See United Nations (1984).

23.   These issues belong primarily to the first group of variables discussed in this paper.

24.   See, in the context of the impact of juvenile justice procedures, Martin *et al.* (1981: 217).

25.   Cf. the discussion of 'Outstanding Problems' below.

26.   Cf. note (1) above.

27. See the paper of Verhellen in this volume.
28. This proposition is of course somewhat problematical. In some instances (two illustrations of which were referred to above) the choice between legalism and welfarism seems to be a straight dichotomy. More usually there is a continuum of possibilities, but these are finite and discrete, as illustrated by the description of Israel's juvenile justice system, with its five gradations on the legalism-welfarism axis.
29. Alternative solutions along these lines may doubtless be proposed. Blumstein (1991) observes that the problem of multi-criterion decision-making 'has received considerable attention in the literature of economics, operations, research, and management science . . .' He himself has suggested a model for the purposes of reconciliation of the conflicting aims of sentencing (in particular deterrence, incapacitation, and desert). Unlike the issues being considered here, however, the dependent variable is in the context of Blumstein's analysis primarily quantitative in character, i.e., the duration of the term of imprisonment deemed appropriate. (Blumstein appears to regard this as a *disadvantage*.) Nevertheless there is clearly a similarity in the subject matter.
30. In Blumstein's model (see preceding note), which focuses exclusively on the sentencing stage in adult criminal courts, the policy decision would vary in accordance with *type of offence*.

REFERENCES

Adler, R.M., *Taking Juvenile Justice Seriously*, Edinburgh: Scottish Academic Press (1985).
Aries, P., *Centuries of Childhood*, London: Jonathan Cape (1962).
Blumstein, A., 'Making Sentencing Policy More Rational and More Effective', *Israel Law Review* 25 (1991).
Blumstein, A., Cohen, J. and Nagin, D. *Deterrence and Incapacitation: Estimating the Effects of Criminal Sanctions on Crime Rates*, Washington: National Academy of Sciences (1978).
Clemmer, D., *The Prison Community*, New York: Holt, Rinehart and Winston (1940).
Cohen, S., 'The Punitive City: Notes on the Disposal of Social Control', *Contemporary Crises* 3 (1979), 339.
Cressey, D.R., *Delinquency, Crime and Differential Association*, Martinus Nijhoff (1964).
Dahl, T.S., 'The Scandinavian System of Juvenile Justice: A Comparative Approach', in M. Rosenheim (ed.), *Pursuing Justice for the Child*, Chicago: University of Chicago Press (1976).
Farson, R., *Birthrights*, Harmondsworth: Penguin (1978).
Feld, B.C., 'The Juvenile Court Meets the Principle of Offense: Punishment, Treatment and the Difference it Makes', *Boston University Law Review* 68 (1988), 821.
Freeman, M.D.A., *The Rights and Wrongs of Children*, London: Frances Pinter (1983).
Goldstein, J., Freud, A., and Solnit, A., *Beyond the Best Interests of the Child*, New York: Free Press (1979).
Hagan, J., *Modern Criminology*, New York: McGraw-Hill (1987).
Hassin, Y., 'Raising the Age of Criminal Responsibility in Israel', *Israel Law Review* 16 (1981), 225.
Kittrie, N. N., *The Right to Be Different*, Baltimore: Johns Hopkins (1971).
Landever, A., 'The Rights of Children in America: the Different Perceptions', *Poly Law Review* 5 (1) (1979), 19.
Martin, F. M., Fox, S. J., Murray, K., *Children Out of Court*, Edinburgh: Scottish Academic Press (1981).
Martinson, R., 'What Works? – Questions and Answers About Prison Reform', *Public Interest* 35 (1974), 22.
Melton, G.B., 'Taking *Gault* Seriously: Towards a New Juvenile Court', *Nebraska Law Review* 68 (1989), 146.

Parker, H., Casburn, M. and Turbull, D., *Receiving Juvenile Justice*, Oxford: Basil Blackwell (1981).

Peterson, M., 'Children's Understanding of the Juvenile Justice System: A Cognitive-Developmental Persepctive', *Canadian Journal of Criminology* 30 (1988), 381.

Pratt, J., 'Corporatism: The Third Model of Juvenile Justice', *British Journal of Criminology* 29 (3) (1989), 236.

Rawls, J., *A Theory of Justice*, Oxford: Clarendon Press (1971).

Sebba, L., 'Legalism versus Welfarism in Israel's Juvenile Justice System', *Israel Law Review* 16 (1981), 461.

Sebba, L., 'Victims and the Parameters of a Justice System', in Separovic, Z. P., *Victimology: International Action and Study of Victims*, Zagreb: University of Zagreb (1989), p. 13.

Sykes, G., *The Society of Captives*, Princeton: Princeton University Press (1958).

United Nations, *Report of the Interregional Preparatory Meeting for the Seventh United Nations Congress on the Prevention of Crime and the Treatment of Offenders on Topic IV: 'Youth, Crime and Justice'*, United Nations General Assembly (1984).

United Nations, *Standard Minimum Rules for the Administration of Juvenile Justice*, New York: United Nations Department of Public Information (1986).

United Nations, *Report of the Eighth United Nations Congress on the Prevention of Crime and the Treatment of Offenders* (1990).

MIEK DE LANGEN*

19. The Meaning of Human Rights for Children

INTRODUCTION

By the end of the 19th century, as in most other European countries, so also in the Netherlands public authorities and private organisations became very much concerned about neglected, mistreated and exploited children. After a period in which children were considered the property of their fathers or parents, who could do with them what they wanted, laws were introduced to protect children against neglect or mistreatment by their parents and also against heavy child labour and the withholding of children from education. Care for children became a public concern and the state felt responsible for these children and could, as *parens patriae*, interfere in certain families to protect the interest of the child, deprive parents of their parental custody and take their children away. This state interference in the family and in many social policy areas has grown immensely during this century.

It was assumed that the state could judge what should happen in the interest of the child. This led to a lot of rules and provisions in social policy areas and to a judicial system in which, on the one hand, judges and other responsible authorities were given a very comprehensive competence to decide and, on the other hand, the child concerned had nothing to say about this interference as it was considered to be actually in the interest of the child. Even today judges – in this case juvenile court magistrates – are supposed to know what is in the best interest of the child and have, on the basis of this assumption, a far-reaching competence to act and interfere in family life. In modern terms this means that, with this state interference, the rights of parents are violated. This violation is only justifiable when the state has done everything to make it possible for these parents to care for their children. The Preamble of the Convention on the Rights of the Child accepted by the United Nations on November 20, 1989 also refers to this first obligation of the state, stating: . . . 'that the family, as the fundamental group of society and the natural environment for the growth and well-being of all its members and particu-

---

* Faculty of Law, University of Amsterdam, The Netherlands.

M. Freeman and P. Veerman (eds.), The Ideologies of Children's Rights, 255–264.
© 1992 *Kluwer Academic Publishers. Printed in the Netherlands.*

larly children, should be afforded the necessary protection and assistance so that it can fully assume its responsibilities within the community'. It is only when parents are still unable or unwilling to take care of their children and keep mistreating or neglecting them that the state is allowed and required to protect the rights of the children against their parents. But even then the question remains when and who can say that the protection of children's rights requires this interference and that these rights will be more protected after this.

Bearing in mind that interference in family life can also be a violation of the child's right to respect for his private and family life, it is hard to weigh this violation of rights against the assumed protection, as long as we are not taking any account of what children themselves think and wish. It is quite possible that the interpretation of the interests of children by the state is entirely different from the child's point of view. But still many adults – including judges – think and say that children, because of their limited level of development, knowledge and experience, cannot judge what is in their interests or what will be the consequences of their thoughts and behaviour. The fact that children are not yet grown up has been and is used as an excuse by parents, social workers, teachers, judges and many other adults to follow their own inter- pretation of the child's interests and to set demands and make decisions that may have far-reaching consequences for children which no one can foresee. This seems to be a question of rationalization on the part of the adults, who pretend it is their duty to protect the vulnerable child. The assumption, on the grounds of age, sex, race or whatever characteristic, that certain people are irrational and unable to fend for themselves, is itself usually based on highly irrational arguments. Recognition of the individual identity of the child with her or his ideas, desires and dreams of the future, proves fundamentally un- acceptable again and again. For most adults it also appears to be impossible to communicate with children on an equal basis, as if they are afraid of them.

In the '70s, discussion started about granting certain rights to children of a certain age and about involving children in a procedure concerning their interests and a lot of proposals were made. At that time most people still considered children as a special category and did not think of the meaning of human rights for children and the application of these fundamental rights to children.

HUMAN RIGHTS

But, in the meantime, an emphasis began to be placed increasingly on equal rights for all people, whites and blacks, women and men, children and adults. All international agreements and conventions have included either the equality principle, or a non-discrimination article. These generally valid human rights must in principle apply always and for all, and their scope may only be limited for functional reasons. The other party, usually governmental authorities, will have to demonstrate why these generally recognized human rights do not apply to children or psychiatric patients or convicts – groups often mentioned together – during a certain period or under certain circumstances. The most important reason to demand that these rights apply to children as well, is also the most simple reason: namely the self-evident fact that children are human beings.

After the Convention on Human Rights and Fundamental Freedoms and the international convenants between the United Nations of 1966, which entered into force in 1976, the so-called European Convention signed at Rome in 1950, which entered into force in 1953, it is no longer a question in the legal sense of the word whether the rights and fundamental freedoms mentioned there also apply to children. In addition to these generally recognized human rights, children require special attention or, as stated in the Universal Declaration of Human Rights: 'Special care and assistance', on the grounds of their specific needs. That is, the right to care, to nurture, to protection, to education and to games and recreation. Granting children general human rights does not mean that special or preferential rights no longer apply to them. Nor does the fact that children have special rights mean that the generally recognized human rights should not apply to them. It can be considered as a missed chance that, in the Preamble of the Convention on the Rights of the Child, this has not been included and recognized.

Both in European law and in the law of separate European countries, children are recognized as having equal capacity of rights and their rights are equally weighed against the rights of others. But it remains a question whether, and to what degree, a child can independently appeal to these material rights, such as the right to respect for his private or family life or the right to freedom of thought, conscience and religion or the right to freedom of speech. Even though children are recognized as having the capacity of rights, in general they are not regarded as competent to assert their rights. It is, however, possible for them, in cases of violation by the authorities of the rights mentioned in the Convention, to file a complaint against these authorities with the European Commission for Human Rights.

Although age is not specifically mentioned as such as a prohibited ground for differential treatment, it could be included in the concept of 'other status' referred to in Article 14 of the Convention: the non-discrimination article. Anyway this has not been argued in any of the applications examined by either the European Commission or the Court.[1] It is clear that this is not an obvious step for children. But it appears from a few dozen cases where complaints by or on behalf of children from various European countries have been filed and treated seriously, it does occur.

The conclusion of Buquicchio-de Boer is:

That in spite of the absence of an express provision enshrining children's rights, the Convention is not ineffective as regards their protection. A common feature of the applications brought by children in their capacity as purported victims in their claim for respect as individuals worthy of respect. . . . In order to give any practical significance to the task of the Convention organs in this area, even if it is a subsidiary one, it is essential that the point of view of all those concerned, including the children, should be reflected in the relevant domestic proceedings.

Donna Gomien is less optimistic about the evolution of children's rights in European jurisprudence in her article about State powers and the best interests of the child under Article 8 of the European Convention of Human Rights, which reads: 'Everyone has the right to respect for his private and family life, his home and his correspondence.' This right can also be found in the Convention on the Rights of the Child and has been formulated as follows: 'No child shall be subjected to arbitrary or unlawful interference with his or her privacy, family, home or correspondence, nor to unlawful attacks on his or her honour and reputation' (Article 16-1). In her analysis of the cases of state interference in the family,[2] she comes to the conclusion that

the Commission and Court continue to take a nineteenth century view of children as objects rather than subjects of the law, accepting without question that many disputes under Article 8 properly belong to parents and the State, but not to the child as a third and directly affected party.

Although claiming a high level of interest in and concern for children's rights to family life under Article 8, the European Commission and Court of Human Rights belie their claims by allowing States the freedom to exercise their *parens patriae* powers and police powers in increasingly arbitrary and potentially destructive ways.

. . . This endorsement of broad State powers under Article 8, compounded by the almost total acceptance of the State's view of a child's 'best interests', has created dim prospects for the European Convention's protection of children's rights to family life.[3]

The Child and the State

This statement by Donna Gomien is not on its own and we have to ask ourselves again and again what the position is of 'the child as a third and directly affected party' in relation to the State and to parents. We have to face the paradoxical question whether it is or must be possible for a child to take action against the State as the protector of his rights or as the *parens patriae*. This is of particular interest when the child is taken away from his home and placed with a foster family or in an institution where it does not feel at home and does not want to be. These placements can be viewed by the child as a violation of his rights to liberty, also one of the most fundamental human rights. When children complain about unlawful deprivation of their liberty with European judicial organs they are confronted with the specially formulated ground for detention of minors in Article 5-1d of the Convention: 'The detention of a minor by lawful order for the purpose of educational supervision or his lawful detention for the purpose of bringing him before the competent legal authority'.

This again means that the State can easily say that the deprivation of the liberty of a child is justified by the purpose of educational supervision, which fits in quite well in the *parens patriae* concept. It must be made very clear that this justification is not acceptable before a claim of a minor will be held as a violation of Article 5-1 of the Convention by the European Court, as was proved twelve years ago in the case of X *vs* Switzerland.[4]

In another and more recent case, however, where a minor, who had been placed nine times in a remand prison, had stated that the detention could not be viewed as a measure for the purpose of educational supervision, the European Court concluded: 'The fruitless series of nine placement orders, which did not further any educational aim, cannot be compatible with sub-paragraph d of Article 5-1'. Moreover, the Court in this case came to the conclusion: 'It has not been established that counsel for the applicant were either present during the hearings preceding placement at the remand prison or had access to all the documents in the file'.[5] And furthermore: 'The available remedies were also not compatible with the requirements of Article 5-4'. It was accepted that Articles 5-1 and 5-4 had been violated. Concerning the divergent rules, such as Article 5-1d and different treatments for juveniles, the European Court considered thought: 'that the protective nature of the procedure applied to juveniles provides an objective and reasonable justification for the difference of treatment'.

We can learn from this case that a child who has been given the opportunity to complain about his fundamental rights, as in this case the violation of his right of liberty had been alleged to be, has a chance with his complaint about the lawfulness of the deprivation of his liberty and also about the lawfulness of the followed procedure. So there is an opening for children to put their claims about unlawful detention before the European juridical organs. As shown in the above-mentioned survey of Buquicchio-de Boer, there is also the possibility for complaints of children about being subjected to torture or to inhuman or degrading treatment or punishment, mentioned in Article 3 and about other rights covered in this Convention and those claims have not all been unsuccessful.[6] Even more than in the case of other court decisions, the individual child may not really benefit, but the result is that certain problems of children are exposed, such as flogging in schools or detaining children, even in prisons, without proper legal procedures; in these cases the government concerned is called to answer before an international forum.

Using this possibility of highest appeal may have considerable consequences, since certain forms of abuse would be publicly exposed and no government appreciates the honour of being requested to answer for its actions in the dock, certainly not before the European Commission in Strasbourg, and least of all on the initiative of a child.

The Child and the Parents

When we look at the relation between parents and children we can see, on the one hand, that some parents today are much more concerned about their children then before and see them as individuals with their own needs, thoughts and rights. Emotional relations between parents and children have grown more intense and the emotional aspects of family relations have come to dominate the economic ones. On the other hand, we see that a large number of parents consider their children more and more as their property or as a consumption-good, like so many things in modern society.

As a result of a growing individualisation in Western democratic societies,[7] including the family, couples can decide to have children or not, and if this cannot be achieved by natural means there are other, different ways to get one: the medical ways of artificial insemination, *in vitro* – fertilisation or embryo transfer, and the judicial way of adoption. They can also order a child, let a surrogate mother bear it, and even refuse it if the product does not suit them.

The possibility of planning to have children or not and to get them through different artificial ways boils down to the fact that some people think that they have a right to have a child. This process of increasing individualisation is also demonstrated by a rising divorce rate and growing numbers of one-parent families, stepfamilies and all kinds of family forms, which can break down again. People can afford today to quarrel with their relatives and friends, and having children is no longer considered an obstacle to pursuing a life of one's own. This disappearance of family relations that were once taken for granted can lead to a lot of uncertainty and fear for the children and sometimes even to a feeling that is was their fault. However, it can under certain circumstances also give children a sense of freedom.

When a marriage breaks up, for which parents are responsible, rather than the children, and parents do not agree on joint custody or on who will have custody, both will claim it and a court has to decide. After the court has made the decision the parent who was not appointed as a guardian can start further proceedings if he can prove that circumstances have changed. With the possibilities of appeal to a higher court these procedures can take years; procedure about what and why? Is it really concern for the child, a feeling of responsibility, or is it purely a fight with the other parent, the ex-spouse, and a question of no loss of face?

It is evident that these procedures cause a lot of uncertainty and will do much harm to the child, who is the object and victim of the fight and is viewed as property. The question can be raised whether it is wise that these procedures about custody can go on for many years and can be started any moment once again. Most procedures within the family law of the last decade in the Netherlands – and as far as I know in most European countries – are about access to the child by parents after their divorce, by unmarried parents after their relationship has broken up, by grandparents, or by foster parents. All kinds of parents claim this access as part of their right to respect for their private and family life, based on their biological ties, their judicial relationship or their social parenthood. Instead of showing their concern or responsibility for this child they claim their right to keep in contact with this child. Respect for family life – one of the human rights – has been interpretated so widely, at least by the Dutch Supreme Court, that all kinds of family ties can be used, and all people who call themselves a parent in some way, since nobody can be excluded because of the principle of equality, can request access. This has been stretched so far that this human right, which was meant originally to be a protection for family life against unlawful interference by the State, has been emptied of its actual meaning.

It looks as if the individualistic assumptions on Western Family law combined with the concept of equality of rights have many problematic aspects. However, when parents are admitted to the procedure their request for access – or, for the European Commission, their application – can be rejected, because this request from one of the parents can at the same time be an infringement of the rights and even of the same right to respect for private and family life of other family members, namely the children or the other parent. So it can happen that all family members appeal to the same right, but – and this is very important – they all mean something quite different by this respect for their private and family life, because they have a different concept of family life. Children will ask for care, attention and continuity in their educational and living circumstances. In a thorough research which I have carried out on the jurisprudence of the Dutch Supreme Court decisions in the last decade[8] it appears that the rights of children to respect for their private and family life have had prevalence, which is as it ought to be; not only because children are the weakest party in divorce cases, but also because the meaning of their private and family life is most important.

ACCESS TO A COURT

In these cases, too, we see that only parents can request access to their child, although it is called a reciprocal right. But weighing their rights against the rights of children, their request can be rejected. Most legislators are very hesitant to give children the right of access to a court, although: 'In the determination of his civil rights and obligations or of any criminal charge against him, everyone is entitled to a fair and public hearing within a reasonable time by an independent and impartial tribunal established by law', as Article 6-1 of the European Convention says. Although children are given no access by the legislator, they do receive it in actual judicial practice, which is usually – slightly – better at adopting to social change than the legislature is. If the child's legal representatives, parents or guardians, who must usually initiate action on behalf of the child, are absent, or unable or unwilling to act for the child for any other reason, or if the child's conflict is with her or his legal representative, children are enabled to act independently in so-called summary proceedings in emergency cases, when no time can be lost. Thus, even children under 12 of foreign descent, who lived in the Netherlands without their parents, but with relatives, have taken this action against the State when they were in danger of being expelled.[9] And on very few occasions older children have taken action against their parents.[10] This was possible because bringing a conflict to an impartial court is a generally recognized human right, which should also apply to children.

An important case for the European Commission concerning the right of a minor girl to respect for her private life against parental custody and concerning the justification, the interference in her private life by public authorities, was the application of X and Y *vs* the Netherlands,[11] although it was dealt with fifteen years ago. The girl alleged:

> Discrimination on the grounds of age should not take place when weighing the interests of a minor against those of the parents. The rigidity of the law which only favours the restoration of the parents' right destroys the right of a minor to privacy or in any case is a restriction thereof. By using the legal competence, the police acted against the interests of the minor and thus there is a violation of this Article.

The Commission considered at that time:

> as a general proposition, and the absence of any special circumstances, the obligation of children to reside with their parents and to be otherwise subjected to a particular control is necessary for the protection of children's health and morals, although it might constitute from a particular child's point of view, an interference with his or her own private life

and furthermore:

> that any interference by reason of her being forced to return to her parents, as provided for in the relevant Netherlands legislation and as enforced by the authorities, was both an exercise of respect for the life of her family and also necessary for the protection of her health and morals within the meaning of Article 8(2) of the Convention.

Although the result of these considerations was for many people disappointing, what was important was that for the first time an application of a minor was treated seriously and that the child's point of view was at least mentioned.

VIOLATION OF CHILDREN'S RIGHTS

Furthermore, it remains an open question to what degree these judicially recognized rights are also recognized by any society at large. It is quite clear that the most basic rights of children are in fact still massively violated, in families and in schools, in jobs or on the street. Unfortunately, the examples are telling, universal and all too familiar: violation of physical integrity by physical abuse, incest or other forms of sexual violence, violation of personal privacy by forcing a child to certain thoughts or actions instead of leaving him or her alone, ignoring the right to family protection by intervening in family structures or not permitting families to be reunited, ignoring the right to freedom of speech by imposing censorship, refusal of necessary schooling by providing a limited or not generally accessible education system, trafficking of children and worse, negation of an individual's autonomy by claiming to know best what the child needs, and so on. One major question that arises is why these rights are still violated every day and everywhere, by parents, teachers, social workers and many other adults, including policy-makers; followed by the question how to end or at least restrict these violations.

Children's Law Centre

These developments, where on the one hand children's rights were recognized by the different courts and incompetence was waived in some cases and, on the other hand, these rights were actually violated daily in many ways led me to set up the first Children's Law Centre or Centre for Children's Legal Aid in Amsterdam.

This centre primarily seeks to give children information, advice and support in legal affairs. This can be done by:
- explaining the rules and how they are to be applied in each particular case; naturally children shall be told what is possible and what is not;
- writing a letter together with the child to a family member, a store or a firm in order to explain a case very clearly and tell them what the opinion of this child is;
- accompanying the child to all kinds of people, such as the police, a school, a children's home or a juvenile court magistrate, and helping to explain the case or to clear up a situation very explicitly;
- if necessary assuring the child that its case can be submitted before the court.
The starting point is the child's point of view. Nothing is to be done behind the child's back: this does not mean that what the child wants can always be done. Experience teaches us that, particularly in divorce cases, children in most cases know quite well what they want; this means where and with whom they want to stay and live, and whether they want to meet and keep in contact with the other parent.

It appears that even very young children, of four years of age and upwards, can make clear what they want, can give their view on the case and can articulate their rights very well. It is also impressive to see how children find solutions for their own problems and a way to get their rights realized.

NOTES

1. M.F. Buquicchio-de Boer, 'Children and the European Convention on Human Rights', in *Protecting Human Rights: The European Dimension, Studies in Honour of G. J. Wiarda*, Köln (1988), p. 73.

2. For instance: European Court 8-7-1987, BCHD and W vs United Kingdom. Publ. ECHR, Series A, Vol. 120/126; and judgement of 24-3-1988, Olsson vs Sweden, Publ. ECHR, Series A, vol. 130.

3. D. Gomien, 'State Powers and the Best Interests of the Child under Article Eight of the European Convention on Human Rights', *Netherlands Quarterly of Human Rights* 7 (1989), p. 450.

4. European Commission 14-12-1979, Application nr 8500/79, X vs Switzerland, D&R 18 (1980), p. 238.

5. European Court 29-2-1988, Bouamar vs Belgium, Publ. ECHR series A, Vol. 129.

6. See also an article in Dutch by M.L. van Emmerik, 'Klachten van Kinderen bij de Europese Commissie voor de Rechten van de Mens te Straatsburg', in: M. de Langen, J.H. de Graaf en F.B.M. Kunneman (eds.), *Kinderen en Recht* (1989), pp. 59–71.

7. D. Popenoe, *Disturbing the Nest*, New York (1988).

8. M. de Langen, 'De Betekenis van Artikel 8 EVRM voor het Familierecht', in: Artikel 8 EVRM, Preadviezen van J. de Boer, M. de Langen en A.H.J. Swart, *Handelingen Nederlandse Juristen Vereniging* 120e jrg. (1990) I.

9. J.M. Sassenburg, 'Proces(recht) voor Jeugdigen', in: M. de Langen, J.H. de Graaf en F.B.M. Kunneman (eds.), *Kinderen en Recht* (1989), p. 318.

10. See the same article of Sassenburg and de Langen, 'Het Recht van Kinderen op Eerbiediging van hun Privé en Gezinsleven door de Overheid, in: M. de Langen, J.H. de Graaf en F.B.M. Kunneman (eds.), *Kinderen en Recht* (1989), p. 296.

11. European Commission 16-12-1974. X and Y (Sosjale Joenit) vs the Netherlands, D&R Vol. 2, 1975.

LUDWIG SALGO*

20. Child Protection in Germany

1. INTRODUCTION

This paper is a report about our research program on family law. I would like to draw the reader's attention to some developments in the field of legislation, jurisdiction, legal and social policy in Germany in respect of child protection.

Our research is funded by the Federal Minister of Justice in Bonn. The complete comparative study will be finished in 1992. It concentrates on questions concerning the representation of children in civil courts, especially in the family and guardianship court.[1] The family court deals with all questions related to divorce, such as custody and visitation rights, whereas the guardianship court decides about state intervention in cases of child abuse, neglect, sexual abuse, adoption, foster care, etc. I shall not and cannot go into the field of the defence and representation of minors in criminal courts, where minors are liable to punishment from the age of 14:[2] nevertheless in the Federal Republic experts are debating the question of the necessity of legal representation for minor offenders in criminal courts.[3] Unfortunately I am able here to present neither a ready formula nor recommendations as results of our research, because we are still right in the middle of our research program. I hope, nevertheless, that our method of questioning and our approach will be of some interest.

In the latter half of the paper I present a short account of the reforms to family law over the last few years, the developments in the relevant constitutional areas, the reform of the Youth Welfare Act (Jugendwohlfahrtsgesetz = JWG), and the recent discussion about the right to representation of children and minors in the political and parliamentary arena.

* School of Social Work, Esslingen and J. W. Goethe University, Frankfurt am Main.

M. Freeman and P. Veerman (eds.), The Ideologies of Children's Rights, 265–288.
© 1992 Kluwer Academic Publishers. Printed in the Netherlands.

2. The Need for Special Representation of Children in Civil Protection Proceedings

2.1. *The Representation of Children in the Context of Recent Developments in Family Law*

The representation of children in courts has been demanded in Germany for some time.[4] The voices in support of such a right are many, from different disciplines, and the matter is viewed favourably not only in the media, but also in academic publications and scholarly conferences.[5] It is striking that – in contrast to earlier discussion – the suggestions made in this respect are much more specific. Thus two organisations with the aim to establish that right have already been founded and have started work.[6] But at the same time it is the general consensus that 'more' in that context does not necessarily mean 'better'. The mere increase in numbers of experts concerned about children's rights does not necessarily mean a change for the better.

The background to such attempts can be found in a general change of paradigms in family law in western countries. These reforms originate from the changing character of the family in society.[7] One sign of this process is that formal criteria which, until recently, were the main pillars of family and child law, are crumbling: e.g. the legitimate/illegitimate or married/unmarried categories. There can be no doubt that the diminished importance of the principle of priority for biological parenthood and of the 'tender years', which implies that children up to a certain age always belong to their mother and not to their father, are clear indications of this development. Another example is the regulation of custody in the case of divorce: one or two decades ago, without any question, the faultless party obtained custody. This doctrine has been abolished with the reform of divorce. Equally, the former, nearly unlimited care and control of parents has been restricted. The disappearance of such clear criteria has made the decision making process an extremely difficult task. The new formula – 'the best interest of the child'[8] or 'Kindeswohl' – is to be found in almost every legislation, worldwide, but it is not a clear-cut line of guidance: it just is a sort of vague direction, which the judge has to define anew in every case. By granting the right of self fulfillment, the right to emancipation to every family member, the recent modifications and adaptations in family law simultaneously create – in case of conflict – new dependencies on the judiciary and on legal procedure: with the acknowledgement of legally guaranteed rights of the individual within the family and with the stronger emphasis on the position of the single parties during the procedure, the representation of the child's point of view gains considerable importance – considering the child's particular vulnerability and his/her need to be protected. Therefore, in a growing number of countries the independent representation of children in courts is demanded, or has already been introduced.

The focus of the following reflections are thus not institutions concerned with the preventive 'policy for the child', such as consulting services, hotlines and other advisory support – I will mention the institutionalization of an 'ombudsman for children' later on – but the judicial intervention on behalf of the children's best interests before civil courts. It is evident, of course, that the form, extent and effects of such judicial decisions and the chance to safeguard the children's interests in this context, are extremely dependent on the existence and quality of a general child policy.

2.2. Traditional Institutions for the Protection and (Co-)representation of Children

First we have to look at the traditional manner of child protection in the legal system and its shortcomings. We have already had quite a few institutions posing as advocates of the child's interests, some of which were even authorized by law.

2.2.1. The Public Prosecutor

As long as the child protection policy of the state was mainly built on the foundations of the criminal law, legal child protection had almost exclusively been the domain of the police and the public prosecutor. Public prosecutors still act as the guardians of the children's interests in case of child abuse. But of course here we have to deal with a special situation: the interest of the child has already been gravely violated, and the reaction of the state always reflects the general interests of society and state: general prevention, stabilization of the legal system and perhaps also retaliation. The interest of this particularly violated child competes with all these and other interests. Often, in cases of conflicting interests, it is necessary to look for ways to restrict the criminal prosecution on behalf of the child. The disadvantages and burdens of every judicial procedure – but especially of a criminal procedure – for a child are immense. The efforts in our guardianship court proceedings, which work with inquisitorial but nevertheless civil procedures, have much more impact and importance for the future of the child than the criminal prosecution of the parents.[9]

2.2.2. The Youth Welfare Office ('Das Jugendamt')

By founding a special Youth Welfare Office and by defining their tasks in the Youth Welfare Act 1922 (JWG) in Germany the idea of this kind of representation of minors' interests has been publicly acknowledged for the first time. However the tasks of these authorities in family conflicts ending at the family or guardianship court are not clearly defined by law. The Child and Youth Service Act (The Kinder- und Jugendhilfegesetz = KJHG), which came into operation on January 1st, 1991,[10] and which replaces the Jugendwohlfahrtsgesetz, stipulates a reporting duty of the Youth Welfare Office in the court in cases of ongoing procedures. This does not mean that there are mandatory reporting obligations in cases of child abuse or neglect in Germany as there are in the USA. But frequently the Youth Welfare Office reports to the court evaluate its own good work, done in the past. The suggestions for the solutions of conflicts reflect the notoriously deficient work of the Youth Welfare Office, understaffed and overworked as it is. Scepticism is therefore appropriate in respect of these suggestions.

Another problem is that in many cases the Youth Welfare Office remains in charge of the social service to the whole family, even after a judicial procedure questioning the parental care of the child. That is one of the reasons why the Youth Welfare Office cannot always be regarded as the true defendant of the child's best interests in court. The goals of public child welfare bureaucracies are not necessarily identical with the best interest of a single child. These bureaucracies are in many ways dependent on the given political structure and public resources. Hierarchical structures help to guard the political priorities. Moreover, these structures favour tendencies of inappropriate centralization. The Youth Welfare Authorities often neglect to make use of the existing possibilities within the court system: for instance they very rarely file an appeal, although the decision compromises their claims. One reason for this is a well-known truth: bureaucracies are ruled by and through their own best interests: professionals from the local social services may not be the best at social welfare, but many times they certainly are the best at bureaucratic order. To sum up: there are several structural barriers which prevent youth welfare bureaucracies from being efficient in fighting for the rights and best interest of the child.[11]

2.2.3. *The Judge Within the Governing Rules of Procedure*

The procedural legislation in Germany, the 'Gesetz über Angelegenheiten der Freiwilligen Gerichtsbarkeit' (FGG) (i.e. matters of non-contentious jurisdiction), as in many other continental European states, gives the judge in the family, guardianship and other competent courts in this field a wide range of discretion to investigate the circumstances in custody and care matters. The public interest in the subjects at stake can be seen in the ruling principle of judicial intervention, which is an inquisitorial system in most countries in continental Europe.[12]

This means that the judge does not depend on any application by one of the parties. We observe very interesting tendencies in Great Britain towards the introduction of inquisitorial elements into the adversary procedure, when the rights of minors are at the centre of family rights conflicts.[13] Although the guardian *ad litem* system in Great Britain, as well as other similar systems in the United States, Australia and various other countries (whatever the names and titles of such new instruments of the courts tell us), basically simply change or soften the traditional adversarial procedure and with it the role, involvement and responsibilities of the courts, the guiding principle for the judge in continental Europe, as in Anglo-American systems and elsewhere, should be the protection of the rights and interests of the child. Nevertheless the judge, in conformity with his or her official role as judge, has to consider all the relevant interests: of the child, as well as those of the parents. If a judge is too partial to the child for instance, there will be some danger that the other parties will not accept the judge as an unbiased mediator or independent judge. There are many reasons why these traditional principles of procedural and substantive law do not succeed. Mostly the barriers are structural. To name some explicitly: the lack of interdisciplinary education of judges, and the high case load.

In my comparison of different types of court procedures, I found that a purely inquisitorial proceeding, as in many countries in continental Europe, has as many advantages and disadvantages as a purely adversary procedure, as in Anglo-American law. Robert Mnookin nevertheless defends this Anglo-American tradition of adversarial techniques: 'There is no reliable evidence that the use of non-adversarial procedure achieves greater accuracy than the method which American courts of civil and criminal jurisdiction generally employ. Nor, for that matter, is there good reason to believe that civil law courts, which typically employ a modified inquisitorial mode of proof, systematically reach more accurate, just results'.[14] Just as we often have difficulty in deciding or teaching our students whether family law is public or private law – I would sometimes say neither, it is something in between or probably a third or an *aliud* – my impression is that the future of family procedure law will in some areas go beyond this classical differentiation between the adversarial and inquisitorial principle. In my studies of different systems for the representation of the child in civil child protective procedures, I have found a lot of different modifications of these traditional ruling principles. The general trend I have observed is (and this development is all but complete) on one hand the introduction of some inquisitorial elements into adversarial proceedings in systems with Anglo-American traditions and, on the other, the implementation of some adversarial elements into inquisitorial proceedings in countries with the continental European traditions. This trend would not change an inquisitorial system to an adversarial one, nor an adversarial one to an inquisitorial one. Rather it brings some stimulating impulses to modify these paternalistic proceedings on one side or too adversarial proceedings on the other side; to bring them into compliance with the constitutionally guaranteed status of the involved participants – especially of minors – in a democratic society. But in using this traditional vocabulary of 'adversarial' versus 'inquisitorial' I find myself bound within the thinking we should overcome in this field of procedure.

2.2.4. *The Psychological/Psychiatric Expert*
Psychological or psychiatric experts often imagine themselves as the only competent advocates of the child. Even if they are now consulted in increasing numbers of cases – this might look like a real advantage to the innocent bystander, but it harbours its own disadvantages and creates new dependencies – they will act as instruments of the court in helping to find a better decision; but they do not act as advocates for one of the involved parties,

even if they have an academic reputation and expertise in handling child affairs.

2.2.5. *The Parents*

Parents, as parents, are the genuine representatives of their children since Adam and Eve. But today, as one result of the child's changed status in the family (it is now acknowledged as a full member of the family), there can follow a clash of interests within the family. If this is the case and the child's further development is in danger, then the state's *parens patriae* doctrine – which in Germany is constitutionally guaranteed along with the parents' rights (Article 6 II Grundgesetz)[15] – demands the protection of the child. If all other efforts to help the parents and child fail, the state is forced to intervene (§§ 1666, 1666a BGB, German Civil Code). More and more we are becoming aware of the extent of abuse and neglect of children and of the psychological harm caused by long-term divorce fights. It is evident that an ever growing number of children and parents in such conflicts need external help. In this situation we cannot rely on the parents' advocates, if they have any. These lawyers are loyal to their adult clients, not to the client children.

2.3. *Chances and Insufficiencies of an Independent Representation of Children's Interests in Present German Law*

The family law of the FRG, as currently valid, acknowledges possible conflicts of interest between parents and their children. In case of a considerable conflict, the law gives the court the possibility to exclude the parents as legal representatives of their child (§§ 1629 Abs .2, S.3, 1796 Abs .2 BGB). It is certainly no accident that traditional family law shows a high degree of sensitivity and protection for the property concerns of the child in cases of possible conflicts between child and parents.[16] In the field of custody and care such regulations are rarely to be found. German family law has always incorporated the role of such independent custodians and guardians for the property concerns of the child and in adoption and legitimacy matters.

Eventually the Constitutional Court of the FRG (das Bundesverfassungsgericht) acknowledged, in a decision of October 17th, 1984, the restrictions of parents' representational rights in respect to their child, if a collision of interests between child and parents happened.[17] In two further decisions the Constitutional Court confirmed the appointment of a special curator in cases of obviously conflicting interests, at least on the level of the constitutional court.[18] But the Court clearly states that deficiencies in the representation of the child's interest, and the finding of any conflict of interest as may possibly exist, have to be checked in advance by the courts of competent jurisdiction – in Germany these are the Guardianship and Family Courts. The effects of these Constitutional Court decisions have up to now been rather small; hence only a few court decisions have ordered a special, independent representative for the procedure. Until now only some supporting voices have been heard in the academic field, as well as from two groups of professionals and volunteers, already mentioned, which founded special private agencies to further and to help to install independent representation with an interdisciplinary background. But the response and public support is growing gradually, and is not as adverse as a few years ago.

2.4. *Starting Point for a Further Concept*

Let me remind you, that, as early as the 4th World Conference of the International Society on Family Law at the Harvard Law School in 1982, Giller and Maidment from Great Britain presented an instructive paper entitled *'Representation of Children'*, with a sceptical undertitle: 'Does more mean better?' These authors concluded: 'Until we confront fully the nature of the decision-making process over children, more representation will not necessarily mean better. It may, in fact, mean merely different or even a whole lot worse'.[19] After nine years of fundamental change in substantive as well as in procedural law in different countries in this area of representation of rights and interests of minors, the well-known and highly respected British scholar and jurist Stephen Cretney sums up the experiences with guardians *ad litem* and solicitors teams (introduced in Great Britain by the 1975 Children Act, but fully in force only since 1984): 'This innovation (i.e. the guardian *ad litem* as a person to be appointed in care and related proceedings to safeguard the rights and interests of the child) has been one of the success stories of our time . . .".[20] I would maintain that both Cretney and Giller and Maidment were right. It would be too simple just to say Giller and Maidment were wrong. These authors could not foresee the astonishing experiences after 1982 in different countries. Moreover we have good reason to be very cautious or even sceptical when Cretney or others speak about 'success' or a 'success story'. What does success mean in this context of representation during civil child protection proceedings? Very soon and very quickly we find ourselves in the middle of the well-known discussion about the definition of the famous term 'best interest'. What does this formula or general standard mean in open societies? We know very well how different assumptions about the success or failure of state intervention can be made in this delicate field. For a child who has been sexually abused for years by a family member, one has to regard it as a success if this abuse is stopped even by a placement of the child outside the family. But this success has its price, as is frequently the case with unavoidable state intervention: the abuse is stopped, but the intervention causes a loss of relationships with friends, school companions and (last but not least) with the other family members. Still, stopping sexual abuse is regarded as a success *per se*. We cannot – beyond the discussion about intervention or non-intervention: 'What the state does is sometimes *so bad* that people would rather it did nothing – which of course is not possible'[21] – avoid all its negative consequences and implications. For another child who has been neglected at home – and for whom neglect could not be stopped within the family – a time limited placement and a speedy return home (as soon as it is safe) – is no doubt a success,[22] especially if, during this placement, we try to keep up the relationships between the child and its family and surroundings. These two examples suggest that the same solution can be seen to be a success or a failure. From whose point of view is such an assessment made? From the point of view of the child, the parents, the foster parents or even the state? In order to measure the success of representatives in court procedures, we have to deal with such questions. Whereas Giller and Maidment could not build on evaluations by socio-legal and other scientists, we can use some important and valuable research results about activities, successes and shortcomings of different systems of children's representation in court procedure, especially from Great Britain[23] and the United States.[24] Most of these evaluations were made by institutions and scientists which were independent of the government, even if the state paid the money for such research projects. Their results sometimes had a direct impact on legislation and state policies, as well as on professional organizations of judges, lawyers and social workers.

The better the family life functions, and the more it is supported by social structure, the less its members are dependent on legal intervention and in need of a special legal representative for any family member. But if the structure is destroyed or imperiled, family and social welfare law, here especially child protection law, becomes all the more important. In a critical situation family and youth law does not limit individual freedom, but tries to restore freedom and to create and guarantee new possibilities for the endangered family. This is the situation and the setting for an independent child representation. The question is not whether the parents should be deprived of their power or whether the state should acquire new possibilities for intervention; it is rather to define more precisely the 'ifs' and the 'hows' of state intervention. It is not a matter of expanding, but a matter of raising the quality and possibly decreasing the quantity of coercive state intervention. The family law reforms in the 1970s in substantive law, especially dealing with the legal position of minors within the family, have not consistently dealt with the procedural necessities and effects. In recent family law reforms, in Germany, too, more legal definitions of special conflicts are found which call for intervention.[25] These developments try to specify the general clause in child law 'the best interest of the child'.[26] At the end of this analysis we can possibly develop a casuistic catalogue of special conflicts and respective procedural provisions for an independent legal representation of children in courts. There are a lot of central questions beyond the already mentioned 'if' and 'how' questions.

2.4.1. *Beyond the If Question*
In many countries for a long time the if question, that is the question *if* we need a separate representation of children during the court procedure, was – in some countries it still is – at the centre of passionate discussions, although in recent years the focus has increasingly been to the *who question*. A focus

on who represents the child raises questions about the qualification of such a representative. The courts and the social welfare authorities, as the traditional institutions for safeguarding children, have long felt the bare demand for separate representation to be a criticism of them. Therefore the discussion in the past was often defensive and accusative. These institutions regarded themselves as being the only legitimate representatives to carry out the *parens patriae* function of the state.[27] During the '80s, however, it was slowly accepted that there are structural limits on these traditional state authorities and on the judiciary that make it difficult or impossible for them to fulfill their tasks. Only after these institutions of the state had accepted the existence of such structural limitations did the often passionate debate of the if question switch to other important issues. A remark made during a plenary session of the Deutsche Bundestag, i.e. the German Parliament, on February, 21st, 1991, by the Federal Minister of Justice of the FRG, would only a few years ago have caused a storm of opposition and indignation: 'Until now the interests of children have been represented in different ways. Partly by their parents, partly by youth welfare authorities, partly by judges and by public prosecutors. Since all these participants represent their own interests, the children's interests are not always in the centre. That's why we really do not have to consider whether the rights of children should not be represented by a qualified person, a separate representative of the child'.[28] There were no negative reactions when he made that comment. On the contrary, the very detailed stenographic official record documents applause by the liberals (FDP) and the conservatives (CDU/CSU) after this remark, which was a part of a long speech on the ratification of the UN Convention on the Rights of the Child.[29]

While the if question – dealing especially with the role of parents, public social workers and courts, and of their structural barriers – is gradually becoming less important, there are a number of further questions which are connected with the if question. In answering these questions various experiences from different countries are helpful:

– In which cases should separate representation be ordered? Do we need enumerated case constellations within the legislation which oblige the judge to order separate representation?
– Do we need a special legislative basis in substantive as in procedural law or should the decision be left to the discretion of the single judge acting in his or her function as *parens patriae*?
– Who is best suited to this undoubtedly difficult task? Social workers, solicitors, other professionals, or even trained volunteers? Can and should we combine different abilities?
– How does the involvement of such a separate representative change the dynamics of the court procedure?
– What is the guiding source for such a representative: the explicit wish or the 'best interest' of the child? How does he or she achieve one of these goals? If a child is not able or not willing to speak with a desig-

nated representative, from where can the representative obtain information and orientation?
- Is he or she an 'officer of the court' or 'the arm of the court' or has she/he
  the same responsibilities towards adult clients?
- How can the representatives' independence from parents, as well as from
  courts and from state welfare authorities, be guaranteed?
- Should he or she be active outside the court or even control/monitor the
  implementation of the court decision after the procedure?
- How and by whom would such a field of work be organized, managed,
  financed and controlled? Children do not have controlling abilities, and other
  types of controlling mechanisms like market, professional ethics and standards hardly exist for this new field. An exception to this lack is the recently
  published Code of Ethics of the National Association of Guardians *ad Litem*
  and Reporting Officers in Great Britain.[30]

These are only a few of many questions. For all of them no one, simple solution
exists, nor a single answer or a universal panacea. But it was surprising, at
the beginning of my studies, how similar problems and questions came up
in many countries. But these developments are not so astonishing with the
general changes and trends within families in mind. I have found a volume
of answers and sometimes already evaluated experiences to these questions,
which could keep us, and probably others, away from unnecessary experimentation, and I have seen legislation, already implemented systems, state and
private agencies and initiatives, which are more than encouraging. Even if there
are a lot of historical and cultural differences including the different legal
traditions of many countries, we have gleaned new ideas and stimulation
from different countries for our suggestions here in Germany by comparing
different systems of legal representation of children and by evaluating foreign
experiences. At the same time we are testing, in cooperation with judges,
students of law, social work and educational sciences, concepts of practical
representation in a few exemplary cases.

There are no simple answers to all these questions. But meanwhile we
have a lot of experiences to consider possible answers and to balance advantages against disadvantages. For reasons of time I can only deal with the
'who question' and the quality issues.

2.4.2. *Who Should Represent Children?*

Many hopes raised by the US Supreme Court decision *In Re Gault*[31] have
not been fulfilled. The guaranteed due process of law led to a much more adversarial system of juvenile justice in the United States, while it attempted to serve
the interests of children who had previously been dealt with in a benevolent,
but also paternalistic and unfair manner. The US and the British experiences
indicate the limits of the traditional private bar in helping children within
the judicial system, as well as providing good examples of creative, new, interdisciplinary coalitions and approaches. These new approaches not only accept
and reconfirm that 'the child is a person, not an object of concern' as Lord

Justice Butler-Sloss in the Cleveland Inquiry Report 1987 stated,[32] but could also play an important monitoring role in the implementation of the intent of the court decision. Even if it sounds contradictory and illogical in terms of the reasons for a separate representation of the child, one of the reasons why guardian *ad litem*/solicitor teams or tandems in the USA and in GB have been so successful is that they resolved the difficult conflict, being both an 'officer of the court', who delivers services for the court, as well as the child's true representative.[33] This dual type of approach also developed ways and tools to resolve the important, though uncommon conflict between the best interest of a child and her or his wishes.

The fact that the if question gradually moved from the centre also has to do with the view of children in society, which has changed greatly. There is no better example of this evolution on the national as well as on the international level than the UN Convention on the Rights of the Child of November 20th, 1989.

Judges, Lawyers and their Organisations. Two decades have brought a radically different view of children's rights and interests, which are no longer seen to be automatically identical with those of adults, even when those adults are parents, judges or social workers.[34] Moreover, we have abandoned 'the traditional premise of identity of interests between the state and the juvenile'.[35] One can observe in those different countries that have introduced separate representation of children's rights and interests a similar evolution of attitudes on the part of the groups of professionals involved. Social workers in public service and judges, for instance, initially resisted the changes but, later on, when they knew more about the concepts, the advantages and the disadvantages, these groups often became important and influential supporters of independent representation of children. For example, the National Council of Juvenile and Family Court Judges in the USA now supports that only specialized judges and attorneys should work in this complicated field: 'Juvenile and family courts should not be the "training ground" for inexperienced attorneys and judges'.

But, on the other hand, they demand 'Court Appointed Special Advocates' (CASAs), who should be 'trained volunteer(s) appointed by the court to be an advocate for the best interest and well-being of the child before, during and after court proceedings', and they demand the assistance of such CASAs during the procedure by qualified attorneys.[36] Meanwhile the American Bar Association (ABA) has, since 1989, officially supported dual types of representation of children by experienced lawyers combined with chosen, trained, and supervised volunteers. This decision seems revolutionary, because lawyers usually tell us that they alone are able to manage all problems.[37] But the results of solo attorney representation in the USA were so negative that the attorneys could no longer deny the need for an alternative representation.

In Great Britain you could observe similar developments: scepticism and rejection first, then real support by different professional organisations afterwards. I interviewed Magistrates Court Judges and justices' clerks and I noticed a deep acceptance and even satisfaction with the system of guardian *ad litem* which was completely introduced in 1984. I have been told that the Magistrates Court Judges as well as the Justices' Clerks in these courts could not now imagine working without the guardians, who are combined in Great Britain with an experienced solicitor.[38]

2.5. *Key Elements for the Future of Representation*

2.5.1. *Cross-Disciplinary Methods*
In answering the question who is best suited for this undoubtedly very difficult task we should not let ourselves be dominated by economic arguments, for this could impede innovative and constructive considerations. Moreover, which solution is the cheapest cannot easily be answered. A seemingly 'cheap' solution of state intervention can in the long run be very expensive. Based on the existing experiences and evaluations, there is every reason to believe that a dual type, that is a cross or interdisciplinary model of representation of children in courts, is best.

The British solution with its 'tandem model' comes up to the highest professional standards as far as can be said at present. This 'tandem model' is superior to all other solutions, apart from its expense. Independent, experienced social workers, who have to be a member of a special panel, represent the children *together with* a solicitor, who also has to be a proven expert in this field and who has to participate in relevant training programs. The solicitor also has to be a member of the panel of the British Law Society specifically installed for this purpose. In this unique combination, the individual *wishes* of the child are represented as well as his or her *interests*. Although a clash of the two spheres – the wishes of the child and his or her interests – is relatively rare, with this dual solution we can resolve such a complicated conflict of representation. We need the services and systems of representation which represent the child's expressed views, no matter how ill-funded they may be[39] in the opinion of the guardian *ad litem* or the child's legal representative. But if we only installed mechanisms for securing this we would create a substantial disservice to children,[40] because children are not adults. So we have to secure at the same time effective services and mechanisms for the independent representation of children's rights *and* interests.

2.5.2. *Professionals and/or Volunteers?*
We should not be ignorant or arrogant towards the CASA Movement in the United States: selected, trained, and supervised volunteers have produced remarkable results there. There are 434 CASA programs in 47 states, with approximately 19,000 CASA volunteers. These volunteers spoke on behalf of about 81,000 abused and neglected children in the year 1990.[41] Their involvement, the quality of their work, and even their roles in court proceedings

differ from state to state. But a recent National Study of Guardian *ad Litem* Representation of 1990 (conducted by CSR on the basis of the Federal Child Abuse Prevention and Treatment Act, P.L. 93-247, which provides the representation of children by a guardian *ad litem* in civil abuse and neglect judicial proceedings) confirms the results of other studies, that the team model, where volunteers are paired with experienced attorneys to assist in Guardian *ad Litem* representation, is one of the most successful and effective models in the United States.[42] It is certainly more effective than solo attorney representation. One director of a state program[43] in the United States, which I could observe myself and which seems to me one of the best there, explained the reasons for the success of their program: 'The purpose of dual volunteer/attorney representation is to provide a thorough, cost-effective investigation by the volunteer out of court, coordinated with representation in court by an attorney who specializes in representing children (. . .). The investment in volunteers has been both productive and cost-effective. Volunteers are the secret of the program's success. They have one characteristic in common – dedication to children they are appointed to represent'.[44] I would add from my observations in the United States, and with the bad earlier experiences with poor attorney representation in mind: such volunteers make lawyers work in effective ways for children. Their enthusiasm – and sometimes naivety – combined with knowledge about the children, their problems and their family background and with information about possibilities and shortcomings of the given local social service, can make a system work. There are many possible ways to guarantee education, training and the independence of CASAs or of guardians *ad litem*, as one can observe in Great Britain and the United States. The lawyers themselves profited from such new coalitions and do not feel themselves any less an independent representative of the child: 'The degree to which guardians and solicitors have come to rely on each other's complementary skills and knowledge was one of the most striking features of the research'.[45]

3. Some Important Issues of Family and Youth Law Development in the FRG

3.1. *Constitutional Law*

Two different developments in this field seem remarkable to me: The Federal Constitutional Court ('das Bundesverfassungsgericht') has jurisdiction to hear claims based on the infringement of a person's basic constitutional rights by a public authority, that means by a court decision or the administration.[46] The Federal Constitutional Court gradually extends the protection of the fundamental rights towards children and juveniles. A review of the Constitutional Court's jurisdiction in the period between 1980 and 1988 dealing with the best interest and the rights of the child[47] came to the conclusion that the jurisdiction contains a lot of positive elements towards child protection, even if it is not free of contradictions. The strengthening of the child's procedural position has to be appreciated,[48] although the decisions could have been more explicit. The 'Leitmotiv' of the court's rule here is the principle that in case of relevant conflicts between child and parents the best interest of the child has become predominant. This can be seen, for instance, in the court's decree regarding foster care and state intervention.[49] Unfortunately the court gave up this principle in its jurisdiction regarding the parental rights of cohabiting parents.[50] Here another hidden principle seems to have been at work: cohabitation is not to be favoured, even if the best interest of the child is overruled. Meanwhile the Constitutional Court corrected its own position in this field.[51] This Court, as well as the whole legal system, takes children, their needs and worries more seriously than in the past. But that does not imply that we can be content. As in other fields we have, as a result of our history of the last five decades, a special German aspect. The courts' strong inclination towards parental rights in the first two decades after World War II can be seen as a reaction to the incredible violations of parental and children's rights during the NS era. During one generation after this catastrophe the communist state of the GDR and its political system also abused the family in general and in many cases intervened in families for mere political reasons.[52] The past, with which Germany, especially its judiciary, has not yet come to terms, has caused new harm here. But stronger differentiations are increasingly gaining ground. A virtual change in the constitutional rights theory must be seen in the same context. While, until recently, the majority of constitutional jurists insisted that minors usually are not allowed to exercise constitutional rights on their own, the recent positions assume that minors, too, are subjects of constitutionally guaranteed rights.[53] This does not exclude existing reservations and inherent barriers of the constitution, which can restrict the fundamental rights of minors. But these restrictions only have the goal of protecting the minor himself or third persons from damage by the minor. This opinion is increasingly becoming accepted. The burden of proof will now lie on the parents, but also on the legislature, if they want to restrict the minor's fundamental rights. This view takes account of the imbalance of power between children and adults: not the naturally weaker part, but the evidently stronger one, the parents, respectively the state, has to justify each restriction of the minor's fundamental rights.[54]

3.2. *Reform Strategies*

3.2.1. *Family Courts*
We look mainly upon positive experiences with family courts and their jurisdiction during the last fifteen years.[55] All matters connected with divorce and separation of the married partners are concentrated in these courts. This is considerable progress compared to the earlier situation, where different courts had jurisdiction, and when only the principle of fault ruled the divorce procedure. With the introduction of family courts it was acknowledged that specific

procedures, competence and responsibilities for the judicial solution of family problems are necessary.[56] Family courts in the FRG, meanwhile, have a respected position, even by other civil law judges. Family court judges, especially of the first generation, are now interested in interdisciplinary training and education. Many of these judges have founded an organization 'Deutscher Familiengerichtstag' for that purpose.[57] The situation of judges in the guardianship court is much more difficult; they have exclusive jurisdiction over minors beyond the responsibility of family courts; for example in cases of neglect, abuse, illegitimate children, adoptions etc. Their legal reputation is not as high as that of the family court judges. The rate of transfer is very high in relation to the judges of the family courts. But in this field, too, the Constitutional Court ruled in 1991 that it is against the Constitution if the matters of children born out of wedlock are not dealt in the same stages of appeal as those of the legitimate children.[58]

3.2.2. *The Reform of the Care Law of 1979*
This legislation ('das Sorgerechtsgesetz') is the final result of a long-lasting reform discussion which promised at the start more self- and co-determination for the child than finally is to be found in the Act. Two central issues, among others, of the reform act have been: foster care finds some marginal regulation in the Civil Code ('Bürgerliches Gesetzbuch' = BGB)[59]; and judges have to hear children personally. This question of communication between court and minors is regulated in the relevant procedure law (§ 50 b FGG).[60] Whenever the attachments, inclinations and wishes of the child are of importance, the judge in the family and/or guardianship court *has* to hear the child. This regulation is not limited to very young children. Only if the hearing is causing undue psychological damage to the child should the judge forgo the hearing. The Federal Constitutional Court approved this regulation,[61] but its application causes difficulties, so there are still controversial discussions. The legislation took into account that the judges would have problems in communicating with minors. Paying due respect to this problem the legislators promised an interdisciplinary further education of family and guardianship court judges.[62] Parts of the promises have been realized, but there remains a lot to be done. The judge has to cope with similar problems in communicating with children as a representative of the child during procedure:
– Where and how should he communicate with the minor?
– Which questions is he allowed to ask?
– Is there an obligation to record the hearing?
The first comprehensive evaluation[63] of the child's hearing by court, done by a child psychiatrist in cooperation with a team of social scientists, favors this hearing obligation and reports a mainly positive echo from judges, minors and their parents, even if the hearings will cause some stress. But one should also mention that a considerable number of judges tend to disregard the hearing regulations.

3.2.3. *The Child and Youth Service Act of 1990 (Kinder- und Jugendhilfegesetz – KJHG)*

The Youth Welfare Act of 1922, the Jugendwohlfahrtsgesetz (JWG), is, up to December 31, 1990, the most important legal basis for the activities of public and private youth welfare activities. The need for reform was not questioned by anybody in the FRG, because this law was ruled by the idea of public order and police law. Supervision and control over children, juveniles and their families do not correspond to the demands of modern social service legislation. The barriers for a reform have been very different:

– Youth welfare as a social right is not publicly prized. Therefore it was very difficult to reach a consent in the Federal Parliament about the financing of the reform.

– There have been, again and again, ideologically overheated debates about subjects like state intervention and about the questions of independence of juveniles or, as the most recent example, about day care for children below the age of three during the working hours of the parents.

After an ongoing debate lasting more than 20 years the 'Kinder- und Jugendhilfegesetz' was passed by the Bundestag, the German Parliament, on March 28th, 1990 and received the required approval by the Bundesrat, the Federal Council, on May 11th, 1990. The Act took effect on January 1st 1991.[64] During the debate on the draft proposals within the last two years before 1991 the volume of money needed for real reform was reduced by more than 50%. Nevertheless the new Act is an improvement compared to the ruling police law-like JWG. The Child and Youth Service Act of 1990 is strongly family oriented and it builds heavily on prevention. Many critics fear an overestimation of its family orientation. Their criticism is founded on the family, but not the single child or juvenile, gaining rights to different services under this law.[65] In the field of care and placing out endangered children from their homes the Act tries to implement the philosophy of planned, time-limited and goal-oriented intervention.[66]

3.2.4. *The Presentation of Children's and Juveniles' Interests in the Political and Parliamentary Arena*

3.2.4.1. The Federal Level. Finally, I want to point out more recent developments which could offer promising prospects and chances. During the last ten years a 'policy for children' has been discussed.[67] But the issue of a representation of children's interests in politics was for a long time seemingly of no interest in our country. As early as 1977 the Council of Europe urged 'an official instance (ombudsman for the child) . . .. to safeguard the interest of the child in a number of fields'.[68] Referring to the positive experiences with the ombudsman for children in Norway,[69] many organizations demanded such an institution in our country on the federal, the state and the local level. These voices point out that, although children have no voting rights, their parents are frequently not able to represent their children's interests politically, and that there is a need for a definite and responsible authority to coordinate and concentrate all the various efforts and activities for the child. In fact, the task of a policy for children is very complex, there are indeed jungle-like interconnections in the different political and administrative resorts.[70] There are preliminary – even if small – results in the implementation of such an office on the federal level in our Parliament, the 'Bundestag'. But until now these activities have mainly been ruled by parliamentarian idealism,[71] since they are quite symbolic. Since summer 1987 all parties in parliament have nominated one representative as 'Kinderbeauftragter', a commissioner for children. We now have four representatives. Their legal position in the Parliament is not clearly defined, and even if they are not yet adequately equipped with a sufficient staff and legal instruments, the four representatives have created more sensitivity for such a new field of policy in Parliament. The traditional structures in the organization of our Parliament are somehow fitted to these new tasks, but this could open a chance for a new policy. One cannot predict the long-term future of this remarkable attempt. There are various open and hidden forms of resistance: especially on all levels of the state administration, but also in the parliamentary administration. The four nominated representatives have various other duties as parliamentarians beside this very special task. Much depends on how the public, the youth welfare organizations, the media, and especially minors and/or their parents, and also professionals and others will make use of this new instrument.

The nonexistence of the usual controlling mechanisms and influencing factors such as market, lobby in the traditional sense, the nonexistent right to vote etc., demands a specific, new and differentiated system of checks and balances on behalf of minors. The growing loss of the power of parliament to control the bureaucracy has often been complained about in western democracies. With new instruments such as ombudspersons for children established by and only responsible to the parliament, the legislator – on the federal, the state and the local community level – could regain a part of its competence, which has been lost to the executive. We therefore have to convince the members of our parliaments that with these new instruments not only children but also they, i.e. parliamentarians, could win.[72]

3.2.4.2. *The Local Level.* There is a remarkable development in some cities in Germany and Austria, in which you can find social-democratic majorities in the local parliament. The mayors (of some cities like Frankfurt am Main, Essen, Vienna, etc.) themselves, as the top of the local government, promise to deal with the problems of children and juveniles more seriously and with more effective means than before. These efforts seem to go far beyond the traditional 'baby kissing' of established politics, i.e. that which uses children for their goals. The instruments of these communities are very different: annual children reports, the establishment of subcommittees for children, of a 'Kinderbüro', a 'Geschäftsstelle Kinder', a 'Koordinationsstelle Kinder', Children's Conferences and networks in the neighbourhoods etc.

The common characteristics of these new efforts is that they are established within the bureaucracy and work with the means of bureaucracy, but they seem to go beyond the traditional bureaucratic methods: on one hand by their direct link to the top of the administration, on the other hand by a number of other ties to the everyday life of children in their neighbourhoods. But at the same time, with the establishment of these new structures within the bureaucracies, the danger that the interests of children cannot succeed, lies within the bureaucratic structures. Warnings against such constructions within the authorities cannot be ignored. Studies in comparative political science have proved that it is a typically German variation of the international development, to establish commissioners or ombudspersons within the administration and not with a link to the parliament.[73]

After all, the above-mentioned cities do not hesitate to spend comparatively high communal resources on manpower and on equipment. Possibly the discussion about ombudspersons will stir up the traditional youth welfare bureaucracies, who now have to justify the uselessness of ombudspersons. The more farsighted representatives of youth authorities, however, see better chances to push through the rights and interests of minors together with ombudspersons with greater effect.

As far as I know there has been no survey of these recent local developments[74] which would meet scientific standards. On one hand these developments on the local level are still too new to predict anything about their effects; on the other hand it is not easy to measure and qualify them.

Our experiences to date support more than ever before the insistence on a concept of the Children's Commissioner or Ombudsperson for Children with the following standards:

- nominated by the parliament with responsibility only to this;
- someone with a friendly and accessible personality instead of an anonymous bureaucrat;
- power of the authority and autonomy by law and with it a permanent status;
- she shall not be a member of the administrative authorities;
- periodic reporting obligations to the parliament;
- an interdisciplinary staff of assistants;
- free access to files and information and
- access to children in institutions;
- reporting obligations for all institutions, which deal with children, towards the Ombudsperson, if requested;
- the right to be heard in all legislative procedures relevant to children;
- independent public relations;
- a 'brains trust' for scientific assistance;

- everybody - this includes children - even public employees, should have the right to inform the ombudsperson informally;
- right of the ombudsperson to protect sources.[75]

4. RESUMÉ

General Trends
1. In this paper I have reported on many questions, efforts and developments, but also on the rising of a new sensitivity to problems in state and society on behalf of children. My main emphasis is on legal developments, but I know that the situation of children and juveniles within and outside their families in state and public is depending on a lot more than law, legislation, jurisdiction, administrative rules and others. Nobody will question this seriously. Not until minors are accepted in family and society as equals will there be a new chance beyond legal regulation. Only then, and only to a certain degree, could intervention and administration by law be diminished. In societies adhering to the protection of the weak, there will always be increased attention paid to children. The last two decades' developments have accelerated a still ongoing - perhaps never ending - evolution and with it a radically different view of children's rights and interests, which are not viewed as being automatically identical with those of adults, irrespec-tive of their status as parents or of their involvement as judges or social workers.[76]

The Micro Level: Developments in the Field of Representation
2. While the reforms in family and especially in juvenile law in the 60s and in the 70s in many countries concentrated on the substantive law, the procedural aspects, which had been neglected earlier, became gradually more important during the 80s.
    3. For a long time the 'If Question', that is if there is a need for a special representation of the interests and rights of children during the court proce-dure beside the traditional institutions ('Does more mean better?') was at the centre of discussion. These debates were often defensive and accusative because the traditional institutions for child protection, like social welfare authorities and the courts, felt challenged and critizised by the demand for a separate representation of children. During the 80s, however, it was increas-ingly accepted that there are structural limits for these traditional state authorities and for the judiciary in fulfilling their tasks.
    4. Meanwhile we have various encouraging but also disappointing experi-ences from different countries with separate representation of children. There now exist very accurate observations and evaluations of such activities inside and outside the courts, so that we cannot but draw consequences from these experiences.
    5. One of the consequences of these evaluations is that both traditional procedural approaches, both 'adversarial' and 'inquisitorial', are unable to draw

attention to the rights and interests of minors within the procedure. Neither Anglo-American experiences with adversarial techniques nor the continental European experiences with an inquisitorial procedure can claim decisive advantages in protecting the separate rights and interests of children. Although the impulses of the US Supreme Court in the post-Gault era have been important, the disadvantages and the limits of a procedure which builds only on adversarial techniques can be clearly seen. On the other hand, in the procedures which are more or less based on inquisitorial principles, as in many countries in continental Europe, we often find a paternalistic attitude in the judges. This inquisitorial procedure assumes that the state's interests are identical with those of the child. The relevant rules of procedure often neglect constitutionally protected rights of the participants. But this is not surprising, since many of these rules of procedure date back to the 19th century and therefore are often paternalistic and guided more by a philosophy of police law and order and not so much by the rights of the individual, not to speak of the rights of children.

6. At present, the multidisciplinary concepts of children's representation as they exist since 1984 in Great Britain and recently in similar ways in some states in the United States seem to be the most successful ones. The consequences and lessons which can be learned from experiences in the USA are definite: the traditional bar, not specialised to deal with problems, rights and interests of minors, offers no considerable advantages. The participation of such legal representatives of the child in the United States frequently led to results which would equally have been reached without them; that is, their participation was merely symbolic. Unfortunately we know of too many cases where such representatives never met the child before the hearing of the case in court or sometimes five minutes before the hearing started.

In contrast to this, the dual types of representation of children by experienced lawyers combined with chosen, trained, and supervised volunteers have produced remarkable results. Whether this successful combination in some US states – which is meanwhile the officially proposed concept for children's representation of the American Bar Association (ABA) – gets close to the unique British model with a very high professional standard, is difficult to say. As far as can be said today, the British 'tandem model' is superior to all other solutions – apart from the expense. Independent, experienced social workers, who have to be a member of a special panel, represent the child, together with a solicitor who also has to be an expert in this field and a member of the panel of the British Law Society created especially for this purpose. In this unique combination the individual rights of the child are represented as well as his or her interests in cases where these two diverge.

The Macro Level: Participation and Representation of Minors in Politics
7. On the macro level, i.e. the representation and participation of children in the political and parliamentary arena, there are also encouraging as well as disappointing developments. In recent years we find a lot of activities, promises

and models which all claim to take children more seriously and which pretend to give them more rights of participation and decision making in some political fields than in the past. Such offers and invitations of politicians towards children hold chances, but they also hold dangers. Children and juveniles will very quickly notice whether they are only needed and used, i.e. instrumentalized, as accessories for the self-representation of politicians in the media for 'Baby Kissing' or whether their concerns are taken seriously. Social scientists should evaluate these new developments.

NOTES

1. These two courts are divisions of the Amtsgericht, which is the lowest court of record in Germany.
2. See, para. 19 StGB (= Strafgesetzbuch) – this is the German penal code – in connection with paras. 1, 3 JGG (= Jugendgerichtsgesetz), which regulates the criminal procedure against juveniles.
3. See, *Verteidigung in Jugendstrafsachen*, Bundesministerium der Justiz (ed.), Bonn (1987).
4. Salgo, 'Brauchen wir den Anwalt des Kindes? – Vorüberlegungen', *Zentralblatt für Jugendrecht* (1985), 259–270 with further references.
5. See, *Der Anwalt des Kindes als Konsequenzen heutigen Verständnisses von Kindeswohl*, Protokoll 14/83, Bad Boll (1983).
6. Verband Anwalt des Kindes (VAK), Hannover and Verein 'Anwalt des Kindes', Hamburg.
7. See Glendon, *The Transformation of Family Law*, Chicago (1989) and Eekelaar, *Family Law and Social Policy*, 2nd. ed., London (1984).
8. See Goldstein, Freud and Solnit, *Beyond the Best Interest of the Child*, New York (1973) and *Before the Best Interest of the Child*, New York (1979) and Goldstein/ Freud/Solnit/Goldstein, *In the Best Interest of the Child*, New York (1986).
9. See Zenz, *Kindesmißhandlung und Kindesrechte*, p. 390 ff., Frankfurt am Main (1979).
10. Wiesner and Zarbock (eds.), *Das Neue Kinder- und Jugendhilfegesetz*, Köln (1991).
11. See Salgo (Note 4), p. 261 ff.
12. For an overview of the family court movement in many countries and the ruling principles in proceedings see, Nakamura, in: Nakamura, *Familiengerichtsbarkeit*, p. 8, Tokio (1984).
13. The introduction of the 'tandem-model' itself, with the guardian *ad litem and* the solicitor, stands on one hand for some inquisitorial links in a traditionally adversarial system; on the other hand, it strengthens the position of the child. 'Care proceedings were not adversial in nature', see R.v. Birmingham *Juvenile Court Ex Parte G. and R.* (1988) 2 FLR 423, the judge followed here the dictum of Lord Widgery, C. J. in Humberside CCv DPR (1977) 3 All ER 964, ibid. 967: care proceedings are 'an objective examination of the position of the child'. See Freeman, *The Rights and Wrongs of Children*, London (1983), pp. 162–163.
14. R. Mnookin and D. K. Weisberg, *Child, Family and State*, 2nd ed., Boston (1990) p. 1081.
15. This constitutionally guaranteed obligation of the state in Germany towards minors is called 'Staatliches Wächteramt'.
16. See Limbach, 'Der Anwalt des Kindes aus Juristischer Sicht, in: *Der Anwalt des Kindes* . . . (Note 5) p. 14.
17. BVerfGE 72, 122.
18. BVerfGE 75, 201 and BVerfGE 79, 51.
19. Giller and Maidment, 'Representation of Children: Does More Mean Better?', in: Eekelaar and Katz, *The Solution of Family Conflict*, Toronto (1984), pp. 405 and 419.

20. Cretney, foreword, in: Monro and Forrester, *The Guardian ad Litem*, Bristol (1991), p. v.
21. Olsen, The Myth of State Intervention in the Family, *U. Mich. J. L. Ref.* 18 (1985), pp. 835–863.
22. For a comparative study of different foster care systems see Salgo, *Pflegekindschaft und Staatsintervention*, Darmstadt (1987).
23. The differentiated and extraordinarily important and influential studies of the Socio-Legal Centre for Family Studies at the University of Bristol directed by Mervyn Murch helped me to learn about the British system. Mr. Murch and his team did their research for the Department of Health. They are funding a book concerned with the system of child representation. Meanwhile Murch, Hunt and Macleod published a *Summary of Conclusions and Recommendations for the Department of Health*, Bristol (January 1990). Another British survey was carried out by The Social Services Inspectorate of the Department of Health: *In the Interest of Children, An Inspection of the Guardian ad Litem and Reporting Officer Service*. London (1990). For an overview of the latest developments and the future of the guardian *ad litem* system in Great Britain see Fortin, 'The Guardian *ad Litem* in Care Proceedings', *Family Law* 20 (1990), p. 303.
24. In the United States it was Donald N. Duquette who evaluated different systems of representation; he is the scholar with the greatest familiarity with the diverse types of children's representatives; he is the director of the Child Advocacy Law Clinic at the University of Michigan Law School. See: Duquette *Advocating for the Child in Protection Proceedings*, Lexington, Massachusetts (1990). See also the *National Study of Guardian ad Litem Representation*, Edited by the Administration for Children Youth and Families, Office of Human Development Services, US Department of Health and Human Services, Prepared by CSR, Inc., Washington (1990).
25. See paras. 1631a, 1631b, 1632 Abs. 4 BGB (Bürgerliches Gesetzbuch), i.e. the German Civil Code.
26. See Coester, *Das Kindeswohl als Rechtsbegriff*, Frankfurt am Main (1983).
27. For the development of such discussions in Germany see Salgo (Note 4).
28. Bundesminister der Justiz Dr. Kinkel, Deutscher Bundestag (Plenarprotokoll 12/9) – 12. Wahlperiode – 9. Sitzung, Bonn, Donnerstag, den 21. Februar 1991, p. 445.
29. The Convention was ratified by the Deutscher Bundestag on November 14th 1991, the Bundesrat gave its consent on December 19th 1991. Steindorff reports some instrumentalizing attempts by the further rights movement in Germany: 'Die UN-Kinderrechtskovention als Legitimationsgrundlage für Elternrechte', *Familie und Recht* (1991), 214–216.
30. National Association of Guardian *ad Litem* and Reporting Officers, *Code of Ethics for Guardian ad litem and Reporting Officers* (1991). The Law Society in Great Britain and the American Bar Association both have developed ethics and rules for lawyers who work in this field.
31. In re Gault, 387 US (1967).
32. *Report of the Inquiry into Child Abuse in Cleveland 1987*, p. 245, Cm 412 HMSO, London (1988).
33. Also Murch *et al.* (Note 23), p. 19 f.
34. Ibid. p. 82–83.
35. Mnookin and Weisberg (Note 14).
36. National Council of Juvenile and Family Court Judges (ed.), *Deprived Children: A Judicial Response: 73 Recommendations*, Reno, Nevada (1987), p. 15.
37. Recommendation of the House of Delegates of the American Bar Association, August 8–9, 1989, Report No. 12.
38. The research findings of Murch *et al.* as well as the Social Services Inspectorate's Report (Note 23) are proof of such subjective observations.
39. See Murch *et al.* (Note 23), pp. 83–84.
40. Ibid.
41. For this and other information about the CASA movement in the United States, see The Connection, 6 (Spring 1991), ed. by the National CASA Association, Seattle, Washington.

42. See the CSR study (Note 24) as well as Duquette and Ramsey, Representation of Children in Child Abuse and Neglect Cases: An Empirical Look at What Constitutes Effective Representation, *U. Mich. J. L. Ref.* 20, 341; the CSR Report as well as Duquette's book (Note 24) present an overview of different types of representation in the United States.

43. My special thanks for information about the Guardian *ad Litem* Program in North Carolina go to Virgina G. Weisz, the former State Administrator, and to Cy Guerney Elkins, Program Coordinator in Durham County.

44. *Children and the Law in North Carolina, A Casebook For Practice*, V.G. Weisz (ed.), Raleigh, North Carolina (1987), pp. XIII–11.

45. Murch *et al.* (Note 23), p. 47. The Social Services Inspectorate's evaluation (ibid.) comes to very similar conclusions.

46. See Art. 93 GG (= Grundgesetz), i.e. the Constitution of Germany.

47. See Salgo, 'Das Kindeswohl in der Neueren Rechtsprechung des Bundesverfassungsgerichts', in: du Bois (ed.), *Praxis und Umfeld der Kinder- und Jugendpsychiatrie*, Bern (1989), pp. 156–169.

48. See Notes 17, 18.

49. BVerfGE 68, 176; 75, 201 and 79, 51.

50. BVerfGE 56, 363.

51. BVerfGE, FamRZ 1991, pp. 913–918.

52. About adoptions, where the parental consent was neglected for politically motivated reasons in the GDR, reports Raack, *Zentralblatt für Jugendrecht* 1991, pp. 449–451; see also, concerning the shadows of the past in German family law practice after World War II, Salgo, 'Das Verhältnis von Eltern, Kind und Staat in der Verfassungsordnung der Bundesrepublik Deutschland, *Familie und Recht* (1990), pp. 363–366.

53. See Roell, *Die Geltung der Grundrechte für Minderjährige*, Berlin (1984), and Hohm, *Grundrechtsträgerschaft und 'Grundrechtsmündigkeit' Minderjähriger am Beispiel Öffentlicher Erziehung*, NJW (1986), pp. 3107–3115.

54. See Salgo (Note 47), p. 167.

55. The Book of Nakamura about family law litigation (Note 12) also contains a report from the FRG by Firsching, pp. 81–105; see also Müller-Freienfels, *Über 'Familiengerichte', insbesondere in den USA*, ZVglRWiss (1973), 117–175, who compares systematically these developments.

56. As the Constitutional Court also acknowledges, see BVerfGE 55, 171 and 180; see about the implications of the introduction of family courts in the FRG and its shortcomings Salgo, *Soll die Zuständigkeit des Familiengerichts Erweitert Werden?*, FamRZ (1984), pp. 221–228.

57. The Deutscher Familiengerichtstag is a membership organisation mainly consisting of Family Court judges and of lawyers with some influence on politics; its registered office is at Brühl. The Guardianship Court judges also founded a similar membership organization the Vormundschaftsgerichtstag: its office is in Hamburg.

58. BVerfGE, FamRZ (1992), pp. 157–160.

59. Paras. 1630, 1632 Abs. 4 BGB.

60. These innovations were introduced with the 'Sorgerechtsgesetz' from July 18th, 1979, in force since January 1st 1980.

61. BVerfGE 55, 171 and 179.

62. See Note 56.

63. Lempp and others, *Die Anhörung des Kindes Gemäß § 50b FGG*, Bonn (1987).

64. But there are a lot of implementation problems with this new, innovative legislation.

65. See for example Kiehl, *Die Rechtsstellung Minderjähriger und Sorgeberechtigter im Neuen Kinder- und Jugendhilfegesetz*, ZRP (1990), pp. 94–99.

66. See Salgo, 'Die Regelung der Familienpflege im Kinder- und Jugendhilfegesetz (KJHG)', in: Wiesner/Zarbock (Note 10), pp. 115–150.

67. See *Politik für das Kind, Loccumer Protokolle 14/88*, ed. Evangelische Akademie Loccum (1989).

68. Council of Europe, Explanatory Memorandum, Doc. 4376, 3 October 1979, p. 5.
69. See Flekkøy, *A Voice for Children*, London (1991) and the evaluation of Melton, 'Lessons from Norway: the Children's Ombudsman as a Voice for Children', *Journal of International Law*, Case Western Reserve (1991), 23(3).
70. See Uppendahl, 'Mittel und Strategien einer Politik für das Kind, in: *Politik für das Kind* (Note 67), pp. 56–72.
71. Ibid.
72. See Salgo, 'Die Funktion eines Kinder- und Jugendlichenbeauftragten im internationalen Vergleich', *Materialen zur Heimerziehung* (1990), nr. 4, pp. 4–6.
73. See Uppendahl (Note 70).
74. A small survey has just been started by the Institute für Sozialarbeit und Sozialpädagogik, Frankfurt am Main.
75. I have tried to compile the most important legal and structural elements on the base of experiences we have had until now.
76. See Murch and others (Note 23) p. 83.

STANLEY S. HERR*

21. The Development of Equitable Remedies for Children with Disabilities

1. INTRODUCTION

Equitable remedies are described as extraordinary remedies. In the 20th century, children with disabilities have certainly needed extraordinary relief. Societies have witnessed their exclusion from education, their relegation to barren institutions, and the extinction of their very lives. These events did not happen only in Nazi Germany or in decades long past. They have also happened in liberal democracies and in recent years. Without the efforts of children's rights advocates and the provision of equitable remedies, such human rights tragedies can reoccur.

This chapter will focus on three questions. What are some origins of the equitable powers to protect children or adults with disabilities? In the United States, how have advocates used equitable judicial remedies to defend such children's rights to education, treatment, and habilitation? What are the implications of this public law litigation for the defence of children's rights?

The American judiciary has often played a leading role in the protection of children's rights. As Professor Louis Henkin concluded, 'the courts have become principal guardians of rights in the United States, scrutinizing legislative and executive acts as well as those of the courts, in the light of constitutional limitations.'[1] To realize their potential as defenders of children's rights, American courts have had to loosen the restraints of technical equity rules and of prudential reasons that limit judicial review in certain human rights cases.[2] They have also been challenged to create new remedies to match new rights of wide contour. If every legal wrong must have its legal remedy, or as the maxim of equity puts it, *ubi jus, ibi remedium*,[3] then considerable judicial ingenuity would be required to protect 5,000 dehumanized inmates of 'state schools' from harm or to enroll 10,000 school-excluded children denied their rights to education.[4]

* University of Maryland, Baltimore, Maryland.

M. Freeman and P. Veerman (eds.), The Ideologies of Children's Rights, 289–310.
© 1992 *Kluwer Academic Publishers. Printed in the Netherlands.*

2. Historical Origins of Equitable Powers

2.1. *Parens Patriae Concepts*

English law provided an early example of equitable protection for persons with mental disabilities, including children. Under the de Praergative regis (Royal Prerogatives), a so-called statute of the 13th century, the king gained powers of custody over 'lunatics' and 'natural fools'. The distinction between lunatics and idiots had practical consequences. According to Blackstone, lunatics were 'to live and be maintained competently', while idiots were only to receive 'their necessaries' with the king having the right to the rest of their properties.[5] Originally vested in the Exchequer, jurisdiction over the property and person of the idiot was shifted to the Court of Wards and then to Chancery along with other profitable rights claimed by the king as *pater patriae*.[6] In *Beverly's Case*, the royal power of custody over such persons and their property was justified on the basis that 'every subject is in the King's protection; an idiot who cannot defend or govern himself, nor order his lands and tenements, goods and chattels, the King of right ought to have him, and to order him, his lands, goods, and chattels . . ..'[7]

Guardianship over minors was also within the crown's parens patriae and equity powers. English treatise writers on equity traced the Court of Chancery's jurisdiction over minors to the 'prerogative of the Crown as *parens patriae*, the exercise of which was delegated to the Chancellor'.[8] Wardship of court, for example, was an equitable jurisdiction traditionally connected to property disputes and the minor's entitlement to property.[9] Not until 1949 was the statute changed to conform the law to the practice of permitting the wardship of children without property for matters of child welfare.[10] It is interesting to note that one of the first such wardship cases for children without property dealt with the protection of Jewish refugees during World War II. Generally, however, equity was more concerned with the property rather than the personal well-being of the child.

Over the centuries, English equity powers reached an assortment of society's relatively vulnerable. According to Holdsworth, the supervisory jurisdiction of the chancery court was long exercised over the affairs of infants, idiots, lunatics, married women, and other presumptively incapacitated categories of persons.[11] As of the Judicature Act of 1873, the appointment of a guardian of a minor's estate was classified as but one of the twelve branches of chancery jurisdiction.[12]

In theory, children – let alone children with disabilities – were the ideal supplicants for equity. For many of their injuries, the common law gave them no remedy. Even if the law appeared to offer a remedy, their prospects for recovery were slight, for 'if the parties were unequally matched in wealth and influence the weaker party often had little chance of obtaining a judgment in his favour or, if he obtained it, of enforcing it'.[13] Professor Maitland in his famous 1906 lectures on equity characterized the typical petitioner in equity as complaining that 'for some reason or another he cannot get a remedy in the ordinary course of justice and yet he is entitled to a remedy. He is poor, he is old, he is sick, his adversary is rich and powerful, will bribe or will intimidate jurors . . .. The petition is often couched in piteous terms, the king is asked to find a remedy for the love of God and in the way of charity'.[14] That the young are not included in Maitland's list of petitioners probably reflects their inability to bring such appeals to the keepers of the king's conscience.

2.2. *Ancient Jewish Equity*

An older tradition of equity sought to protect children from harm. Justice Haim Cohn, formerly of the Israel Supreme Court, wrote that Jewish equitable practice depended 'on the fear of God and the uprightness of the individual rather than on any legal sanction administered on earth'. As an example, he cites the biblical law against oppression of orphans: 'Ye shall not afflict any widow or fatherless child. If thou afflict them in any wise, and they cry at all unto me, I will surely hear their cry; And my wrath shall wax hot, and I will kill you with thy sword; and your wives shall be widows and your children shall be fatherless'.[15] Among the believers, this is certainly an injunction not to be ignored.

Other duties of Jewish equity, however, were made enforceable through less divine intervention. Civil and criminal sanctions attached for failures to pay charitable assessments to a communal welfare fund. Cohn viewed this duty as deriving from the scriptual text, 'and if thy brother be waxen poor, and fallen in decay with thee, then thou shalt relieve him: yea, though he be a stranger or a sojourner; that he may live with thee.'[16]

Then, as now, the resources for relieving the poor were finite. The Bible thus recognized a hierarchy of competing claims, with a rank ordering of the individual's obligation to aid the poor that starts with one's parents, then children, brothers and sisters, other relatives, the learned in town, and other needy persons in town. From these developments in equity, Justice Cohn finds a unique example of 'the enforceability of charity', and a foretaste of 'compulsory tax in a welfare state.'[17]

3. EQUITABLE REMEDIES AND THE AMERICAN EXPERIENCE

3.1. *Background*

Lacking resort to regal power or religious cohesion, the American people often turn to their Constitution and courts for answers to vexing social and political problems. As De Tocqueville observed, private rights are endangered 'if the judicial power does not grow more extensive and stronger to keep pace with the growing equality of conditions', a view reflected in the current campaign to defend the rights of children with disabilities.[18] In a tidal wave of litigation, federal and state courts have enforced the provision of treatment and special services for children with mental handicaps on a variety of grounds, with some courts noting that this duty 'flows from the state's inherent *parens patriae* jurisdiction'.[19] In asserting this jurisdiction over minors and other persons under a disability, the courts have recognized a wide array of powers to secure their affirmative assistance (e.g. education and other habilitation services) and to protect them from harm (e.g. nonconsensual sterilization).[20] As Maryland's highest court in 1982 declared, 'it is [a] fundamental common law concept that the jurisdiction of courts of equity over such persons is plenary so as to afford whatever relief may be necessary to protect the individual's best interests'.[21]

Until the 1970s, there was little affirmative human-rights litigation for children (or adults) with disabilities.[22] Black children and their parents, however, pioneered the use of the courts to secure equality rights. In *Brown v. Board of Education*[23] and its progeny, the US Supreme Court authorized the lower courts to make extensive use of equitable powers for the purpose of desegregating racially separate school systems.[24] These precedents inspired a cadre of activist attorneys for disabled persons to seek similarly far-ranging judicial relief, often through civil rights injunctions of both prohibitory and mandatory character. Under the American constitutional system, they could obtain judicial review of legislation that excluded their clients from public entitlement or denied due process. A regime of checks and balances also permitted the judiciary to enjoin executive decisions that would violate constitutional rights. Judicial intervention often produced catalytic results rather than comprehensive relief for the larger problems identified by the litigation. Thus, the cases described in this chapter led to a mobilizing of political support for children as an insular, powerless minority, and to new legislation and appropriations for their benefit.

3.2. *Injunctions in Special Education Cases*

Broad equitable remedies were at the heart of civil rights cases that required public school systems to offer free, appropriate education to any handicapped child. In *Pennsylvania Association for Retarded Children v. Commonwealth of Pennsylvania* (hereinafter *PARC*), the federal district court issued a permanent injunction that restrained the state and local school districts from denying or postponing free education and training to any child with mental retardation aged 6 to 21. This very specific decree, negotiated by the consent of the parties after preliminary stages of the litigation resulted in rulings favorable to the plaintiff class, included children in institutions. In 1972, the federal court in Washington, D.C. adjudicated the broader claims of all physically or mentally handicapped children excluded from schooling for a variety of reasons, including school discipline, disability, budgetary constraints, and lack of classrooms and specialized instruction. *Mills v. Board of Education of the District of Columbia* held that the plaintiffs' equal protection and due process rights had been violated, and imposed an intricate injunctive remedy. Its main elements included:

- a mandate to educate all handicapped children, regardless of the degree or type of disability, in some individually appropriate form of publicly supported education;
- a 'childfind' program of outreach to identify excluded children;
- new procedural safeguards such as written notice prior to any change in a child's educational placement from a regular classroom, the opportunity to review the child's school records, and the right to request an independent educational evaluation of his or her condition;
- the right to obtain an impartial due process hearing;
- the rights in such a hearing to be represented by a lawyer or lay advocate, to examine and cross-examine witnesses, to introduce documents, and to appeal any adverse decision;
- timetables for the identification, evaluation, and placement of affected children;
- new procedural and substantive safeguards for handicapped and non-handicapped children subject to disciplinary suspension or expulsion.

Cases like *Mills* and *PARC* pioneered the use of an array of extraordinary equitable remedies in education cases. The creation of a new forum – the due process hearing before an impartial hearing officer – offered a fair process for individualizing the relief for members of large class actions and 'for determining what is best for the child in instances when parents and school personnel disagree'.[25] The courts retained continuing jurisdiction over the cases, often for five to ten years, thus permitting the 'finetuning', modification and enforcement of the equitable decrees. To provide ongoing oversight of the defendant's implementation activities, some judges appointed special masters with social science and/or legal expertise.[26] Although plaintiffs' attorneys might seek or threaten to seek contempt citations for breach of court degrees, judges generally managed to induce the defendant's compliance without such draconian sanctions.

Through direct and indirect effects, the so-called 'right-to-education' cases ushered into a new regime in special education. Three years after the *Mills* and *PARC* decrees, with similar lawsuits pending or recently decided for plaintiff children in more than half the states,[27] Congress enacted the Education for All Handicapped Children Act of 1975.[28] Borrowing heavily from the *Mills-PARC* decrees, this legislation represents an 'ambitious congressional attempt' to guarantee an appropriately designed free public education suited to the unique needs of each handicapped child and young person aged 3 to 21.[29] Indeed, the US Supreme Court in tracing the legislative history for this Act recognized its underpinnings in these two federal court decrees and the Congressional intention to apply nationally their substantive and procedural remedies.[30] Public Law 94-142 also helped to ease the financial burdens on those states which assured, *inter alia*, that children with handicaps were 'mainstreamed' (educated to the maximum extent appropriate with nonhandicapped children).[31] The infusion of funds now in excess of $2.123 billion annually to states under Public Law 94-142 has obviated some of the financial difficulties encountered in implementing the early court degrees.[32]

For example, in discussing the financing of the *Mills* decree through reallocation of resources, Judge Waddy opined that 'if sufficient funds are not available to finance all of the services and programs that are needed and desirable in the system then *the available funds must be expended equitably in such a manner that no child is entirely excluded from a publicly supported education consistent with his needs and ability to benefit therefrom.*'[33] With such bold steps, jurists like Judge Waddy helped to empower parents of children with disabilities, and to draw attention to the federal courts as a source of leverage for children's rights advocates.

3.3. *Injunctions in Student Misclassification Cases*

Intelligence quotient (IQ) tests and their use to label and to classify school-age children have also come under judicial scrutiny. In most states, such tests were the primary means of identifying children as mildly retarded and their scientific mystique masked their limitations as a tool for special education placement. As of 1952, the IQ score was used as the sole criterion to define mental retardation; by 1959 impairment in adaptive behavior became another element of the definition.[34] In the 1960s, social science researchers and civil rights activists began to highlight the problem of the so-called 'six-hour retarded' – children who were only considered retarded during their school time – and the over-representation of minorities in classes for the mildly retarded.[35] In the early 1970s, litigants began to mount strong challenges to the misclassification of racial and linguistic minorities and the testing procedures that resulted in a disproportionate percentage of such children being labeled mentally retarded.[36] Through biased placement processes, white children often avoided these classes. Instead they were disproportionately directed to the less stigmatizing classes for the 'learning disabled' or 'educationally handicapped' whose students were presumed capable of returning to regular education after supplemental assistance.

Larry P. v. Riles[37] is a notable example of court intervention to spare children the harms of erroneous placement in segregated, stigmatizing, and often 'dead-end' special classes. The gravamen of plaintiffs' complaint was that primary reliance on culturally biased IQ tests resulted in many false diagnoses of mental retardation in violation of the black students' equal protection and other civil rights. The federal district court enjoined the use of such tests as the basis for placement of black students in public school classes for the 'educable mentally retarded' (EMR). The court gave particular weight to statistical evidence of racial imbalance, specifically the discrepancy between the rates of black and white children labeled mentally retarded. Although black students represented only 9% of the state-wide school population, they totaled 28%

of the students in EMR classes.[38] In the San Francisco school district, for example, 66% of EMR students were black, even though blacks totaled only 28.5% of the total school population.[39] Rejecting theories that genetic inferiority or socio-economic disadvantage explained the over-representation of blacks in EMR classes, the court found that the tests were culturally and racially biassed in their content, and had not been validated for the placement of black children in such classes. This bias was held to violate not only statutory rights to be free from discriminatory effects (under the Education for All Handicapped, Rehabilitation, and Civil Rights Acts), but to constitute intentional discrimination under state and federal equal protection guarantees.

In devising an equitable remedy, the *Larry P.* court took many innovative steps. At the preliminary injunction phase, the defendants were barred from placing black students in EMR classes on the basis of primary reliance on IQ tests results, 'if the consequence of use of such criteria is racial imbalance in the composition of such classes.'[40] Even though this relief changed the status quo prior to the final adjudication, the Court of Appeals for the Ninth Circuit affirmed, citing precedents that such interim relief would not be disturbed 'unless contrary to some rule of equity'[41] and that courts of equity faced with a 'variety of situations' must have considerable discretion in fashioning such relief.[42]

In 1979, the court exercised even broader discretion in ordering a permanent injunction with three major elements. First, the injunction barred future use of standardized intelligence tests for the identification or placement of black children in EMR classes, unless the court's approval would be first obtained. The stringent criteria for such approval included assurances by the state board of education that (1) the tests were not culturally or racially biased, (2) would not be administered in a discriminatory manner, (3) were validated for determining EMR status. The Board was also required to make a written authorization for the use of such tests; and to conduct a prior public hearing on any proposed test. (This relief, in fact, maintained the defendants' voluntarily imposed moratorium on IQ testing for purposes of any EMR placement in California, a result which followed a 1975 state-wide court order restraining educators from performing any psychological evaluations of black school-age children using IQ tests which did not 'properly account for the cultural experiences of these children'.[43]) Second, the court ordered the elimination of the disproportionate placements of blacks in EMR classes. This relief included the development of plans to foster racial balance over a three-year period, with special review procedures by the court for school districts which still evidenced grossly disproportionate placement of black students in EMR classes after this period. Third, school districts were ordered to reevaluate every plaintiff child (i.e., all black students currently in EMR classes). This reevaluation would rely on diagnostic tests of specific learning needs, adaptive behavior observation, and the child's developmental and health histories. Unless the court had approved a specific test for this purpose, IQ tests results were specifically excluded from this reevaluation process. In addition, students who had been misplaced in such classes were to receive compensatory relief in the form of an individualized education plan (IEP) and supplemental assistance to allow the child's return to a regular classroom.

Some of the plaintiff's proposed remedies were rejected by the court as unduly burdensome or tangential to the trial record. For instance, the court declined to order supplemental assistance for former EMR students who were already in regular classes but might need extra help to catch up with their peers. Similarly, no expungement or other relief was provided for pupils identified as of EMR status but not placed in special classes. In justifying such limitations on the scope of relief, and the affected class of beneficiaries, Judge Peckham stated: 'It is not the role of the court to reach out to order [for minority and disadvantaged students] what would amount to a massive expenditure of funds for supplemental assistance'.[44]

After protracted legal maneuvers, Judge Peckham's decree was affirmed by appellate opinions issued in 1984 and 1986.[45] The Ninth Circuit held that the defendants had not discharged their burden of proving that the IQ tests were valid for the purpose of placing children in EMR classes, a classification intended for those 'whose mental capabilities make it impossible for them to profit from the regular education program even with remedial instruction'.[46] The court upheld the trial court rulings of statutory violations on the basis of defendants' failures to validate the tests for the specific purpose for which they were intended, and to use the variety of statutory-mandated evaluation tools. The panel, however, reversed the constitutional rulings. Since those rulings were superfluous to the result, the trial court's equity decree was preserved intact.

The Court of Appeals rejected the defendants' arguments that the court could only eliminate the tests and not correct the erroneous placement of blacks in EMR classes. To the contention that the special review procedure for school districts with racially imbalanced classes greater than one standard deviation constituted an impermissible numerical quota, the court upheld the order since it fixed no racial balance numbers and permitted school districts to maintain imbalanced classes if they could present data that all the black children had been properly placed.[47] One dissenting judge, however, viewed this remedy as an arbitrary restraint on placement that would cause defendants 'to make the numbers fit' and would lead to improperly race conscious evaluations.[48]

The *Larry P.* case has significantly affected placement of minority students in classes for the mildly retarded. First, this 15-year litigative battle over such practices in the Nation's most populous state gave misclassification problems national publicity and attention. Second, courts elsewhere were inspired by that precedent to correct other abuses of IQ tests and related classification procedures. In a federal New York case, the court sought to eliminate discriminatory placement of racial minorities in special day schools for emotionally handicapped and 'acting-out' students. There Chief Judge Jack

Weinstein concluded that 'the isolation of minority students in special education settings with small hope of truly fruitful education or movement into less restrictive environments constitutes a denial of equal protection'.[49] Citing *Larry P.*, a New York court cast doubt on the constitutionality of using IQ tests as a factor in terminating the parental rights of a Spanish-speaking young mother, particularly given the risk of cultural bias in such circumstances.[50] Lastly, beyond its precedential value, *Larry P.* has had considerable indirect impact as test designers searched for ways to market less biased instruments nationally, and as school districts in other states sought to avoid similar litigation.

3.4. *Judicial Relief in Institutional Reform Cases*

American courts have also devoted considerable time and energy to the civil rights denied to the residents of grossly sub-standard institutions. *Wyatt v. Stickney*[51] was the first class action of this kind and became the model for many similar cases in the fields of mental health, juvenile services, and mental retardation. The graphic evidence of the experts who toured the Alabama institutions revealed the urgent need for reform. In recounting a visit to a unit for mildly retarded teenage girls, one expert witness described the range of their needs in these terms:

> These girls were very verbal, spoke with me at length. They were concerned because they had little or no contact with boys. Girls of that age should now typically show some interest in that type of activity. They indicated that they viewed the facility as a prison, which was the word they used. They demanded loudly and strongly to be discharged. I found that the bathroom facility for these girls to contain two toilets with no partition, with no attempt to give these girls any type of privacy. The girls spoke to me of punishment and discipline, including having to sleep on the floor, being deprived of dinner, . . . and in some instances being sent to a building housing profoundly mentally retarded girls and being assigned there as a working resident.[52]

The federal court found that these and other degrading and dehumanizing conditions violated the residents' constitutional right to adequate minimum habilitation. In a parallel decree for the patients of Alabama's state mental hospitals, Judge Frank Johnson upheld the analogous constitutional right to adequate treatment as grounded in substantive due process.[53] 'To deprive any citizen of his or her liberty', the court reasoned, 'upon the altruistic theory that the confinement is for humane therapeutic reasons and then fail to provide adequate treatment violates the very fundamentals of due process'.[54] The court's remedial approach to securing these rights involved incremental (and ever more intrusive) forms of judicial intervention. Initially, the court had simply declared the state officials' violation of the right to adequate treatment, and given the defendants three months to submit a specific plan on how they would provide

the plaintiff class with appropriate and adequate treatment.[55] *Wyatt* further directed the defendants to 'implement fully' within six months a treatment program that would give each resident 'a realistic opportunity to be cured or to improve his or her mental condition'.[56] To spur implementation, the court invited the United States government and granted the motions of leading professional organizations to participate in the case as amici curiae (with the powers of a party), to evaluate institutional conditions, and to advise the court on appropriate standards and implementation steps.[57] When the defendants' plan, proposed standards and interim report proved wholly inadequate, the court defined three conditions as essential to the provision of minimum constitutionally required treatment in public mental institutions:
1. a humane psychological and physical environment;
2. qualified staff in numbers sufficient to administer adequate treatment; and
3. individualized treatment plans.[58]
The district court then requested the parties and the so-called 'litigating amici' to submit proposed standards that would meet medical and constitutional requirements, and to present expert testimony in support of their respective sets of standards. As a result of intensive negotiations and the deadline of an approaching court hearing, the parties stipulated on detailed and comprehensive 'minimum standards of adequate treatment' (along with comparable standards of adequate habilitation for persons with mental retardation). These standards dealt with topics as diverse as the requirement of least restrictive modes of treatment, specific staffing ratios, environmental conditions, civil rights, patient dignity, supervised interaction between members of the opposite sex, and individualized treatment plans. Additional treatment provisions for juveniles required their suitable education, outdoor recreation, strengthened contacts between the hospital and their families, and sufficient teachers and other staff 'with specialized skill in the care and treatment of children and young adults'.[59] Of the 49 standards promulgated by the court as the minimum requirements of the constitutional right to habilitation, only four were not the product of the amici's and parties' agreement. These litigated standards barred the use of locked-room seclusion, regulated medication practices, set hot-water safety levels, and created human rights committees.

The human rights committees had a broad mission. They were intended to ensure that 'the dignity and human rights of patients are preserved.'.[60] Their specific functions included reviewing all research proposals and rehabilitation programs, and advising patients of their legal rights in the event of alleged rights violations or noncompliance with the courts's decree. Exemplifing the flexibility of the equitable remedy, this court-created entity was assigned prospective tasks and wide powers 'to pursue within the limits of reasonableness, whatever action is necessary to accomplish its functions'.[61] These standing committees for each institution were composed of professionals and concerned lay persons who received *per diem* expenses to act as the court's eyes and ears.

The Court of Appeals for the Fifth Circuit upheld these standards and underlying constitutional rights. The right to treatment was expressly held to raise justiciable matters. The unanimous panel substantially affirmed the propriety of Judge Johnson's institutional standards approach; i.e. requiring a program institution-wide in scope that would be capable of formulating individual plans of treatment. One question left undecided was the means to fund these new constitutional obligations. Although the lower court had reserved ruling on plaintiffs' motion to direct the state mental-health board to sell or encumber some of its large land holdings to finance implementation, the Fifth Circuit warned that 'such serious constitutional questions . . . in the event the governing authorities fail to move in good faith to ensure what all parties agree are minimal requirements, should not be adjudicated unnecessarily and prematurely'.[62] Instead, the appellate panel urged the parties, amici and trial judge to move together to 'meet the constitutional requisites' while remaining sensitive to the concerns of federalism.

The district court had also reserved judgment on plaintiffs' motions for the appointments of a special master and a professional advisory committee to oversee implementation. Other enforcement threats were the plaintiffs' request for the creation of an advocacy unit to protect patient's rights and, if financing was lacking, an injunction against the state treasurer barring expenditures for 'nonessential State functions'.[63] Ultimately, the court applied none of these possible remedies. Instead, in response to persistent motions for enforcement action by the plaintiff class, the court placed the Alabama Board of Mental Health under receivership in an attempt to end violation of the *Wyatt* standards dealing with adequate habilitation, least restrictive services in the community, sufficient staff, client privacy, proper medication, and the prevention of client abuse. At his own request, the Governor of Alabama was appointed receiver and charged with the responsibility of overseeing the state's public mental institutions to ensure their operation in compliance with the court's decree. In 1987 – fifteen years after the *Wyatt* standards were first issued – Alabama agreed to a final settlement of the case whereby the defendants promised to adhere to the right to treatment and to implement the standards in exchange for termination of the court's direct receivership and active supervision. Thus the *Wyatt* mandate remains in force, with state officials making quarterly reports to enable the court to monitor their compliance, and with patients retaining legally enforceable rights to treatment under least restrictive conditions.[64]

New York's Willowbrook State School for the mentally retarded was the site of another epic case of judicial intervention into the lives of children and adult mental inmates. There in New York City, as many as 6,200 persons were crammed into understaffed and inhumane wards where each year they suffered some 2000 reported injuries. Locked in buildings giving off an 'overpowering stench of sweat, urine, and human excrement',[65] the residents of the world's largest mental-retardation institution suffered conditions hazardous to health, safety, sanity, and human development. Ruling on the basis of a constitutional right to protection from harm predicated under the Eighth and

Fourteenth Amendments, the court granted a preliminary injunction and ordered interim steps to prevent the residents' further deterioration. These orders included the hiring of additional attendants, physicians, nurses, recreation therapists, and physical therapists; the total ban on locked seclusion; relief from oppressive environmental conditions; and periodic reporting on the defendants' implementation of health, safety, and care measures.[66] After two years of further litigation and a full evidentiary hearing on plaintiffs' request for permanent relief, the parties jointly submitted and the court approved a consent order to transfer most Willowbrook residents to 'non-institutional community facilities and programs'.[67] In the words of the court's judgment and decree, the steps, standards and procedures set out under 23 headings of the *Willowbrook* order were based 'on the recognition that retarded persons, regardless of the degree of handicapping conditions, are capable of physical, intellectual, emotional and social growth, and . . . that a certain level of affirmative intervention and programming is necessary if that capacity for growth and development is to be preserved, and regression prevented'.[68]

The two most striking features of this exercise of equitable power were the creation of the Willowbrook Review Panel and the plans for radical deinstitutionalization. From the onset, the parties and the court accepted the need for an elaborate mechanism for monitoring the order's implementation, resolving disagreements of interpretation, and offering any resident, parent, guardian, or next-of-kin a venue for remedial action. The seven-member Panel, composed of recognized experts in the field of mental retardation and other appointees of the parties, received stipends, the aid of a full-time staff, office space, and other support services – all at the defendants' expense. Its duties included:

- assessing the defendants' progress in upgrading Willowbrook and creating new community services;
- making informal suggestions to spur compliance;
- issuing formal recommendations to defendants on steps to comply with the consent judgment;
- receiving reports from the defendants, the Consumer Advisory Board and the Professional Advisory Board (entities created under the consent order to investigate alleged dehumanizing practices and/or violations of human rights and advise on professional plans and programs);
- producing reports to the court and the parties on implementation progress, disagreements resolved, problems unresolved, any modifications of the court judgment recommended, and other appropriate matters; and
- seeking further orders of the court to interpret, modify, or enforce the court judgment.

Not surprisingly, this avenue for further resort to the court was often invoked by the Panel or the objecting parties. Over the next ten years, the federal district court was to issue orders on such tangled disputes as the exclusion of Hepatitis B carrier plaintiff children from the public schools; appropriations for community placement; the Panel's powers and procedures; staffing for the

Consumer Advisory Board; the plaintiffs' several motions for contempt of court for violations of the consent order; and the proposed transfer of plaintiffs to a newly constructed institution.[69]

The most heated battles centered on meeting the timetables for community placement of all but 250 of Willowbrook's residents. At the time the lawsuit was filed, 5,209 persons were residents. By transfers or deaths, the census had dropped over the next nine months to 4,727. Yet under the consent order, the defendants had fixed a period of six years – until April 1981 – as the deadline for reducing Willowbrook to a 250-bed facility for local residents. To fulfil this ambitious undertaking and avoid dumping residents into the streets or other inadequate institutions, the order required the defendants to supply a complex array of additional group homes, hostels, halfway houses, foster homes, sheltered workshops, day-care training programs, and other community placement services.[70] In a standard that was subsequently modified, the bulk of these community residential placements were to be made in small facilities with ten or fewer beds.[71] To finance this surge in community services, the state defendants in both specific and general terms were ordered to 'take all steps necessary to ensure the full and timely financing of this judgment, including, if necessary, submission of appropriate budget requests to the legislative branch of government'.[72] Although the legislature eventually chafed at the pressure created by the Willowbrook case, the community placements went forward, albeit at a slower pace than the consent order anticipated. While the deadlines were moved back, all of Willowbrook's residents were ultimately transferred to other locations. In the end, even with a new name and a new mandate to exist as a small institution, the stigma and horror attached to living or working on the grounds of Willowbrook (renamed the Staten Island Developmental Center) led to its closure by the state.

This decision also resulted from the mounting evidence that institutions such as Willowbrook could not offer integrated, normalizing and habilitative services meeting professional and legal standards. This observation had particular pertinence for the children of Willowbrook. Many of them had suffered neglect and isolation from families and the rest of society. In the now infamous Hepatitis virus experiments, some of these children were purposefully injected with the virus and contracted that disease in a program of nontherapeutic experimental research.[73] As a result, the consent order was studded with provisions intended to protect children. Taking specific note of the history of medical experimentation at Willowbrook, no further bio-medical research or experimentation was to be performed on its residents.[74] On the subject of education for plaintiffs under age 21, eleven specific provisions guaranteed each child 'a full and suitable education program, regardless of chronological age, degree of mental retardation or accompanying disabilities or handicaps'.[75] These standards provided for six-hour school days, maximum class sizes, some access to educational services in the community, year-round educational services for those requiring it, and staffing and other special-education standards generally equivalent to those provided for New York

City pupils.[76] In addition, resident living groups would in the future separate children from adults.[77] Toys, previously nonexistent or locked away, were now ordered to be readily accessible to children during their waking hours.[78] Children and other residents who lacked the active representation of a parent, relative or legal guardian would now be offered a spokesperson acting *in loco parentis*. These volunteers supplied by the Consumer Advisory Board (CAB) were to look out for their interests in such decisions as community placement, and the development of 'specific programming for an individual's normalization, including a projected date for his or her progress to a community setting . . ..'[79]

In the end, the CAB representatives, the Willowbrook Review Panel, and the court would conclude that normalization could not occur at Willowbrook or other large institutions.[80] The evidence further demonstrated that the educational and other programs for children on the institution's grounds remained inferior to those afforded their community counterparts. Therefore the Panel recommended that children receive a higher priority for transfer from Willowbrook than adults and that off-campus school placements be used more frequently until such residential transfers were effected.[81]

Symbolically and practically, the Willowbrook case, stands as a reminder that society can eliminate custodial warehouses for children with mental retardation. It also offers important lessons on the role and limitations of courts acting as beacons in that struggle.

Other cases have focused exclusively on institutions for juveniles. In *Gary W. v. Louisiana*, the federal district court examined the adequacy of the treatment programs offered to mentally disabled children transferred by public official to out-of-state facilities. In examining the 'State's historic role as *parens patriae* for mentally ill, mentally retarded, and physically handicapped children', the court held that 'mere custodial care far from home' would not discharge constitutional obligations.[82] Stressing the constitutional right to treatment in the least restrictive alternative, the court ordered the development of a treatment plan for each child individually tailored to his or her needs and the provision of such care, education, medical treatment, and personal treatment as will enable the child 'to realize his fullest potential, and equip him to live as normally as possible'.[83] After two years of defendants' failures to evaluate hundreds of children and to implement recommended plans for a majority of those already evaluated, the district court appointed a special master to act as a fact finder, monitor and hearing officer.[84] In Florida, the *Bobby M. v. Martinez* decree[85] required the creation of many small community-based programs for residents of state training schools. This state-wide class action on juvenile correctional services also ordered increased special-education services, restrictions on admission criteria, and the provision of on-site legal aid for residents. As a result of reports by the court-appointed monitors of noncompliance with community-care provisions, the court issued a new implementation order. In response, the Florida legislature passed the Juvenile Justice Reform Act of 1990 and appropriated $ 52 million for additional community services, including programs for juvenile delinquents with mental health needs.[86] Baltimore's foster children also prevailed in obtaining 'equitable relief in the form of an injunction that would require reforms of the foster care system'.[87] In another dramatic federal case, civil rights lawyers in Maryland brought a class action for the residents of the 450-bed Montrose State School, charging that its juvenile offender population was confined in prison-like conditions that produced alarming rates of suicide and mental disorder.[88] After extensive pre-trial discovery, negotiations between the parties, and lobbying of the legislature for new resources, the parties reached a settlement, enforced by court order, that closed Montrose and substituted a network of community-based services.

This pattern of extensive court-ordered community care is emerging in a number of states and treatment contexts. In the 1980s, for example, 38 class action suits on the right-to-habilitation were reported in 27 states and Washington, D.C. In many instances, the state defendants and governors requested their legislatures to approve substantial new funds for additional community services initiatives in order to satisfy the court judgments in those suits.[89] With those requests generally granted, plaintiffs' lawyers have been encouraged in the pursuit of injunctive remedies for a variety of classes of juveniles.

4. IMPLICATIONS OF PUBLIC LAW LITIGATION FOR CHILDREN'S RIGHTS

In the United States, children have become one of the under-represented groups who seek judicial protection from an indifferent majority and unresponsive officials. Their resort to the courts, particularly in the case of children with disabilities, came after the legislative and executive branches of government had failed to heed powerful pleas to aid those persons 'locked-up in institutions, shunned and neglected in their communities'.[90] However, the large-scale problems of exclusion from school, racial bias in special-education placement, brutal institutions, and the absence of decent community alternatives were beyond the capacity and competence of the courts to resolve alone.

Cases like *Wyatt* and *Mills* demanded a complex dynamic between the three branches of government, and between advocacy forces and the different levels of government. From the perspective of plaintiffs' lawyers, the courts were involved in exposing executive nonfeasance and malfeasance, crafting innovative remedies, stimulating Congress and state legislatures to respond with comprehensive laws and fresh appropriations, and then struggling to enforce both constitutional and statutory commands to apply new children's rights.

If these lawsuits had taken place in an ideal world, the image might have resembled a relay race in which the advocates handed off to the judiciary, the judiciary ruled and then passed the baton to the executive, the executive implemented the new rights within the available resources, and the executive routinely received from the legislature the requested resources to bring the race to a successful conclusion.[91] The realities, of course, all too often reflected adversarialness rather than teamwork, professional territoriality rather than children-centered concerns, competing priorities rather than consensus, and abdication of responsibilities rather than governmental accountability. To issue an equity decree on the right to treatment or the right to a suitable education, as judges soon discovered, was to begin, not end the legal implementation process. In an observation equally apt to other cases analyzed in this chapter, the *Larry P.* judge stated: 'The history of this litigation has demonstrated the failure of legislators and administrative agencies to confront problems that clearly had to be faced and it has revealed an all too typical willingness either to do nothing or to pass on issues to the courts'.[92]

The cases described in this chapter also exemplified a new mode of public interest litigation that flowered in the 1970s. Harvard Law professor Abram Chayes termed this model of class actions in the federal courts to change how governmental agencies treated disadvantaged groups as 'public law litigation'.[93] Its hallmark was prospective relief, generally through equitable injunctions that were specific, comprehensive and flexible enough to remedy broad-scale wrongs. Because this remedial process was not static, courts inevitably retained jurisdiction for many years and accepted the need for close judicial supervision of the decree. This supervision could be direct or indirect. The courts often forged a monitoring apparatus – such as a special master, human rights committee, review panel, or advisory board – to act as extensions of their judicial power. Although the decree was binding and coercive, its elements were frequently the result of negotiation between the parties and affected professional organizations participating as amici curiae. This type of litigation often mobilized many groups and actors to aid the plaintiff class. Through the rules of civil procedure and the inventiveness of judges, broad participation in the suit was possible, and even encouraged through wide definitions of plaintiff and defendant class, liberal opportunities for intervention by affected parties, amicus curiae motions, and public meetings organized by review panels and others to communicate with interest constituencies.

This type of litigation provided a visible focus for reform activity in the fields of mental health, mental retardation, and children's services. In many cases, it proved capable of bringing both tangible and intangible benefits to a class of children who otherwise lacked the champions, money, and political muscle to gain those benefits through alternative courses of action. The results in terms of increases in budget, staffing, and the quantity and quality of services provided were sometimes impressive. For example, total spending for mental-retardation community services programs soared nationally from $ 879 million in 1977 to $ 5.6 billion in 1988 (a 226% increase over this period after adjusting for inflation), a development correlated on a state-by-state basis with civil rights litigation and consumer advocacy variables.[94]

This litigation also had its drawbacks and critics. Similarly situated children who were not under the umbrella of a class action equitable decree might see resources drained away from their needs. Lawyers for classes of thousands of plaintiffs often had little opportunity to gauge first-hand the effects of sweeping judicial orders on, in one commentator's phrase, the 'unconsenting footsoliders' in these judicial wars.[95] Since there was no sharp line between law and policy in defining and enforcing children's treatment and education rights, courts could be accused of acting as an imperial judiciary, usurping political prerogatives, and adding to the woes of schools and institutions already saddled with awesome responsibilities. One of the difficulties of permanent injunctions and their ongoing judicial supervision was the lack of certainty as to the duration of the court's involvement and the preconditions for ending that regime. Whether through lack of will or adequate resources, defendants were often found in only partial compliance with the court's decrees. Eventually the gap between the ambitious ends of the litigation and the partial results achieved might erode respect for the rule of law. To minimize that risk, courts sometimes relied too heavily on procedural relief that, while more familiar to judges and thus easier to frame, might misdirect attention from the deeper reforms needed.

In the 1990s, suits for broad injunctive relief for persons with disabilities are going forward. Despite more conservative judicial tendencies as a result of recent Supreme Court opinions[96] and wholesale changes in the composition of the bench, such judicial complaints are still routinely filed. Courts continue to be called upon to fill the gaps in legislative or executive provision through a mixture of formal and informal means (e.g., cajoling, publicizing abuses). The use of the sturdy equitable injunction remains the mainstay of civil rights enforcement. Its effectiveness has been demonstrated in cases aiding juvenile clients and reforming systems of special education, child care, and disability services long resistant to other advocacy strategies.[97] As one recent empirical study concludes, class action litigation has emerged as a key form of interest group activity and the 'linkage between interest group activity and spending [for new community services] can be direct and powerful'.[98]

The impact of cases like *Wyatt*, *Willowbrook*, and *Mills* is also reflected in their concepts, standards and principles that have now firmly entered into statutory law and professional practice. The concepts of individual treatment plans, individual education plans, least restrictive environments, and accessible advocacy services accessible to isolated clients – first pioneered in the disability field – have also taken root in statutes and precedents for various juvenile populations.[99] Although equitable remedies often produce only partial compliance, it is important to recall that legislative and executive commands to respect children's rights are no less prone to be ignored or compromised. Indeed, the steady flow of new filings on behalf of disabled children – as well as more recently recognized classes of vulnerable children such as homeless children[100] – suggests that equitable relief works and is still perceived as a productive means to realize children's rights.

5. CONCLUSION

Equitable relief for children with disabilities has undergone many transformations. Ancient forms of such relief focused on the property rather than the well-being of such a child. In addition to the wardship or guardianship process of throwing some judicial protection over the individual, there are now class-oriented actions and remedies to aid large groups of victimized children.

This chapter suggests that principles of equity coupled with the modern powers of constitutional jurisprudence can offer powerful engines for the defense of children's rights. Whether countries without written constitutions, or legal cultures of judicial activism can achieve comparable results is beyond the scope of this discussion.[101] Certainly the Convention on the Rights of the Child and the incorporation of its basic outlines in domestic children's charters raise anew the role of courts in turning children's paper rights into real rights.[102] The United States experience suggest that a judiciary can tailor injunctive relief to meet wide-scale problems of child mistreatment once a fundamental rights violation has been adjudicated. As this disability-rights litigation reveals, equity decrees have also indirectly spurred remedial legislation, regulations, and additional spending at state and federal government levels. Perhaps its most critical contribution is that the needs and rights of distressed children have become more visible. The trials, the bold remedies, and the attendant publicity have alerted the citizenry to alarming gulfs between myths of a child-centered culture and the realities of neglected disabled youth. Like the equity petitions of old, the young now cry out in 'piteous terms' for remedies from the powerful.

NOTES

1. L. Henkin, *The Age of Rights* (1990) pp. 159–160.
2. 'The rights idea so depends on the judiciary as to require less concern with the niceties of old equity practice, deriving from a tradition that did not count on the judiciary to vindicate rights against government, and to warrant greater imagination in the use of remedies by state as well as by federal courts, under state and federal constitutions'. Id. at 105.
3. 'Equity will not suffer a wrong to be without a remedy'. This maxim has been described as a central idea of equity since 'no wrong should be allowed to go unredressed if it is capable of being remedied by courts of justice, and this really underlies the whole jurisdiction of equity'. R. Megarry and P. Baker, *Snell's Principles of Equity* (27th ed. 1973), London, Sweet and Maxwell, 27.
4. For discussion of cases of that type, see Part 3 on equitable remedies and the American experience, *infra*.
5. W. Blackstone, I *Commentaries on the Laws of England* (1765) 292, 294.
6. S. Herr, *Rights and Advocacy for Retarded People* (1983) D.C. Heath, Lexington, Mass., p. 10.
7. 4 Co. Rep. 123, 125b, 76 Eng. Rep. 1118, 1124 (K.B. 1604).
8. R. Megarry and P. Baker, *supra* note 3, at 531.
9. See G. Keeton and L. Sheridan, *Equity* 5 (2nd ed. 1976).

10. R. Megarry and P. Baker, *supra* note 3, at 531 (citing the Law Reform (Miscellaneous Provisions) Act, 1949, s. 9).

11. W. Holdsworth, *A History of English Law* vol. 6 648–650 (2nd ed. 1937, reprinted 1966); W. Holdsworth vol. 5, *supra*, 309–315, Methuen & Co., London.

12. G. Keeton and L. Sheridan, *supra* note 9, at 55.

13. W. Ashburner, *Principles of Equity* (D. Browne 2nd ed. 1933), London, Butterworth, p. 21.

14. F. W. Maitland, in J. Brunyate (ed.), *Equity: A Course of Lectures* (1969), Cambridge University Press, London, 4.

15. Exodus 22: 20–23, quoted in H. Cohn, *Ancient Jewish Equity*, in *Equity in the World's Legal Systems: A Comparative Study Dedicated to Rene Cassin* (1973), Brussels, Etablissement E. Bruylant, 51.

16. Id. at 61, quoting Leviticus 25: 35.

17. Id. at 63.

18. 2 A. de Tocqueville, in Reeves (ed.), *Democracy in America* (1954) Vintage Books, NY, 343. See Rabinowitz v. New Jersey State Board of Education, 550 F. Supp. 481, 482 (DNJ 1982) ('For centuries the handicapped and retarded have been treated with neglect and too often with abuse. Belatedly such persons have been accorded the respect, dignity and assistance to which they are entitled.').

19. J. Bishop, 'Children Who Slip Through the Cracks' *Md. Bar Journal* (Nov. 1990), at 23.

20. For the decision of Canada's Supreme Court prohibiting, under the parens patriae power, non-therapeutic sterilization without the consent of a person with mental retardation, see *Re Eve* (1986), 2 S.C.R. 388.

21. Wentzel v. Montgomery General Hospital, 293 Md. 685, 702 (1982), *cert. denied*, 459 US 1147 (1983) (refusing to authorize sterilization of a mentally retarded teenager based on the court's inherent equitable powers).

22. P. Wald, in M. Kindred, J. Cohen, D. Penrod and T. Shaffer (eds.), 'Basic Personal and Civil Rights', in *The Mentally Retarded Citizen and the Law* 3 (1976), Free Press, NY ('The past few years have seen an explosion of litigation on behalf of mentally retarded persons').

23. 347 US 483 (1954).

24. E.g., Swann v. Charlotte-Mecklenburg Board of Education, 402 US 1 (1971) (defining equitable powers to eliminate one-race schools, change school-attendance zones, and use bussing for the purpose of desegregation).

25. M. Ziegler, 'Future Strategies for Advocacy', in *The Legal Rights of Citizens with Mental Retardation* 274, 276 (L. Kane, P. Brown & J. Cohen eds., 1988) University Press of America: London. Such due process hearings first required in *Mills* and *PARC* were subsequently mandated by Congress nationally under Public Law 94-142.

26. S. Herr, 'The Right to an Appropriate Free Public Education' in *The Mentally Retarded Citizen and the Law*, *supra* note 22, at 251, 256.

27. P. Friedman, *The Rights of Mentally Retarded Persons* (1976), Avon Books, NY, 103. For a list of those states, see S. Herr, *supra* note 26, at 262.

28. Public Law No. 94–142, codified 20 USC Sections 1401-1461 (1976).

29. Rabinowitz v. New Jersey State Board of Education, 550 F. Supp. 481, 485, 486-7 (DNJ 1982) (interpreting domicile and age eligibility requirements for those under age 5 and over age 18). See generally, L. Rothstein, *Special Education Law* (1990); H. Turnbull, *Free Appropriate Public Education: The Law and Children with Disabilities* (1990).

30. Board of Education of the Hendrick Hudson Central School District v. Rowley, 458 US 176, 192–200 (1982).

31. 20 USC section 1412(5).

32. US Department of Education, *Tenth Annual Report to Congress on the Implementation of the Education of the Handicapped Act* (1988).

33. Mills v. Board of Education, 348 F. Supp. 866, 876 (DDC 1972) (emphasis added).

34. D. Biklen, *Mental Retardation: Advances in Education and Rehabilitation Technology*, *supra* note 25, at 241.

35. US President's Committee on Mental Retardation, *The Six Hour Retarded Child* (1969); J. Mercer, *Labeling the Mentally Retarded* (1973); *Placing Children in Special Education: A Strategy for Equity* (K. Heller, W. Holtzman & S. Messick eds., 1969); J. Mercer, 'Sociological Perspectives on Mild Mental Retardation', in *Social-Cultural Aspects of Mental Retardation* 378, 391 (C. Haywood ed., 1970) (questioning whether the assignment to the deviant status of mentally retarded during the school years for persons who later escape that status was necessary or desirable), Appleton Century Crofts, NY.

36. E.g., Diana v. Board of Education, No. C-70-37 RFP (ND Cal. June 18, 1973) (stipulating that Hispanic children should receive nondiscriminatory special education placement). See M. Sorgen, 'Classification and Labeling', in *The Mentally Retarded Citizen and the Law*, *supra* note 22, 214–44; J. Mercer, *Sociological Perspectives on Mild Mental Retardation*, *supra* note 35, at 288 (documenting that Spanish-surnamed children had higher probability of being labeled mental retarded than other white or black children).

37. 343 F. Supp. 1306 (ND Cal. 1972), *aff'd*, 502 F.2d 963 (9th Cir. 1974), 495 F. Supp. 926 (ND Cal. 1979) (permanent injunction), *aff'd in part & rev'd in part*, 793 F.2d 969 (9th Cir. 1984).

38. 343 F. Supp. at 1311.

39. Id.

40. Id. at 1315.

41. 502 F.2d 963, 964–965, citing with approval Prendergast v. N.Y. Telephone Co., 263 US 43, 50 (1923).

42. Id., citing with approval, Tanner Motor Livery, Ltd. v. Avis. Inc., 316 F.2d 804, 809 (9th Cir. 1963).

43. 495 F. Supp. at 934.

44. Id. at 991. Q 992.

45. Larry P. by Lucille P. v. Riles, 793 F.2d 969 (9th Cir. 1984), opinion amended in denying request for rehearing (1986).

46. Id. at 980.

47. Id. at 984.

48. Id. at 988 (Enright, J., dissenting).

49. Lora v. Board of Education of City of New York, 456 F. Supp. 1211, 1276 (EDNY 1978), *vacated in part & aff'd in part*, 623 F.2d 248 (2nd Cir. 1980), *on remand*, 587 F. Supp. 1572 (EDNY 1984) (approving stipulations on retraining teachers and clinicians and other steps to avoid bias in special education referral, assessment, classification, and placement; implementing 'nondiscriminatory standards and procedures' designed to eliminate linguistic, cultural and ethnic bias and to assure each child's placement in the appropriate least restrictive environment). Id. at 1574–1581.

50. Matter of Ana Maria R., 98 Misc.2d 910, 414 N.Y.S.2d 982, 986–7 (Fam. Ct., N.Y. Co. 1979).

51. 325 F. Supp. 781 (M.D. Ala. 1971), 334 F. Supp. 1341 (1972), 344 F. Supp. 373 (1972), 344 F. Supp. 387 (1972), *aff'd sub nom.* Wyatt v. Aderholt, 503 F.2d 1305 (5th Cir. 1974).

52. Wyatt v. Stickney No. 3195-N, Memorandum Transcript of the Testimony of Dr. Phillip Roos, Feb. 29, 1972 (M.D. Ala 1972), reprinted in M. Perlin, II *Mental Disability Law – Civil and Criminal* 75, 88 (1989), Michie: Charlottesville, VA.

53. 325 F. Supp. at 784 ('Adequate and effective treatment is constitutionally required because, absent treatment, the hospital is transformed 'into a penitentiary where one could be held indefinitely for no convicted offense.' Ragsdale v. Overholser, 281 F.2d 943, 950 (DC Cir. 1960).').

54. Id. at 785.

55. 325 F. Supp. at 785.

56. Id.

57. The amici included the American Association on Mental Deficiency, the American

Psychological Association, the American Orthopsychiatric Association, and the American Civil Liberties Union.

58. 344 F. Supp. 373, 375.
59. Wyatt v. Stickney, 344 F. Supp. at 386, App. A, Standard 32. (a), (c)–(e).
60. Id. at 387.
61. Id. at 392 n. 10.
62. Wyatt v. Aderholt, 503 F.2d 1305, 1318 (5th Cir. 1974).
63. 344 F. Supp. 373, 377 (placing defendants on notice that their failure to make satisfactory and timely compliance with the decrees would obligate the court to appoint a special master).
64. Barnes v. Dale, 530 So.2d 770, 780, 785 (Ala. 1988) (conferring immunity on state employees who discharge patients pursuant to the *Wyatt* standards even though a patient may harm a member of the public, since discharge power is an exercise of a discretionary public function).
65. New York State Association for Retarded Children v. Rockefeller (hereinafter *Willowbrook* case), No. 72-C-356/357, Complaint at 22 (EDNY, filed March 1972).
66. 357 F. Supp. at 768–770.
67. *Willowbrook Case* Consent Order, App. A, Standard V.1., No. 72-C-356/357, April 30, 1975, *approved*, 393 F. Supp. 715 (EDNY 1975).
68. Id. at para. 1.
69. 544 F. Supp. 330, 334 n. 3 (EDNY 1982).
70. *Willowbrook Case* Consent Order, *supra* note 67, at V.1–V.14.
71. Id. V.4. For mildly retarded persons, the size of community residences was limited to fifteen beds. Id. In 1983, the appellate court ordered a modification of these limits up to fifty beds in response to defendants' pleas for greater flexibility in the face of housing shortages and other factors delaying the creation of new group homes in the New York City area. In cases involving the ongoing judicial oversight of a complex remedy, the court emphasized the need for oversight of a complex remedy, the court emphasized the need for flexibility in the face of changed conditions and for 'phased implementation and small alterations in strategic objectives as new knowledge is acquired'. *The Willowbrook Case*, 706 F.2d 956, 970 (2nd Cir. 1983) (quoting Note, 'Implementation Problems in Institutional Reform Litigation', *Harvard Law Review* 91, 428, 436 (1977)).
72. *Willowbrook Case* Consent Order, *supra* note 67, at para. 3. *See also* standards V.4.–5., 8., 14.
73. See New York University Medical Center, Urban Health Affairs Program, *Proceedings of the Symposium on Ethical Issues in Human Experimentation: The Case of Willowbrook State Hospital Research* (May 4, 1972).
74. *Willowbrook Case* Consent Order, *supra* note 67, at P. 4.
75. Id. at F. 1.
76. Id. at F. 1.–11. Other specific standards required bilingual/bicultural instruction for residents from Spanish-speaking backgrounds; specially designed services for blind, deaf, and multi-handicapped pupils; and the availability of all necessary classroom materials and equipment. Id. at 6, 8, 11.
77. Id. at A. 3.
78. Id. at B. 7.
79. Id V. 11., W. 3., 7.
80. See New York State Association for Retarded Children v. Carey, No. 72 Civ. 356/357 (EDNY June 10, 1977) (barring transfers to new developmental center on the grounds that parties had agreed on normalization as the ultimate goal and community care as the ultimate placement for Willowbrook class members).
81. Willowbrook Review Panel, Report to the Court 49–50 (Dec. 1978).
82. 437 F. Supp. 1209, 1222–23 (E.D. La. 1976).
83. Id. at 1225.
84. Gary W. v. Louisiana, 601 F.2d 240 (5th Cir. 1979) (affirming trial court's discretion

to appoint a special master and noting that such relief is not extraordinary in institutional reform cases).

85. No. TCA 83-7003 MMP (ND Fla. May 7, 1987), summarized in *Mental & Physical Disability Law Reporter* 11, 237 (1987).

86. 'Update on Florida Juvenile Justice Class Action', *Mental & Physical Disability Law Reporter* 14, 389 (1990).

87. L.J. by and through Darr v. Massigna, 699 F. Supp. 508, 509 (D. Md. 1988) (ordering preliminary injunction and approving consent decree to prevent maltreatment of children in foster homes, set caseworkers case-load maximums, and require additional services and process safeguards for children and their natural families).

88. R.L. v. Maryland, Settlement and Order (D. Md. July 1988).

89. D. Braddock and G. Fujiura, 'Politics, Public Policy, and the Development of Community Retardation Services in the United States', *American Journal of Mental Retardation* 95, 369, 372 (1991) (No. 4, 369–387).

90. Telegram of President John F. Kennedy to all state governors, July 24, 1963, reprinted in White House Conference on Mental Retardation, *Proceedings* 7 (1963).

91. For one judge's view of interactions between governmental branches and other actors in this type of litigation, see Bazelon, 'Institutionalization, Deinstitutionalization and the Adversary Process', *Columbia Law Review* 75, 897 (1975) ('The process of accountability . . . which the court must guarantee, starts with self-scrutiny and includes *ongoing oversight* by peers, by other concerned disciplines, by the legislature, and ultimately by the public at large.'). Id. at 911–912.

92. Larry P. v. Riles, 495 F. Supp. 926, 932 (ND Cal. 1979).

93. Chayes, 'The Role of the Judge in Public Law Litigation', *Harvard L. Rev.* 89, 1281 (1976).

94. Braddock and Fujiura, *supra* note 89, 376–377, 382–383.

95. R. Mnookin, *In the Interest of the Child: Advocacy, Law Reform, and Public Policy* (1985, Freeman, NY), 10.

96. E.g., Youngberg v. Romeo, 457 US 307 (1982).

97. See, e.g. Martin A. v. Gross, 546 N.Y.S.2d 75 (A.D. 1 Dept. 1989) (upholding preliminary injunctions to provide preventive services reasonably calculated to preserve family integrity for homeless children, to permit them to live in adequate housing with their families rather than foster homes, and to restrain state from imposing a 90-day limit on emergency shelter care for homeless families).

98. Braddock and Fujiura, *supra* note 89, at 372.

99. See text accompanying notes 85–88. In the Montrose School case, the plaintiffs relied on mental disability law precedents and implementation experience to obtain stipulated relief closing an institution for juvenile delinquents, developing individual treatment plans, and providing least restrictive services in the community. Previous efforts to accomplish such reforms through lobbying efforts with the legislature had failed.

100. Herr, 'Children Without Homes: Rights to Education and to Family Stability', *U. Miami Law Review* 45, 337 (1990–91).

101. On the narrower use of injunctions by English courts and equity's 'special care concerning minors', see H. Hanbury and R. Maudsley, *Modern Equity* 694–763 (J. Martin ed. 13th ed. 1989), London, Stevens & Sons.

102. Convention on the Rights of the Child, UN Doc. A/Res/44/23 (1989), reprinted in I.L.M. 28, 1448 (1989). See generally, *Children's Rights in America: UN Convention on the Rights of the Child Compared with United States Law* (C. Cohen and H. Davidson, eds., 1990), American Bar Association: Washington.

JANET R. FINK*

22. Cocaine's Smallest Victims: Advocacy on Behalf of Drug-exposed Infants

1. INTRODUCTION

The epidemic of drug abuse, which has swept across the United States since the mid-1980's, has had its most devastating effects upon the young. Far more than opiates or other substances, usage of 'crack', a smokeable derivative of cocaine which has been called the 'junk-food of the drug business',[1] has become especially pervasive among young people, particularly women of prime child-bearing ages, i.e., sixteen to twenty-five. A new generation of cocaine-exposed children, now approaching school-age, is growing up with a myriad of special needs; as a wealth of medical evidence demonstrates, these children are afflicted with a disproportionate share of physical and developmental disabilities and present special challenges to the legal system.

The intense debate over appropriate legal responses – e.g., civil child abuse and neglect actions, criminal prosecutions of mothers for pre-natal transmission of drugs to infants, civil commitment or criminal intervention during pregnancy – have strained the already-delicate balance existing between the rights and interests of children, their parents and the State and have all-too often left questions of how to secure vital treatment and other services to meet the critical needs of these children unanswered.

The dilemma facing child advocates is multi-faceted and the issues numerous. If voluntary efforts either fail or are not available to serve families in their communities, what coercive role, if any, should the legal system assume to protect children at risk? At what point, if any, does a recognition of independent children's rights require parents' rights to be superseded or even terminated in order to secure needed services? Can the needs and interests of children be protected without causing a seemingly-inevitable clash of parental and children's rights? How can children's fundamental rights to healthy births and nurturing, safe development be accommodated with established constitutional conceptions of parental bodily integrity, familial autonomy and

* State Assembly, New York.

M. Freeman and P. Veerman (eds.), The Ideologies of Children's Rights, 311–322.
© 1992 *Kluwer Academic Publishers. Printed in the Netherlands.*

privacy? This article addresses these quandaries from the standpoint of the children's legal advocates, delineates the role of attorneys for children in drug-exposure cases and articulates an appropriate role for the legal system in meeting the unmet needs of these innocent victims of the scourge of drugs.

2. COCAINE-EXPOSED CHILDREN: ACUTE PROBLEMS, ACUTE NEEDS

While research on the harmful effects of crack is still in its infancy – as recent as 1982, high-risk obstetrics texts maintained that cocaine had no dele-terious effects upon fetuses[2] – numerous recent studies have documented that cocaine readily passes across the sponge-like placenta and 'almost no cocaine-exposed baby fully escapes its damaging effects'.[3] While the most serious teratogenic effects occur during the first trimester of pregnancy, when the brain and other vital organs are in formation, cocaine-induced complications have been reported in all phases of pregnancy; post-natal damage has occurred as well through breast-feeding.[4]

The risk of infant mortality, exacerbated by the prematurity and low birth-weight endemic to this population, is considerable. The high incidence of maternal hypertension has been shown to cause *abruptio placentae*, a tearing of the placenta from the uterine lining causing premature labor, and placental haemorhage.[5] Sudden Infant Death Syndrome is five to ten times more likely to occur among cocaine-exposed than drug-free infants and is considerably more prevalent than among infants exposed to heroine and methadone.[6] Hepatitis, syphilis and AIDS, transmitted in utero, correlate highly with, although are not directly caused by, cocaine exposure, due to the frequent poly-substance abuse and sexual activity of crack-users. Indeed, AIDS is the ninth leading cause of death among children aged one to four and, within three to four years, is expected to be the fifth leading cause of death among Americans up to the age of twenty-four.[7] Thus, children who survive early childhood and reach school-age have already overcome significant odds.

Congenital deformities, such as the absence of middle fingers and malformed kidneys and genitals, have been observed in disproportionate numbers among cocaine-exposed infants. Motor difficulties, which impact upon children's abilities to explore and learn about their environments, are estimated to be forty times more prevalent among cocaine-exposed infants than the population at large.[8]

However, the greatest challenges to policy-makers and to the legal system may stem, not so much from the serious medical difficulties encountered by drug-exposed children, as much from the severe neuro-behavioral deficits they experience. The low birth-weight, as well as below-average length and head circumference, manifested in a significant number of these children may be predictors of learning disabilities.[9] While displaying normal, although low-range intelligence, many cocaine-exposed children display such severe deficits in relating and reacting to adults and their environments, as well as organizing creative play, that they resemble mildly autistic or personality-disordered children.[10]

Although it is premature to assess whether the emotional and organizational deficits manifested in cocaine-exposed children are entirely reversible, it is clear that early intervention, both in pre-school and medical milieus, have proven promising. The Perinatal Center for Chemical Dependence in Chicago, for example, has developed specialized protocols for caring for, and training parents or other care-givers in caring for, cocaine-exposed infants – methods which have shown progress in addressing the infants' agitation and rapid mood-swings and facilitating bonding, stimulation and capacity for engaging in play.[11] New York City's Northside Early Childhood Center in Harlem, a preschool program for children with learning disabilities, many of whom were exposed to crack before birth, has had demonstrable success; half of its graduating five-year olds have been able to enter regular, rather than special education, kindergarten classes after one year of intensive one-on-one intervention.[12]

Although preliminary indications from research at Brookwood Child Care, a Brooklyn foster care agency, imply that perhaps half of the drug-exposed children develop *without* drug-induced developmental delays,[13] it is clear that a large number of the children will require special education, as well as other medical and therapeutic assistance, during their critical pre-school years. While a few model programs exist or are in development nationally, waiting lists abound and many children remain unserved.

Special education services are not yet in place to handle the influx of drug-exposed children now entering their pre-school and school years. Public Law 99–457, the 1986 amendment to the federal Education for the Handicapped Act (EHA), mandates, under Section 619, that states provide comprehensive services to children aged three to five, either directly or by contract, or face a loss of their entire EHA allocation. Family involvement must be encouraged and 'Individualized Education Plans' must encompass teaching parenting skills, if appropriate. Part H of the Act requires that, during a five year phase-in period, states must provide a comprehensive range of child and parenting services to children from infancy through age two exhibiting developmental delays in one or more areas and may provide services to children *at risk* of such delays. 'Individualized Family Service Plans' utilizing a 'least restrictive alternative' standard must be developed within forty-five days, with a multi-disciplinary assessment and significant parental involvement. New York, California, Florida, New Hampshire, New Jersey, Oregon and Utah are in their third year of planning. All other states are in their fourth year, during which programs must be put into place in readiness for the fifth year when such programs must be available to all who are eligible. However, as the Mental Health Law Project has documented, compliance with the planning provisions and timetables of Public Law 99–457 has been erratic nationally.[14]

Likewise, many of these children require child welfare services which are all too often not available in their communities. Preventive programs geared to avert the need for placement by providing intensive assistance to parents and children together are insufficient to meet the ever-growing need. 'Home-builders' and other models for intensive, home-based services exist but on a woefully small scale. Comprehensive programs providing a multiplicity of needed services, including drug treatment, both for pregnant women and women with small children, are scarce.[15]

While empowering more families to care for children at home is critically important, appropriate foster care options need to be enhanced for those children who require it. Child abuse and neglect tripled in the United States between 1986 and 1988; in New York City, the child abuse and neglect caseload of the Legal Aid Society's Juvenile Rights Division jumped over 600% between 1983 and 1989. These increases were largely traceable to the crack epidemic, as 2/3 of the Juvenile Rights Division's child protective cases included allegations of parental substance abuse. A similar percentage of cases resulted in placement of children out of their homes, placing incalculable strains on an already-overburdened foster care system.[16] New York City, Los Angeles and Washington, D.C. were not alone among metropolitan areas caught with insufficient foster homes when the crack epidemic hit; unfortunately, 'boarder baby' became a nationally-recognized term of art. Enhanced foster home recruitment efforts, prompted at least in New York City by class action litigation, has eased the shortage of foster homes for 'boarder babies' and young children bounced from one overnight placement to another. However, the continued vigor required for this effort, in order that the supply of homes can keep pace with the ever-increasing demand and so that children are not relegated inappropriately to congregate care settings, has proven difficult for the deficit-ridden City government to sustain.

While drug exposure *per se* does not dictate the need for foster care, many cocaine-exposed infants are abandoned at birth and face no alternative; the pervasive pattern of multi-generational drug use,[17] effectively converting some homes to crack dens, places an additional segment of this population in imminent risk if they remain at home.

Optimally, foster care for drug-exposed children should be therapeutic and geared to meet their special needs, but therapeutic foster home programs, such as the 'cluster' or 'satellite' model of community-based homes sharing clinical and preventive services utilized by the Center for Family Life in New York City, are in their infancy. Kinship foster homes represent an untapped resource for many children who otherwise might require placement with strangers, but these homes, too, must be carefully screened, supervised and therapeutically supported. As a result of a lawsuit, as well as legislative and regulatory reforms, New York City currently places approximately half (over 20,000 children) of its vast foster care population in kinship foster homes, but problems remain in securing prompt evaluations, adequate supervision and clinical and financial resources for these homes.

3. ROLE OF ATTORNEYS FOR DRUG-EXPOSED CHILDREN

The acute medical, educational and affective needs of drug-exposed children compel an especially rigorous role for counsel, even for children in a pre-verbal stage of development. To the degree that the capacities of these young children are not sufficiently developed to assume full competence when confronted with the maze of complex legal decisions inherent in the judicial process, the need for counsel becomes ever-more compelling.[18] Counsel is critical in order to secure children's entitlements proactively and to protect their rights and interests in the many cases which reach the juvenile and family courts. Assurance of adequate counsel for children in child protective proceedings nationally, and, in particular, for special needs children including many of the drug-exposed population, however, remains an elusive goal, as many have no access to advocates at all or, at minimum, to effective advocates.

Unfortunately, although with the impetus of the children's advocacy mandate of the federal Child Abuse Prevention and Treatment Act of 1974 [42 USC. 5101–5115], forty-one states have enacted mandates for representation of children in child protective proceedings, only twenty-five of these require the advocates to be trained attorneys and only two of these states (New York and New Jersey) specifically include articulation of the children's wishes as part of the attorney's function.[19] While lay advocates, such as those provided by the growing Court Appointed Special Advocates movement, can be helpful in performing certain functions, including monitoring compliance with court orders, children require attorneys to assure that their rights and interests are protected on a par with those of other parties.

Children stand at the center of such proceedings as subject and object and have enormous stakes in the outcome. Facing possible removal from their homes and severance or suspension of ties with siblings and other family members, they may have the most to lose by the courts' decisions, even if the proceeding is geared toward meeting their special treatment needs. Representation of children in child protective proceedings includes conveying their wishes and preferences, if these are discernible, but extends way beyond this advocacy function, particularly for younger children. Children who are the subjects of such proceedings have rights and interests in remaining alive, in having their special needs fulfilled so that they can develop adequately, in being protected from physical injury and psychological damage and in being fed, clothed and educated. They have an interest in remaining in their own homes and in maintaining parental, sibling and extended family ties; they thus have a right to have every effort made to maintain them at home or, at minimum, with family members unless this would subject them to imminent risk of maltreatment or neglect. If such efforts fail and they cannot be maintained or returned home, they have a right to permanence and stability within a caring, nurturing family, rather than to be wards in institutions or bounced through a succession of temporary shelters or homes.[20]

The attorney's zealous role is dictated, not only by the statutory and constitutional obligation to ensure protection of children's rights, but also by compelling ethical concerns. Canon 7 of the *Lawyer's Code of Professional Responsibility* states that '[a] lawyer should represent a client zealously and within the bounds of the law', – educating the client as to the options pursuant to the attorney's 'counsellor-at-law' function, but ultimately deferring to the client for decisions on the case and resolving doubts as to the bounds of the law in the client's favor.[21] Significantly, although authorizing attorneys to make legal arguments, the *Code* specifically prohibits attorneys from expressing personal opinions about the merits of a case.[22]

For a client with verbal skills and judgmental capacity, the attorney's role as described above may be straightforward but in the case of infants and young children, it is far more complex. The *Lawyer's Code* recognizes that the attorney's responsibilities necessarily vary according to the age or other disabilities of the client, with the magnitude of these responsibilities increasing for young children. However, regardless of disability, 'if the client is capable of understanding . . . or contributing to the advancement of his interests, . . . the lawyer should obtain from him all possible aid'. Even where the child is too young to make judgments binding upon the lawyer, the lawyer must look to the child for whatever degree of assistance the child can provide. Where a guardian *ad litem* has been appointed, the attorney can look to the guardian for decisions otherwise made by clients. However, the *Code* provides that:

> if the disability of a client and lack of legal representative compel the lawyer
> to make decisions for his client, the lawyer should consider all circumstances
> then prevailing and act with care to safeguard and advance the interests
> of his client.[23]

These dictates are mirrored as well in the American Bar Association's various standards applicable to lawyers. The *Model Rules of Professional Conduct*, applicable in some states, provide that, notwithstanding a client's disabilities, including age, 'the lawyer shall, as far as reasonably possible, maintain a normal client-lawyer relationship with the client'. Under the *Rules*, the lawyer may seek appointment of a guardian *ad litem* or take other protective action 'only when the lawyer reasonably believes the client cannot adequately act in the client's own interest'.[24] Similarly, the Institute for Judicial Administration/American Bar Association *Juvenile Justice Standards* emphasize advocacy of client's wishes where they can be determined and appointment of a guardian *ad litem* if substituted judgment is necessary. In the absence of a separate guardian, the *Standards* authorize attorneys either to remain neutral and simply test the evidence adduced or to 'adopt the position requiring the least intrusive intervention justified by the juvenile's circumstances'.[25]

Representation of the children's complex interests compel complex training and inter-disciplinary expertise on the part of the advocate, as well as access to adequate social work and clinical assistance.[26] Because the juvenile and family courts are 'socio-legal' in nature,[27] courts whose decisions must be grounded in social services and clinical disciplines, the tasks of the children's lawyer must be performed with an extra measure of sensitivity and competence. In short, the child's lawyer must be a 'lawyer-plus'.[28]

4. LEGAL SYSTEM RESPONSES: CRIMINAL AND CIVIL INTERVENTION

The sad plight of children of drug abusers has spawned a variety of responses from policy-makers and participants in the court system, all too often of marginal utility in meeting the desperate needs of these children. From the standpoint of children's advocates, developing an appropriate and constructive response is a delicate task which can be likened to treading rocky shoals in dangerous waters. What is most clear, however, is that policies and modes of intervention which strengthen families and communities are likely also to meet the needs of children; punitive responses, which exacerbate deterioration in the fabric of families and communities, are likely to produce the opposite effect.

Calls for criminalization of pre-natal transmission of drugs, criminal intervention against mothers of drug-exposed infants, civil commitment of drug-abusing pregnant women and removal of drug-exposed infants to large, congregate-care facilities constitute an assault upon the already sensitive balance of children's, parental and governmental rights and interests and are of dubious efficacy in serving the children such policies are ostensibly designed to protect.

Indeed, the consequences of such intervention must be carefully assessed, so that the cure for the pediatric drug problem does not become worse than the disease. Former American drug 'czar' William Bennett's 'dark prophecy' of wholesale removal of drug-exposed infants from their families into orphanages must be a rallying point for both parents' and children's advocates.

> His ideas . . . belong to an American tradition of authoritarian reform that has over the long run achieved very little. The authoritarian approach to problems is typically both paternalistic and punitive, and its reliance on criminalization . . . has tended to weaken the very social institutions it claims to want to serve.[29]

Even apart from the complex constitutional questions raised by such initiatives, practical considerations from the children's standpoint cast serious doubt as to the appropriateness of these initiatives. Resort to coercive measure, in particular, through the criminal justice system, is not likely to deter drug use during pregnancy but is instead likely to deter women from seeking needed pre-natal care, drug treatment even where available, and medical and other services for children once born. Moreover, few jails, prisons or psychiatric facilities have facilities for children or drug treatment programs and many are woefully deficient in the quality of medical care afforded to inmates or patients. The conditions of confinement can be injurious to fetal and children's health, overcrowding, unsanitary conditions, shackling and exposure to infectious diseases may exacerbate the risks to children. Thus, a unity of interest can be said to exist between parents and children in opposition to punitive, criminal intervention approaches to addressing the drug crisis.

The far more prevalent trend toward civil child abuse and neglect prosecutions presents a more difficult dilemma for children's advocates, as civil intervention may well be necessary to ensure protection of children's medical, psychological and educational needs. Viewed against the backdrop of a dearth of voluntary, community-based treatment opportunities and a tendency toward discriminatory intervention against poor, minority families, however, application of child protective statutes may not be an appropriate systemic response. While removal from home may not necessarily be warranted in all drug-exposure cases, all too frequently it has been the reflex reaction of child protective agencies and courts in the absence of sufficient alternatives to guarantee children's safety. Moreover, although drug abuse cuts across racial and class lines, substance-abusing, black women have been shown to be ten times more likely than their white counterparts to be reported to authorities, thus casting a cloud over the fairness of proceeding against them.[30] Additionally, as noted, drug treatment programs are notorious in their discrimination against pregnant women, which thus raises the question of whether it is fair to proceed against them for prenatal damage to their children.

Yet child protective proceedings are ostensibly designed not to be punitive, but to serve the interests of children and are often a child's only recourse for protection. Care must be taken, therefore, to assure that utilization of coercive civil court intervention is a last resort – i.e., one prong of a multi-track strategy which includes major emphases upon widespread drug education and treatment, elimination of treatment obstacles for pregnant women and mothers of young children, enhancement of child and maternal health and nutrition programs and replication of successful community-based models for comprehensive day and residential programs to meet the needs of children and families.

To the extent that child protective proceedings are utilized, each critical decision point from child neglect/abuse reporting at the outset through post-dispositional monitoring must serve, rather than impede, the interests of children. Reporting laws must, therefore, be specific both as to who must report and what constitutes a sufficient threshold level of risk to warrant a report. Testing protocols, whether by statute, administrative regulation or hospital procedure, must not discriminate on ethnic or class grounds and must ensure accuracy and thoroughness; medical indicators warranting testing, confirmatory and other testing procedures and 'chain of custody' and documentation requirements should be specified.

Once a child abuse or neglect report is made, whether based upon medical testing or other indicators, a thorough investigation must be performed to assess whether preventive services or other alternatives to court action would be efficacious and to marshall the evidence required, should court action be deemed necessary. Although some court cases nationally have sustained child protective proceedings initiated solely predominantly on the basis of positive toxicological results,[31] protocols instituted in New York City and urged by practitioners elsewhere include sound requirements for more evidence to be gathered to support petitions.[32]

Equally critical to children's and parent's joint interests in family preservation and integrity, the narrow standard of imminent risk must be strictly applied as the criterion for removal of children from their homes, as it can not be assumed that all children exposed to drugs must be put into foster care. Significantly, the mandates of the federal Adoption Assistance and Child Welfare Act of 1980 [Public Law 96–272] must be applied in conjunction with this standard – i.e., to the extent that reasonable efforts, if appropriate in light of an assessment of potential risks, can avert the need for foster care placement or shorten its duration, such efforts should be extended. Courts making foster care placements must render the required reasonable efforts findings.

Finally, options both for pretrial diversion and disposition upon fact-finding must be enhanced so that children's, as well as parents', interests can be furthered. Resource constraints can not be allowed to impede provision of comprehensive services so that the continuum of services available to drug-exposed children is truly a continuum. As noted above, community-based treatment centers should be available to facilitate retention of children in their homes or, if inappropriate, in therapeutically-supported kinship and other foster homes. For those children for whom return home is clearly unlikely, especially those abandoned at birth, efforts toward permanency must proceed apace. Where grounds to terminate parental rights exist, statutory timetables should be followed so that children do not spend prolonged periods of time in limbo.[33]

As one journalist noted, '[i]f cocaine use during pregnancy were a disease, its impact on children would be considered a national health care crisis'.[34] The need to marshall the resources to meet that crisis, particularly as the child victims of parental cocaine abuse enter the school system, stands as one of the most major challenges facing the United States. An unprecedented level of collaboration between health, child welfare, educational and legal professionals in which sensitivity is accorded to both children's and parents' rights and interests, is critically needed, as the nation can ill-afford to sacrifice a generation to the ravages of drug abuse and its attendant effects.

NOTES

1. Crack is widely available and low in cost; while $ 40 per vial in 1985, by 1988, the price had dropped to $ 5 to $ 10 per vial. See J. Plaut and T. Kelley, *Childwatch: Children and Drugs*, New York Interface Development Project (1989).
2. Revkin, 'Crack in the Cradle', *Discover* (Sept., 1989), pages 63–69.

3. Brody, 'Cocaine: Litany of Fetal Risks Grows', *New York Times*, Sept. 6, 1988, p. C 1. See also Schneider and Chansnoff, 'Cocaine Abuse During Pregnancy: Its Effects on Infant Motor Development: A Clinical Perspective', *Topics in Acute Care and Trauma Rehabilitation* 2 (July 1987), pp. 59–69; Chasnoff, Lewis and Squires, 'Cocaine Intoxication in a Breast-fed Infant', *Pediatrics* 80 (Dec., 1987), pp. 836–838.

4. Blakeslee, 'Crack's Toll on Infants Found to be Emotional Devastation', *New York Times*, Sept. 17, 1989, p. 1, col. 2; Revkin, *supra*; Brody, *supra*; National Association of Perinatal Addiction Research and Education (NAPARE), 'Substances Most Commonly Abused During Pregnancy and their Risks to Mother and Baby' (1989).

5. NAPARE, *supra*; Chasnoff *et al.*, *supra*; Chasnoff, 'Newborn Infants with Drug Withdrawal Symptoms', *Pediatrics in Review* (March, 1988), pp. 273–276; Church, Dintcheff and Gessner, 'Dose-dependent Consequences of Cocaine on Pregnancy Outcome in the Long-Evans Rat', *Neurotoxicology and Teratology* 10 (1988), pp. 51–58; Oro and Dixon, 'Fetal and Neonatal Medicine: Perinatal Cocaine and Methamphetamine Exposure: Maternal and Neonatal Correlates', *Journal of Pediatrics* 111 (1987), pp. 571–570.

6. See Chasnoff, 'Newborn Infants with Drug Withdrawal Symptoms',*Pediatrics in Review* 9, pp. 273–276 (1988); Howard, 'Annotation: Cocaine and Its Effects on the Newborn', *Developmental Medicine and Child Neurology* 31, pp. 255–257 (1989); Chasnoff, Hunt, Kletter and Kaplan, 'Prenatal Cocaine Exposure is associated with Respiratory Pattern Abnormalities', *American Journal of Disabled Children* 143, pp. 583–587 (1989); Chasnoff, Burns and Burns, Cocaine Use in Pregnancy: Perinatal Morbidity and Mortality', *Neurotoxicology and Teratology*, pp. 291–293 (1987).

7. See Plaut and Kelley, *Childwatch: Children and Drugs*, New York Interface Development Project (1989); Chasnoff, *supra*; Revkin, 'Crack in the Cradle', *Discover* (1989), pp. 63–69.

8. See Howard, *supra*; Chasnoff, Griffith, MacGreyor, Dirkes and Burns, 'Temporal Patterns of Cocaine Use in Pregnancy: Perinatal Outcome', *Journal of the American Medical Association* 261, pp. 1741–1744 (1989); Bingol, Fuchs, Diaz, Stone and Gromish, 'Teratogenicity of Cocaine in Humans', *Journal of Pediatrics* 110, pp. 93–96 (1987); Brody, 'Cocaine: Litany of Fetal Risks Grows', *New York Times*, Sept. 6, 1988, p. C1.

9. Chasnoff, 'Perinatal Effects of Cocaine', *Contemporary Ob/Gyn* (1987), pp. 163–179; Howard, 'Annotation: Cocaine and its Effects on the Newborn', *Developmental Medicine and Child Neurology* 31 (1989), pp. 255–257; Cro and Dixon, *supra*; Ryan, Erlich and Finnegan, 'Cocaine Abuse in Pregnancy: Effects on the Fetus and Newborn', *Neurotoxicology and Teratology* 9 (1987) pp. 295–299; Chouteau, Namerow and Leoppert, 'The Effect of Cocaine Abuse on Birth Weight and Gestational Age', *Obstetrics and Gynecology* 72 (1988), Pt. I, pp. 351–354.

10. See Howard, *supra*; Howard, Beckwith, Rodning and Kropenske, 'The Development of Young Children of Substance-Abusing Parents: Insights from Seven Years of Intervention and Research', *Zero to Three: Bull. of the Nat'l. Center for Clinical Infant Programs*, IX (1989), pp. 8–12; Chasnoff, 'Perinatal Effects of Cocaine', *Contemporary Ob/Gyn* (1987), pp. 163–179; Blakeslee, 'Crack's Toll on Infants Found to be Emotional Devastation', *New York Times*, Sept. 17, 1989, p. 1, col. 2.

11. See Schneider and Chasnoff, 'Cocaine Abuse During Pregnancy: Its Effects on Infant Motor Development: A Clinical Perspective', *Topics in Acute Care and Trauma Rehabilitation* pp. 59–69 (1987).

12. Hemphill, 'A Tormented Cry: As Crack Babies Grow, so Do Their Problems', *Newsday*, Sept. 28, 1990, p. 29.

13. Id.

14. See generally, reports of the Early Intervention Advocacy Network of the Mental Health Law Project, Washington, D.C.; Morrow, 'Early Intervention Programs May Help Drug-exposed Children', *Youth Law News* XI (1990), 31.

15. Although modest increases are expected, New York City, for example, currently has only one residential mother-child drug treatment program (Odyssey House), which has a sub-

stantial waiting list, and only a modest number of community-based treatment slots. The dearth of drug treatment for pregnant women is even more severe; discrimination by drug treatment programs against pregnant women is the subject of a pending lawsuit by the American Civil Liberties Union and has been well-documented in surveys by the House Select Committee on Children, Youth and Families and Dr. Wendey Chavkin. Significantly, Dr. Chavkin found, in a survey of 78 drug treatment programs in New York City (95% of the total), that fully 54% categorically exclude pregnant women, 67% exclude pregnant women on medicaid and 87% had no services for indigent, crack-addicted pregnant women. Similarly, two-thirds of the hospitals surveyed by the House Select Committee on Children, Youth and Families reported that they had *no* drug treatment programs to which their pregnant patients could be referred. See, House Select Committee on Children, Youth and Families, 'Principal Findings on Addicted Infants and their Mothers', and 'Hearing Summary, Born Hooked: Confronting the Impact of Perinatal Substance Abuse' (Apr. 27, 1989).

16. See Kerr, 'Addiction's Hidden Toll: Poor Families in Turmoil', *New York Times*, June 23, 1988, p. A1; Fink, 'Effects of Crack and Cocaine Upon Infants: A Brief Review of the Literature', *Children's Legal Rights Journal* 10 (1989), 8, n. 4.
17. Surveys have shown that up to 70% of individuals referred for drug treatment report that they represent the second or third generation of drug abusers in their homes. See Plaut and Kelley, *supra*.
18. Fink, 'Determining the Future Child: Actors on the Juvenile Court Stage', in Hartmann (ed.), *From Children to Citizens: Vol. II: The Role of the Juvenile Court*, Springer-Verlag (1987), p. 279.
19. See Fink, 'Determining the Future Child: Actors on the Juvenile Court Stage', in F. Hartmann (ed.), *From Children to Citizens: Volume II, The Role of the Juvenile Court*, Springer-Verlag (1987), p. 291; Butz, 'Lawyering for the Abused Child: You Can't Go Home Again', *UCLA Law Review* 29, 1216, 1222, 1229 (1982).
20. See generally, Fink, 'Determining the Future Child: Actors on the Juvenile Court Stage', in Hartmann (ed.), *From Children to Citizens: Volume II, The Role of the Juvenile Court*, Springer-Verlag (1987), p. 289 and accompanying notes.
21. *Lawyer's Code of Professional Responsibility*, Ethical Considerations 7-3, 7-7.
22. Id., Ethical Consideration 7-24.
23. Id., Ethical Consideration 7-11, 7-12.
24. American Bar Association, *Model Rules of Professional Conduct*, Section 1.14(a), (b) (Approved Draft, 1983).
25. Institute for Judicial Administration/American Bar Association Juvenile Justice Standards Project, *Standards Relating to Counsel for Private Parties* 3.1 (Approved Draft, 1979).
26. The Juvenile Rights Division of The Legal Aid Society in New York City pioneered multi-disciplinary team representation of children, a concept which has been replicated in several jurisdictions nationally. Since the early 1970's, a professional staff of social workers, with access to independent clinical experts, work in teams with the attorneys – assisting in a variety of tasks, including assessment, exploration of community and family resources, referral to and procurement of needed services or placement resources, presentation of expert testimony, proffering of dispositional plans to the court and post-dispositional monitoring of cases. See generally, Fink, 'Determining the Future Child: Actors on the Juvenile Court Stage', *supra*, pp. 289–290; 'Clout and Credibility: A Powerful Combination for Lawyers and Social Workers', *Practice Digest* 7, pp. 13–16 (National Association of Social Workers, Fall, 1984).
27. C. Schinitsky, 'The Role of the Lawyer in Children's Court', *Record of the Association of the Bar of the City of New York* 17, p. 25 (1962).
28. C. Silberman, *Criminal Violence, Criminal Justice* (1978), p. 365.
29. 'Talk of the Town', *New Yorker Magazine*, July 23, 1990.
30. Sherman, 'Keeping Babies Free of Drugs', *National Law Journal* 12 (1989).
31. See, e.g., 'Matter of Stefanel Tyesha C.', *New York Law Journal*, May 31, 1990 (N.Y.

App. Div., 1st Dept.); *In Re Troy D.*, 263 Cal. Rptr. 869 (Cal. App., 4th Dist., 1989); *In Re Baby X.*, 293 N.W.2d 736 (Ct. App., Mich., 1980)

32. See, e.g., English, 'Prenatal Drug Exposure: Grounds for Mandatory Child Abuse Reports', *Youth Law News* XI (1990), pp. 3–8.

33. New York State, for example, recently enacted an amendment to its child protective disposition statute authorizing an order for diligent efforts to locate the parent(s) in abandonment cases and for timely filing of a parental rights termination petition on abandonment grounds in six months if such efforts are unsuccessful.

34. Revkin, 'Crack in the Cradle', *Discover* (Sept., 1989), pp. 63–69.

GEORGE KENT*

23. Little Foreign Bodies:
International Dimensions of Child Prostitution

Child prostitution refers to situations in which children under the age of 16 engage in regularized sexual activity for material benefits for themselves or others. These are institutionalized arrangements – sustained, patterned social structures – in which children are used sexually for profit. Child prostitution is an extreme form of sexual abuse of children and an especially intense form of exploitative child labor. The core concern here is the highly exploitative character of child prostitution. Most prostitution is exploitative, but for mature men and women there may be some element of volition, some consent. The assumption here is that children under the age of 16 do not have even the capacity to give valid, informed consent on such matters.

Child Prostitution is widespread, but it is not possible to assess its magnitude with any precision. Except in some centers of pedophilia, children account for only a small segment of the prostitution trade overall. Even so, the numbers are large. The Ministry of Social Services and Development in the Philippines acknowledges that child prostitution rivals begging as the major occupation of the 50,000 to 75,000 street children who roam metropolitan Manila. There is a consensus that the number of underage prostitutes in Bangkok numbers at least in the tens of thousands.[1]

This is not a general survey of child prostitution around the world, but rather it is an examination of the ways in which child prostitution activities in different countries are *linked* with one another. And the point here is not to present individual incidents, but to show that these linkages are regularized and institutionalized. Child prostitution activities cross national borders in several ways. There is *trafficking*, the movement of prostitutes, and those who will become prostitutes, from one region to another. And there are *traveling customers*. These include not only tourists but also business and military travelers. In response to all this, there are efforts at *international control*, by governmental and nongovernmental organizations working internationally to limit the practice of child prostitution. This study focuses on the linkages

* University of Hawaii.

M. Freeman and P. Veerman (eds.), The Ideologies of Children's Rights, 323–346.

specifically as they relate to child prostitutes, defined here as those under 16 years of age.

In some places, such as India and Thailand, child prostitution was deeply ingrained as part of the culture well before foreign soldiers or tourists appeared in large numbers. There are many local customers. Some Japanese and other tourists may use the child prostitutes in the 'tea houses' in the Yaowarat district of Bangkok, but traditionally most of their customers have been locals, especially local Chinese.[2] Similarly, 'data from interviews in the Philippines indicate . . . that more than half the customers near the American military bases, Clark and Subic Bay, are local people'.[3] There is big money associated with the foreign trade, but there are bigger numbers in the local trade. This study focuses on international liaisons, but this does not mean that most customers of child prostitutes are foreigners.

TRAFFICKING

International trafficking for purposes of prostitution has a long history that is well documented and widely ignored. In the middle of the 19th century there was trafficking of young children from England to the continent, especially to Belgium, France, and Holland for purposes of prostitution. At the turn of the century many young girls were purchased in China, taken to the United States, and sold in open markets or directly to individuals.[4] There was large-scale trafficking of Chinese women into Malaya: 'In 1884, at least 2,000 out of 6,600 Chinese women in Singapore were prostitutes. Most of these girls were between the ages of 13 and 16'.[5] By the 1930s, under the *Mui Tsai* system, there was extensive traffic in women and girls between southern China and Malaya:

> Although the young girls entered Malaya supposed for the domestic labour market, many mui tsai were sold to brothels. Often they came under the strict control of the secret societies which were involved in their importation into Malaya and Singapore. In 1863 alone, 500 young girls were coerced from China by secret societies . . . . These girls were between the ages of 13 and 16. These young girls were meant not only for the brothels in Singapore but were also distributed to the mining and other commercial towns in Malaya, and other parts of South-East Asia.[6]

During the 19th century there was extensive traffic in Jewish girls from Eastern Europe. In 1903 Arthur Moro of London's Jewish Association for the Protection of Girls and Women reported:

> We have positive evidence that to almost all parts of North and South Africa, to India, China, Japan, Philippine Islands, North and South America and also to many of the countries in Europe, Yiddish speaking Jews are maintaining a regular flow of Jewesses, trafficked solely for the purpose of

prostitution. We know that they were taken to brothels owned by Yiddish speaking Jews.[7]

Many others were involved in international trafficking early in this century:

> Overseas at Buenos Aires, The Rand, Manchuria, and other stops on the international vice circuit, the French were equally well-represented in all aspects of commercial vice. Italians and Greek traffickers sent their tribute to the voracious brothels of the Middle East and North Africa. Furthermore, in terms of participants, the Chinese and Japanese played the biggest role of all . . .[8]

With Stroessner's rise to power in 1955, Paraguay became a major source:

> The large demand for prostitutes in the cities, combined with the easy availability of girls from the countryside, has stimulated the traffic in women to other countries. There is evidence that young peasant girls from Paraguay are taken to the United States and Europe for prostitution. In the past several years over 700 girls from the rural area of Caraguatay are reported to have come into the United States in groups of ten to twenty, passed through Miami and Chicago, and then by bus to New York City.[9]

Eleven-year-old girls have been taken from the hill tribes of Burma and smuggled into Bangkok.[10] In 1981 a representative of a Hong Kong nightclub, working with collaborators in Guangdong Province, took 41 girls from China to be forced into prostitution in Hong Kong.[11] Undoubtedly most international trafficking is in women over the age of 16, but some children do get swept up in the tide. Specific ages are rarely reported, but it seems reasonable to infer that at least some under-16s are included.

Some migration that is normally for other purposes has effect of supplying prostitutes. For example, sometimes children who are supposedly being adopted are in fact used for sexual purposes. In one case a 14-year-old Filipino girl was 'ostensibly adopted by a Dutch woman of Filipino origin who brought the girl into the Netherlands where she forced her to engage in prostitution'.[12] An NBC report shows 'the ease with which children can be adopted abroad and then brought to the United States to be sexually abused'.[13] 'Catalog' or 'mail order' brides often end up as prostitutes. After the young woman arrives in the new country, the marriage may not take place, or if it does it might come apart after a very short period. In some cases the abandoned woman, stranded in a strange country, turns to prostitution. In some cases she is turned over to a specific pimp or brothel, in accordance with the broker's original intent.

In the 19th century, ritual marriages, undertaken without the required civil registration, were used as the means of procuring young Jewish girls from Eastern Europe:

> Procurers were known to go through the traditional ritual and then take their legally unmarried and largely unprotected partners off to a domestic or foreign brothel. . . . In 1892 twenty-two men were convicted in Lemberg

for procuring girls from small Galician towns with promises of jobs as servants, and selling them to brothels in Constantinople, Alexandria and points east of Suez. The Austrian consul in Constantinople had rescued sixty of them from virtual imprisonment the year before.[14]

Similar means are still being used. The German ambassador to Thailand has said that 'a terrifyingly high number of marriages of German men in Thailand – who appear there as tourists – aim only at bringing young Thai women to the Federal Republic in order to force them into prostitution there'.[15]

In India, fake marriages are a common means for drawing young women into the trade. In some cases the woman may sustain both an arranged marriage and prostitution simultaneously:

> Says Beena, a Delhi prostitute originally from Tibet: 'Most of us came as child brides and were sold off to brothels. Once we got in there was no way of getting out'. Today Beena lives a double life. In the morning she helps her husband sell readymade garments on the streets of New Delhi and at night, she paints her face and solicits customers in the notorious G.B. Road area. 'My husband wants me to do this', she says in a tone of pain mixed with anger. 'Men only want our money. No one wants to love us'.[16]

Women who travel to new countries for arranged marriages are particularly vulnerable because they do not have any local family support system to provide an alternative. The age distribution of those drawn into fake marriages and then forced into prostitution is not known, but it is likely that at least some of them are younger than 16. In many societies girls are sold into prostitution directly by their parents. Undoubtedly most of these girls are under 16. Most girls that are sold work locally, but some are taken by their procurers to distant countries, to replenish the stock in their brothels.

In many parts of the world there are patterns of circular migration in which poor people go off to richer countries to work, but with the intention of returning home after a time. Often these are men or women who travel without their families, to work in various forms of unskilled labor. These migrations of 'guest workers' are encouraged by the sending countries because they have severe underemployment problems, and the repatriation of earnings may account for a large share of the poor countries' income. Migrating men often become the customers of prostitutes. In Peru:

> The history of the exploitation of Peruvian Amazonian resources of wood, rubber, and oil has been paralleled by a history of prostitution in the same area. Short-term migrant workers live in camps or enclaves, and companies supply prostitutes for their sexual needs. It has been reported that the demand for very young girls (12 to 16 years) is very high in Inquitos, and that virgins are offered as gambling prizes.[17]

Migrating women are likely to become prostitutes. Young women travel abroad with the expectation that they will work in factories or as entertainers, waitresses, or servants. Some, deceived from the outset, are channeled directly into brothels where they are held by force. Some drift into prostitution after the original work arrangements deteriorate or disappear. Many go to work abroad in a form of international indenturing in which children from poor families serve as house servants for rich families.

Unfortunately, indenturing often leads to exploitation and abuse of children. The seduction or rape of the parlor maid by the master of the house was the subject of many a nineteenth century novel. The woman was frequently blamed and cast out either pregnant or with a young child. A long way from home, unable to return to her family because of shame or the financial burden resulting from the penalty clause in her indenture contract, she turned to prostitution as her only means of survival.

The realities of contemporary indenturing are just as harsh. Children as young as 8 in Thailand, the Philippines, and other countries are sold by impoverished parents to agents from Bangkok and Manila. Instead of being placed with rich families, the minors are diverted to brothels in distant cities. A 15-year old prostitute whom we interviewed had traveled from Santo Domingo to St. Maarten and told a story almost identical to the Victorian melodrama just mentioned. She went to work as a maid in the house of a radio personality at the age of 12. He seduced or raped her, and she was pregnant by the age of 13. After the infant was born, the baby was taken from her, and the offender applied to the courts for custody on the grounds that the mother was immoral. She was expelled from the house and resorted to prostitution.[18]

The pattern of domestic service functioning as a path to prostitution was well established in central Europe by the turn of the century: 'At Lemberg in 1909 for example the police reported that two-thirds of the registered prostitutes had been in service beforehand'.[19] It remains an important path to prostitution. Reports from Haiti say that young girls are employed as domestic help specifically to provide sex for the family's sons. There is a pattern followed by young girls hired as household help in Haiti:

Exploited, ridiculed, lost in the big city, girls who are totally cut off from their parents are the most victimized . . . Without any options, they are led to prostitution. After being abused by the sons of the house and then its master, the family throws them out. To survive, they become prostitutes and later they become abandoned single mothers.[20]

Most international travel occurs in the procurement stage, but there is also some travel of prostitutes after they are already in the trade. Many move to more lucrative markets, especially Japan.[21] Sometimes the move is only temporary. For example, major events such as world fairs or major sports events that draw large numbers of people attract prostitutes as well. Some may travel of their own volition, and some may be brought or sent by their pimps.

However, there is no indication of extensive international travel by child prostitutes after they are recruited. They do travel within countries under the control of their pimps.

TRAVELING CUSTOMERS

While international trafficking refers to the delivery of prostitutes to the countries of customers, there are also systematic means for delivering customers to the countries of the prostitutes. Tourism plays an important role, and there is a steady international traffic of pedophiles to particular areas. Business travelers often use prostitutes. Military 'rest and recreation' programs, and the location of military bases in less developed countries also bring in customers from richer countries to prostitutes in poorer countries.

Tourism

Many tourist destinations have flourishing prostitution industries, and many of them make special efforts to accommodate tastes for very young girls. A visitor to Hong Kong in the 1960s describes a 'special massage establishment on Cameron Road'.

> The special massage establishments use very young girls from twelve to fifteen or sixteen as masseuses. There are hundreds in the Kowloon areas, tucked away in the rear rooms of apartments, and the young girls there are slaves in every sense of the word. Since the Communist take over of the mainland there has been a steady flow of refugees, many landed illegally from 'snake-boats', to Hong Kong. They are only too willing to sell their young daughters to the traffickers. The usual price the traffickers pay for a ten-year-old virgin girl is HK\$ 1600. As I discovered that night in the special massage establishment, they get their investment back on the first night she works for them, as they charge HK\$ 1,600 for the services of a virgin.[22]

Some prostitution evolves to accommodate ordinary tourists on ordinary excursions. The availability of child prostitutes may be just one of the many amenities that make their vacations interesting. In some cases, however, tours are established specifically for tourists for whom sex is the primary objective. In the Philippines, for example, child prostitution appears to be promoted as a direct result of government policy:

> In the early 1970s the country deliberately went in for tourism as an important source of income. Every effort was to be made to attract tourists to the Philippines and schemes were deliberately laid to use sexual services in the marketing of tourism and as a tourist attraction. Red light districts sprang up with brothels, 'massage-parlors' and so on, both in the capital,

Manila and in tourist areas such as Puerto Galera and Boracay. The hotels started up so-called 'hostess services'. Child prostitution developed to add to the variety in the market'. Certain people understood that this was a niche for making a lot of money. More and more paedophiles in many places in the world became aware of the fact that the Philippines had developed almost into a sanctuary for them.[23]

There is sex-oriented tourism to some richer countries, particularly Holland and some of the Scandinavian countries, but tourism focused on child prostitutes is based in poorer countries. The customers are relatively rich, whether they come from rich or poor countries. Most are from the United States, Europe, and Japan, and some come from the Middle East.

Comfortably off men from the Middle East constitute a considerable proportion of those creating a demand for prostitution in Asian countries, India included. It is claimed, for instance, that approximately 1 in 10 of the customers in Bombay's red light district is a man from the Middle East. It is also claimed that Arabian businessmen have pseudo-marriages arranged for them by middle men for a price. The 'marriage' lasts just for the length of the man's holiday or business stay in India. As soon as he returns home, the relationship, as far as he is concerned, is as though it had never existed. The girl is left behind, defiled, cast out and often pregnant.[24]

Apparently they have a special interest in child prostitutes:

Tourists from the Middle East are particularly enthusiastic about 'deflowering' virgin girls. They are thus easy prey to enterprising pimps who know how to sell their experienced child prostitutes as 'virgins'.[25]

In the Philippines:

The biggest number of customers are white males from the industrialized countries and prefer girls who are less than 12 years old and boys a little older. They pay them in cash. The Japanese come second and they are fond of older teenage girls and give clothes, jewelry, cameras and other amenities as payment. A small but significant group are Filipinos. These are older men locally referred to as dirty old men, DOMs. But generally child prostitutes still prefer to have sex with foreign men.[26]

The demands of wealthy tourists lead to increasing supplies of child prostitutes. The Centre for the Protection of Children's Rights in Thailand found that 'during 1985–88 when tourism was heavily promoted by the government, the sale of children into prostitution boomed. Of all the families they spoke to who had sold their daughters into prostitution, 35% had sold one daughter in the 12–16 age group and 25% had sold two daughters'.[27] The demand is explained by one visitor to Bangkok who said he was there for just one reason, girls: 'Fourteen-, fifteen-year old girls. I've already been to Sri Lanka and

Korea, but this is the best place to find them: the girls are real fresh here, straight from the hills'.[28]

In 1984 fire destroyed a brothel in Phuket, Thailand, a major resort area. Five girls, ranging in age from 9 to 12, were found dead in the ruins of the locked basement. A film, *Tomorrow Will There Be a Rainbow*, was made to tell the story of how their poor family in northern Thailand had sent them out to earn money.

The children are exploited economically, not only by being paid very little, but also by being cheated. A 14-year-old from Cebu in Manila's red light district 'was sold to a brothel where she was devirginized by a Japanese. She stayed with the Japanese for a week, returned to the casa to get her pay but was told she still owed them money'.[29]

The children pimp for each other:

> At the casas we visited, the recruitment process was simple: you brought in your friends who needed cash. As one ages, you start pimping for the younger ones. Glenda is 14 . . . semi-retired after two years as a child prostitute and now manages younger girls who she beats up when they don't follow her orders.[30]

The child prostitutes work long hours:

> Robinson's Plaza, Harrison Plaza, Ali Mall, Luneta – you see them especially on week-ends, hanging around, sending out signals to prospective customers. Spartacus, an international guide for pederasts, once described Harrison Plaza as a 'fist market', open from ten in the morning to ten at night with 'several hundred boys available at one time in that area'.[31]

Few children operate wholly independently, but some are much freer than others. Street children come and go more or less as they wish, and undertake a variety of different activities, while other children may be permanently confined to a brothel. One study found that with regard to child prostitution

> Street children have, on average, only a few customers. As a rule they only use this way of making money when absolutely necessary. In the sample of 1,000 children in the Philippines only 17% had customers every day. Conditions are in general completely different for children controlled by the syndicates. These children may be forced to have sexual intercourse up to 20 times a day.[32]

Some organized sex tours specialize in sex with children. Investigative reporters for the National Broadcasting Company found travel agencies in West Germany and in England offering child sex tours to Thailand. One of the reporters 'purchased a child sex tour from a London travel agent. When he arrived in Thailand at his destination, a pimp whom he met through the Bangkok branch of the multinational travel agency delivered a 13-year-old girl to his hotel room'.[33] Apart from the sex tours, tourism promotes prostitution indirectly. There is the symbolic effect of rich tourists demonstrating lavish lifestyles, and tempting young people to go after easy money. In addition, there are strong economic pressures. The tourist trade brings in wealthy people who can afford to pay high prices for all kinds of things. Accordingly, local merchants increase their prices, which leads to rapid inflation. The many local people whose incomes do not increase as a result of tourism find they can no longer afford the inflated prices. Desperate for new sources of income, many of them turn to prostitution.

Business people sometimes use their opportunities to travel, or to relocate for extended periods, to take advantage of young children. Consider this account of a British businessman working in the Philippines for a multinational oil company:

> Steve has an apartment in the Malate area and both invites young kids (mostly boys-but also a few girls) not only to his apartment but to eat in restaurants etc. he also gives a small amount to kids who bring other kids. Usually the age range of the kids would be 8–14 with a few a little older. Sometimes, he has them take a shower or play with each other naked on the bed while he makes video documentaries. Sometime early this year, the police raided his apartment and found him and five other boys playing naked.

Testimony regarding his behavior was taken from children by Bahay Tuluyan, a church-based program responding to the needs of women and children in Malate-Ermita, the major red-light district of Manila. The organization staged a march to the immigration authorities asking that he be deported. They were not successful.

Military Travelers

Prostitution, including child prostitution, occurs on a large scale near military bases and military 'rest and recreation' areas. This occurs at both domestic and overseas bases. Since there has been so much projection of US military power abroad since World War II, frequently it has been US servicemen and civilians attached to bases in foreign countries who are the customers.

The pattern is particularly visible in the Philippines. Thousands of Americans are stationed at 25 bases and other military facilities in the Philippines. The largest are Clark Air Base (55,000 hectares) and Subic Naval Base (26,000 hectares). Thousands of American military personnel are stationed at Subic Bay, but the numbers go up sharply when the Seventh Fleet visits. There are also many American civilians working at the base. Thus businesses in the nearby town of Olongapo are geared toward accommodating the Americans at the base. There are thousands of 'hospitality girls'. Olongapo has been described as Asia's biggest brothel.

In 1982 a serious outbreak of venereal disease led to the hospitalization of 12 girls between the ages of 9 and 14. It was this incident that triggered Father Shay Cullen, who had been running a drug rehabilitation center, to launch a campaign to end the prostitution in Olongapo. In 1989 he reported that naval intelligence agents at Subic had found out that children from 11 to 14 were being offered by an organized group to pedophile servicemen. In addition, he says 'hundreds of people from Europe, the United States, and Australia come to Olongapo City to buy and sell sex with children between 6 and 16'.[35] The local mayor, prosecutor, and other officials have refused to act on the information. Cullen has been asked to leave the country, and pressured by the base commander. He has had his life threatened many times, but he persists in his campaign.

In Thailand, the American presence during the Indochina war accelerated the development of prostitution. During 1962–76 there were tens of thousands of US military personnel stationed at seven air bases in different parts of Thailand supporting operations in the Indochina war. Hundreds of thousands flew into Thailand for 'rest and recreation' visits. Bars and brothels mushroomed near the bases and the R & R centers, especially in the Northeast. In 1964 the police department estimated there were 400,000 prostitutes in Thailand. After the departure of the United States forces the women in the trade shifted to resort areas such as Pattaya, or went overseas, to work in Japan, Singapore, Hong Kong, Germany, Switzerland, Holland and elsewhere.

Many establishments are operated by local people and appear to be local operations but in fact are owned and controlled by foreigners. For example, it has been estimated that Americans own a majority of the bars in Barrio Barreto and Subic City, two smaller prostitution areas outside Olongapo in the Philippines: 'They are able to own bars through marriage to a Filipino or using a Filipino front. Bar owners are the 'upstanding' members of the city – the Lions Club, the Rotary Club etc. and have their own Bar Owners Association'.[36]

Too little attention has been given to the children of prostitutes and the problems they encounter. They are prime candidates for entry into the trade. In Honduras, children born to women who have been forced to work in brothels 'are taken over by the owners and become part of the establishment'.[37] The prospects of prostitutes' children may depend on whether they are the products of international liaisons. In the Philippines, for example, it has been found that relatives of the prostitute were more willing to look after the child if he or she were a pure Filipino than if the child resulted from a relationship with a Caucasian. 'Amerasian' children were more likely to remain in the prostitution environment.[38]

Pedophiles

Most of the traveling customers of child prostitutes are men. In some cases they are women, such as the middle-aged white European women who travel as tourists along the coast of Kenya. The customers may be heterosexuals, homosexuals, or pedophiles. Pedophiles prefer sexual relationships with children. They may or may not be homosexual. Pedophiles – mostly men, but occasionally women – constitute a very distinctive group of customers.

Certain areas have become known as centers of pedophilia. In the Philippines, international pedophilia was recognized as a problem as far back as 1599, when the Spanish Royal Audiencia issued an ordinance prohibiting Chinese settlers from practicing 'sodomia' with the 'Moro and Indian boys of these inlands'.[39] In modern times the city of Pangsanjan, about 40 miles southeast of Manila, has become an international center of pedophilia. It seems 'local residents discovered the easy money in male prostitution when American filmmakers came to town to shoot scenes for 'Apocalypse Now'.' Then the word spread and foreign men took up residence, including an American who ran a prostitution business. That American was arrested in 1988, 'along with six other Americans, five West Germans, three Australians, two Belgians, a Japanese and a Spaniard. Most have since left the country'. But one Swiss national 'married the sister of his 15-year-old male lover and has applied to return home not with his wife but with his new brother-in-law'. It has been estimated than in the town of 22,000, 65 percent are under 18, and one-third of these – almost 5,000 – are child prostitutes.[40]

Manila has its share of the child prostitution trade:

In Manila, as in other similar centers, the growth of child prostitution is alarming. In this case, the pimps visit the poor rural areas and negotiate to buy children or lease them for about $ 50.00 per year. Young children, both girls and boys from the age of about eight, are taught to perform sexual acts for voyeurs and later placed in brothels which cater to pedophiliacs.[41]

Pedophilia has become a major concern in Sri Lanka only recently, as a result of the vigorous promotion of tourism that began in the 1970s. By 1980 child prostitution was well established, especially in the resort areas. Tim Bond has provided details on how 'men from all parts of the world come each year to Sri Lanka to satisfy their sexual and emotional needs, and, having visited once, they come back again and again. . . . Boys as young as ten years old . . . are easily attracted into prostitution'.[42]

The 'beach boys' that cruise the resort areas are numerous and well organized:

It has been found that though a rough estimate of about 10,000 boys are 'moved' from resort area to resort area by their 'agents' with whom the 'deals' are made, there are others boys from the ages 8–16 who have now emerged acting independently, and making their contacts individually or in small groups. They ape the older boys who are "professionals" in these practices. What is disturbing is that paedophiles are coming in search of still younger and younger boys for the purposes of sexual pleasure. In a season or two these sexually exploited children are abandoned.[43]

Many of the pedophiles take rooms in small hotels on a monthly basis, and re-enter the country annually to make contact with 'their boys'. Tourism in general has fallen sharply because of the ethnic and political violence in the country since 1983, but the hotels catering to pedophiles have maintained high occupancy rates.

Jack Andersen, a famous newspaper columnist, describes Bangkok as 'the hub for international child prostitution. . . . Europeans and Americans make up a big share of the clientele and have even cashed in on the business side'.[44] Andersen also mentioned the case of a Utah man arrested by Thai police because he was suspected of running a house of prostitution for pedophiles under the guise of an orphanage. Two other Americans were arrested in 1989 for running a child sex ring. American men have been arrested in Manila for similar reasons.

Pedophiles around the world have established vigorous communication networks through publications such as the *Spartacus Gay Guide* and *PAN* magazine from the Netherlands, and the Paedo Alert News, and through organizations such as the Lewis Carroll Collector's Guild and the North American Man-Boy Love Association (NAMBLA).[45]

INTERNATIONAL CONTROL

International Governmental Organizations

Many organizations work within individual countries to combat child prostitution, but our concern here is limited to those that work internationally. Several international governmental organizations (international organizations whose members are national governments) play a role.

The International Criminal Police Organization (INTERPOL) began as an international nongovernmental organization, but in 1971 it was recognized as an international governmental organization. INTERPOL acts as an information exchange and as a liaison body between police forces of different countries; it does not have the power to investigate specific crimes. The international effort to control 'white slavery' was one of the major factors leading to INTERPOL's creation.[46] In 1974 INTERPOL's General Secretariat prepared a document on *Traffic in Women: Recent Trends*. Its sketchy information did not include any data on the ages of the women.[47] In 1988 INTERPOL conducted an International Symposium on Traffic in Human Beings.

The International Labour Organization (ILO) has sponsored some studies on conferences on child labor, and child prostitution has been mentioned in those contexts, but the organization does not address the issue systematically. As an international governmental organization, the ILO is constrained in much the same way that UNICEF is constrained.

The United Nation's Children's Fund (UNICEF) is the leading international governmental agency responsible for issues relating to children. Born out of the need to care for the thousands of children who faced famine and disease as a result of World War II, UNICEF was formally created in December 1946 by the United Nations General Assembly. It works with national governments all over the world to help formulate national programs for child survival and development. As an international governmental organization obligated to work with national governments, it cannot undertake activities contrary to the wishes of national governments. Thus UNICEF cannot be outspoken on human rights issues. It will not be a major implementing agency for the new Convention on the Rights of the Child. The organization has a program on Children in Especially Difficult Circumstances that includes the issues of labor exploitation and child abuse, but it has not done any programmatic work on child prostitution.

With the United Nations system, in addition to UNICEF and ILO, the Working Group of Experts on Contemporary Forms of Slavery (ECOSOC) also is concerned with the exploitation of children. Human rights in general is the responsibility of the Economic and Social Council of the United Nations. ECOSOC has a subsidiary Commission on Human Rights, which in turn has a Sub-Commission on Prevention of Discrimination and Protection of Minorities. That Sub-Commission receives reports from a number of Working Groups, one of which is the Working Group of Experts on Contemporary Forms of Slavery. Since 1975 it has held sessions each summer at United Nations headquarters in Geneva.[48] The 1986 meeting of the Working Group of Experts on Contemporary Forms of Slavery was canceled because of the United Nations system's economic crisis, precipitated by the United States' and the Soviet Union's failure to keep up with their payments. Cancellation of the slavery meeting suggests that human rights issues are of low priority even within the United Nations system. Indeed, even in normal years only 0.7 per cent of the United Nations budget is allotted specifically for the promotion and protection of human rights'.[49]

In 1982 ECOSOC commissioned 'a synthesis of the surveys and studies on the traffic in persons and the exploitation of the prostitution of others'. The report spoke of the traffic of north African women to Europe, South Americans to Melbourne, women from Hawaii and California to Japan, and Thai women to Switzerland, giving special attention to the traffic based on fake marriages. It also attacked sex tours. The report said that 'confined in the bondage of prostitution, women and children await their liberation. This fight is as necessary as the fight against the drug traffic and the fight against racism'.[50] Apparently the report did not lead to any significant action.

International Nongovernmental Organizations

For the purposes of this discussion, international nongovernmental organizations (INGOs) are nongovernmental organizations that work in several different countries, not necessarily those with membership from several different countries. While there is no INGO for which child prostitution is the central concern, several give it a prominent place on their agendas.

The Anti-Slavery Society in London, founded in 1839, is the world's oldest human rights organization. It gives a great deal of attention to child labor, and in that context it frequently addresses the problem of child prostitution.

Child Workers in Asia, headquartered in Bangkok, publishes a journal under the same name. The journal frequently carries items about cases of child prostitution, and in April-June 1990 it devoted a special issue to the theme.

Defence for Children International (DCI) advocates children's interests worldwide. It has national offices in many countries, and publishes the quarterly *International Children's Rights Monitor*. DCI-USA and DCI-Netherlands have given particular attention to child prostitution.[51]

End Child Prostitution in Asian Tourism (ECPAT) is an organization and international campaign intended to carry out the objective spelled out in its name. It grew out of an Ecumenical Consultation on Tourism and Child Prostitution organized by the Ecumenical Coalition on Third World Tourism in Chiang Mai, Thailand in May 1990. This is the first focused campaign designed to stop child prostitution on a regional basis. A new headquarters office for ECPAT is to be established in Bangkok.[52]

The International Abolitionist Federation (IAF) was founded by Josephine Butler, a woman from Liverpool who worked to abolish prostitution in England in the 19th century. (She was joined in her efforts by Alfred Dyer, whose special concern was the rise of child prostitution in England. He campaigned to raise the age of consent from 12 to 18, to curtail procuring of young girls for prostitution. He focused on the traffic of young English girls to the continent, where they were forced into prostitution.[53]) The Federation, founded in 1875, is headquartered in Lausanne, Switzerland. The IAF's major objective is controlling traffic in persons and the exploitation of the prostitution of others. It opposes the regulation of prostitution itself. The IAF has organized numerous conferences to further its cause. The main theme of its September 1990 conference in Geneva was 'The Exploitation of Prostitution: Violation of Human Rights; Children, The First Victims'.

The International Catholic Child Bureau, headquartered in Geneva, has been working actively on children's rights issues, and on child prostitution in particular. It published a periodical on Children Worldwide.

The International Feminist Network Against Female Sexual Slavery grew out of the Global Feminist Workshop to Organize Against Traffic in Women held in Copenhagen in 1980. The IFN's first meeting in Rotterdam in 1983 led to the creation of a network of local groups to address the problems of prostitution in every region of the world.[54] In 1984, with the assistance of the United Nations Non-Governmental Liaison Service, the group conducted a consultation to examine prostitution and other forms of exploitation of women.[55]

The International Save the Children Alliance has supported a variety of projects relating to child prostitution, including a study by its Norwegian arm, REDD BARNA, on the sexual exploitation of children in several developing countries.

Terre des Hommes is a private social services organization headquartered in Lausanne, Switzerland. It has supported work in Sri Lanka and Thailand on the problem of child prostitution.

International Law

In many countries the law regarding prostitution is applicable to children, and in some cases there are laws relating specifically to child prostitution. The concern here, however, is with international law.

Many international human rights declarations and agreements over the past century are related to child prostitution. One stream is centered on prostitution, slavery, and the exploitation of women, and the other is centered on children. The two come together in Article 34 of the new Convention on the Rights of The Child. After ten years of negotiation and drafting by a working group of the Commission on Human Rights, on November 20, 1989 the United Nations General Assembly adopted a new Convention on the Rights of the Child. Weaving together the scattered threads of earlier international statements of the rights of children, the convention's articles cover civil, political, economic, social and cultural rights. The convention addresses not only basic survival requirements such as food, clean water, and health care, but also rights of protection against abuse, neglect, and exploitation, and the right to education and to participation in social, religious, political, and economic activities. It is a comprehensive legal instrument, binding on all nations that accept it. The minimum number of 20 ratifications required for the convention to come into force were obtained as of September 2, 1990. By the conclusion of the World Summit for Children held at the United Nations on September 29–30, 1990, 126 nations had signed the convention, and 49 had ratified it. The United States was not among them.

Article 34 addresses the issue of child prostitution directly:

> States Parties undertake to protect the child from all forms of sexual exploitation and sexual abuse. For these purposes States Parties shall in particular take all appropriate national, bilateral and multilateral measures to prevent:
> (a) the inducement or coercion of a child to engage in any unlawful sexual activity;
> (b) the exploitative use of children in prostitution or other unlawful sexual practices;
> (c) he exploitative use of children in pornographic performances and materials.

To implement the Convention, Article 43 calls for the creation of a Committee on the Rights of the Child consisting of ten elected experts whose main functions are to receive and transmit reports on the status of children's rights. Article 44 requires signatory nations to submit 'reports on the measures they have adopted which give effect to the rights recognized herein and on the progress made on the enjoyment of those rights'. Article 46 entitles UNICEF and other agencies to work with the committee within the scope of their mandates.

The Convention on the Rights of the Child is an important advance, and should be vigorously supported by all governments and all advocates of children's interests. But its implementation mechanisms are much too weak. The same problem arises with respect to the implementation of earlier human rights agreements. The United Nations has a number of committees in place to implement human rights law such as the Committee on the Elimination of Racial Discrimination, the Human Rights Committee, the Committee on Economic, Social, and Cultural Rights, the Committee on the Elimination of Discrimination against Women, and the Committee against Torture. They do useful work, but their resources and their mandates are not nearly adequate to the needs in these areas. The Committee on the Rights of the Child is not likely to be any more effective.

Cultural Relativism

Intervention in other people's lives always raises serious ethical questions. Interventions across borders, across cultures, and across political worlds raise even more questions. Should powerful white men from rich countries ever involve themselves with disadvantaged people in poor countries? Intervention that is not only across borders, across cultures, and between worlds but also involves the most intimate issues of sexuality raises an enormous swarm of ethical problems. They seem almost unmanageable. Confronting all these difficult issues, one might leap to the conclusion that no one should ever mess with anyone else's life. But being unresponsive to problems can be unethical too.

Perhaps we can say a little about just one issue. A crucial question in dealing with child prostitution, or with human rights more generally, is whether rights should be recognized as different in different cultural settings. If in Samoa fathers traditionally twist their children's ears to discipline them, should you intervene, or should you say, 'that's all right, he's Samoan?' What does the answer depend on? Do you intervene if you witness the incident in California but not if you see it happen in Samoa?

The problem of cultural relativism is especially important in international work, but the problem comes up with individual countries as well. In most Asian countries it is Christian women's groups that are most outspoken in their concern about child prostitution. There are considerable differences between them and their Buddhist and Muslim counterparts, even if there is never any direct confrontation over those differences.

At a children's advocacy conference in the summer of 1989 a young woman from a Muslim country was upset about the draft Convention on the Rights of the Child. She was outraged that its negotiators made special accommodations for Muslim countries because their laws and customs with respect to adoption and other practices were different from those in western countries. She asked why Muslim children should not be entitled to the same rights and the same protection as other children throughout the world. The charge was not that the Westerns who dominated the negotiations were being cultural insensitive, but that they were being too sensitive!

Certainly there are great variations in cultural attitudes toward child prostitution. What is regularly accepted as simple fondling in some cultures may be viewed with horror as child sexual abuse in other cultures. One way to make the issue less problematic is to be careful about definitions. What exactly is it that we want to have controlled? Article 34 speaks specifically of 'the exploitative use of children' in prostitution. This language is comparable to that in Article 6 of the Convention on the Elimination of All Forms of Discrimination Against Women of 1979 which calls for the suppression of the 'exploitation of prostitution of women'. The International Abolitionist Federation works to implement this objective. Following the convention and the federation, we should emphasize that the issue is not prostitution as such but the *exploitation of the prostitution of others* that is important. The core problem is exploitation.

Of course there are cultural variations in tolerance for exploitation, too. How do we handle that? My personal answer is that I want to show respect for others' views of what is right and wrong, but I also want to act with integrity, with respect for my own views of what is right and wrong. I want to take account of others' ways, but ultimately my action must be based on my own values and my own understanding of the situation. I would not accept, say, the killing of children, in any society just because those who did it thought it was right. I would try to be culturally sensitive in how I approached the problem, but that would be more a matter of strategic considerations (how could I be most effective?) than a concern about the propriety of intervention.

One way to deal with the problem of cultural relativism is to say that the international law of human rights is about *universal minimum human rights*. International conventions on human rights should be based on universally recognized rights. Of course this means that international law can codify only the 'lowest common denominator' of rights that are widely accepted. Individual countries should be free to make more stringent specifications of human rights, and to vary among themselves, provided that they recognize and work within that baseline universal minimum. This understanding implies that international human rights law would cover only a narrow base of issues. But the fact that the law focuses on only a few major issues, and is codified without exceptions, could make it much more powerful.

CONCLUSION

Large differences in the income levels of the peoples of different countries have little effect when everyone stays home. But when poor people travel to rich countries, or rich people travel to poor countries (whether as tourists, business people, or soldiers), the inducements promoting prostitution are enormous. With large differences in wealth levels and increasing ease of transportation, beginning in the 19th century, 'prostitution became a multinational enterprise'.

> In the late-nineteenth century commercial prostitution changed in one crucial respect. Routes of supply lengthened and the traffic became international. . . . the popularity of brothels diminished among clientele and inmates, both of whom began to find them confining. . . . This change of taste squeezed the profits of commercial vice, based as they were on the economies of scale of the large brothel. Fortunately for the entrepreneurs, the sex imbalances created by the disproportionate emigration of European men meant that there was a foreign requirement for prostitutes. The steamship and the telegraph made it possible to respond to the new market situation. There is an uncanny parallel between the real crisis of commercial prostitution and the alleged crisis of capitalism in the same period, each resolved by expansion overseas.[56]

International prostitution accelerated rapidly in the 20th century, largely as a result of the expansion of international relationships of every kind. The process is economic:

> The demand for sexual service is most significant where men congregate in large groups separated from home and family. The sexual demands of military men, traveling, businessmen or sailors, and immigrant laborers create a major market for women's bodies. That market is kept supplied through procurers and gangs that run the traffic in women and children.
>
> Procurers work the poverty-stricken countryside of Third World nations as well as bus and train stations of major cities, acquiring girls and young women. They maintain a constant supply to serve the market.[57]

Trafficking for purposes of prostitution follows general patterns of international trade: there is a net flow from poorer to richer countries, and the more highly valued commodities go to the richer countries, or at least to richer people.

In some places the market in women is institutionalized enough to sustain regular auctions. There have been reports of women being sold through auction in Buenos Aires in the 1920s.[58] An unconfirmed report speaks of auctions in Zanzibar, the island part of Tanzania, as recently as the 1970s.[59] In India 'the slave bazaar is so well organized a woman can be kidnapped in Bangladesh and moved across India for sale in Pakistan. Some women are auctioned like cattle at transit centers located just outside big cities'.[60] One reporter tells of a row of business hotels along Showa Avenue in Ueno, Tokyo that has become an auction block for human bodies':

Young Thai girls were being auctioned off left and right at knock-down prices before my eyes. I couldn't stand to watch it. . . . Dealers came from all around – Nara, Osaka, the Kansai area. The highest bid was 750,000 yen (about US$ 3,000) for six months service, but one little black girl went for only 200,000 yen (US $ 800).[61]

In China, according to one report:

The women are transported hundreds of miles from their home and sold at auctions in many of the provinces in the north-west and the coastal regions. Some are only 13 or 14. They are displayed at markets or, in one notorious case in 1988, paraded semi-naked down the main street of a town in Central China.[62]

Child prostitution activities are economic, but there is a fundamentally political dimension as well. Many analysts recognize the importance of power relationships in child prostitution:

The main issue that must be confronted in pedophilia and child prostitution is the element of exploitation. Exploitation exists where the relationship is unequal in terms of power. We speak of exploitation in several senses:

There is the *exploitation of the child*, who is often too young to be aware of the implications of the relationships they enter. . . .

Second, we deal with *class exploitation*. The child prostitutes are often recruited from economically depressed families, who also lack the political power to fight excesses of the pedophiles. . . . In the context of capitalism, there is massive commodification of sex. The child is reduced to a commodity to be exchanged mainly for money. . . .

Finally, we deal with *national exploitation*. We [in the Philippines] have become so desperate about earning dollars that we now prostitute our children to fuel our dying economy. . . .[63]

The idea that the receiving country earns substantial amounts of money from sex tourism may be an illusion because of the foreign control. Yayori Matsui, describing Japanese sex tours to the Philippines, says 'very little foreign money stays in the Philippines; most of it ultimately goes back to Japan':

Japanese tourists are buying package tours from Japanese travel agencies, travelling on Japan Air Lines, staying at hotels owned by Japanese capital, enjoying sight-seeing tours arranged by Japanese travel agency branches, picking up women at Japanese-managed clubs, dining at Japanese restaurants, buying souvenirs at department stores backed by Japanese investments, and returning to Japan the same way they came – Japan Air Lines.[64]

Sex tourism can be compared with the use of foreign labor by multinational corporations in overseas plantations or factories. In many countries, laborers on plantations owned by foreigners are better off than laborers on locally-owned plantations. Similarly, prostitutes serving tourists are likely to be better off than those serving local clients:

> Indeed, whatever the contribution of tourism to the growth of prostitution in Thailand, it should be emphasized that the women working with *farangs* are in many respects the 'elite' among the prostitutes: they earn significantly more than those working with Thais, enjoy greater independence, and are rarely controlled by pimps or pushed into prostitution against their will – which is otherwise quite a common phenomenon.[65]

The objection to multinational corporations, and the objection to foreign clients of prostitutes, is not that they are *foreign* exploiters.

Historically the sexual abuse of young children occurred on a limited, localized scale, but modernization, and the internationalization of prostitution in general has changed that. Several major factors account for child prostitution and its growth. Persistent poverty, and the increasing awareness of the rich-poor gap, create enormous pressure toward prostitution either of oneself or one's children. Females are recruited into lives of prostitution while still under 16. With elaboration of the pedophile trade, there is more interest in the prostitution of children as children. There is widespread interest in pornography involving children. And now it appears that with the rapid growth of the AIDS epidemic, customers prefer encounters with child prostitutes, in the belief that they will be safer. The prospects are grim.

Actions have been taken to control child prostitution, both nationally and internationally, but they have not been enough. It is going to take much more than publicity to end the outrage. In Pangsanjan, some parents dependent on their children's incomes have resisted attempts to end child prostitution. In many places agencies of government, including police forces, are actively involved in prostitution, including child prostitution. In the late 1970s, when a film was made on child prostitution in the Philippines, the government was furious – at the film.[66] In Thailand, the large-scale development of prostitution for the promotion of tourism was critically reviewed in a British documentary film, 'Foreign Bodies' (whose title I have borrowed). Many government officials in Thailand were more upset with the negative publicity created by the film than by the facts that it portrayed. The same thing happened in 1989 when ABC-TV in the United States produced a documentary on child prostitution in Thailand.

International law has not been very effective in limiting prostitution in general or child prostitution in particular. The means for implementing the new *Convention on the Rights of the Child* are not adequate. Legal principles need to be joined to economic and political analyses and actions to combat child prostitution.

The best hope may be to join clearly articulated principles of international law to the implementation capacities of international organizations, especially international nongovernmental organizations. Agencies such as the

International Committee of the Red Cross and Amnesty International suggest the potential for effective action on human rights issues by nongovernmental organizations. The ways in which international organizations take up the pressing issue of child prostitution should not be left to evolve on a fragmentary *ad hoc* basis. It should be well thought out and carefully designed.

Children are being robbed of their childhoods, childhoods which cannot be returned to them later. Vigorous, coordinated legal, economic, and political action is needed, and it is needed urgently.

NOTES

1. Kenneth J. Herrman, Jr. and Michael Jupp, 'International Sex Trade', in Daniel S. Campagna and Donald L. Poffenberger, *The Sexual Trafficking in Children: An Investigation of the Child Sex Trade* (Dover, Massachusetts: Auburn House, 1988), p. 147. Judith Ennew, in *The Sexual Exploitation of Children* (Cambridge: Polity Press, 1986) suggests that much of the published information on child prostitution is exaggerated and sensationalized.
2. Yayori Matsui, *Women's Asia* (London: Zed Books, 1987), pp. 64–66.
3. Ove Narvesen, *The Sexual Exploitation of Children in Developing Countries* (Oso: REDD BARNA, 1989), p. 26.
4. Kathleen Barry, *Female Sexual Slavery* (New York: New York University Press, 1984), pp. 22, 24, 35.
5. Lai Ah Eng, *Peasants, Proletarians and Prostitutes: A Preliminary Investigation into the Work of Chinese Women in Colonial Malaya* (Singapore: Institute of Southeast Asian Studies, 1986), p. 28.
6. Noeleen Heyzer, *Working Women in South-East Asia: Development, Subordination and Emancipation* (Philadelphia: Open University Press, 1986), pp. 62–63.
7. Quoted in Edward J. Bristow, *Prostitution and Prejudice: The Jewish Fight Against White Slavery 1870–1939* (New York: Schocken Books, 1982), p. 1. For a time in central Europe the taint on the Jewish community was relieved by 'the requirement that Jewish women be baptized before being allowed to practise licensed prostitution' (p. 16).
8. Bristow, *Prostitution and Prejudice*, p. 2.
9. Barry, *Female Sexual Slavery*, p. 68.
10. 'Thai Report Highlights Child Slavery Problem', *International Children's Rights Monitor* 2, 1(1985).
11. INTERPOL, *International Symposium on Traffic in Human Beings*, 21st–23rd September 1988, p. 10.
12. INTERPOL, *International Symposium . . .*, p. 9.
13. Herrman and Jupp, 'International Sex Trade', p. 143.
14. Edward J. Bristow, *Vice and Vigilance: Purity Movements in Britain Since 1700* (Totowa, New Jersey: Rowman and Littlefield, 1977), p. 179.
15. Quoted in Ulla Ohse, *Forced Prostitution and Traffic in Women in West Germany* (Edinburgh, Scotland: Human Rights Group, 1984), p. 12.
16. Ramesh Menon, 'Child Prostitutes: Nobody's Children', *India Today*, April 15, 1989, p. 126.
17. Anti-Slavery Society, 'Sexual Exploitation of Children', *Response* 8, No. 2 (Spring 1985), pp. 13–14.
18. Herrman Jupp, 'International Sex Trade', p. 150.
19. Bristow, *Prostitution and Prejudice*, p. 98.
20. Quoted in *Restavek: Child Domestic Labor in Haiti* (Minneapolis, Minnesota: Minnesota Lawyers International Human Rights Committee, 1990), p. 22.

21. Tsukamoto Yumi, 'Trafficking in Women: Sex Tours Come Home to Japan', in *Female Sexual Slavery and Economic Exploitation: Making Local and Global Connections*. Report of a Consultation Organized by the Non-Governmental Liaison Service (New York), San Francisco, California, October 25, 1984, pp. 57–59.

22. Sean O'Callaghan, *The Yellow Slave Trade: A Survey of the Traffic in Women and Children in the East* (London: Anthony Blond, 1968), p. 26.

23. Narvesen, *The Sexual Exploitation of Children in Developing Countries*, p. 46.

24. Narvesen, *The Sexual Exploitation of Children in Developing Countries*, pp. 46–47.

25. Nanya Pancharoen, 'Prostitution is a Lucrative Booming Industry in Thailand', *The Nation*, February 27, 1989.

26. *Child Prostitution and Tourism: Philippines Country Report*, presented at the Ecumenical Consultation on Tourism and Child Prostitution, Chiang Mai, Thailand, May 1990, p. III: 3.

27. 'Child Prostitution: An Unending Vortex', *Thai Development Newsletter*, No. 17 (1989), p. 27.

28. Pico Iyer, *Video Night in Kathmandu: And Other Reports from the Not-So-Far-East* (New York: Knopf, 1988), p. 292.

29. *Pom Pom: Child and Youth Prostitution in the Philippines* (Quezon City, Philippines: Health Action Information Network), 1987, p. 27.

30. *Pom Pom*, p. 27.

31. *Pom Pom*, p. 28. The quotation is from *Spartacus Holiday Help Portfolio: Manila*, published in Amsterdam in 1980.

32. Narvesen, *The Sexual Exploitation of Children in Developing Countries*, p. 27.

33. Kenneth J. Herrman, Jr. and Michael Jupp, 'International Sex Trade', in Campagna and Poffenberger, *The Sexual Trafficking in Children*, p. 143.

34. Aihwa Ong, 'Industrialization and Prostitution in Southeast Asia', in *Female Sexual Slavery and Economic Exploitation*, pp. 13, 18.

35. Linda Hosek, 'Priest to Meet Navy Officials About Philippine Child Sex', *Star-Bulletin* (Honolulu), August 29, 1989, p. A-7.

36. Brenda Stoltzfus, *Situationer on Prostitution in Olongapo*, May 1987, p. 2.

37. Lucy Komisar, 'In a Honduran Red-Light District', *Utne Reader* (April/May 1985), p. 89.

38. Narvesen, *The Sexual Exploitation of Children in Developing Countries*, p. 33.

39. *Child Prostitution and Tourism: Philippines Country Report*, presented at the Ecumenical Consultation on Tourism and Child Prostitution, Chiang Mai, Thailand, May 1990, p. II: 1.

40. Seth Mydans, 'Philippine Town's Parents Battle Effort to Stop Their Children's Sex Trade', *New York Times*, February 25, 1989, p. 3.

41. Ron O'Grady, *Tourism in the Third World: Christian Reflections* (Maryknoll, New York: Orbis Books, 1982), p. 37.

42. Tim Bond, *Hello, What's Your Name, Then? Tourists, Boys, and Sri Lanka. The Results*, July 1980 (From Terre des Hommes, Switzerland).

43. *Sri Lanka National Report*, presented at the Ecumenical Consultation on Tourism and Child Prostitution, Chiang Mai, Thailand, May 1990, p. 3. For an interview with a 14-year old child prostitute in Sri Lanka, see 'My Best Customers are the Tourists', *Child Workers in Asia* 6, No. 2 (June 1990), pp. 16–17.

44. Jack Anderson, 'Bangkok's Kiddy Sex Market', *San Francisco Chronicle*, June 1990.

45. A statement by a NAMBLA spokesman on the organization's philosophy may be found in David Hechler, *The Battle and the Backlash: The Child Sexual Abuse War* (Lexington, Massachusetts: Lexington Books, 1988), pp. 293–299.

46. Michael Fooner, *Interpol: Issues in World Crime and International Criminal Justice* (New York: Plenum Press, 1989); Malcolm Anderson, *Policing the World: Interpol and the Politics of International Police Cooperation* (Oxford: Clarendon Press, 1989).

47. Barry, *Female Sexual Slavery*, pp. 283–298.

48. For a report on the 1989 meeting, see Commission on Human Rights, Sub-Commission on Prevention of Discrimination and Protection of Minorities, Forty-First Session, *Slavery and Slavery-Like Practices: Question of Slavery and the Slave Trade in All Their Practices and Manifestations, Including the Slavery-Like Practice of Apartheid and Colonialism, Report of the Working Group on Contemporary Forms of Slavery on its Fourteenth Session* (Geneva: Economic and Social Council, E/CN.4/Sub.2/1989/39, 28 August 1989).

49. Roger Sawyer, *Children Enslaved* (London: Routledge, 1988), p. 177. See pp. 189–190 for an account of the limited scope of the Working Group's activity.

50. Department of International Economic and Social Affairs, *Activities for the Advancement of Women: Equality, Development and Peace; Report of Jean Fernand-Laurent, Special Rapporteur on the Suppression of the Traffic in Persons and the Exploitation of the Prostitution of Others* (New York: United Nations, 1985).

51. *International Children's Rights Monitor*, Vol. 2, No. 1 (1985).

52. 'Children Caught in Modern Slavery: Conclusions of the Chiang Mai Consultation on Tourism and Child Prostitution', *Contours: The Quarterly Newsletter of the Ecumenical Coalition on Third World Tourism* 4, No. 6 (June 1990), pp. 12–15.

53. Barry, *Female Sexual Slavery*, pp. 23–24.

54. Kathleen Barry, Charlotte Bunch, and Shirley Castley (eds.), *International Feminism: Networking Against Female Sexual Slavery* (New York: International Women's Tribune Center, 1983).

55. *Female Sexual Slavery and Economic Exploitation: Making Local and Global Connections.* Report of a Consultation Organized by the Non-Governmental Liaison Service (New York), San Francisco, California, October 25, 1984.

56. Bristow, *Prostitution and Prejudice*, pp. 2–3, 33–34.

57. Barry, *Female Sexual Slavery*, p. 70.

58. Bristow, *Prostitution and Prejudice*, p. 135.

59. Barry, *Female Sexual Slavery*, pp. 53–58.

60. Arthur Bonner, *Averting the Apocalypse: Social Movements in India Today* (Durham, North Carolina: Duke University Press, 1990), p. 45. Also see K. T. Suresh, *A Contextual View of Tourism and Child Prostitution in India*, presented at the Ecumenical Consultation on Tourism and Child Prostitution, Chiang Mai, Thailand, May 1990. Details may be found in M. Rita Rozario, *Trafficking in Women and Children in India (Sexual Exploitation and Sale)* (New Delhi: Uppal Publishing House, 1988).

61. Quoted in Yumi, 'Trafficking in Women: Sex Tours Come Home to Japan', in *Female Sexual Slavery and Economic Exploitation*, p. 57.

62. Simon Long, 'Chasing the Dragons of the Flesh Trade', *The Sunday Correspondent* (London), January 14, 1990.

63. M. L. Tan, 'An Overview of Pedophilia and Child Prostitution in the Philippines', in *Pom Pom*, pp. 12–13.

64. Matsui, *Women's Asia*, pp. 70–71.

65. Erik Cohen, 'Thai Girls and Farang Men: The Edge of Ambiguity', *Annals of Tourism Research* 9 (1982), p. 409.

66. M. L. Tan, 'Preface', in *Pom Pom*, p. 1.

REFERENCES

Barry, Kathleen. *Female Sexual Slavery*. New York: New York University Press, 1984.

Barry, Kathleen; Bunch, Charlotte; and Castley, Shirley, eds. *International Feminism: Networking Against Female Sexual Slavery*. New York: International Women's Tribune Center, 1984.

Bristow, Edward J. *Prostitution and Prejudice: The Jewish Fight Against White Slavery 1870–1939*. New York: Schocken Books, 1982.

Bristow, Edward J. *Vice and Vigilance: Purity Movements in Britain Since 1700.* Totowa. New Jersey: Rowman and Littlefield, 1977.

Campagna, Daniel S. and Poffenberger, Donald L. *The Sexual Trafficking in Children: An Investigation of the Child Sex Trade.* Dover, Massachusetts: Auburn House, 1988.

Department of International Economic and Social Affairs. *Activities for the Advancement of Women: Equality, Development and Peace; Report of Jean Fernand-Laurent, Special Rapporteur on the Suppression of the Traffic in Persons and the Exploitation of the Prostitution of Others.* New York: United Nations, 1985.

Ennew, Judith. *The Sexual Exploitation of Children.* Cambridge: Polity Press, 1986.

Female Sexual Slavery and Economic Exploitation: Making Local and Global Connections. Report of a Consultation Organized by the Non-Governmental Liaison Service, New York. San Francisco, California, October 25, 1984.

Matsui, Yayori. *Women's Asia.* London: Zed Books, 1987.

Narvesen, Ove. *The Sexual Exploitation of Children in Developing Countries.* Oslo: REDD BARNA, 1989.

Pom Pom: Child and Youth Prostitution in the Philippines. Quezon City, Philippines: Health Action Information Network, 1987.

Rozario, M. Rita. *Trafficking in Women and Children in India (Sexual Exploitation and Sale).* New Delhi: Uppal Publishing House, 1988.

FRANÇOISE KRILL*

24. The Protection of Children in Armed Conflicts

1. INTRODUCTION

The Convention on the Rights of the Child was adopted by the United Nations General Assembly on 20 November 1989. It marks the culmination of a long legislative process initiated by the Polish government in 1978.

Whereas most of the Convention's provisions are concerned with human rights as a whole, only one – Article 38 on children in armed conflicts – relates to international humanitarian law. There can be no doubt that in time of war children are in even greater need of protection and assistance than in peacetime. The concern of States to protect children in such situations is therefore fully justified, and Article 38 reflects that concern. But, to be effective, any new law must mark an improvement over existing law instruments, in this case the Geneva Conventions of 1949 and their Additional Protocols of 1977, many of whose provisions afford special protection to children in armed conflicts. The present text will examine whether Article 38 represents such an improvement.

2. HISTORICAL REVIEW

2.1. *The International Committee of the Red Cross (ICRC) and International Humanitarian Law*[1]

The ICRC has long been concerned about the welfare of children, especially those caught in armed conflicts. In January 1939, the ICRC and the Save the Children Fund International Union drew up a draft convention for the protection of children in armed conflicts. Unfortunately, the outbreak of the Second World War prevented its adoption. Immediately after the war, the ICRC resumed its attempts to create special provisions for the protection of children. The Fourth Geneva Convention relative to the Protection of Civilian Persons

* International Committee of the Red Cross, Geneva.

M. Freeman and P. Veerman (eds.), The Ideologies of Children's Rights, 347–356.
© 1992 *Kluwer Academic Publishers. Printed in the Netherlands.*

in Time of War was adopted in 1949. It contains no less than seventeen Articles specifically protecting children.

In the conflicts which have taken place since the Convention was adopted, the victims have for the most part been civilians, and above all women and children. The fact that so many civilians, including children, have been killed is largely due to the use of new, indiscriminate methods and means of warfare. Moreover, the most prevalent type of recent conflict – regular troops pitted against guerilla forces – has too often seen young adolescents brandishing weapons and ready to use them indiscriminately. The participation of children in hostilities puts not only the children themselves in mortal danger but also those who become their targets. To meet this new situation, the 1949 Geneva Conventions needed to be supplemented. This was achieved on 10 June 1977, when the Protocols additional to the Geneva Conventions were adopted by the Diplomatic Conference on the Reaffirmation and Development of International Law. These two new instruments afford special protection to children and, for the first time, deal with the participation of children in hostilities.

2.2.   *The United Nations and Human Rights*

The League of Nations and later the United Nations have also given their attention to the protection of children.[2] Only in 1974, however, did the UN General Assembly deal with children in war in its Declaration on the Protection of Women and Children in Emergency and Armed Conflict. Among other things, the Declaration prohibits attacks on the civilian population and all forms of repression and cruel and inhuman treatment of women and children.[3] Fifteen years later, the Convention on the Rights of the Child, Article 38 of which is on the protection of children in armed conflict, was adopted.

3.   THE RELATIONSHIP BETWEEN INTERNATIONAL HUMANITARIAN LAW AND THE CONVENTION ON THE RIGHTS OF THE CHILD

3.1.   *Protection of Children under International Humanitarian Law*

3.1.1.   *Definition of a Child*
It is difficult to decide at what age a person is still a child and when that person becomes an adult. International humanitarian law gives no precise definition of a child, but in several provisions it sets the age of fifteen as that below which a child must enjoy special protection.[4] Other provisions set a higher age. Article 68 (4) of the Fourth Geneva Convention 1949 provides that 'in any case, the death penalty may not be pronounced on a protected person who was under eighteen years of age at the time of the offence'. This age of eighteen is also repeated in Article 77 (5) of Additional Protocol I 1977 and Article 6 (4) of Additional Protocol II. Thus, some flexibility is appropriate, for there

are persons who in many respects remain children, both physically and mentally, after the age of fifteen.[5]

According to the Convention on the Rights of the Child, 'a child means every human being below the age of eighteen years unless, under the law applicable to the child, majority is attained earlier'. However, paragraphs 2 and 3 of Article 38 have adopted the wording of Article 77 (2) of Protocol I, which, as we will see later, sets the age of fifteen as that below which children may not take part in hostilities.

3.1.2. *Protection of Children as Members of the Civilian Population*

3.1.2.1. *General Protection.* Children are protected in a general way by internal humanitarian law as persons not taking part in hostilities. To begin with, they are protected against abuses by the party to the conflict in whose power they find themselves and are included in the category of persons protected by the Fourth Geneva Convention for the protection of civilians in wartime. As such, they benefit from all the provisions based on the fundamental principle of humane treatment. In a non-international armed conflict, such persons are protected by Article 3 common to the four Geneva Conventions. In addition, as civilians they benefit from the rules set down by international humanitarian law concerning the conduct of hostilities. These rules, which stipulate that a distinction must be made between civilians and combatants and ban attacks against the civilian population, are set forth in the 1977 Additional Protocols.

3.1.2.1. *Special Protection.* As particularly vulnerable persons, children who do not take part in the hostilities also enjoy additional special protection. Although the Fourth Geneva Convention contains many provisions protecting children, the principle on which these provisions are based was not clearly stated until the two Protocols were adopted:

> Children shall be the object of special respect and shall be protected against any form of indecent assault. The Parties to the conflict shall provide them with the care and aid they require, whether because of their age or for any other reason (Protocol I, Article 77).

For non-international conflicts, Article 4 of Protocol II applies. The Geneva Conventions of 1949 and their Additional Protocols of 1977 contain no less than 25 Articles affording special protection to children. First, they are protected against the effects of hostilities (admission to hospital and safety zones of children under fifteen, of expectant mothers and mothers of children under seven years of age: Fourth Convention, Article 14; evacuation of children and maternity cases from besieged or encircled areas: Fourth Convention, Article 17).

The right to care and assistance is guaranteed (children under fifteen, expectant mothers and maternity cases are entitled, within the terms of Article 23 of the Fourth Convention, to be sent medical supplies, food and clothing; other provisions such as those of Articles 50, 81, 89 and 91 of the said Convention and Article 70 of Protocol I prescribe similar assistance). There are also guarantees concerning personal rights (Fourth Convention, Article 50). In addition, the principle of preferential treatment is set forth in Articles 38 and 50 of the Fourth Convention.

Children's cultural environment, education and the unity of their families must be preserved (Articles 24, 25, 50, 51, 82 and 94 of the Fourth Convention; Articles 74 and 78 of Protocol I).

Children who are arrested, detained or interned must be held in quarters separate from the quarters of adults (Protocol I, Article 77). The death penalty may not be carried out on persons who have not attained the age of eighteen years at the time the offence was committed (Fourth Convention, Article 68, and Protocol I, Article 77).

There are also special provisions for children who have been orphaned or separated (Articles 24 and 50 of the Fourth Convention).

Finally, the Fourth Convention calls for the release, repatriation, return to the place of residence or accommodation in a neutral country of children, pregnant women and mothers with young children (Fourth Convention, Article 132). These rules were to some extent included in Protocol II for the protection of victims of non-international armed conflict.

3.1.3. *Participation by Children in Hostilities*
It has not been possible absolutely to prohibit participation by children in hostilities. The Additional Protocols have, however, made significant progress by specifically banning the recruitment of persons below the age of fifteen (Protocol I, Article 77, para. 2, and Protocol II, Article 4, para. 3). Moreover, Protocol I encourages the parties to a conflict, if they recruit persons between the ages of fifteen and eighteen, to give priority to the oldest (Article 77, para. 2).

If, despite the provisions of the Protocols, children who have not attained the age of fifteen years take a direct part in hostilities and are captured, they continued to benefit from the special protection afforded by the Protocols (Protocol I, Article 77, para. 3, and Protocol II, Article 4, para. 3d).[6]

3.2. *Article 38 of the Convention on the Rights of the Child*

At its thirty-fourth session in February 1978, the UN Commission on Human Rights decided to add the question of a convention on the rights of the child to its Agenda. To expedite the process of drawing up the Convention, an open-ended (i.e. not restricted to government representatives) Working Group was set up in 1979 and chaired by Mr. Adam Lopatka of Poland (the country that had initiated the entire process).[7]

At the Working Group's seventh session (28 January to 1 February 1985), which preceded the forty-first session of the Commission on Human Rights, the Netherlands, Swedish and Finnish delegations, supported by Belgium, Peru and Senegal, proposed the incorporation of an article on children in armed conflicts, there having been no such provision in the initial draft.[8] This Article was added, with the backing of a number of NGOs. It had already been included in the latter's 1984 draft, though there it had taken a somewhat different form. That same year, the Islamic Republic of Iran had also submitted a proposal. Also in 1986, the Iraqi delegation tabled a new provision but withdrew it during the debate. In 1986, the NGOs submitted a slightly modified version of their 1984 text. In the end, it was the proposal submitted by Sweden, the Netherlands and Finland which was discussed at the Working Group's eighth session in 1986. After lengthy debate, Article 20 (later to become Article 38) passed the first reading. It read as follows:

1. The States Parties to the present Convention undertake to respect and to ensure respect for rules of international humanitarian law applicable to them in armed conflicts which are relevant to the child.
2. States Parties to the present Convention shall take all feasible measures to ensure that no child takes a direct part in hostilities and they shall refrain in particular from recruiting any child who has not attained the age of fifteen years into their armed forces.
3. In accordance with their obligations under international humanitarian law to protect the civilian population in armed conflicts, States Parties to this Convention shall take all feasible measures to ensure protection and care of children who are affected by an armed conflict.[9]

Since this provision failed to preserve the essential headway that had been made in the Geneva Conventions of 1949 and their Additional Protocols of 1977, the Swedish and Swiss delegations, supported by the Netherlands and Venezuela, urgently asked the Working Group (at its ninth session in 1987) to reopen debate on Article 20.[10] The Swedish and Swiss representatives invoked the resolution (No. IX) on the protection of children in armed conflicts which had been adopted by the 25th International Conference of the Red Cross in Geneva in 1986. Point 7 of that resolution '. . .stresses that the protection accorded by the new Convention should be at least the same as that accorded boy the Geneva Conventions and the two Additional Protocols.[11]

At the tenth session in 1988, Sweden proposed amendments to the Working Group based on the above-mentioned resolution and UN General Assembly resolution 41/120. The Netherlands also proposed amendments but withdrew them in favour of the Swedish proposal. In the discussion that followed, most delegates showed willingness to make improvements to the text during the second reading in order to bring it into line with international humanitarian law; some were even prepared to go further. It was thereupon decided at the 1988 session to add to paragraph 2 of Article 20 the second sentence in paragraph 2 of Article 77 of Protocol I:

> In recruiting among those persons who have attained the age of fifteen years but who have not attained the age of eighteen years, States Parties shall endeavour to give priority to those how are oldest.[12]

At the same session, it was also decided to carry out a technical review of the draft Convention to facilitate the second reading.[13] UNHCR, UNICEF and the ICRC all made their views known during 1988.[14]

The Working Group met from 28 November to 9 December 1988 and examined the text that had passed the first reading with the amendments proposed by UNICEF. It also examined another text submitted by a drafting committee composed of representatives of France, India, Italy, Mozambique, Norway and the United States and observers from Angola, Australia, Austria, the Netherlands, Sweden, UNHCR, the ICRC and Rädda Barnen International.[15] After lengthy debate,[16] the following text passed the second reading by the Working Group on 7 December 1988:

1. States Parties undertake to respect and to ensure respect for rules of international humanitarian law applicable to them in armed conflicts which are relevant to the child.
2. States Parties shall take all feasible measures to ensure that persons who have not attained the age of fifteen years do not take a direct part in hostilities.
3. States Parties shall refrain from recruiting any person who has not attained the age of fifteen years into their armed forces. In recruiting among those persons who have attained the age of fifteen years but who have not attained the age of eighteen years, States Parties shall endeavour to give priority to those who are oldest.
4. In accordance with their obligations under international humanitarian law to protect the civilian population in armed conflicts, States Parties shall take all feasible measures to ensure protection and care of children who are affected by an armed conflict.

The question of a Convention on the Rights of the Child was then referred to the forty-fifty session of the Commission on Human Rights and was tabled for consideration (agenda item 13) on 8 March 1989.[17]

Article 38 (the former Article 20) was adopted without amendment by the Commission and later by the UN Economic and Social Council. Finally, it was adopted along with the rest of the Convention by the UN General Assembly on 20 November 1989.[18]

3.3. *Article 38 in Relation to International Humanitarian Law*

3.3.1. *First Paragraph*
This paragraph refers directly to international humanitarian law, i.e. the Geneva Conventions of 1949. Since 165 States – virtually the entire international community – are party to those instruments today, it follows that children enjoy

the special protection of 17 Articles thereof and, obviously, of the four Geneva Conventions as a whole. As for the Additional Protocols, it is true that they are not binding on States which have not yet ratified them. But there are, today, 99 States party to Protocol I and 89 to Protocol II. Moreover, although certain States have for various reasons not ratified the Protocols, the eight Articles relating to children have never been disputed. Some States even regard those provisions as being part of customary law.[19]

3.3.2. *Second Paragraph*

The drafters of Article 38 could have taken advantage of the opportunity to improve protection by requiring that the States Parties should take '*all necessary measures*' instead of '*all feasible measures*'. As it stands, the wording of the second paragraph means that voluntary participation by children is not totally prohibited. At the 1974–1977 Diplomatic Conference, the ICRC had suggested the words '*necessary measures*' but this was, unfortunately, not accepted.[20]

Likewise, the drafters could have given more extensive protection by removing the word 'direct'. The ICRC had suggested this, too, during the Diplomatic Conference, but the proposal was not approved. It can thus reasonably be inferred from Article 38 that indirect acts of participation are not covered, for example gathering and transmitting military information and transporting weapons, munitions and other supplies.[21] Article 38 therefore offers no improvement in protection over Protocol I; it even represents a regression vis-à-vis Protocol II (Article 4, para. 3c) which uses neither the words 'feasible measures' nor 'direct'.[22]

The minimum age for participation was finally set at fifteen. Here again, protection could have been extended. Some delegations had expressly declared that eighteen was the age set by legislation in their countries and would continue to apply.[23]

3.3.3. *Third Paragraph*

This paragraph uses wording taken from Protocol I, Article 77, para. 2 (end of first sentence, second sentence). This wording is the result of a compromise, just as it was at the 1974–1977 Diplomatic Conference. Although one delegation there had proposed in an amendment that the limit on non-recruitment should be raised from fifteen to eighteen years, the majority was opposed to extending the prohibition of recruitment beyond fifteen years. However, to take this proposal into account, it was provided that in the case of recruitment of persons between fifteen and eighteen, priority should be given to the oldest.[24]

3.3.4. *Fourth Paragraph*

The words 'feasible measures' in this paragraph go further than anything else in the Article to weaken international humanitarian law. The drafters of Article 38 did not include the rule prohibiting attacks on civilians and *a fortiori* on children. One of the fundamental rules of international humanitarian law applicable in armed conflict is the one stating that all parties to the conflict shall, at all times, distinguish between the civilian population and the combatants in such a way that civilians and civilian objects are spared. Neither the civilian population as such nor individual civilians may be the object of attack; attacks may be directed only against military objectives. This principle conveys the content of the humanitarian rules applicable in any of the situations normally faced by armed forces. These rules are set forth in greater detail in treaties such as the 1907 Hague Regulations and the 1949 Geneva Conventions, while the two Additional Protocols of 1977 reaffirm and further develop them. Under these treaties, the ban on attacks against the civilian population is absolute (Protocol I, Article 51, para. 2), as is the right to care and assistance. Article 23 of the Fourth Geneva Convention, for example, stipulates that 'each High Contracting Party shall permit the free passage of all consignments of essential foodstuffs, clothing and tonics intended for children under fifteen, expectant mothers and maternity cases'. Several other provisions of the Fourth Convention and Protocol I prescribe similar assistance (see Chapter 1, subheading 'Special protection').[25]

3.3.5. *Safeguard Clause*

After the second reading, the ICRC saw that there was no prospect of improving Article 38 and therefore proposed the elimination of paragraphs 2, 3 and 4, to leave only the first paragraph with its reference to international humanitarian law.[26] First, the inclusion of such a safeguard clause alone would have avoided the introduction into an instrument entirely devoted to human rights of a provision dealing with international humanitarian law, whose nature and mechanisms of implementation are quite different. The fields of application of those two bodies of law are also different: human rights law is normally applied in peacetime whereas international humanitarian law is applicable in times of armed conflict. Moreover, human rights law essentially governs the relations between the State and its own citizens, while international humanitarian law governs those between the State and enemy aliens.[27] Secondly, a simple safeguard clause would have obviated the risk of the other provisions that afford special protection to children in such situations being ignored; limiting the Article to a reference to international humanitarian law would thus have avoided confusion, ambiguity and erroneous interpretation.

In the end, Article 38 was adopted by the General Assembly in 1989 with no amendment following the second reading.

4. CONCLUSION

Article 38 does not fulfil all the hopes that were placed in it. However, Article 41 of the Convention does contain a general safeguard clause and, as we have seen, Article 38 refers to international humanitarian law in its first paragraph. Thus, the rules of international humanitarian law, in particular the 25 provisions specifically protecting children, remain preponderant.

Like the other provisions of the Convention, Article 38 is the result of a compromise and must be considered as the lowest common denominator. Any State that so wishes may provide for greater protection through domestic legislation.[28] It would also be desirable for governments to indicate their intention by making a declaration on their ratification. The Convention is undeniably a step forward compared with the 1924 and 1959 Declarations on the Rights of the Child, which did not have the same force in law. Lastly, the Convention provides for a Committee on the Rights of the Child, consisting of 10 experts, to be established six months after its entry into force with the purpose of examining the progress made by the States Parties in fulfilling their obligations under the Convention. This will, of course, include Article 38. Thus the Convention is unquestionably a major new tool to ensure increased respect for the provisions of international law according special protection to children in armed conflict.

NOTES

1. The Geneva Conventions of 1949 and their Additional Protocols of 1977.
2. – Geneva Declaration of 1924;
   – Declaration of the Rights of the Child (1959);
   – Universal Declaration of Human Rights;
   – International Covenant on Civil and Political Rights (Articles 23 and 24);
   – International Covenant on Economic, Social and Cultural Rights (Article 10).
3. *Human Rights, a Compilation of International Instruments*, United Nations, New York (1983), pp. 130–132.
4. Dutli, M. T., 'Captured child combatants', *International Review of the Red Cross*, No. 278 (1990), p. 423.
5. *Commentary on the Additional Protocols*, ICRC, Geneva 1987, pp. 899–900, para. 3179.
6. Plattner, D., 'Protection of Children in International Humanitarian Law', *International Review of the Red Cross*, No. 240 (1984), p. 150.
7. Note from the Secretary-General on the adoption of the Convention on the Rights of the Child (A/44/616) and the Report of the Third Committee (A/44/736).
8. The proposed article reads as follows:

   1. States Parties to the present Convention undertake to respect and to ensure respect for rules of international humanitarian law applicable in armed conflicts which are relevant to children.
   2. In order to implement these obligations, States Parties to the present Convention shall, in conformity with the relevant rules of international humanitarian law, refrain in particular from recruiting children into the armed forces and shall take all feasible measures to ensure that children do not take part in hostilities.

9. UN document of 13 March 1986 (E/CN.4/1986/39), pp. 26–30.
10. UN document of 9 March 1987 (E/CN.4/1987/25), pp. 41–42.
11. See also statements made by Rädda Barnen International (UN document E/CN.4/1987/WG.1/WP.3) and the ICRC (UN document E/CN.4/1987/WG.1/WP.4).

12. UN document of 6 April 1988 (E/CN.4/1988/28), pp. 19–20.
13. Ibid., pp. 49–52.
14. Technical review of the draft Convention on the Rights of the Child, UN document of 15 October 1988 (E/CN.4/1988/WG.1/CRP.1), pp. 43–45.*
15. UN document of 2 March 1989 (E/CN.4/1989/48), p. 108–110.*
16. Ibid., p. 110–114*; 'Debate on children in armed conflicts', document compiled by Rädda Barnen International.
17. 'Debate of 8 March 1989', Rädda Barnen International.
18. Report of the Economic and Social Council (A/44/3, chapter V, section A); Note from the Secretary-General on the adoption of the Convention on the Rights of the Child (A/44/616); Report of the Third Committee (A/44/736).
19. During a discussion organized by the American Society of International Law, a representative of the US State Department said that the United States views 'Article 77, paragraph 1 as already part of customary international law and Article 77, paragraphs 2, 3 and 4 as supportable for inclusion in customary law through State practice' (M. J. Matheson, 'The United States' position on the relation of customary international law to the 1977 Protocols additional to the 1949 Geneva Conventions', published in *The American University Journal of International Law and Policy*, p. 419 ff.
20. *Commentary on the Additional Protocols*, paragraph 3184.
21. Ibid., para. 3187.
22. Ibid., para. 4557.
23. UN document of 2 March 1989 (E/CN.4/1989/48), p. 113.*
24. *Commentary on the Additional Protocols*, para. 3188.
25. See also ICRC statement (UN document E/CN.4/1987/WG.1/WP.4).
26. ICRC statement on point 13 to the forty-fifth session of the UN Commission on Human Rights (Geneva, March 1989) (see also *L'enfant dans la guerre*, International Red Cross and Red Crescent Museum, Geneva 1990, p. 90–91).
27. Schindler, D., 'Human Rights and Humanitarian Law – Interrelationship of the Laws', *American University Law Review*, 31 (1982), pp. 935–943. Sassoli, M., 'Mise en Oeuvre du Droit International Humanitaire et du Droit International des Droits de l'Homme: une Comparaison', *Annuaire suisse du droit international* XLIII (1987), pp. 24–61.
28. Circular of 26 March 1990 from the ICRC and the League of Red Cross and Red Crescent Societies to the National Societies concerning the UN Convention on the Rights of the Child (see also footnote 26).

* Numbers refer to the pages in the French-language version.

PHILIP E. VEERMAN*

25. Towards a More Integrated Basis for the Children's Rights Movement

The Aims and Outcome of the First International Interdisciplinary Study-Group on Ideologies of Children's Rights

The idea of a Study-Group on children's rights was the brainchild of Dr. Menachem Horovitz, the first ombudsman for children in Israel[1] and chairman of the Israel section of Defence for Children International. Dr. Horovitz enlisted the support of Prof. Michael Freeman of the Faculty of Laws of University College London. On September 22, 1988, Dr. Horovitz brought together representatives of the Faculty of Law of the Hebrew University of Jerusalem, the Center for the Study of Youth Policy of Haifa University and the Israel Section of Defence for Children International (DCI).

Dr. Mike Saltman of the Anthropology Department of Haifa University, who joined the local organizing committee, proposed to look at children's rights comparatively. It was a proposal for serious reflection on the different theories, policies and practices in the children's rights field.

The Scandinavian School of Legal Realism[2] relativises the concept of rights. In their opinion 'rights' are merely beliefs of people and expressions of feelings. It was from them that Mike Saltman[3] got his idea to include the term *ideologies* in the name of the Study-Group. This approach about rights fitted very well with studies of the *concept of childhood*[4] arguing that this was both historically and culturally relative. Melton[5] added that the concepts of childhood and rights are imbedded in broader authority relations with society.

Many colleagues involved in children's rights have no time to reflect upon their work. They have to adopt a 'shoot from the hip' approach: they see a violation of children's rights and act. Before they have time to reflect upon what they have done, they already have to deal with other violations. The Study-Group wanted to create such a moment of reflection. This Study-Group came at a crucial time for the children's rights movement. With the entering into force of the new UN Convention on the Rights of the Child on September 2, 1990, the Children's Rights Movement could not afford to be amateurish.

We did not have illusions that our efforts would lead to a new *science*. Such romantic ideas were cherished, for instance, in the first half of our century

* Defence for Children International, Jerusalem.

M. Freeman and P. Veerman (eds.), The Ideologies of Children's Rights, 357–363.
© 1992 *Kluwer Academic Publishers. Printed in the Netherlands.*

by the Polish-Jewish educator and pediatrician Janusz Korczak.[6] He thought about 'a great synthesis of a child, concerning which I had daydreams in the libraries of Paris, while excitedly reading the great and extraordinary French classics of clinical medicine'. In 1899 the first issue of a journal called *the Paidologist* appeared in the United Kingdom with the aim to establish such a new integrated science of the child. Our aims were ambitious, but not *so* ambitious. We wanted to stimulate interdisciplinary thinking, further cooperation and a serious foundation for practical work. We hoped to break the splendid isolation of the different disciplines, to link the different scientific components, without trying to create a supra-disciplinary paradigm.

According to Cutler[7] who spoke at the First International Conference on Interdisciplinary Research Groups, 'interdisciplinary research evokes strong reactions. One widespread view holds' (according to him) 'that mamy important scientific and social problems cut across the boundaries of the scholarly disciplines and, therefore, the interdisciplinary approach is a "must".'

Rossini and Porter[8] reported in the book *Problems in Interdisciplinary Studies* 'that interdisciplinarity is not stimulated by Universities, and there is hardly any training for such an approach. They state that *integration* will emerge as the eminent criterion of interdisciplinarity'. Children's rights is 'par exellence' a field in which an interdisciplinary approach can be helpful. However, the subject of children's rights is so diffuse that it must be ultimately reduced to highly specific problems for any kind of focussed dispassionate analysis. It does not only bring into question the meaning of the idea of *right* as a legal concept, but also raises the problematic issue of cultural relativity underlying the status of children in a universal context.

Is it possible to categorize under the same heading of *children's rights* such phenomena as 'child slavery' and the issue of 'the rights of children in the media and advertising'? What may be perceived by a Westener as 'child slavery' may be nothing more than a normative cultural pattern in other cultures that is necessary for the efficient functioning of a traditional economy. Alternatively, and perhaps more realistically, the idea of children's rights may be the product of that traditional economic system's adaptation to its transformation into a market economy. The legislation of children's rights under these circumstances does not necessarily constitute a remedy.

The concepts 'right' and 'child' are themselves subject to change, and we need the participation of philosophers of law and historians of childhood to explain to what extent this has influenced our present thinking on children's rights.

An important input has to be made by developmental psychologists, since their insight in developmental stages and needs of children is essential. Other disciplines[9] are equally important.

A fascinating but sometimes complicating factor is that *within* the disciplines there are such differences of opinion. As organizers of the Study-Group we took the stand that the different opinions and world pictures are enriching our undertaking rather than disturbing it. A precondition was that the world pictures (the 'Weltanschauungen' as the Germans say) of the participants were open enough. As the Dutch psychologist Van Parreren[10] has explained this means that it is recognized that 'a world picture that accepts that a person's discipline and point of view only explains *certain* aspects of man, but does not pretend to comprise the "total human being"'.

Nauta[11] has pointed out that 'the theory resulting from the end product of an interdisciplinary project depends on the organization of the project'. He called this interdependence of organization and theory the first law of interdisciplinarity. The role of the organizer becomes clear when we realize that it was his task to invite the representatives of the different disciplines. Nauta pointed out that an interdisciplinary project can only be fruitful if you have a minimum number of experts in your project. As the organizer, I invited maybe too many experts. My collegues were afraid that too many would come and we would have a Conference instead of a Study-Group. But I was greatly helped by fate (some invited experts fell ill or had other problems) as well as by President Saddam Hussein of Iraq and President Bush of the United States! Quite a few experts were advised not to travel to a country where war could break out any day. Those who came figured that the war would not start before the deadline given to Iraq (to leave Kuwait) had passed. Now we know that they were right. Although the tension of a coming war could already be felt, everybody tried to continue their work as normally as possible. The Study-Group started on December 9, 1990. One of the participants, Hans-Joachim Heintze[12] wrote about the time of the Study-Group: 'Timing and planning for a First International Study-Group could not have been better. Shortly after the coming into force of the UN Convention on the Rights of the Child, the Study-Group met in a region in crisis in which children would more and more be feeling the consequences of that conflict'.[13] When the Study-Group took place, distribution of gas masks and other protective material had already been started in Israel.[14] On the night of January 16 the first scud missiles were fired at Israel. On February 28 gasmasks could be stored away.

At a time when all other scheduled international academic meetings in the region were called off due to participants' cancellations, this group of highly motivated professionals worked hard and came to know each other quite well. The atmosphere was cordial. A rich program of events contributed to this atmosphere. In addition to the academic sessions informal discussions took place with persons and agencies working on children's issues in Israel and the occupied territories. There was a visit to the Holocaust Memorial (in particular the Children's Memorial) and we gathered around the statue of the pioneer in the field of children's rights, Janusz Korczak[15], who perished with the children of his orphanage in the death camp Treblinka. The Study-Group visited the youth wing of the Sharon prison[16] and the youth village Yemin Orde where many new immigrant Ethiopian Jewish adolescents study. The YMCA in East Jerusalem hosted a meeting where the Study-Group met with representatives of human rights organisations working for Palestinian children in the occupied territories. Speakers included representatives from the YMCA

Rehabilitation Center for wounded Palestinian youngsters[17], the Hotline for the rights of the individual, the Quakers' legal aid program, B'tselem, the Information Center on Human Rights in the Occupied Territories, Prof. Charles Greenbaum (of the Association for Civil Rights in Israel) and Dr. Awni Habash, DCI's lawyer who represents Palestinian minors arrested for security offences when their parents cannot pay for a lawyer.[18]

Participants appreciated the mixture of theory and discussion with field workers. The confrontation with the reality of the world of children's rights in Israel and the occupied territories was respectively interesting and shocking.

The Conference was a 'closed' event. Sessions were attended by the overseas participants and a small number of local experts. Three sessions, however, were open to the general public and advertised accordingly. One was held (in observance of International Human Rights Day) in the Senate Hall at the Hebrew University. The subject was 'children's rights and human rights', and participants included Prof. Alexander Minkowski of France, Trevor Davies, Secretary General of Defence for Children International, Prof. Adam Lopatka of the Polish Academy of Sciences in Warsaw[19], and Albert Likhanov (Lenin Children's Fund, Moscow).[20] A special session was held on 'Equity and Children's Rights'.[21] This reflected the close connection between the development of child protection and equity law, originating in the policy of the Chancery Courts in medieval times to supervise guardians. A third public session was held at Haifa University. Child abuse and neglect was the topic of the evening.

The Goethe Institute made the participation of three leading German experts (one from former East Germany) possible, and the Swedish Institute subsidized the participation of Prof. Ulla Jacobsen (Faculty of Law, University of Lund). On the evening of December 12, 1990, almost all participants came to discuss my idea to start an *International Interdisciplinary Journal of Children's Rights*. Although many problems were expected (for instance how to make a journal academic and still be accessible to people in the field) the plan was met with great enthusiasm. The idea of an international journal has kept all the participants of the Study-Group in touch with each other. A foundation (the 'Children's Rights Publication Foundation') was founded in 1991 by the undersigned in Amsterdam, the Netherlands, with the aim to develop and realize plans to start an academic journal on children's rights.

In April 1992, Study-Group participant Michael Longford (the European Center for Social Welfare and Research), Chairman of the new Foundation, signed a contract with Martinus Nijhoff. In 1993 the first issue of the new journal will appear. Almost all participants of the Study-Group are either in the 'International Editorial Advisory Committee' or became members of the board of the Foundation. Others promised to contribute in other ways to the realization of the initiative.

On December 14, 1990, when the participants left, the real work – to try to give the children's rights movement a more integrated basis – really started. Because the academic sessions of the Study-Group had concentrated on the discussion on the different papers presented by the participants (most of which are published in this book), there was no time to reflect more on, for instance, what kind of philosophies[22] of children's rights were expressed in the different papers. What we realized was that the Study-Group would have been more interdisciplinary if more anthropologists, philosophers, educators, physicians, psychologists, social workers and historians had participated. There was still an 'overweight' of legal discussion and legal issues on the agenda. But it was the first such Study-Group and the field has been dominated by the legal profession until now. It would have been better if we had more practitioners[23] in our Study-Group (such as Gwen James of the 'Voice for the Child in Care' from London who participated). And last but not least: representatives from the Third World were missing and missed. For them (and the practitioners) it was mostly the financial obstacle that prevented them from participating. The organizers[24] approached quite a few colleagues in the Third World and we approached foundations. However, travel grants are not something foundations like to give. The next Study-Group will have to do better. Such a second event is in preparation, and will be held in Paris, probably already in the winter of 1993. Under consideration is to start an 'Association for the Advancement of the Study of Children's Rights' to organize that event and similar activities.[25]

If we evaluate what was achieved, we have to be modest. We did not come to a real integrated vision on children's rights, but that aim was too high to achieve in five days. We also did not succeed in discussing what kind of children's rights ideology was expressed in each paper, since this could not happen without a joint framework of analysis. However, stimulated by an interesting group process and each other's enthusiasm, the very first steps on the way towards a more integrated basis for the children's rights movement were made. The mechanisms (an interdisciplinary journal and a plan for more Study-Groups) were created to reach that goal in the future. We hope that the enthusiasm of the Study-Group will also have got through to the readers of this book.

NOTES

1. Dr. Horovitz worked as Ombudsman for Children for the Jerusalem Council for Children and Youth. See: Flekkøy, Malfrid Grude, *Models for Monitoring the Protection of Children's Rights Meeting Report*, Florence, 1991. UNICEF/International Child Development Center, pp. 38–41 (about the work of the Ombudsman in Jerusalem).
2. See: Olivecrona, Karl, *Law and Facts*, 1939; Hagerström, Axel, *Inquiries into the Nature of Law and Morals*.
3. Saltman, Mike, *The Demise of the Reasonable Man; Crosscultural Study of a Legal Concept*, New Brunswick, J.J. (1991), Transaction Publications.
4. Veerman, Philip, E., *The Rights of the Child and the Changing Image of Childhood*, Dordrecht Martinus Nijhoff (1992).
5. Melton, Gary, *Child Advocacy, Psychological Issues and Interventions*, New York/London, Plenum (1983), p. 200.

6. Lax, Elisabeth, 'Korczaks Auffassung von der Entwicklung des Kindes – Ein Beitrag zu Korczaks Bild vom Kinde', in: Beiner, Friedhelm (ed.), *Zweites Wuppertaler Korczak-Kolloquium 1984*, Wuppertal (1984), Universitäs-Druck, pp. 74–109.

7. Cutler, R. S., 'A Policy Perspective on Interdisciplinary Research in US Universities', in: *Proceedings of the First International Conference on Interdisciplinary Research Groups*, Barth, R. T. and Steck, R. (eds.) (1980).

8. Rossini, F. A. and Porter, A. L., 'Interdisciplinary Research: Performance and Policy Issues', in: Jurkovich, R. and Paelinck, I. H. P. (eds.), *Problems in Interdisciplinary Studies*, Aldershot, Hampshire, 1984, pp. 26–46.

9. Silverman, Marvin, 'Children's Rights and Social Work', in: *The Social Service Review* 51 (1977), pp. 171–178. Downing, Theodore, E., 'Human Rights Research: The Challenge for Anthropologists', in: Downing, Theodore, E., and Kushner, Gilbert (eds.), *Human Rights and Anthropology*, Cambridge, Mass (1988), Cultural Survival Inc., pp. 9–19.

10. Parreren, C. F. van, 'Verscheidenheid van Mensbeelden – Eenheid in de Psychologie?', in: Parreren, C. F. van, and Bend, J. G. van der (eds.), *Psychologie en Mensbeeld*, Baarn, Ambo (1983), pp. 98–115.

11. Nauta, D., 'Introduction to the Volume', in: Jurkovich, R. and Paelinck, J. H. P., op. cit., pp. 2–10.

12. Heintze, Hans-Joachim, 'Erstes Treffen der Internationalen und Interdisziplinären Studiengruppe zu den Rechte der Kinder – Tagung, Organisiert von der Israelische Sektion der Defence for Children International (DCI)', in: *Humanitäres Völkerrecht* 1/2 (1991), pp. 72–73.

13. Miller, Jossi (ed.), *The Effect of the Gulf War on Children*, Report of a Conference organized by the Israel-Section of Defence for Children International (DCI), Jerusalem (1991).

14. The Israel-Section of DCI and the Association for Civil Rights in Israel (ACRI) jointly petitioned the High Court of Justice also to distribute gasmasks in the occupied territories.

15. Veerman, Philip, 'Janusz Korczak and the Rights of the Child', in: *Concern* 62 (1987), publication of the National Children's Bureau, London, pp. 7–9.

16. DCI-Israel is monitoring the situation of youngsters in detention. The main concern about the Sharon prison (better known as the Tel Mond prison) is that the Palestinian security detainees (there are also Jewish and Arab-Israeli kids, 'criminal cases') are sitting 22 hours in small cells while neither teachers from outside nor adult inmates who are teachers are allowed to give them an education.

17. At the time this book goes to the press the YMCA estimates that from the start of the intifada 120,000 people are wounded of whom 40,000 will remain handicapped. A large percentage of them are adolescents.

18. In the meantime DCI-Israel started also a legal aid project for (mostly Jewish) children in the Tel Aviv area and in the Bethlehem area (Palestinian children who appear before the military court for security offences).

19. Prof. Adam Lopatka (former Chairman of the UN Working Group which created the UN Convention on the Rights of the Child) was made possible by the Raoul Wallenberg Chair for the study of Human Rights at Bar Ilan University. He delivered the first annual Janusz Korczak lecture. A Dutch group of friends, headed by Mr. Z. Hartog, also contributed to this Korczak lecture, which is now an annual event (in 1991 the lecture was delivered by Malfrid Grude Flekkøy).

20. The Israeli Foreign Ministry sponsored the participation of Mr. Likhanov and his two colleagues (Sergei Abramov, editor of *Familia* magazine, Moscow and Mephodii, the metropolitan of Vornez and Lipetsk). At that time there were no diplomatic relations between Israel and the USSR (and the USSR still existed!).

21. This session was made possible by the Israel B. and Sara Mann Greene Fund for Equity Studies.

22. At the request of the organizers, a Canadian participant of the Study-Group, Robert Vyncke (of the DCI Canada Francophone Section) brought, for instance, a text from his colleague

Renée Joyal (lawyer and professor at the Université du Québec at Montreal) to stimulate such discussion. She questioned the notion of *the best interest of the child* (and its place in the UN Convention). She asked, for instance, the following questions: 'Does this notion of the child's best interest, conceived at a time when the child was perceived more as object than subject, retain its *raison d'être* within a context of rights? Is it better to dispense with it altogether? If so, must it be replaced? If not, how can the notion of a meaningful role be given, which does not enter into conflict with the rights themselves?' It would have been better if such basic concepts as *the best interests of the child*, the *Juvenile Court* etc. would have been discussed more in depth.

23. Marian Wright Edelman (the Director of the Children's Defense Fund in Washington DC) pointed out (in an interview with Rochelle Beck, published in the *Harvard Educational Review* 44 (February 1974) that there is 'a lack of understanding from the academic community of what we need to know and do for children with immediate needs'.

24. Defence for Children International – Israel-Section; The University of Haifa – Center for Youth Policy; The Hebrew University of Jerusalem – Faculty of Law.

25. The idea raised at the Study-Group was that the Association and the publishing house would together publish the *International Journal of Children's Rights*. That might still be possible. However, for practical purposes a Foundation (Stichting Children's Rights Publication Foundation) was incorporated in Amsterdam, the Netherlands. The statutes of the 'Stichting' state that if such an Association will be formed, the board of the 'Stichting Children's Right Publications Foundation' will be appointed by that Association.

Index

Editorial Advisory Committee for this Book

International Studies in Human Rights

International Studies in Human Rights

This series is designed to shed light on current legal and political aspects of process and organization in the field of human rights.

MARTINUS NIJHOFF PUBLISHERS – DORDRECHT / BOSTON / LONDON